TREATISE

ON

THE POLICE

OF

THE METROPOLIS.

PATTERSON SMITH REPRINT SERIES IN
CRIMINOLOGY, LAW ENFORCEMENT, AND SOCIAL PROBLEMS

1. Lewis: *The Development of American Prisons and Prison Customs, 1776-1845*
2. Carpenter: *Reformatory Prison Discipline*
3. Brace: *The Dangerous Classes of New York*
4. Dix: *Remarks on Prisons and Prison Discipline in the United States*
5. Bruce *et al: The Workings of the Indeterminate-Sentence Law and the Parole System in Illinois*
6. Wickersham Commission: *Complete Reports, Including the Mooney-Billings Report.* 14 Vols.
7. Livingston: *Complete Works on Criminal Jurisprudence.* 2 Vols.
8. Cleveland Foundation: *Criminal Justice in Cleveland*
9. Illinois Association for Criminal Justice: *The Illinois Crime Survey*
10. Missouri Association for Criminal Justice: *The Missouri Crime Survey*
11. Aschaffenburg: *Crime and Its Repression*
12. Garofalo: *Criminology*
13. Gross: *Criminal Psychology*
14. Lombroso: *Crime, Its Causes and Remedies*
15. Saleilles: *The Individualization of Punishment*
16. Tarde: *Penal Philosophy*
17. McKelvey: *American Prisons*
18. Sanders: *Negro Child Welfare in North Carolina*
19. Pike: *A History of Crime in England.* 2 Vols.
20. Herring: *Welfare Work in Mill Villages*
21. Barnes: *The Evolution of Penology in Pennsylvania*
22. Puckett: *Folk Beliefs of the Southern Negro*
23. Fernald *et al: A Study of Women Delinquents in New York State*
24. Wines: *The State of the Prisons and of Child-Saving Institutions*
25. Raper: *The Tragedy of Lynching*
26. Thomas: *The Unadjusted Girl*
27. Jorns: *The Quakers as Pioneers in Social Work*
28. Owings: *Women Police*
29. Woolston: *Prostitution in the United States*
30. Flexner: *Prostitution in Europe*
31. Kelso: *The History of Public Poor Relief in Massachusetts: 1820-1920*
32. Spivak: *Georgia Nigger*
33. Earle: *Curious Punishments of Bygone Days*
34. Bonger: *Race and Crime*
35. Fishman: *Crucibles of Crime*
36. Brearley: *Homicide in the United States*
37. Graper: *American Police Administration*
38. Hichborn: *"The System"*
39. Steiner & Brown: *The North Carolina Chain Gang*
40. Cherrington: *The Evolution of Prohibition in the United States of America*
41. Colquhoun: *A Treatise on the Commerce and Police of the River Thames*
42. Colquhoun: *A Treatise on the Police of the Metropolis*
43. Abrahamsen: *Crime and the Human Mind*
44. Schneider: *The History of Public Welfare in New York State: 1609-1866*
45. Schneider & Deutsch: *The History of Public Welfare in New York State: 1867-1940*
46. Crapsey: *The Nether Side of New York*
47. Young: *Social Treatment in Probation and Delinquency*
48. Quinn: *Gambling and Gambling Devices*
49. McCord & McCord: *Origins of Crime*
50. Worthington & Topping: *Specialized Courts Dealing with Sex Delinquency*

PUBLICATION NO. 42: PATTERSON SMITH REPRINT SERIES IN CRIMINOLOGY, LAW ENFORCEMENT, AND SOCIAL PROBLEMS

A TREATISE ON THE

POLICE of the METROPOLIS

By

PATRICK COLQUHOUN

Reprinted from the seventh London edition, 1806

Montclair, New Jersey
PATTERSON SMITH
1969

The first edition of this work was published in1795.
The seventh (and last) edition,
corrected and considerably enlarged,
was published in 1806.
This facsimile of the seventh edition is published by
Patterson Smith Publishing Corporation
Montclair, New Jersey

SBN 87585-042-1

Library of Congress Catalog Card Number: 69-14918

A

TREATISE

ON THE

POLICE OF THE METROPOLIS;

CONTAINING A DETAIL OF THE

VARIOUS CRIMES AND MISDEMEANORS

*By which Public and Private Property and Security are, at present,
injured and endangered:*

AND

SUGGESTING REMEDIES

FOR THEIR

PREVENTION.

THE SEVENTH EDITION, CORRECTED AND CONSIDERABLY ENLARGED.

BY P. COLQUHOUN, LL.D.

*Acting as a Magistrate for the Counties of Middlesex, Surry, Kent, and Essex.—
For the City and Liberty of Westminster, and for the Liberty of the Tower of London.*

Meminerint legum conditores, illas ad proximum hunc finem accommodare;
Scelera videlicet arcenda, refrænandaque vitia ac morum pravitatem.

Judices pariter leges illas cum vigore, æquitate, integritate, publicæque utili-
tatis amore curent exequi; ut justitia et virtus omnes societatis ordines prevadant.
Industriaque simul et Temperantia inertiæ locum assumant et prodigalitatis.

LONDON:

PRINTED FOR J. MAWMAN, CADELL AND DAVIES, R. FAULDER, CLARKE AND
SONS, LONGMAN, HURST, REES AND ORME, VERNOR, HOOD, AND SHARPE,
H. D. SYMONDS, LACKINGTON, ALLEN, AND CO. SCATCHERD AND LETTER-
MAN, R. LEA, B. CROSBY AND CO. WYNNE AND SON, R. PHENEY, BLACKS
AND PARRY, J. ASPERNE; AND WILSON AND SPENCE, YORK.

1806.

TO THE SOVEREIGN,

Who has graciously condescended to approve
of the Author's Efforts " To establish a
" System of Morality and good Order in
" The Metropolis :"

AND TO HIS PEOPLE;

In every Part of the British Dominions; whose
favourable Reception of these Labours, for
the Good of their Country, has contributed
in a considerable degree, to the Progress which
has been already made, towards the Adoption of
the Remedies proposed for the Prevention of
Crimes, the Comfort of Society, and the Security
of the Peaceful Subject :

This Improved and Enlarged Edition of

THE TREATISE ON THE POLICE
OF THE METROPOLIS,

LONDON, *is humbly*

Jan. 1, 1800. *and respectfully*

DEDICATED.

ADVERTISEMENT.

OCCUPIED in a variety of laborious pursuits, which afford little time either for study or recreation, the Author once more presents this Work to the Public with an unfeigned diffidence, arising from his consciousness, that under such circumstances it must require their indulgence. This, he trusts, will be granted when it is considered, that his employments are of a nature unfriendly to that critical accuracy and precision, the necessity of which is impressed on his mind, not less by a sense of his own personal character, than of his obligations to the long experienced candour and liberality of his readers.

In the present Edition much new matter has been brought forward, and considerable improvements have been attempted by the introduction of official facts, and authentic details calculated to elucidate and explain the general system first placed by the Author under the review of the Public. Their extensive approbation (although his only reward) is of a nature which can never be too highly estimated. That approbation has not only been confirmed by many of the first and most respectable characters in these kingdoms, not less conspicuous for talents and abilities than for that genuine patriotism which distinguishes the good subject, and the valuable member of Society ; but also by several Foreigners eminent for learning and virtue.

While we deplore the miserable condition of those numerous delinquents who have unfortunately multiplied, with the same rapidity that the great wealth of the metropolis has increased: while their errors and their crimes are exposed only for the purpose of amendment; while the tear of pity is due to their forlorn state, a prospect happily opens through the medium of *the Report of the* SELECT COMMITTEE *of the* HOUSE *of* COMMONS, for the adoption of those remedies which will unquestionably give a seasonable check to immorality and delinquency; so as by their prevention not only to protect the rights of innocence, but also increase the number of the useful members of the community, and render punishments less frequent and necessary.

To witness the ultimate completion of legislative arrangements, operating so favourably to the immediate advantage and security of the Metropolis, and extending also similar benefits to the country at large, will prove to the Author of this Work a very great and genuine source of happiness.

To the Public, therefore, in general, and to the Legislature in particular, does he look forward with confidence for that singular gratification which, by giving effect to his well-meant endeavours for the prevention of Crimes, will ultimately crown with success the exertions he has used in the course of a very intricate and laborious investigation, in which his only object has been the good of his country.

LONDON,
1st *January*, 1800.

PREFACE.

PoLICE in this Country may be considered as a *new Science;* the properties of which consist not in the Judicial Powers which lead to *Punishment,* and which belong to Magistrates alone; but in the PREVENTION and DETECTION OF CRIMES, and in those other Functions which relate to INTERNAL REGULATIONS for the well ordering and comfort of Civil Society.

THE POLICE OF THE METROPOLIS, in every point of view, is a subject of great importance to be known and understood; since every innocent and useful Member of the Community has a particular interest in the correct administration of whatever relates to the Morals of the People, and to the protection of the Public against Fraud and Depredation.

Under the present circumstances of insecurity, with respect to property, and even life itself, this is a subject which cannot fail to force itself upon the attention of all :—All are equally concerned in the

Information

Information which this Work conveys; the chief part of the details in which are entirely novel, not to be found in books. and never laid before the Public through the medium of the Press, previous to the first Publication of this Treatise.

It may naturally be imagined, that such an accumulation of delinquency systematically detailed, and placed in so prominent a point of view, must excite a considerable degree of astonishment in the minds of those Readers who have not been familiar with subjects of this nature; and hence a desire may be excited to investigate how far the amazing extent of 'the Depredations upon the Public here related, can be reconciled to reason and possibility.

Four years have, however, elapsed, since these details have been before the Public, and they still stand on their original ground, witout any attempt which has come to the Author's knowledge, to question the magnitude or the extent of the evil.—On the contrary, new sources of Fraud and Depredation have been brought forward, tending greatly to increase the general mass of Delinquency*.

* See Mr. Middleton's interesting Report on the County of Middlesex, and the extracts from thence in Chapter III. of this Work.

In

In revising the present Edition, the Author felt a strong impulse to reduce his estimates; but after an attentive review of the whole, excepting in the instances of the Depredations on Commercial Property, (which have been greatly diminished by the establishment of a *Marine Police*, applicable to that particular object,) he was unable to perceive any ground for materially altering his original calculations.—If some classes of Theft, Robbery, and Depredation, have been reduced, others have been augmented; still leaving the aggregate nearly as before.

The causes of these extensive and accumulated wrongs being fully explained, and accounted for, in various parts of the Work, a very short recapitulation of them is, therefore, all that is necessary in this Preface.

The enlarged state of Society, the vast extent of moving property, and the unexampled wealth of the Metropolis, joined to the depraved habits and loose conduct of a great proportion of the lower classes of the people; and above all, the want of an appropriate Police applicable to the object of prevention, will, after a careful perusal of this work, reconcile the attentive mind to a belief of the actual existence of evils which could not otherwise have been credited.

dited.—Let it be remembered also, that this Metropolis is unquestionably not only the greatest Manufacturing and Commercial City in the world, but also the general receptacle for the idle and depraved of almost every country; particularly from every quarter of the dominions of the Crown—Where the temptations and resources for criminal pleasures— Gambling, Fraud and Depredation, almost exceed imagination; since besides being the seat of Government, it is the centre of *fashion, amusements, dissipation and folly.*

Under such peculiar circumstances, while immorality, licentiousness and crimes are known to advance in proportion to the excessive accumulation of wealth, it cannot fail to be a matter of deep regret, that in the progressive increase of the latter, the means of checking the rapid strides of the former have not been sooner discovered and effectually applied.

It is, however, earnestly to be hoped that it is not yet too late—Patriots and Philanthropists who love their country, and glory in its prosperity, will rejoice with the Author in the prospect, that the great leading features of improvement suggested and matured in the present Edition of this Work will ultimately receive the sanction of the Legislature.

May

May the Author be allowed to express his conviction that the former Editions of this book tended, in no small degree, to remove various misconceptions on the subject of Police: and at the same time, evidently excited in the public mind a desire to see such remedies applied as should contribute to the improvement of the Morals of the People, and to the removal of the danger and insecurity which were universally felt to exist?

An impression, it is to be hoped, is generally felt from the example of the Roman Government, when enveloped in riches and luxury, that National prosperity must be of short duration when public Morals are too long neglected, and no effectual measures adopted for the purpose either of checking the alarming growth of depravity, or of guarding the rising generation against evil examples.

It is by the general influence of good Laws, aided by the regulations of an energetic Police, that the blessings of true Liberty, and the undisturbed enjoyment of Property, are secured.

The sole object of the Author in pointing out the accumulated wrongs which have tended in so great a degree to abridge this Liberty, is to pave the way for the adoption of those practical remedies which he

has

has suggested, in conformity with the spirit of the Laws, and the Constitution of the Country, for the purpose of bettering the state of Society, and improving the condition of human life.

If in the accomplishment of this object the Morals of the People shall undergo a favourable change, and that species of comfort and security be extended to the inhabitants of this great Metropolis, which has not heretofore been experienced, while many evils are prevented, which in their consequences threaten to be productive of the most serious mischief, the Author of this Work will feel himself amply rewarded in the benefits which the System he has proposed shall be found to confer upon the Capital of the British Dominions, and on the Nation at large.

Published, by the Author of this Work,

A TREATISE

ON THE

COMMERCE AND POLICE

OF

THE RIVER THAMES:

CONTAINING

AN HISTORICAL VIEW OF
THE TRADE OF THE PORT OF LONDON :
THE DEPREDATIONS COMMITTED
ON ALL PROPERTY IMPORTED AND EXPORTED THERE;
THE REMEDIES HITHERTO APPLIED;
AND THE MEANS OF FUTURE PREVENTION,
BY COMPLETE SYSTEM OF
RIVER-POLICE.

WITH AN ACCOUNT OF
THE FUNCTIONS OF THE VARIOUS MAGISTRATES AND OTHERS
EXERCISING OR CLAIMING JURISCTION ON THE RIVER;
AND OF THE
PENAL STATUTES AGAINST MARITIME OFFENCES
OF EVERY DESCRIPTION.

Printed for J. MAWMAN, *in the Poultry.*

CONTENTS.

CHAP. I.

GENERAL VIEW OF EXISTING EVILS.

PAGE

*Ineffective System of Criminal Jurisprudence.—
Facility of eluding Justice.—Severity and inequality of Punishments.—Necessity of revising
our Penal Code.—Certain dangerous Offences
not punishable.—Receivers of Stolen Property.
—Extent of Plunder in the Metropolis, &c.—
Proposed Restrictions on Receivers.—Coiners
and Utterers of Base Money; the extent of
their crimes.—Defects in the mode of prosecuting Offenders.—-Pardons.—-Periodical Discharges of Prisoners—Summary of the causes
of the present inefficacy of the Police, under
nine different heads*   1

CHAP. II.

ON THE SYSTEM OF PUNISHMENTS:
THEORETICALLY CONSIDERED.

*The mode of ascertaining the Degrees of Punish-
ment.—The object to be considered in inflicting
Punishments—Amendment, Example, and Retribution. —- In order to render Criminal
Laws*

PAGE

Laws perfect, prevention ought to be the great object of the Legislature.—General Rules suggested for obtaining this object.—Reflections on the Punishments authorised by the English Laws, and their disproportion.—The necessity of enforcing the observance of religious and moral Virtue.—The leading Offences made Capital by the Laws of England considered, with the Punishments allotted to each; compared with, and illustrated by, the Custom of other Countries; with Reflections.—The Code of the Emperor JOSEPH *the Second, shortly detailed.—Reflections thereon* · · · · · · · · · · · · · · · 29

CHAP. III.

THE CAUSE AND PROGRESS OF SMALL THEFTS.

The numerous Receivers of Stolen Goods, under the denomination of Dealers in Rags, Old Iron, and other Metals.—The great Increase of these Dealers of late years.—Their evil tendency, and the absolute necessity of restraining them by Law.—Petty Thefts in the Country round the Metropolis.—Workhouses' the causes of Idleness.—Commons.—Cottagers.—Gypsies. —Labourers and Servants—Thefts in Fields and Gardens.—Frauds in the Sale and Adulteration of Milk · 74

CHAP.

C H A P. IV.

ON BURGLARIES AND HIGHWAY ROBBERIES.

PAGE.

These Crimes more peculiar to England than to Holland and Flanders, &c.—A General View of the various classes of Criminals engaged in these pursuits, and with those discharged from Prisons and the Hulks, without the means of support.—The necessity of some antidote previous to the return of Peace.—Observations on the stealing Cattle, Sheep, Corn, &c.—Receivers of Stolen Goods, the nourishers of every description of Thieves.—Remedies suggested, by means of detection and prevention · · · · · · · · · **93**

C H A P. V.

ON CHEATS AND SWINDLERS.

A considerable check already given to the higher class of Forgeries, by shutting out all hopes of Royal Mercy.—Petty Forgeries have, however, increased. — The qualifications of a Cheat, Swindler and Gambler.—The Common and Statute Law applicable to Offences of this nature, explained.—Eighteen different classes of Cheats and Swindlers, and the various tricks and devices they pursue.—Remedies proposed· · · · · · **110**

CHAP.

CHAP. VI.

ON GAMING AND THE LOTTERY.

PAGE

The great anxiety of the Legislature to suppress these Evils, which are however encouraged by high sounding names, whose houses are opened for purposes odious and unlawful.—The civil Magistrate called upon to suppress such mischiefs.—The danger arising from such Seminaries.—The evil tendency of such examples to Servants and others.—A particular statement of the proceedings of a confederacy of Persons who have set up Gaming-Houses as regular Partnership-Concerns, and of the Evils resulting therefrom.—Of Lottery Insurers of the higher class.—Of Lottery Offices opened for Insurance.—Proposed Remedies.—Three Plans for drawing the Lottery so as to prevent all Insurance · 133

CHAP. VII.

ON THE COINAGE OF COUNTERFEIT MONEY.

The Causes of the enormous increase of this Evil of late years.—The different kinds of false coin detailed. —— The process in fabricating each Species.—The immense profits arising therefrom.
—The

PAGE

—*The extensive Trade in sending base Coin to the Country.—Its universal circulation in the Metropolis.—The great grievance arising from it to Brewers, Distillers, Grocers, and all Retail Dealers, as well as to the Labouring Poor.— Counterfeit Foreign Money extremely productive to the Dealers.—A summary View of the Causes of the Mischief.—The Defects in the present Laws explained;—And a Detail of the Remedies proposed to be provided by the Legislature* · · · · 171

C H A P. VIII.

ON RIVER PLUNDER.

The magnitude of the Plunder of Merchandize and Naval Stores on the River Thames.—The wonderful extent and value of the Floating Property, laden and unladen, in the Port of London in the course of a year.—The modes heretofore pursued in committing depredations through the medium of various classes of Criminals, denominated River Pirates;—Night Plunderers: —Light Horsemen:—Heavy Horsemen:— Game Watermen:—Game Lightermen:—Mudlarks:—Game Officers of the Revenue:—And Copemen, or Receivers of Stolen Property.— The effects of the Marine Police Institution in checking these Depredations.—The advantages which

PAGE

which have already resulted to Trade and the Revenue from this system partially tried.—The further benefits to be expected from Legislative Regulations, extending the System to the whole Trade of the River · 213

C H A P. IX.

ON PLUNDER IN THE DOCK-YARDS, &c.

Reflections on the causes of this Evil.—Summary view of the means employed in its perpetration.— Estimate of the Public Property exposed to Hazard.—A Statement of the Laws at present in force for its protection:—Proofs adduced of their deficiency.—Remedies proposed and detailed, viz:—1st. A Central Board of Police.—2d. A Local Police for the Dock-yards. —3d. Legislative Regulations in aid thereof.— 4th. Regulations respecting the sale of Old Stores.—5th. The Abolition of the Perquisite of Chips.—6th. The Abolition of Fees and Perquisites, and liberal Salaries in lieu thereof. —7th. An improved Mode of keeping Accounts. —8th. An annual Inventory of Stores in hand. —Concluding Observations · · · · · · · · · · · · · · · · 249

CHAP.

CHAP. X.

ON THE RECEIVERS OF STOLEN GOODS.

PAGE

Receivers more mischievous than Thieves.—The increase of their number to be attributed to the imperfection of the Laws, and to the disjointed state of the Police of the Metropolis.—Thieves, in many instances, settle with receivers before they commit robberies :—Receivers always benefit more than Thieves :—Their profit immense : —They are divided into two classes :—The immediate Receivers connected with Thieves, and those who keep shops and purchase from Pilferers in the way of trade :—The latter are extremely numerous.—The laws are insufficient effectually to reach either class:—The existing statutes against Receivers examined and briefly detailed, with Observations thereon.— Amendments and improvements suggested, with means to ensure their due execution · · · · · · · · 288

CHAP. XI.

ON THE ORIGIN OF CRIMINAL OFFENCES.

The increase of Crimes imputed to deficient Laws and ill-regulated Police :—To the habits of the Lower Orders in feeding their families

PAGE

families in Alehouses:—To the bad Educa-
tion of Apprentices:—To the want of Indus-
try:—To idle and profligate menial Servants
out of Place:—To the Lower Orders of the
Jews of the Dutch and German Synagogues:—
To the depraved Morals of aquatic Labourers:
—To the Dealers in Old Metals, Furniture,
Clothes, &c.—To disreputable Pawnbrokers:—
And finally, to ill-regulated Public Houses.—
Concluding Reflections. 310

CHAP. XII.

THE ORIGIN OF CRIMES CONTINUED:

FEMALE PROSTITUTION.

The pitiable condition of the unhappy Females,
who support themselves by Prostitution:—The
progress from Innocence to profligacy.—The
morals of Youth corrupted by the multitude of
Prostitutes in the streets.—The impossibility
of preventing the existence of Prostitution in a
great Metropolis.—The propriety of lessening
the Evil, by stripping it of its Indecency and
much of its immoral tendency.—The advantages
of the measure in reducing the mass of Turpi-
tude.—Reasons offered why the interests of
Morality and Religion will thus be promoted.
—The example of Holland, Italy, and the East-
Indies

PAGE

Indies quoted.—Strictures on the offensive manners of the Company who frequent Public Tea Gardens:—These places under a proper Police might be rendered beneficial to the State. —Ballad-Singers—Immoral Books and Songs —Necessity of Responsibility for the execution of the Laws attaching somewhere. 334

CHAP. XIII.

THE ORIGIN OF CRIMES CONTINUED:

STATE OF THE POOR.

The System with respect to the Casual Poor erroneous.—The effect of Indigence on the Offspring of the Sufferers—Estimate of the private and public Benevolence amounting to 850,000l. a year.—The deplorable state of the Lower Ranks, attributed to the present System of the Poor Laws.—An Institution to inquire into the cause of Mendicity in the Metropolis explained.—A new System of Relief proposed with respect to Casual Poor, and Vagrants in the Metropolis—The distinction between Poverty and Indigence.—The Poor divided into five classes, with suggestions applicable to each.—The evil Examples in Work-Houses.—The stat. of 43 Eliz. considered.— The defective system of Execution exposed.—

A Public

PAGE

*A Public Institution recommended in the nature
of a Pauper Police, under the direction of three
Commissioners :—Their Functions.—A proposition for raising a fund of 5,230l. from the
Parishes for the support of the Institution,
and to relieve them from the Casual Poor.—
Reasons why the experiment should be tried.—
Assistance which might be obtained from Gentlemen who have considered this subject fully. . 351*

CHAP. XIX,

ON THE DETECTION OF OFFENDERS.

*The present state of the Police on this subject ex-
plained.—The necessity of having recourse to
known Receivers.—The great utility of Officers of Justice.—The advantages of rendering
them respectable in the opinion of the Public.—
Their powers by the common and statute Law.
—Rewards granted to Officers in certain cases
of Conviction.—The statutes quoted, applicable to such rewards.—The utility of Parochial
Constables, under a well-organized Police.—
A Fund for this purpose might arise from the
reduction of the expences of the Police, by the
diminution of Crimes.—The necessity of a competent Fund.—A new System for prevention
and detection of Crimes proposed.—The functions*

PAGE

*tions of the different classes of Officers.—
Salaries necessary to all.—Improvements in the
system of Rewards suggested.—1040 Peace-
Officers in the Metropolis and its vicinity, of
whom only 90 are stipendiary Constables.—Defects and abuses in the system of the Watch explained.—A general Plan of Superintendance
suggested.—A view of the Magistracy of the
Metropolis.—The inconvenience of the present
System* ·381

CHAP. XV.

ON THE PROSECUTION OF OFFENDERS.

*The prevailing Practice when Offenders are
brought before Magistrates.—The duty of Magistrates in such cases.—Professed Thieves seldom intimidated when put upon their Trial,
from the many Chances they have of escaping.—
These Chances shortly detailed.—Reflections on
false Humanity towards Prisoners.—The delays
and expences of Prosecutions a great discouragement to Prosecutors.—An account of the different Courts of Justice, for the trial of Offences
committed in the Metropolis.—Five inferior
and two superior Courts.—A statement of
Prisoners convicted and discharged in one year.
—Reflections thereon.—The advantage which
would arise from the appointment of a Public
Prosecutor,*

PAGE

Prosecutor, in remedying Abuses in the Trial of Offenders.—From 2500 to 3000 Persons committed for trial, by Magistrates, in the course of a year.—The chief part afterwards returned upon Society · · · · · · · · · · · · · · · · · ·422

CHAP. XVI.

ON THE SYSTEM OF PUNISHMENTS CONSIDERED PRACTICALLY.

The mode authorised by the Ancient Laws.—The period when Transportation commenced.—The principal Crimes enumerated which are punishable with Death.—Those punishable by Transportation and Imprisonment.—Number of Persons tried compared with those discharged.— The system of Pardons examined; and Regulations suggested.—An historical Account of the rise and progress of Transportation.—The system of the Hulks; and the Laws as to provincial and National Penitentiary Houses.— Number of the Convicts confined in the Hulks for twenty-two years.—The enormous expence of maintenance and inadequate produce of their Labour.—The impolicy of the System.—The system of Transportation to New South Wales examined, and Improvements suggested.—Erection of National Penitentiary Houses recommended.

PAGE

mended.—The National Penitentiary House (according to the Proposal of Jeremy Bentham, Esq.) considered:—Its peculiar advantages with respect to Health, productive Labour, and Reformation of Convicts.—General Reflections on the means of rendering Imprisonment useful. ·435

CHAP. XVII.

CRIMINAL POLICE OF THE METROPOLIS.

The Police of the Metropolis examined, and its Organization explained.—The utility of the system, established in 1792, examined and explained.—Its great deficiency from the want of Funds to reward Officers for the detection and punishment of Offenders.—Suggestions relative to stipendiary Justices, and the benefits likely to result from their exertions in assisting the City Magistrates.—The vast labour and weight of duty attached to the chief Magistrate and Aldermen in London.—The benefits to result from Established Police Magistrates exemplified by the System already adopted under the Act of 1792.—The advantages which would arise from the various remedies proposed in the course of this Work, only of a partial nature, for want of a centre-point and superintending Establish-

PAGE

Establishment.—The ideas of Foreigners on the Police of the Metropolis—Observations on the Old Police of Paris, elucidated by Anecdotes of the Emperor JOSEPH II. *and Mons. de Sartine.—A Central Board of Commissioners for managing the Police, peculiarly necessary on the return of Peace.—This measure recommended by the Finance Committee.* • • • • • • • • • 501

C H A P. XVIII.

PROPOSED SYSTEM OF CRIMINAL POLICE.

A proposition to consolidate the two Boards of Hawkers and Pedlars, and Hackney Coaches, into a Board of Police Revenue.—The whole Revenue of Police from Fees, Penalties and Licence Duties, to make a common Fund.— Accounts to be audited.—Magistrates to distribute small rewards.—A Power to the Board to make Bye-Laws.—A concurrent jurisdiction recommended —The Penitentiary House for reforming Convicts.—Measures proposed after the Board is established—namely, a Public Prosecutor for the Crown.—A Register of Lodging Houses.—The Establishment of a Police Gazette.—Two leading objects; the prevention of Crimes: and raising a Revenue for Police purposes.—The enumeration of the Dealers,

PAGE

*Dealers, who are proposed to be licenced.—A
general View of the annual Expence of the
present and proposed Police System.—Suggestions respecting a chain of connections with
Magistrates in the Country.—The Functions of
the proposed Central Board of Police.—Specification of the Trades to be regulated and
licenced.—The advantages likely to result from
the adoption of the Plan.* ···················536*

CHAP. XIX.

MUNICIPAL POLICE OF THE METROPOLIS.

*Extent and Opulence of the City of London, its
Streets, Lanes, Alleys, Courts, and Squares, estimated at 8000.—Churches, &c. 400.—Seminaries for Education 4000.—The various Institution and Societies for Learning, for the
fine Arts, and for charitable and humane Purposes.—The Courts of Law.—The Prisons—
Suggestions as to improving the System of Imprisonment for Debt, particularly as relating to
small Debts: and as to dividing the judicial
and ministerial Labours among more Officers.—
The internal or municipal Regulations established in the Metropolis by several Statutes;
respecting Paving — Watching — Sewers —
Hackney Coaches — Carts — Watermen — and
Buildings.*

8

PAGE

Buildings.—Necessity of rendering these Laws uniform and extensive, so as to consolidate the System of Municipal Police.—Expence calculated at 1,000,000l. a year.—Suggestions for reducing it.—The present Epoch calls for Improvements. 567

CHAP. XX.

CONCLUSION.

A summary View of the Evils detailed in the preceding Chapters.—Arguments in favour of a more energetic Police as the only means of remedying these Evils.—A general View of the estimated Depredations annually in the Metropolis and its Vicinity, amounting in all to Two Millions Sterling.—A View of the Remedies proposed—1st. With respect to the Corruption of Morals.—2d. The means of preventing Crimes in general.—3d. Offences committed on the River Thames.—4th. Offences in the Public Arsenals and Ships of War.—5th. Counterfeiting Money and fabricating Bank Notes; 6th. Punishments.—7th. Further advantages of an improved System of Police.—Concluding Reflections. 602

A

TREATISE, &c.

CHAPTER I.

A general view of the Evils existing in the Metropolis, and the causes from which they arise.—Necessity of a well-regulated Police.—Ineffective system of Criminal Jurisprudence.—Facility of eluding Justice. Severity and inequality of Punishments.—Necessity of revising our Penal Code.—Certain dangerous Offences not punishable.—Receivers of stolen property.—Extent of plunder in the Metropolis, &c.— Proposed restrictions on Receivers.—Coiners and Utterers of Counterfeit Money; the extent of their crimes.—Defects in the mode of prosecuting Offenders.—Pardons.—Periodical discharges of Prisoners.—Summary of the causes of the present inefficacy of the Police, under nine different heads.

NEXT to the blessings which a Nation derives from an excellent Constitution and System of general Laws, are those advantages which result from a well-regulated and energetic plan of Police, conducted and enforced with purity, activity, vigilance, and discretion.

Upon

Upon this depends, in so great a degree, the comfort, the happiness, and the true liberty and security of the People, that too much labour and attention cannot possibly be bestowed in rendering complete the domestic administration of Justice in all cases of criminal delinquency.

That much remains to be done in this respect no person will deny; all ranks must bear testimony to the dangers which both life and property are at present subjected to by the number of criminal people, who, from various causes (which it is the object of the Writer of these pages to explain), are suffered with impunity to repeat acts of licentiousness and mischief, and to commit depredations upon individuals and the Public.

In vain do we boast of those liberties which are our birthright, if the vilest and most depraved part of the Community are suffered to deprive us of the privilege of travelling upon the highways, or of approaching the Capital in any direction after dark, without risk of being assaulted and robbed; and perhaps wounded or murdered.

In vain may we boast of the security which our Laws afford us, if we cannot lie down to rest in our habitations, without the dread of a burglary being committed, our property invaded, and our lives exposed to imminent danger before the approach of morning.

Imperfect must be either the plan or the execution, or both, of our Criminal Code, if crimes are found
to

to increase; if the moral principle ceases to be a check upon a vast proportion of the lower ranks of the People; and if small thefts are known to prevail in such a degree, as to affect almost all ranks of the Community who have any property to lose, as often as opportunities occur, whereby pilfering in a little way can be effected without detection.

If, in addition to this, the peace of Society can, on every specious pretence, be disturbed by the licentious clamours or turbulent effusions arising from the ill-regulated passions of vulgar life, surely it becomes an interesting inquiry, worthy the attention of every intelligent member of the Community, *from what source spring these numerous inconveniences; and where is a remedy to be found for so many accumulated evils?*

In developing the causes which have produced that want of security, which it is believed prevails in no other civilised country in so great a degree as in England, it will be necessary to examine how far the System of Criminal Jurisprudence has been, hitherto, applicable to the prevention of crimes.

If we look back to the measures pursued by our ancestors two centuries ago, and before that period, we shall find that many wholesome laws were made with a view to prevention, and to secure the good behaviour of persons likely to commit offences. Since that æra in our history, a different plan has been pursued. Few regulations have been established to restrain vice, or to render difficult the
commission

commission of crimes; while the Statute Books have been filled with numerous Laws, in many instances doubtfully expressed, and whose leading feature has generally been severe punishment. These circumstances, aided by the false mercy of Juries in cases of slight offences, have tended to let loose upon Society a body of criminal individuals, who under a better Police—an improved system of Legislation, and milder punishments,—might, after a correction in Penitentiary Houses, or employment in out-door labour, under proper restraints, have been restored to Society as useful members.

As the Laws are at present administered, it is a melancholy truth not to be contradicted, that the major part of the criminals who infest this Metropolis, although committed by magistrates for trial on very satisfactory proof, are returned upon the Public in vast numbers year after year; encouraged to renew their former practices, by the facility they experience in evading justice.

But this is not all:—The adroit Thief and Receiver, availing themselves of their pecuniary resources, often escape, from their knowledge of the tricks and devices which are practised, through the medium of disreputable practitioners of the Law; while the novices in delinquency generally suffer the punishment attached to conviction. If, as is the case in some other countries, evidence were allowed to be received of the general character of persons, put upon their trial for offences, and the means by which they obtain their

7   subsistence,

subsistence, so as to distinguish the old reputed Thief and Receiver from the novice in crimes, the minds of Jurymen would be often enlightened, to the further-ance of substantial justice; and a humane and pro-per distinction might be made between the young pupil of depravity, and the finished villain ; as well in the measure of punishment, as in the distribution of mercy.

The severity of the punishment, which at present attaches to crimes regarded by mankind as of an inferior nature, and which affect property in a trivial manner, is also deserving the most serious attention. It is only necessary to be acquainted with the mo-dern history of the *criminal prosecutions, trials, ac-quittals, and pardons in this country,* in order to be completely convinced that the progressive increase of delinquents, and the evils experienced by Society from the multitude of petty crimes, result in a great measure from this single circumstance.

It will scarcely be credited by those, whose habits of life do not permit them to enter into discussions of this sort, that by the Laws of England, there are above *one hundred and sixty* different offences which subject the parties who are found guilty, to death without benefit of Clergy. This multiplicity of capital punishments must, in the nature of things, defeat those ends, the attainment of which ought to be the object of all Law, namely, *The Prevention of Crimes.*

In consequence of this severity, (to use the words of an admired Writer,) " The injured, through
" compassion,

" compassion, will often forbear to prosecute: Juries,
" through compassion, will sometimes forget their
" oaths, and either acquit the guilty or mitigate the
" nature of the offence; and Judges, through com-
" passion, will respite one half the convicts, and
" recommend them to Royal Mercy."*

The Roman Empire never flourished so much as
during the æra of the Portian Law, which abrogated
the punishment of death for all offences whatsoever.
When severe punishments and an incorrect Police
were afterwards revived, the Empire fell.

It is not meant, however, to be insinuated that
this would be, altogether, a proper system of Criminal
Jurisprudence to be adopted in modern times.

In the present state of society it becomes indispensably necessary, that offences, which in their nature
are highly injurious to the Public, and where no mode
of prevention can be established, should be punished
by the forfeiture of life; but these dreadful examples
should be exhibited as seldom as possible: for while
on the one hand, such punishments often defeat the
ends of Justice, by their not being carried into execution; so on the other, by being often repeated,
they lose their effect upon the minds of the People.†
However

---

* Blackstone's Commentaries.

† Can that be thought a correct System of Jurisprudence, which
inflicts the penalty of Death, for breaking down the mound of a
fish-pond, whereby the fish may escape; or cutting down a fruit-
tree in a garden or orchard; or stealing a handkerchief, or any
trifle, privately from a person's pocket, above the value of 12d;—
while

However much we glory (and we ought to glory) in the general excellence of our Criminal Law, yet there is no truth more clear and obvious than this:—"That this code exhibits too much the appear-"ance of a heterogeneous mass, concocted too often "on the spur of the occasion (as Lord Bacon ex-"presses it):—and frequently without that degree "of accuracy which is the result of able and minute "discussion, or a due attention to the revision of "the existing laws, or how far their provisions bear "upon new and accumulated statutes introduced "into Parliament; often without either considera-"tion or knowledge, and without those precautions "which are always necessary, when laws are to be "made which may affect the property, the liberty, "and perhaps even the lives of thousands."

Some steps have, indeed, been taken in Parliament, since this work first appeared, towards a general revision of our Statute Law,* and which, it is hoped, will ere long be adopted. Whenever the time shall arrive that the existing laws, which form the present Criminal Code, shall be referred to able and intelligent men

while a number of other crimes of much greater enormity, are only punished with transportation and imprisonment; and while the punishment of murder itself is, and can be, only Death, with a few circumstances of additional ignominy?

* See the "Report from the Committee of the House of Commons on Temporary Laws," May 13, 1796—and also the "Re-"port from the Committee for promulgation of the Statutes," December 5, 1796; and the "Resolutions of a Committee of the whole House," March 20, 1797.

effectually

effectually to revise, consolidate, and adjust the whole, in a manner best suited to the present state of Society and Manners, the investigation will unquestionably excite no little wonder and astonishment.

Penal laws, which are either obsolete or absurd, or which have arisen, from an adherence to rules of Common Law when the reasons have ceased upon which these rules are founded ; and in short, all Laws which appear not to be consonant to the dictates of truth and justice, the feelings of Humanity, and the indelible rights of Mankind, should be abrogated and repealed*.

But the deficiency of the Criminal Code does not arise solely from an erroneous and undigested scale of penalties and punishments. While on the one hand, we have to lament the number of these applicable to certain offences of a slight nature : we have equally to regret, that there exist crimes of considerable enormity, for the punishment of which the Law has made no provision.

Among the most prominent of these crimes may be ranked the receiving *Cash or Specie, Bank-Notes* or *Bills, knowing them to be stolen.*

To this very high offence, in its nature so productive of mischief in a Commercial Country, no punishment at all attaches; inasmuch as *Specie, Notes, and Bills,* are not considered for this purpose

* Blackstone.

to

to be *Goods and Chattels;* and the law only makes it a crime to receive property so described.

If therefore a notorious Receiver of stolen goods shall be convicted of purchasing a glass bottle or a pewter pot, he is liable to be punished severely; but if he receives ten or twenty thousand pounds in *Cash, Bank-Notes,* or *Bills,* he escapes with impunity?*"

Innumerable almost are the other instances which could be collected from Reporters of Criminal Cases, shewing the deficiency of the Criminal Code; and in how many instances substantial justice is defeated, and public wrongs are suffered to go unpunished, through the objections and quibbles constantly raised in Courts of Justice; and which are allowed to prevail, principally, for want of that revision of our laws and those amendments which the present state of Society and Commerce requires.

One of the chief nurseries of Crimes is to be traced to the Receivers of Stolen Property.

Without that easy encouragement which these Receivers hold out, by administering immediately to the wants of criminals, and concealing what they purloin, a Thief, a Robber, or a Burglar, could not, in fact, carry on his trade.

And yet, conclusive and obvious as this remark must be, it is a sorrowful truth, that in the Metropolis alone there are at present supposed to be

* It is said the same construction of the Law has been made with respect to the Offence of buying or receiving Horses, knowing them to be stolen.

upwards

upwards of Three Thousand Receivers of various kinds of stolen Goods; and an equal proportion all over the Country, who keep open shop for the purpose of purchasing at an under price—often for a mere trifle,—every kind of property brought to them; from a nail, or a glass bottle, up to the most valuable article either new or old; and this without asking a single question.

It is supposed that the property, purloined and pilfered in a little way, from almost every family, and from every *house, stable, shop, warehouse, workshop, foundery, and other repository,* in and about the Metropolis, may amount to about 700,000*l.* in one year, exclusive of depredations on ships in the River Thames, which, before the establishment of the Marine Police System in June 1798, were estimated at half a million more, including the stores and materials!—When to this is also added the Pillage of his Majesty's stores, in ships of war, Dockyards, and other public repositories, the aggregate will be found in point of extent, almost to exceed credibility!

It is a melancholy reflection to consider how many individuals, young and old, who are not of the class or description of common or even reputed thieves, are implicated in this system of depredation; who would probably have remained honest and industrious, had it not been for the easy mode of raising money, which these numerous Receivers of stolen goods hold out in every bye-street and lane

in

in the Metropolis: In their houses, although a
beggarly appearance of old iron, old rags, or second-
hand clothes, is only exhibited, the back apartments
are often filled with the most valuable articles of
ship-stores, copper-bolts and nails, brass and other
valuable metals, West-India produce, household
goods and wearing apparel; purchased from artificers, labourers in the docks, lumpers, and others
employed on the River Thames, menial servants,
apprentices, journeymen, porters, chimney-sweepers,
itinerant Jews, and others; who, thus encouraged
and protected, go on with impunity, and without
the least dread of detection, from the easiness of
access, which their various employments give them,
plundering every article not likely to be missed, in
the houses or stables of men of property; or in the
shops, warehouses, founderies, or work-shops of manufacturers; or from new buildings; from ships in
the river; nay even from his Majesty's stores, and
other repositories, so that in some instances, the
same articles are said to be sold to the Public Boards
three or four times over.

Thus the moral principle is totally destroyed among
a vast body of the lower ranks of the People; for
wherever prodigality, dissipation, or gaming, whether
in the Lottery or otherwise, occasions a want of
money, every opportunity is sought to purloin public
or private property; recourse is then had to all those
tricks and devices, by which even children are
enticed to steal before they know that it is a crime;
and to raise money at the pawnbrokers, or the old

iron

iron or rag shops, to supply the unlawful desires of profligate parents.

Hence also, Servants, Apprentices, Journeymen, and in short all classes of labourers and domestics, are led astray by the temptations to spend money, which occur in the Metropolis; and by the facility afforded through the numerous Receivers of stolen Goods, who administer to their pecuniary wants, on every occasion, when they can furnish them with any article of their ill-gotten plunder.

The necessity of adopting some effectual regulations respecting the numerous class of Dealers in old metal, stores, and wearing apparel, is too obvious to require illustration; and the progressive accumulation of these pests of Society is proved, by their having increased, from about 300 to 3000, in the course of the last twenty years, in the Metropolis alone.

Similar regulations should also be extended to all the more latent Receivers, who do not keep open shop; but secretly support the professed Robbers and Burglars, by purchasing their plunder the moment it is acquired : of which latter class there are some who are said to be extremely opulent.

It would by no means be difficult to form such a plan of Police as should establish many useful restrictions, for the purpose of checking and embarrassing these criminal people ; so as to render it extremely difficult, if not impracticable for them, in many instances, to carry on their business without the greatest hazard of detection.

But

But laws for this purpose must not be placed upon the Statute-Book as a kind of dead letter, only to be brought into action when accident may lead to the detection, perhaps of one in a thousand. If the evil is to be cured at all, it must be by the promotion and encouragement of an active principle, under proper superintendance, calculated to prevent every class of dealers, who are known to live partly or wholly by fraud, from pursuing those illegal practices; which nothing but a watchful Police, aided by a correct system of restraints, can possibly effect.

Nor ought it to be argued, that the restraints, which may hereafter be proposed, will affect the liberty of the Subject. They will assist and protect the honest and fair dealer; and it is perfectly consistent with the spirit of our ancient laws, to restrain persons from doing evil, who are likely to commit offences; the restrictions can affect only a very few, comparatively speaking; and those too whose criminal conduct has been the principal, if not the sole cause, of abridging the general liberty; while it subjected the great mass of the people to the risk of their life and property.

Whenever Dealers, of any description, are known to encourage or to support crimes, or criminal or fraudulent persons, it becomes the indispensable interest of the State, and the duty of the Legislators to prevent them from pursuing, at least, the mischievous part of their trade; and that provisions
should

should be made for carrying the laws strictly and regularly into execution.

While restraints of a much severer nature than those which are hereafter proposed, attach to all trades upon which a revenue is collected; can it be considered as any infringement of freedom to extend a milder system to those who not only destroy liberty but invade property?

The present state of Society and Manners calls aloud for the adoption of this principle of regulation, as the only practicable means of preserving the morals of a vast body of the Community; and of preventing those numerous and increasing crimes and misdemeanors, which are ultimately attended with as much evil to the perpetrators as to the sufferers.

If such a principle were once established, under circumstances which would insure a correct and regular execution; and if, added to this, certain other practicable arrangements should take place, (which will be discussed in their regular order in these pages,) we might soon congratulate ourselves on the immediate and obvious reduction of the number of Thieves, Robbers, Burglars, and other criminals in this Metropolis, being no longer able to exist, or to escape detection.   Without the aid, the concealment, and the opportunities, afforded at present by the multitude of Receivers spread all over the Capital, they would be compelled to abandon their evil pursuits, as no less unprofitable and hazardous, than they are destructive to the best interests of Society.

This

This indeed is very different from what is said to have once prevailed in the Capital, when criminals were permitted to proceed from the first stage of depravity until they were worth forty pounds.—This is not the System which subjected the Public to the immediate depredations of every villain from his first starting, till he could be clearly convicted of a capital offence.—Neither is it the System which encouraged public houses of rendezvous for Thieves, for the purpose of knowing where to apprehend them, when they became ripe for the punishment of death.

The System now suggested, is calculated to prevent, if possible, the seeds of villany from being sown : or, if sown, to check their growth in the bud, and never permit them to ripen at all.

It is proposed to extend this system of prevention to the Coiners, Dealers, and Utterers of base Money, and to every species of theft, robbery, fraud, and depredation.

The vast increase, and the extensive circulation of counterfeit Money, particularly of late years, is too obvious not to have attracted the notice of all ranks. It has become an enormous evil in the melancholy catalogue of Crimes which the Laws of the Country are called upon to assist the Police in suppressing.— Its extent almost exceeds credibility; and the dexterity and ingenuity of these counterfeiters have, (after considerable practice,) enabled them to finish the different kinds of base Money in so masterly a manner, that it has become extremely difficult for
the

the common observer to distinguish their spurious manufacture from the worn-out Silver of the Mint.— So systematic, indeed, has this nefarious traffic become of late, that the great dealers, who, in most instances are the employers of the Coiners, execute orders for the Town and Country, with the same regularity as manufacturers in fair branches of trade.

Scarcely a waggon or coach departs from the Metropolis, which does not carry boxes and parcels of base Coin to the camps, sea-ports, and manufacturing towns. In London, regular markets, in various public and private houses, are held by the principal Dealers; where *Hawkers, Pedlars, fraudulent Horse-Dealers, Unlicensed Lottery-Office-Keepers, Gamblers at Fairs, Itinerant Jews, Irish Labourers, Servants of Toll-Gatherers, and Hackney Coach Owners, fraudulent Publicans, Market-Women, Rabbit-Sellers, Fish-Cryers, Barrow-Women*, and many who would not be suspected, are regularly supplied with counterfeit Copper and Silver, with the advantage of nearly 100*l. per cent.* in their favour; and thus it happens, that through these various channels, the country is deluged with immense quantities of base Money, which get into circulation; while an evident diminution of the Mint Coinage is apparent to every common observer.

It is impossible to reflect on the necessity to which all persons are thus reduced, of receiving and again uttering, Money which is known to be false and counterfeit, without lamenting, that by thus familiarizing

liarizing the mind to fraud and deception, the same laxity of conduct may be introduced into other transactions of life :—The barrier being broken down in one part, the principle of common honesty is infringed upon, and infinite mischief to the very best interests of Society, is the result, in cases at first unthought of.

To permit, therefore, the existence of an adulterated and ill-regulated Silver and Copper Coinage, is in fact to tolerate general fraud and deception, to the ultimate loss of many individuals ; for the evil must terminate at some period, and then thousands must suffer; with this aggravation, that the longer it continues the greater will be the loss of property.

Nor has the mischief been confined to the counterfeiting the Coin of the Realm. The avarice and ingenuity of man is constantly finding out new sources of fraud ; insomuch, that in London, and in Birmingham, and its neighbourhood, Louis d'Ors, Half Johannas, French Half Crowns and Shillings, as well as several coins of Flanders and Germany, and Dollars of excellent workmanship, in exact imitation of the Spanish Dollars issued from the Bank, in 1797, have been from time to time coun terfeited ; apparently without suspicion, that under the act of the 14th of Elizabeth, (cap. 3,) the offenders were guilty of misprision of High Treason.

These ingenious miscreants have also extended their iniquitous manufacture to the coins of India ; and a Coinage of the Star Pagoda of Arcot was
established

established in London for years by one person.—— These counterfeits, being made wholly of blanched copper, tempered in such a manner as to exhibit when stamped, the cracks in the edges, which are always to be found on the real Pagoda, cost the maker only Three Half-pence each, after being double gilt.—When finished, they are generally sold to Jews at Five Shillings a dozen, who disposed of them afterwards at 2s. 3s. or even 5s. each; and through this medium, they have been introduced by a variety of channels into India, where they were mixed with the real Pagodas of the country, and passed at their full denominated value of Eight Shilings sterling.

The Sequins of Turkey, another Gold Coin, worth about five or six shillings, have in like manner been counterfeited in London ;—Thus the national character is wounded, and the disgrace of the British name proclaimed in Asia, and even in the most distant regions of India. Nor can it be sufficiently lamented that persons who consider themselves as ranking in superior stations of life, with some pretensions to honour and integrity, have suffered their avarice so far to get the better of their honesty, as to be concerned in this iniquitous traffic.

It has been recently discovered that there are at least 120 persons in the Metropolis and the Country, employed principally in coining and selling base Money; and this, independent of the numerous horde

of

of Utterers, who chiefly support themselves by passing it at its full value.

It will scarcely be credited, that of Criminals of this latter class, who have either been detected, prosecuted, or convicted, within the last seven years, there stand upon the Register of the Solicitor to the Mint, more than 650 names!—And yet the mischief is not diminished. When the Reader is informed, that two persons can finish from 200*l.* to 300*l.* (nominal value,) in base silver in *six days;* and that three people, within the same period, will stamp the like amount in Copper, and takes into the calculation the number of known Coiners, the aggregate amount in the course of a year will be found to be immense.

The causes of this enormous evil are, however, easily developed.—The principal laws relative to Counterfeit Coin having been made a Century ago, the tricks and devices of modern times are not sufficiently provided against;* when it is considered also, that the offence of dealing in base Money, (which is the main spring of the evil,) is only punishable by a slight imprisonment; that several offences of a similar nature are not punishable at all, by any existing statute; and that the detection of actual Coiners, so as to obtain the proof necessary for conviction, required by Law, is, in many in-

* The partial remedy applied to some of these evils by Statutes passed since the former Edition of this Work, shall be noticed in a subsequent Chapter dedicated to the subject of Coinage.

stances,

stances, impracticable ; it is not to be wondered at where the profit is so immense, with so many chances of escaping punishment, that the coinage of, and traffic in, counterfeit Money has attracted the attention of so many unprincipled and avaricious persons.

Having thus stated many prominent abuses which appear to arise from the imperfections in our Criminal Code, as well as the benefits which an improved system would extend to the country; it now remains to elucidate the further evils arising to Society, from the abuses practised in carrying the existing statutes into execution.—As the laws now stand, little or no energy enters into the system of detection, so as to give vigor and effect to that branch of Police which relates to the apprehension of persons charged with offences; and no sooner does a Magistrate commit a hacknied Thief or Receiver of stolen Goods, a Coiner, or Dealer in base Money, or a Criminal charged with any other fraud or offence punishable by law, than recourse is immediately had to some disreputable Attorney, whose mind is made up and prepared to practice every trick and device which can defeat the ends of substantial justice. Depraved persons, frequently accomplices, are hired to swear an *alibi* ; witnesses are cajoled, threatened, or bribed either to mutilate their evidence, or to speak doubtfully on the trial, although they swore positively before the committing Magistrate.

If bribes and persuasions will not do, the prosecutors

tors are either intimidated by the expence,* or softened down by appeals to their humanity ; and under
such circumstances, they neither employ counsel nor
take the necessary steps to bring forward evidence :
the result is, that the Bill is either returned *ignoramus*
by the Grand Jury; or, if a trial takes place, under
all the disadvantages of a deficient evidence, without
a counsel for the prosecution, an advocate is heard
for the prisoner, availing himself of every trifling inaccuracy which may screen his client from the punishment of the Law, the hardened villain is acquitted
and escapes justice: while, as we before noticed, the
novice in crimes, unskilled in the deficiencies of the
Law, and unable, from the want of criminal connections, or that support which the professed thief receives from the Buyers of stolen goods, to procure
the aid of counsel to defend him, *is often convicted!*

The Registers of the Old Bailey afford a lamentable proof of the evils arising from the present mode
of trying criminals without a public Prosecutor for
the Crown.—In the course of seven years, previous
to the Police Establishment, no less than 4262
prisoners, who had been actually put upon their trial
by the Grand Jury, were let loose upon the Public
by acquittals.

* No hardship can be so great as that of subjecting an individual, under any circumstance whatsoever, to the expence of a public prosecution, carried on in behalf of the King; besides adding,
almost on every occasion, to the loss of the parties, it is productive of infinite mischief, in defeating the ends of justice.

Since

Since that period no material diminution has taken place, except what may be easily accounted for by the war; and when to this dreadful Catalogue of Human Depravity, is to be added, the vast number of criminals who are periodically discharged from the different gaols by proclamation, and of cheats, swindlers, gamblers, and others, who have never yet been discovered or known, we may state with certainty that there are at this time *many thousand* individuals, male and female, prowling about in this Metropolis, who principally support themselves by various depredations on the Public.

Nor does the evil rest here; for even convicted felons, in too many instances, find means to escape without punishment; and to join that phalanx of villains, who are constantly engaged in objects of depredation and mischief.

No sooner does the punishment of the law attach on a criminal, than false humanity becomes his friend. Pardons are applied for; and it is known that his Majesty's great goodness and love of mercy has been frequently abused by the tricks, devices, and frauds, too commonly resorted to, by convicts and agents equally depraved as themselves; who while they have recourse to every species of falsehood and forgery, for the purpose of attaining the object in view, at the same time plunder the friends and relatives of the prisoner, of their last guinea, as the wages of villany and misrepresentation.

By such nefarious practices, it is much to be feared,

feared, that many a hardened villain has eluded the punishment of the Law, without any previous reference to the committing Magistrates, who may be supposed to have accurately examined into his character and connections; and what is still worse, without extending to the Community those benefits which might arise from important discoveries useful to Public Justice: such as convicted felons are always capable of making, and which, in conjunction with transportation, it should seem, ought to be one indispensable condition, upon which pardons should be granted to capital convicts.

Instead of these precautions which appear to be absolutely requisite, it is to be lamented, that without reflecting that a common thief can seldom be restrained by military discipline, many of the worst class of convicts have received his Majesty's gracious pardon, on the simple condition of going into the Army or Navy: This has been no sooner granted, than the Royal mercy has been abused, either by desertion, or by obtaining a discharge, in consequence of some real or pretended incapacity, which was previously concealed. Relieved in so easy a manner, from the heavy load of a capital punishment, the culprits return again to their old practices; and by this means, punishment not only ceases to operate as a prevention of crimes, by example, but becomes even an encouragement; while the labour of detection, and the expence of trial and conviction, are

fruitlessly

fruitlessly thrown on an injured individual, and their effect is wholly lost to the Public.

In addition to the enormous evil arising from the periodical discharge of so many criminals by procla-mations, acquittals, and pardons, *the* HULKS also send forth, at stated times, a certain number of convicts ; who having *no asyluu, no home, no character,* and *no means of subsistence,* seem to have only the alterna-tive of starving, or joining their companions in ini-quity ; thus adding strength to the body of criminals, by the accession of men, who, polluted and depraved by every human vice, rendered familiar to their minds in those seminaries of profligacy and wicked-ness from whence they have come, employ them-selves constantly in planning and executing acts of violence and depredation upon the Public ; and some of them, rendered desperate from an additional de-gree of depravity, feel no compunction in adding the crime of murder to that of robbery, as has been too clearly manifested by many late instances.

From what has been thus stated, is it not fair to conclude, that the want of security which the Pub-lic experiences with regard to life and property, and the inefficacy of the Police in preventing crimes, are to be attributed principally to the following causes?

1, *The imperfections in the Criminal Code ; and in many instances, its deficiency with respect to the mode of punishment : as well as to the want of many other regulations,*

regulations, provisions, and restraints, applicable to the present state of Society, for the purpose of preventing crimes.

2. *The want of an active principle, calculated to concentrate and connect the whole Police of the Metropolis and the Nation; and to reduce the general management to system and method, by the interposition of a superintending agency, composed of able, intelligent, and indefatigable men, acting under the direction and controul of his Majesty's Principal Secretary of State for the Home Department.—On these persons, it is proposed, should devolve the subordinate care and direction of the general Police of the Metropolis; so as to obtain, by the introduction of order and arrangement, and by efforts of labour and exertion, a complete History of the connections, and pursuits of all or most of the criminal and fraudulent persons who resort to the Metropolis; (either natives or foreigners;) forming, from such materials, a register of all known offenders, and thereby establishing a clue for their detection, as often as they are charged with committing depredations on the Public—with power to reward Officers of Justice, and all other persons whose services are found to be useful in the discovery or detection of delinquents of every description.—To keep an Account of property stolen, or procured by swindling or fraudulent transactions in the Metropolis, as well as in other parts of Great-Britain.—To establish a Correspondence with the Magistrates in Town and Country,*

Country, so as to be able more effectually to watch the motions of all suspected persons; with a view to quick and immediate detection; and to interpose such embarrassments in the way of every class of offenders, as may diminish crimes by increasing the risk of detection: All this, under circumstances where a centre-point would be formed, *and the general affairs of the Police conducted with method and regularity: —where Magistrates would find assistance and information; where the greater offences, such as the* Coinage of base Money, *and* Lottery Insurances, *would be traced to their source; the care and disposal of convicts, according to their different sentences, be minutely attended to; and the whole System conducted with that intelligence and benefit to the Country, which must arise from the attention of men of business being directed solely to these objects, distinct from all other affairs of State; and their exertions being confined principally to the preservation of the morals of the People, and the prevention of crimes.*

3. *The want of an Institution of Police Magistrates in the Dock Yards, and in all great Commercial and Manufacturing Towns, where there are no Corporations or Funds for the administration of Public Justice.*

4. *The want of a Public Prosecutor for the Crown, in all criminal cases, for the purpose of preventing fraud, delay, and expence in the administration of Justice.*

6. *The*

5. *The want of a more correct and regular System, for the purpose of obtaining the fullest and most authentic information, to avoid deceptions in the obtaining of pardons.*

6. *The deficiency of the System of the* Hulks.

7. *The want of an improved System with regard to the arrangements and disposal af Convicts—destined for hard labour or for transportation.*

8. *The want of national* Penitentiary Houses, *for the punishment and reformation of certain classes of Convicts.*

9. *The want of a more solemn mode of conducting Executions; whenever such dreadful examples are necessary for the furtherance of Public Justice.*

Having thus explained the general features of the actually existing *Crimes,* and their probable causes, we shall in the next place proceed to some considerations on the present principles of *Punishments,* in this Country, as compared with those in other nations and ages. It will then be requisite to enter into particular and minute details on both these subjects; and to offer some suggestions for the introduction of new and applicable laws to be administered with purity under a correct and energetic System of Police; which may be, in some degree, effectual in guarding the Public against those increasing and multifarious injuries and dangers, which are universally felt and lamented.

CHAP.

CHAP. II.

*Of Punishments in general.—The mode of ascertaining
the degrees of Punishment.—The objects to be considered in inflicting Punishments—namely, Amendment—Example—and Retribution.—The Punishment of Death has little effect on hardened Offenders.—Examples of convicts exhibited in servile
employments would make a greater impression.—Towards rendering the criminal laws perfect, Prevention ought to be the great object of the Legislature.
—General Rules suggested for attaining this object,
with illustrations.—The severity of our laws with
respect to Punishments—not reconcileable to the
principles of morality, and a free government—calculated in their operation to debase the human character.—General Reflections on the Punishments authorised by the English Law.—The disproportion of
Punishments, exemplified in the case of an assault,
opposed to a larceny.—In seduction and adultery,
which are not punishable as criminal offences.—The
laws severe in the extreme in political offences, while
they are lax and defective with regard to moral
Crimes.—The necessity of enforcing the observance
of religious and moral Virtue by lesser Punishments.
—General Reflections applicable to public and private Crimes.—The dangers arising from the progress
of immorality to the safety of the State.—The leading offences made capital by the laws of England
considered,*

*considered, with the Punishment allotted to each;
compared with, and illustrated by, the custom of
other countries, in similar cases, both ancient and
modern : namely, High Treason—Petit Treason :
—Felonies against Life, viz. Murder, Manslaughter, Misadventure, and Self-defence : against the
Body, comprehending Sodomy, Rape, Forcible Marriage, Polygamy and Mayhem.—Against Goods or
Property, comprehending Simple Larceny, Mixt
Larceny, and Piracy,—and against the Habitation,
comprehending Arson and Burglary.—Concluding
Reflections relative to the severity of the Laws, and
their imperfections with regard to Punishment.—
The new Code of the* Emperor JOSEPH *the Second,
shortly detailed.—Reflections thereon.*

PUNISHMENT, (says a learned and respectable author)
*is an evil which a delinquent suffers, unwillingly, by
the order of a Judge or Magistrate; on account of
some act done which the Law prohibits, or something
omitted which the Law enjoins.*

All Punishment should be proportioned to the
nature of the offence committed; and the Legislature, in adjusting Punishment with a view to the
public good, ought, according to the dictates of sound
reason, to act on a comparison of the Crime under
consideration, with other offences injurious to Society: and thus by comparing one offence with
another,

another, to form a scale, or gradation, of Punishments, as nearly as possible consistent with the strict rules of distributive justice.*

It is the triumph of Liberty, says the great Montesquieu, when the criminal laws proportion punishments to the particular nature of each offence.—It may be further added, that when this is the case, it is also the triumph of Reason.

In order to ascertain in what degree the Public is injured or endangered by any crime, it is necessary to weigh well and dispassionately the nature of the offence, as it affects the Community.—It is through this medium that Treason and Rebellion are discovered to be higher and more dangerous offences than breaches of the peace by riotous assemblies ; as such riotous meetings are in like manner considered as more criminal than a private assault.

In punishing delinquents, two objects ought to be invariably kept in view.—

1. The Amendment of the Delinquent.

2. The Example afforded to others.

To which may be added, in certain cases,

3. Retribution to the party injured.

If we attend to Reason, the *Mistress of all Law*, she will convince us that it is both unjust and injurious to Society to inflict Death, except for the highest offences, and in cases where the offender appears to be incorrigible.

* Beccaria on Crimes and Punishments, Cap. 6.

Wherever

Wherever the amendment of a delinquent is in view, it is clear that his punishment cannot extend to death : If expatiating an offence by the loss of life is to be (as it certainly is at present) justified by the necessity of making examples for the purpose of preventing crimes, it is evident that the present System has not had that effect, since they are by no means diminished; and since even the dread of this Punishment has, under present circumstances, so little effect upon guilty associates, that it is no uncommon thing for these hardened offenders to be engaged in new acts of theft, at the very moment their companions in iniquity are launching, in their very presence, into eternity.

The minds of offenders, long inured to the practice of criminal pursuits, are by no means beneficially affected by the punishment of Death, which they are taught to consider as nothing but a momentary paroxysm which ends all their distress at once; nay even as a relief, which many of them, grown desperate, look upon with a species of indifference, bordering on a desire to meet that fate, which puts an end to the various distresses and anxieties attendant on a life of criminality.

The effect of capital punishments, in the manner they are now conducted, therefore, as far as relates to example, appears to be much less than has been generally imagined.

Examples would probably have much greater force, even on those who at present appear dead to shame

and

and the stigma of infamy, were convicts exhibited day after day, to their companions, occupied in mean and servile employments in Penitentiary Houses, or on the highways, canals, mines or public works.—It is in this way only that there is the least chance of making retribution to the parties whom they have injured; or of reimbursing the State, for the unavoidable expence which their evil pursuits have occasioned.

Towards accomplishing the desirable object of perfection in a criminal code, every wise Legislature will have it in contemplation rather to prevent than to punish crimes; that in the chastisement given, the delinquent may be restored to Society as an useful member.

This purpose may possibly be best effected by the adoption of the following general rules.

1. That the Statute-Laws should accurately explain the enormity of the offence forbidden; and that its provisions should be clear and explicit, resulting from a perfect knowledge of the subject; so that justice may not be defeated in the execution.

2. That the punishments should be proportioned and adapted, as nearly as possible, to the different degrees of offences; with a proper attention also to the various shades of enormity which may attach to certain crimes.

3. That persons prosecuting, or compelled so to do, should not only be indemnified from expence; but also that reparation should be made, for losses sustained by the injured party, in all cases where it can be obtained from the labour, or property of the delinquent.

4. That

4. That satisfaction should be made to the State for the injury done to the Community; by disturbing the peace and violating the purity of Society.

Political laws, which are repugnant to the Law of nature and reason, ought not to be adopted. The objects above-mentioned seem to include all that can be necessary for the attention of Law-givers.

If on examination of the frame and tendency of our criminal laws, both with respect to the principles of Reason and State Policy, the Author might be allowed to indulge a hope, that what he brings under the Public Eye on this important subject, would be of use in promoting the good of Mankind, he should consider his labours as very amply rewarded.

The severity of the criminal Laws is not only an object of horror, but the disproportion of the punishments, as will be shewn in the course of this Work, breathes too much the spirit of DRACO,* who boasted *that he punished all crimes with death; because small crimes deserved it, and he could find no higher punishment for the greatest.*

Though the ruling principle of our Government is unquestionably *Liberty*, it is much to be feared that the rigour which the Laws indiscriminately inflict on slight as well as more atrocious offences, can be ill reconciled to the true distinctions of Morality, and strict notions of Justice, which form the peculiar ex-

* He lived 624 years before the Christian æra.

cellence

cellence of those States which are to be charac-
terised as free.

By punishing smaller offences with extraordinary
severity, is there not a risque of inuring men to base-
ness; and of plunging them into the sink of infamy
and despair, from whence they seldom fail to rise
capital criminals; often to the destruction of their
fellow-creatures, and always to their own inevitable
perdition?

To suffer the lower orders of the people to be ill
educated—to be totally inattentive to those wise regulations of State Policy which might serve to guard
and improve their morals; and then to punish them
for crimes which have originated in bad habits, has
the appearance of a cruelty not less severe than any
which is exercised under the most despotic Governments.

There are two circumstances which ought also to
be minutely considered in apportioning the measure of punishment—*the immorality of the action, and
its evil tendency.*

Nothing contributes in a greater degree to deprave the minds of the people, than the little regard
which Laws pay to Morality; by inflicting more
severe punishments on offenders who commit, what
may be termed *Political Crimes,* and crimes against
property, than on those who violate religion and
virtue.

When we are taught, for instance, by the measure
of

of punishment that it is considered by the Law as a greater crime to coin a sixpence than to kill our father or mother, nature and reason revolt against the proposition.

In offences which are considered by the Legislature as merely personal, and not in the class of public wrongs, the disproportionate punishment is extremely shocking.

If, for example, a personal assault is committed of the most cruel, aggravated, and violent nature, the offender is seldom punished in any other manner than by fine and imprisonment: but if a delinquent steals from his neighbour secretly more than the value of twelve-pence, the Law dooms him to death. And he can suffer no greater punishment (except the ignominy exercised on his dead body,) if he robs and murders a whole family. Some private wrongs of a flagrant nature are even passed over with impunity: the seduction of a married woman—the destruction of the peace and happiness of families, resulting from alienating a wife's affections, and defiling her person, is not an offence punishable by the Criminal Law; while it is death to rob the person, who has suffered this extensive injury, of a trifle exceeding a shilling.

The Crime of Adultery was punished with great severity both by the Grecian and the Roman Laws.—In England this offence is not to be found in the Criminal Code.—It may indeed be punished with fine and penance by the Spiritual Law; or indirectly

in

in the Courts of Common Law, by an action for damages, at the suit of the party injured. The former may now (perhaps fortunately) be considered as a dead letter; while the other remedy, being merely of a pecuniary nature, has little effect in re-straining this species of delinquency.

Like unskilful artists, we seem to have begun at the wrong end: since it is clear that the distinction, which has been made in the punishments between public and private crimes, is subversive of the very foundation it would establish.

Private Offences being the source of public crimes, the best method of guarding Society against the lat-ter is, to make proper provisions for checking the former.—A man of pure morals always makes the best Subject of every State; and few have suffered punish-ment as public delinquents, who have not loug re-mained unpunished as private offenders. The only means, therefore, of securing the peace of Society, and of preventing more atrocious crimes, is, to en-force by lesser punishments, the observance of reli-gious and moral duties: Without this, Laws are but weak Guardians either of the State, or the persons or property of the Subject.

The People are to the Legislature what a child is to a parent:—As the first care of the latter is to teach the love of virtue, and a dread of punishment; so ought it to be the duty of the former, to frame Laws with an immediate view to the general im-provement of morals.

" That

" That Kingdom is happiest where there is most virtue," says an elegant writer.—It follows, of course, that those Laws are the best which are most calculated to promote Religion and Morality; the operation of which in every State, is to produce a conduct intentionally directed towards the Public Good.

It seems that by punishing what are called public Crimes, with peculiar severity, we only provide against present and temporary mischiefs. That we direct the vengeance of the Law against effects, which might have been prevented by obviating their causes:—And this may be assigned in part as the cause of Civil Wars and Revolutions.—The Laws are armed against the *powers* of Rebellion, but are not calculated to oppose its *principle*.

Few civil wars have been waged from considerations of Public Virtue, or even for the security of Public Liberty. These desperate undertakings are generally promoted and carried on by abandoned characters, who seek to better their fortunes in the general havoc and devastation of their country.— Those men are easily seduced from their Loyalty who are apostates from private virtue.

To be secure therefore against those public calamities which, almost inevitably, lead to anarchy and confusion, it is far better to improve and confirm a nation in the true principles of natural justice, than to perplex them by political refinements.

Having thus taken a general view of the principles applicable to Punishments in general, it may be

necessary,

necessary, for the purpose of more fully illustrating these reflections, briefly to consider the various leading Offences, and their corresponding Punishments according to the present state of our Criminal Law; and to examine how far they are proportioned to each other.

High Treason is the highest Crime which can be committed by any member of the Community.— After various alterations and amendments made and repealed in subsequent reigns, the definition of this offence was settled as it originally stood, by the Act of the 25th of Edward III. stat. 5. cap. 2. and may be divided into seven different heads:

1. Compassing or imagining the Death of the King, Queen, or Heir Apparent.
2. Levying War against the King in his realm.
3. Adhering to the King's enemies, and giving them aid, in the realm or elsewhere *.

4. Slaying

* It has been thought necessary, by the Legislature, to explain and enlarge these clauses of the Act 25 *Ed.* III. as not extending, with sufficient explicitness, to modern treasonable attempts. It is therefore provided by the Act 36 *Geo.* III. *cap.* 7, " That if any person (during the life of his present Majesty, and until the end of the Session of Parliament next after a demise of the Crown) shall within the realm, or without, compass, imagine, invent, devise, or intend death or destruction, *or any bodily harm, tending to death or destruction, maim, or wounding, imprisonment, or restraint* of the person of the King, his heirs, and successors, or to deprive or depose him or them from his stile, honour, or kingly name; or to levy war against the King within this Realm, in order by force to compel him to change his measures; *or in order to put any force or con-*
straint

4. Slaying the King's Chancellor or Judge in the execution of their offices.

5. Violating the Queen, the eldest daughter of the King, or the wife of the Heir Apparent, or eldest Son.

6. Counterfeiting the King's Great Seal, or Privy Seal.

7. Counterfeiting the King's Money, or bringing false Money into the kingdom.

This detail shews how much the dignity and security of the King's person is confounded with that of his officers, and even with his effigies imprest on his Coin.—To assassinate the servant, or to counterfeit the type, is held as criminal as to destroy the Sovereign.

This indiscriminate blending of crimes, so different and disproportionate in their nature, under one common head, is certainly liable to great objections; seeing that the judgment in this offence is so extremely severe and terrible, *viz. That the offender be drawn to the gallows on the ground or pavement: That he be hanged by the neck, and then cut down alive: That his entrails be taken out and burned while*

straint upon, or to intimidate or overawe, BOTH HOUSES, OR EITHER HOUSE, OF PARLIAMENT; or to incite any foreigner to invade the dominions of the Crown: and such compassings, &c. shall express, utter, or declare, by publishing any printing, or writing, or by any other overt act or deed"—the offender shall be deemed a Traitor, and punished accordingly.

he

*he is yet alive : That his head be cut off : That his
body be divided into four parts : And that his head
and quarters be at the King's disposal.*—Women,
however, are only to be drawn and hanged :—though
in all cases of treason, they were heretofore sentenced to be burned : a cruel punishment, which,
after being alleviated by the custom of previous
strangulation, was at length repealed, by the Act 30
Geo. III. *c.* 48.

There are indeed some shades of difference with
regard to coining money ; where the offender is only
drawn and hanged ; and that part of the punishment which relates to being *drawn* and *quartered* is,
to the honour of humanity, never practised.   But
even in cases of the most atrocious criminality, the
execution of so horrid a sentence seems to answer no
good political purpose.—Nature shudders at the
thought of imbruing our hands in blood, and mangling the smoking entrails of our fellow-creatures.

In most Countries and in all ages, however, Treason has been punished capitally.—Under the Roman
Laws, by the *Cornelia Lex*, of which Sylla, the Dicta-
tor, was the author, this Offence was created—It was
also made a capital crime when the Persian Monarchy became despotic.

By the Laws of China, Treason and Rebellion are
punished with a rigour even beyond the severity of
our judgment, for the criminals are ordained to be
cut in *ten thousand* pieces.

There is another species of Treason, called *Petty
Treason,*

Treason, described by the Statute of the 25th of Edward the III, to be the offence of *a Servant killing his Master, a Wife killing her husband,* or a *Secular or Religious slaying his Prelate.*—The Punishment is somewhat more ignominious than in other capital offences, inasmuch as a *hurdle* is used instead of a *cart.*—Here again occurs a very strong instance of the inequality of Punishments; for although the principle and essence of this Crime is breach of duty and obedience due to a superior slain, yet if a child murder his parents (unless he serve them for wages) he is not within the Statute; although it must seem evident to the meanest understanding that Parricide is certainly a more atrocious and aggravated offence, than either of those specified in the Statute.

By the *Lex Pompeia* of the Romans, Parricides were ordained to be sewn in a sack with a *dog,* a *cock,* a *viper,* and an *ape,* and thrown into the sea, thus to perish by the most cruel of all tortures.

The antient laws of all civilized nations punished the crime of Parricide by examples of the utmost severity.—The Egyptians put the delinquents to death by the most cruel of all tortures—mangling the body and limbs, and afterwards laying it upon thorns to be burnt alive.

By the Jewish Law it was death for children to curse, or strike their parents; and in China, this crime was considered as next in atrocity to Treason and Rebellion, and in like manner punished by cutting the delinquent in *one thousand* pieces.

The

The Laws of England however make no distinction between this crime and common Murder; while it is to be lamented that offences far less heinous, either morally or politically considered, are punished with the same degree of severity ; and it is much to be feared, that this singular inequality is ill calculated to inspire that filial awe and reverence to parents, which all human Laws ought to inculcate.

The offences next in enormity to Treason, are by the Laws of England, denominated Felonies, and these may be considered as of two kinds, *public* and *private.*

Under the head of *Public Felonies,* we shall class the following: having peculiar relation to the State.

1. Felonies relative to the Coin of the Realm.
2. ——————— to the King and his Counsellors, &c.
3. ——————— to Soldiers and Marines.
4. ——————— to embezzling Public Property.
5. ——————— to Riot and Sedition.
6. ——————— to Escape from Prison.
7. ——————— to Revenue and Trade, &c.

We consider as comprehended under *Private Felonies* the following crimes committed, 1. *Against the Life,* 2. *The Body,* 3. *The Goods,* 4. *The Habitation of the Subject.*

Against Life.
1. By Murder.
2. By Man-slaughter.
3. By Misadventure.
4. By Necessity.

Against the Body.
1. Sodomy.
2. Rape.
3. ForcibleMarriage.
4. Polygamy.
5. Mayhem.

Against Goods.
1. Simple Larceny
2. Mixt Larceny.
3. Piracy.

Against the Dwelling or Habitation.
1. Arson.
2. Burglary.

Those

Those Crimes which we have denominated *Public Felonies* being merely of a political nature, it would seem that the ends of justice would be far better answered than at present, and convictions oftener obtained, by different degrees of Punishment short of Death.

With regard to *Private Felonies*, it may be necessary to make some specific observations——

The first, in point of enormity, is *Murder*, which may be committed in two ways:—first, upon *one's self*, in which case the offender is denominated *Felo de se*, or a *Self-murderer*;—secondly, by killing another person.

The Athenian Law ordained, that persons guilty of Self-murder, should have the hand cut off which did the murder, and buried in a place separate from the body; but this seems of little consequence.— When such a calamity happens, it is a deplorable misfortune; and there seems to be a great cruelty in adding to the distress of the wife, children, or nearest kin of the deceased, by the forfeiture of his whole property; which is at present confiscated by Law.

By the Law of England, the judgment in case of Murder is, that the person convicted shall suffer death and that his body shall be dissected.

The laws of most civilized nations, both ancient and modern, have justly punished this atrocious offence with death. It was so by the Laws of Athens, and also by the Jewish and Roman Laws.—By the Persian Law Murderers were pressed to death be-

between

tween two stones; and in China, persons guilty of this offence are beheaded, except where a person kills his adversary in a duel, in which case he is strangled.—Decapitation by the Laws of China, is considered the most dishonourable mode of execution.

In the ruder ages of the world, and before the manners of mankind were softened by the arts of peace and civilization, Murder was not a capital crime: Hence it is that the barbarous nations which over-ran the Western Empire, either expiated this crime by private revenge, or by a pecuniary composition.—Our Saxon ancestors punished this high offence with a fine; and they too countenanced the exercise of that horrid principle of revenge, by which they added blood to blood.—But in the progress of civilization and Society, the nature of this crime became better understood; private revenge was submitted to the power of the Law; and the good King Alfred first made Murder a capital offence in England.

In this case, as in that of Self-murder, the property of the murderer goes to the State; without any regard to the unhappy circumstances of the families either of the murdered or the guilty person, who may be completely ruined by this fatal accident. —A provision which seems not well to accord with either the justice or mildness of our Laws.

Man-slaughter is defined to be *The killing another without malice, either express or implied: which may be be either, voluntarily, upon a sudden heat; or involuntarily, but in the commission of some unlawful Act.* And the Punishment is, *that the person convicted shall be burnt in the hand, and his goods forfeited.*—And offenders are usually detained in prison for a time not exceeding one year, under the Statutes, regulating the Benefit of the Clergy.

Homicide by *Misadventure* is, when *one is doing a lawful act, without intent to hurt another,* and *death ensues.*—For this offence a pardon is allowed of course; but in strictness of Law the property of the person convicted is forfeited; the rigour of which, however, is obviated by a Writ of Restitution of his goods, to which the party is now, by long usage, entitled of right; only paying for suing out the same.

Homicide *by necessity* or in *Self-defence,* is another shade of Murder, upon which no punishment is inflicted: and in this is included what the Law expresses by the word *Chance-medley:* which is properly applied to such killing as happens in self-defence upon a sudden rencounter. Yet, still by strictness of Law, the goods and chattels of the person charged and convicted are forfeited to the Crown; contrary, as it seems to many, to the principles of Reason and Justice.

It should be recollected that in all cases where the Homicide does not amount to Murder or Manslaughter, the Judges permit, nay even direct a verdict of acquittal.—But it appears more consonant with the sound principles of Justice, that the Law itself

self should be precise, than that the property of a man should, in cases of *Misadventure, Chance-medley, and Self-defence,* depend upon the construction of a Judge, or the lenity of a Jury: Some alteration therefore, in the existing Laws, seems called for in this particular.

Having thus briefly discussed what has occurred relative to the punishment of offences against life, we come next to make some observations on what we have denominated *Private Felonies against the Body of the Subject.*

By the Grecian, Roman, and Jewish Laws, the abominable crime of *Sodomy* was punished with death. —In France, under the Monarchy, the offenders suffered death by burning.

The Lombards were said to have brought this detestable vice into England, in the reign of Edward the Third.—In ancient times the men were hanged, and the women drowned: At length by the Act 25th of Henry the Eighth, cap. 6. it was made Felony without Benefit of Clergy.

It has been doubted, however, whether the severity of the punishment of a crime so unnatural, as even to appear incredible, does not defeat the object of destroying it, by rendering it difficult to convict an offender.

The same objection has been made with respect to the crime of committing *a Rape.* A proper tenderness for life makes the Law require a strong evidence, and of course the proof is nice and difficult;
whereas,

whereas, were the punishment more mild, it might be more efficacious in preventing the violation of chastity.

By the Law of Egypt, Rapes were punished by cutting off the offending parts.—The Athenian Laws compelled the ravisher of a virgin to marry her. It was long before this offence was punished capitally by the Roman Law, but at length the *Lex Julia* inflicted the pains of death on the Ravisher.—The Jewish Law also punished this crime with death: but if a virgin was deflowered without force, the offender was obliged to pay a fine, and marry the woman.

By the 18th of Elizabeth, cap. 7, this offence was made Felony without Benefit of Clergy.

It is certainly of a very heinous nature, and, if tolerated, would be subversive of all order and morality; yet it may still be questioned, how far it is either useful or politic to punish it with death; and is worth considering, whether, well knowing that it originates in the irregular and inordinate gratification of unruly appetite, the injury to society may not be repaired without destroying the offender.

In most cases, the injury might be repaired by compelling, (where it could be done with propriety,) the criminal to marry the injured party; and it would be well for Society, if the same rule extended not only to all forcible violations of chastity, but even to instances of premeditated and systematic Seduction.

In

In cases, however, where marriage could not take place, on account of legal disability, or refusal on the part of the woman, the criminal ought to be severely punished, by pecuniary damages to the party injured, and by hard labour and confinement, or transportation for life.

The offence considered as next in point of enormity to Rape, is *Forcible Marriage* or *Defilement of Women:* but it is somewhat remarkable, that by confining the punishment to offences against women of estate only, the moral principles are made to yield to political considerations ; and the security of property in this instance, is deemed more essential, than the preservation of female chastity.

In short, the property of the woman is the measure of the crime ; the statutes of the 3d of Henry the Seventh, cap. 2. and the 39th of Elizabeth, cap. 9, making it Felony without Benefit of Clergy, to take away, *for lucre,* any woman having lands or goods, or being an heir apparent to an estate, by force, or against her will, and to marry or to defile her. The forcible marriage and defilement of a woman without an estate is not punished at all; although, according to every principle of morality and reason, it is as criminal as the other. It is indeed an offence not so likely to be committed.

However, it seems in every point of view, impolitic to punish such offences with death; it might be enough, to expiate the crime by alienating the estate from the husband—vesting it in the wife alone, and
confining

confining him to hard labour; or by punishing the delinquent, in very atrocious cases, by transportation.

Polygamy stands next as an offence against the person :—It was first declared Felony by the statute of James the first, cap. 11, but not excluded from the Benefit of Clergy, and therefore not subject to the punishment of death.

Though, in one view, the having a plurality of wives or husbands, appears only a political offence, yet it is undeniably a breach of religious and moral virtue, in a very high degree.—It is true, indeed, that in the early ages of the world, Polygamy was tolerated both in Greece and Rome, even after the People had arrived at a high pitch of refinement.— But since the institution of Matrimony under the present form, Polygamy must be considered as highly criminal, since Marriage is an engagement which cannot be violated without the greatest injury to Society. The Public Interest, therefore, requires that it should be punished; and the Act 35th George III. cap. 67, which punishes this offence with transportation, is certainly not too severe.

Mayhem, or Maiming, is the last in the Catalogue of *Offences against the Person.* It was first made Single Felony by the 5th of Henry the Fourth, cap. 5.—It is defined to be *maiming, cutting the tongue or putting out the eyes of any of the King's liege people.* The statute of the 22d and 23d of Charles the Second, cap. 1, extends the description of this offence to slitting the nose, cutting off a nose or lip,

or

or cutting off or disabling any limb or member, by malice forethought, and by lying in wait with an intention to maim and disfigure:—And this statute made the offence Felony, without Benefit of Clergy.

To prove malice in this crime, it is sufficient that the act was voluntary, and of set purpose, though done on a sudden.

Mayhem, as explained in the above statutes, is certainly a very atrocious offence; and as the punishment is not followed by corruption of blood, or the forfeiture of the property of the offender, it is, according to the present system, perhaps not too severe.

One particular sort of Mayhem by cutting off the *ear*, is punishable by an Act 37 Hen. VIII. cap. 6, which directs that the offender shall forfeit treble damages to the party grieved, to be recovered by action of trespass; and *l.* 10 by way of fine to the King.

We next come to examine *Private Felonies* against the *Goods or Property of the Individual*, viz. *Simple Larceny, Mixt Larceny,* and *Piracy*.

Simple Larceny is divided into two sorts;—1st, Grand Larceny, and 2d, Petit Larceny.—The first is defined to be *the felonious taking and carrying away the mere personal property or goods of another, above the value of twelve pence.*—This offence is capital, and punished with death, and the forfeiture of property.

Petit Larceny is where the goods, taken in the above

above manner, are under the value of twelve pence ; in which case, the punishment (according to the circumstances of atrocity attending the offence,) is imprisonment, whipping, or transportation, with forfeiture of goods and chattels.

Thus it appears, that by the rigour of the Law, stealing the least trifle above 12*d.* subjects the offender to the loss of life ; a punishment apparently repugnant to reason, policy, or justice: more especially when it is considered, that at the time this *Anglo Saxon Law* was made, in the reign of *Athelstan,* 860 years ago, *one shilling* was of more value, according to the price of labour, than *seventy-five shillings* are at the present period : the life of man therefore may be justly said to be seventy-five times cheaper than it was when this mode of punishment was first established.

By the Athenian Laws, the crime of Theft was punished, by paying double the value of what was stolen, to the party robbed ; and as much more to the public.—Solon introduced a law, enjoining every person to state in writing, by what means he gained his livelihood ; and if false information was given, or he gained his living in an unlawful way, he was punished with death.—A similar law prevailed among the Egyptians.

The *Lex Julia* of the Romans made Theft punishable at discretion ; and it was forbidden, that any person should suffer death, or even the loss of a member, for this crime.—The greatest punishment which

which appears to have been inflicted for this offence, in its most aggravated circumstances, was four-fold restitution.

By the Jewish Law, Theft was punished in the same manner : with the addition of a fine according to the nature of the offence; excepting in cases where *men* were stolen, which was punished with death.

In China, Theft is punished by the bastinadoe, except in cases of a very atrocious nature, and then the culprit is condemned to the knoutage—a contrivance not unlike the pillory in this country.

The ancient Laws of this kingdom punished the crime of Theft differently.—Our Saxon ancestors did not at first punish it capitally.—The Laws of King Ina * inflicted the punishment of death, but allowed the thief to redeem his life, *Capitis estimatione*, which was sixty shillings; but in case of an old offender, who had been often accused, the hand or foot was to be cut off.

After various changes which took place under different Princes, in the rude and early periods of our history, it was at length settled in the 9th of Henry the First, (A. D. 1108,) *that for theft and robbery, offenders should be hanged;* this has continued to be the law of the land ever since, excepting in the county palatine of Chester: where the ancient custom of beheading felons was practised

---

* King of the West Saxons, anno 688.

some

some time after the law of Henry the First; and the Justices of the Peace of that county, received one shilling from the King, for every head that was cut off.

Montesquieu seems to be of opinion that as thieves are generally unable to make restitution, it may be just to make theft a capital crime.—But would not the offence be atoned for in a more rational manner, by compelling the delinquent to labour, first for the benefit of the party aggrieved, till recompence is made, and then for the State?*

According to the present system the offender loses his life, and they whom he has injured lose their property; while the State also suffers in being deprived of a member, whose labour, under proper controul, might have been made useful and productive.

Observations have already been made on one consequence of the severity of the punishment for this offence; that persons of tender feelings conscientiously scruple to prosecute delinquents for inconsiderable Thefts. From this circumstance it is believed, that not one depredation in a hundred, of those actually committed, comes to the knowledge of Magistrates.

---

* That acute Reasoner, the Marquis BECCARIA, who wrote after MONTESQUIEU, holds this last opinion.—" A punishment, (says this able writer) to be just should have only that degree of severity which is sufficient to deter others: perpetual labour will have this effect more than the punishment of death."

BECC. chap. 28.

Mixed

Mixed or *compund Larceny* has a greater degree of guilt in it than simple Larceny; and may be committed either by taking from a man, or from his house. If a person is previously put in fear or assaulted, the crime is denominated *Robbery.*

When a Larceny is committed which does not put the party robbed in fear; it is done privately and without his knowledge, by picking his pocket, or cutting the purse, and stealing from thence above the value of twelve pence: or publicly, with the knowledge of the party, by stealing a hat or wig, and running away.

With respect to *Dwelling Houses,* the Common Law has been altered by various acts of Parliament; the multiplicity of which is apt to create confusion: but upon comparing them diligently, we may collect that the following domestic aggravations of Larceny are punishable with death, without Benefit of Clergy.

First, *Larcenies above the value of twelve pence;* committed—1st. In a church or chapel, with or without violence or breaking the same: 23 Henry VIII. cap. 1: 1 Edward VI. cap. 12.—2d. In a booth or tent, in a market or fair, in the day time or in the night, by violence or breaking the same; the owner, or some of his family, being therein; 5 and 6 Edward VI. cap. 9.—3d. By robbing a dwelling house in the day time, (which *robbing* implies a *breaking,*) any person being therein: 3 and 4 William and Mary, cap. 9.—4th. By the same Act, (and see the Act 23 Henry VIII. cap. 1.) in a dwelling house, by
day

day or by night; without breaking the same, any person being therein, and put in fear: which amounts in law to a Robbery; and in both these last cases the *Accessary before the fact* is also excluded from the benefit of Clergy.

Secondly; *Larcenies to the value of five shillings*; committed— 1st. By breaking any dwelling house, or any out-house, shop, or warehouse thereunto belonging, in the day time; although no person be therein, which also now extends to aiders, abettors, and accessaries before the fact: 39 Elizabeth, cap. 15; see also 3 and 4 William and Mary, cap. 9.—2d. By privately stealing goods, wares, or merchandise in any shop, warehouse, coach-houses, or stable, by day or night: though the same be not broken open, and though no person be therein: which likewise extends to such as assist, hire, or command the offence to be committed: 10 and 11 William III. cap. 23.

Lastly; *Larcenies to the value of forty shillings* from a dwelling house, or its out-houses, although the same be not broken, and whether any person be therein or not; unless committed against their masters, by apprentices, under age of fifteen; 12 Anne stat. 1. cap. 7.

Piracy is felony against the goods of the Subject by a robbery committed at sea. It is a capital offence by the civil law, although by Act of Parliament it may be heard and determined, according to the rules of the common law, as if the offence had been committed on land. The mode of trial is regulated by the 28th of Henry VIII. cap. 15; and further by the
Acts

Acts 11 and 12 William III. cap. 7. and 39 George
III. cap. 37; which also extend to other offences
committed on the High Seas.

Felonies *against the Dwelling or Habitation of a*
man are of two kinds; and are denounced Arson *and*
Burglary.

Arson or *Arsonry* is a very atrocious offence—It is
defined to be *the malicious burning of the House of*
another either by night or by day. It is in this case a
capital offence; but if a man burns his own house,
without injuring any other, it is only a misdemeanor,
punishable by fine, imprisonment, or the pillory.

By the 23d of Henry the Eighth, cap. 1. the capital part of the offence is extended to persons,
(whether principals or accessaries,) burning dwelling
houses; or barns wherein corn is deposited; and by
the 43d of Elizabeth, cap. 13, burning barns or
stacks of corn in the four northern counties, is also
made Felony without Benefit of Clergy.

By the 22d and 23d of Car. II. cap. 7, it is made
felony to set fire to any stack of corn, hay, or grain;
or other outbuildings, or kilns, maliciously in the
night time; punished with transportation for seven
years.

By the 1st George I. cap. 48, it is also made
single felony to set fire to any wood, underwood, or
coppice.

Other burnings are made punishable with death,
without Benefit of Clergy, *viz.* Setting fire to any
house, barn, or out-house, or to any hovel, cock, mow
or stack of corn, straw, hay, or wood: or the rescuing
                                                    any

any such offender: 9 George I. cap. 22.—Setting
fire to a coal-mine : 10 George II. cap. 32.—Burning, or setting fire to any wind-mill, water-mill, or
other mill; (as also pulling down the same:)
9 George III. cap. 29; but the offender must be
prosecuted within eighteen months.—Burning any
ship; to the prejudice of the owners, freighters, or
underwriters : 22 and 23 Charles II. cap. 11 ˉ 1 Anne,
stat. 2. cap. 9; 4 George I. cap. 12.—Burning the
King's ships of war afloat, or building: or the
Dock-yards, or any of the buildings, arsenals, or
stores therein : 12 George III. cap. 24.—And finally,
Threatening by anonymous or fictitious letters to
burn houses, barns, &c. is by the Act 27 George II.
cap. 15, also made felony without Benefit of
Clergy.

Burglary is a felony at common law; it is described
to be *when a person, by night, breaketh into the mansion of another, with an intent to commit a felony;
whether the felonious intent be executed or not.*

By the 18th of Elizabeth, cap. 7, the Benefit of
Clergy is taken away from *The Offence*; and by the 3d
and 4th William and Mary, cap. 9, from *Accessaries
before the fact.*—By the 12th of Anne, stat. 1. cap. 7,
if any person shall enter into a mansion or dwelling
house by day or by night, without breaking into the
same, with an intent to commit any felony; or being
in such houses, shall commit any felony; and shall,
in the night time, *break* the said house *to get out* of
the

the same, he is declared guilty of the offence of burglary, and punished accordingly.

It is, without doubt, highly expedient that this Offence should be punished more severely than any other species of theft; since, besides the loss of property, there is something very terrific in the mode of perpetration, which is often productive of dreadful effects.

The ancient laws made a marked distinction in the punishment, between this Offence, which was called Hamsokne, (and which name it retains at present in the Northern parts of this kingdom) and robbing a house in the day time.

There are many other felonies which have been made capital (particularly within the present century) which do not properly fall within the class above discussed:—for an account of these the reader is referred to the general Catalogue of offences specified in a subsequent Chapter.

The number of these various capital Offences upon which the judgment of death must be pronounced, if the party is found guilty, has been already stated to amount to above *one hundred and sixty.*—And yet if a full consideration shall be given to the subject, it is believed that (excepting in cases of *Treason, Murder, Mayhem,* and some aggravated instances of Arsonry) it would be found that the punishment of death is neither politic nor expedient.

At any rate it must be obvious to every reasoning mind,

mind, that such *indiscriminate rigour*, by punishing the petty pilferer with the same severity as the atrocious murderer, cannot easily be reconciled to the rights of nature or to the principles of morality.

It is indeed true, in point of practice, that in most cases of a slight nature, the mercy of Judges, of Juries, or of the Sovereign, saves the delinquent; but is not the exercise of this mercy rendered so necessary on every occasion, " *a tacit disapprobation of the laws** ?

Cruelty, in punishment for slight Offences, often induces offenders to pass on from the trifling to the most atrocious crime.—Thus are these our miserable fellow mortals rendered desperate ; whilst the laws, which ought to soften the ferocity of obdurate minds, tend to corrupt and harden them.

What education is to an individual, the Laws are to Society. Wherever they are sanguinary, delinquents will be hard-hearted, desperate, and even barbarous.

However much our ancestors were considered as behind us in civilization, yet their Laws were infinitely milder, in many instances, than in the present age of refinement.

The real good of the state, however, unquestionably requires that not only adequate punishments should be impartially inflicted, but that the injured should obtain a reparation for their wrongs.

* Beccaria. *See ante, page* 45.

Instead

Instead of such reparation, it has been already stated, and indeed it is much to be lamented, that many are induced to desist from prosecutions, and even to conceal injuries, because nothing but expence and trouble is to be their lot : as all the fruits of the conviction, where the criminal has any property, go to the State.—That the State should be the only immediate gainer by the fines and forfeitures of criminals, while the injured party suffers, seems not wholly consonant to the principles either of *justice, equity,* or *sound policy.*

Having said thus much on the subject of severe and sanguinary Punishments, it may not be improper to mention a very recent and modern authority, for the total abolition of the Punishment of death. This occurred in the Imperial Dominions, where a new code of criminal law was promulgated by the late Emperor, JOSEPH II. and legalized by his edict in 1787.

This Code, formed in an enlightened age, by Princes, Civilians, and Men of Learning, who sat down to the deliberation, assisted by the wisdom and experience of former ages, and by all the information possible with regard to the practice of civilized modern nations ; with an impression also upon their minds, that sanguinary punishments, by death, torture, or dismemberment are not necessary, and ought to be abolished ; becomes an interesting circumstance in the annals of the world.

" *The*

" THE EMPEROR *in his edict signed at Vienna the* " *13th of January,* 1787, *declares his intention to have* " *been to give a precise and invariable form to Crimi-* " *nal Judicature; to prevent arbitrary interpretations;* " *to draw a due line between criminal and civil offences,* " *and those against the state; to observe a just propor-* " *tion between offences and punishments, and to deter-* " *mine the latter in such a manner as that they may* " *make more than merely a transient impression.—Hav-* " *ing promulgated this new code, he abrogates, annuls,* " *and declares void all the ancient laws which formerly* " *existed in his dominions.*—Forbidding at the same " time every criminal Judge to exercise the functions " of his office, on any but those who shall be brought " before him, accused of a criminal offence expressed " in the new code."

This system of criminal law is so concise as to be comprehended in less than one hundred octavo pages. It commences with laying down certain general principles, favourable in their nature both to humanity and public liberty.—In determining the punishments (which will hereafter be very shortly detailed) the following rules are laid down for the Judges.

" *The criminal Judge should be intent on observing* " *the just proportion between a criminal Offence and* " *the punishment assigned it, and carefully to compare* " *every circumstance.—With respect to the* Offence, " *his principal attention should be directed to the de-* " *gree of malignity accompanying the bad action,—to* " *the importance of the circumstance connected with the*
" *Offence*

" Offence,—to the degree of damage which may result
" from it,—to the possibility or impossibility of the pre-
" cautions which might have been made use of to pre-
" vent it.—With respect to the Criminal, *the attention*
" of the Judge should be directed to his youth,—to the
" temptation or imprudence attending it,—to the punish-
" ment which has been inflicted for the same Offence,
" and to the danger of a relapse."

Those denomi-
nated Crimi-
nal Offences,
viz.
{
1. Offences against the Sovereign and the State; including High Treason.
2. Offences against human life and bodily safety.
3. Offences against honour and liberty.
4. Offences against possessions and rights.

Those denomi-
nated Civil
Offences, *viz.*
{
5. Offences that endanger the life or health of the Citizens.
6. Offences that affect the fortunes or rights of the Citizens.
7. Offences that tend to the corruption of morals.

The offences are divided into seven different classes.

It is impossible, within the narrow compass of this Work, to enter into a particular detail of the various subdivisions of the Crimes and Punishments explained in this Code; which must be perused, in order to form a clear and comprehensive view of the subject. The following specification therefore contains merely the *heads* or outlines of the System; which it is hoped may be found, from the mode of its arrangement, to convey to the reader both amusement and instruction.

ABSTRACT

ABSTRACT
OF THE CRIMINAL CODE
OF THE
E M P E R O R   J O S E P H   II.

CRIMES.	PUNISHMENTS.

High Treason.

1. Laying violent hands on the Sovereign, whether injury results from it or not.

Confiscation of property; imprisonment for not less than 30 years; and branding on each cheek with the mark of a gallows * if the prisoner is remarkably depraved.

2. Attacking the Sovereign by speeches or writings.

Imprisonment 8 years, and not less than 5.

3. Persons conspiring and taking up arms, or entering into alliance with an enemy, &c. are guilty of *sedition and tumult.*

Confiscation of Property and 30 years' imprisonment, with branding as above.

Criminal Offences relative to the Sovereign and the State.

4 He who enters the house or abode of another, and uses violence against his person, goods, or possession, is guilty of *open force.*

Imprisonment, not less than 1 month, nor more than 5 years, and condemnation to the public works.

5. He who violently resists the authority of a Judge, or Officer of Justice, although no wound result, is guilty of *open violence.*

Imprisonment not less than 1 month, nor more than 5 years; but where there is an injury and wounds, not exceeding 8 nor less than 5.

6. Breach of trust, in a Governor, or Charge des Affaires; neglecting the interest of the State, or betraying his Country, &c.

Imprisonment not less than 8, nor more than 12 years, and condemnation to the public works, and in aggravated cases, the pillory.†

7. A.   Im-

---

* In cases where a Criminal appears to be remarkably depraved, and that the apprehensions he may excite require such precautions, he shall be branded on each cheek with the mark of a gallows, so visibly and strongly impressed as not to be effaced either by time or any other means whatever.

† This punishment is different from the pillory in England. In the German Language it signifies an exposure on the public theatre of shame. The Criminal is chained and guarded on an elevated scaffold, and exposed an hour at a time, with a paper on his breast denoting his offence.

CRIMES.   PUNISHMENTS.

Criminal offences against the Sovereign and the State. (Continued.)

7. A Judge, who from corruption or passion is guilty of an *abuse of judicial authority.*

Imprisonment not less than 8, nor more than 12 years, and condemnation to the public works,& in aggravated cases the pillory.

8. Accomplices attempting to corrupt a Judge.

Imprisonment not less than1 month,nor more than 5years; and condemnationtothepublicworks.

9. Forgery, by attempting to counterfeit public bills of the State which circulate as money.

Imprisonment not less than 30 years, and branding with a hot iron.

10. Falsifying a public bill, by changing or altering it, or imitating the signatures.

Imprisonment not less than 12, nor more than 15 years, and condemnation to the public works.

11. Coining false money, resembling the Coin of the Hereditary Dominions, or foreign Coin current by law; even though of equal weight and quality, or superior to the current Coin.

Imprisonment not less than 1 month, nor more than 5 years, with condemnation to the public works.

12. Coining false money by using a bad alloy; and by fraud giving false money the quality of good.

Imprisonment not less than12, nor more than 15 years, and condemnation to the public works.

13. Accomplices in fabricating tools for coining.

Imprisonment not less than 8, nor more than 12 years, and condemnation to the public works.

14. Assisting in the escape of a prisoner.

Imprisonment not less than 1 month,nor more than5years; and condemnation tothepublicworks.

15. Magistrates granting indulgences contrary to law, &c.

Imprisonment not less than12, nor more than 15 years; and deprivation of authority.

Criminal Offences against Human Life and Bodily Safety.

16. *Murder,*—by wounding a man so that death ensues, including all accomplices.

Imprisonment not less than15, nor more than 30 years; the latter in cases of consanguinity.*

17. Killing a man in self-defence, if the slayer exceed the bounds of necessity.

Imprisonment not less than 1 month, nor more than5years, and condemnationtothepublicworks.

18. *Murder.*   Imprison-

* When a criminal is condemned to severe imprisonment, he has no bed but the floor, no nourishment but bread and water, and all communication with relations or even strangers, is refused him. When condemned to milder imprisonment better nourishments is allowed but he has nothing to drink but water.

CRIMES.	PUNISHMENTS.

Criminal Offences against Human Life, and Bodily Safety. (*Cont.*)

18. *Murder,*—with an intention to rob or steal the property of the person, or other property intrusted to his care.

Imprisonment not less than 30 years, with the hot iron; in cruel cases; to be closely chained, with corporal punishment*every year.

19. Assasination by stratagem, arms, and poison.

Condemnation to the Chain,† not less than 30 years.

20. Inducing another to commit Murder; by caresses, promises, presents, or threats, whether death is the result or not.

Imprisonment not less than 5, nor more than 8 years, and condemnation to the public works.—If murder is committed, the criminal shall suffer as a murderer.

21. *Duelling,*—or challenging another to combat with murderous weapons on whatever pretence the challenge be grounded.—The person accepting the challenge is equally guilty, after agreeing to combat with murderous weapons.

If death ensues; condemnation to the chain for 30 years, where the survivor is the challenger. If the survivor be the party challenged, imprisonment, not more than 12, nor less than 8 years, and condemnation to the public works. If neither fall, imprisonment to the challenger, not less than 1 month, nor more than 5 years; and hard labour in the public works.

22. Accomplices acting as assistants and seconds.

Imprisonment not less than 1 nor more than 5 years.

23. A woman with child using means to procure abortion.

Imprisonment not less than 15, nor more than 30 years, and condemnation to the public works: augmented when married women.

24. Accomplices advising and recommending abortion.

Imprisonment not less than 1 month, nor more than 5 years, and condemnation to the public works.—Punishment increased when the accomplice is the father of the infant.

25. Exposing a living infant, in order to abandon it to danger, and

Imprisonment not less than 8 nor more than 12 years; to be increased

---

* Corporal punishment is inflicted with the whip, rod, or stick, publicly, on the criminal; the degree of punishment (within 100 lashes or strokes at one time) depends on the sound prudence of the Judge.

† The punishment of the Chain is inflicted in the following manner. criminal suffers severe imprisonment, and is so closely chained, that he has more liberty than serves for the indispensable motion of his body.—The criminals suffer a corporal punishment once a year, as an example to the P

CRIMES.   PUNISHMENTS.

Criminal Offences against Human Life and Bodily Safety. (Cont.)

and death; or to leave its deli-increased under circumstances of verance to chance; whether the aggravation. infant, so exposed, suffers death or not.

26. Maiming by malignant   Imprisonment not less than 1 assault.   month, nor more than 5 years.

27. Suicide or self-murder,   The body to be thrown into without any sign of insanity.   the earth by the executioner, and the name of the person and crime to be publicly notified and fixed on a gallows.

Criminal Offences against Honour and Liberty.

28. *Calumny*—false accusa-   Imprisonment not less than 1 tion—injuring a man of his   month, nor more than 5 years, right, or robbing him of his   and condemnation to the public good name unjustly and without   works; with corporal punish-proof. (See post. No. 56.)   ment if the party received injury.

29. *Rape*,—or forcibly, by   Imprisonment not less than 8 associates, threatenings, or shew-   years, nor more than 12, and ing weapons, overpowering and   condemnation to the public forcing a woman to submit, and   works. shamefully abusing her by ren-dering her incapable of opposi-tion.

30. Accomplices aiding in the   Imprisonment not less than 5, commission of a rape.   nor more than 8 years; and con-demnation to the public works.

31. *Forcibly carrying a person   Imprisonment not less than 15 out of the State* without his will,   years, nor more than 30 years: or the consent of the Magistrate,   augmented if the criminal is a enlisting men into foreign ser-   natural born subject. vice, &c.

32. *Forcibly, or by address,   Imprisonment not less than 1 secretly carrying away a Minor*   month, nor more than 5 years; if past the years of infancy, under   no injury result—otherwise im-the care of parents or guar-   prisonment, not less than 8, nor dians, &c.   more than 12 years, and con-demnation to the public works.

33. *Forcibly, and by address,   Imprisonment not less than 5 getting possession of any woman*   years, and not more than 8; and contrary to her will, obtaining   condemnation to the public her consent to marriage, or   works. shameful debauchery, and carry-ing

Imprison-

CRIMES.   PUNISHMENTS.

Criminal Offences against Honour and Liberty.   (Continued.)

ing her from her abode: whether
the design is accomplished or not.

34. *Forcibly carrying away a*   Imprisonment not less than 1
woman known to be bound by month, nor more than 5 years,
lawful marriage, or under pro- and condemnation to the public
tection of parents, and without works.
her consent.

35. Accomplices aiding and   The same.
assisting.

36. *Unlawful Imprisonment*,   Imprisonment not less than 1
or keeping a person in confine- month, nor more than 5 years;
ment against his will and of his augumented in case of damages.
own private authority.

Criminal Offences against Possessions and Rights.

37. *Fraud.*—Obtaining the   Various, according to the de-
property of another by stratagem gree of malignity—in general by
with an evil design on his pos- imprisonment not less than 8,
sessions, honour, or liberty; nor more than 12 years; and in
forging title deeds or contracts, smaller offences, not less than 5
or *altering* the same.   nor more than 8; and condem-
                               nation to the public works.

Perjury in a Court of Justice,   The same.
assuming a false name, &c. &c.
bearing false witness.

38. *Theft*, or taking a move-   Imprisonment not less than 1
able from the possession of an- month, nor more than 5 years, if
other by fraud, and without his unaccompanied by aggravating
consent. (See post. No. 47.) circumstances: but in aggravated
                               cases, imprisonment not less than
                               5 nor more than 8 ; or not less
                               than 8, nor more than 12 years.

39. *Accomplices in Theft*,—   Imprisonment not less than 1
abettors and receivers, &c. month, nor more than 5 years, and
                               condemnationto the public works.

40. *Robbery* —— committed   Imprisonment not less than 15
alone or in company, by using years, nor more than 30; if wounds
violence, or forcing a person ensue, in consequence of the vio-
to discover effects, on which the lence used. And if acts of cruelty
offender has felonious views. or wounds, occasioning death,
                               then the punishment of the chain
                               addit onal.

41. *Incendiary*—where one   Imprisonment not less than 8
undertakes an action from which nor more than 12 years; and con-
fire may ensue, or with intention demnation to the public works :
to   when

CRIMES.　　　　　　　PUNISHMENTS.

Criminal Offences against Possessions and Rights. (Continued.)

to prejudice, or cause damage, when the flames have been stifled. with a view to profit by the dis- Setting fire to a Camp, Maga- order that takes place, he shall zine, Barn, Timber-yard, &c. be considered as an *incendiary*, from 15 to 30 years; according whether damage ensues or not. to the circumstances of the case.

42. *Bigamy*—where one bound　Imprisonment not less than 5 by the tie of lawful matrimony, nor more than 8 years, or condem- concludes a second marriage with nation to the public works; if the another person, single or married. person with whom the offender contracts the second marriage was acquainted with the first—If concealed, the imprisonment not exceeding 12 nor less than 8 years.

Civil Offences that endanger the Life or Health of the Citizen.

43. *Misadventure*——where　Imprisonment from 1 month without any ill intention, by to a year, or condemnation to the means of poisonous merchandize, public works, if the offender has or apothecaries selling adultera- caused any immediate damage; ted drugs, any person suffers but if the cause of damage be re- danger or injury. mote, imprisonment from a day to 1 month.

44. Damage to man or child,　Imprisonment from 1 day to occasioned by riding or driving a month; to be augmented, in carriages with too much speed; case death or wound should have or injury received by persons in- resulted from the accident. capable of guarding against dan- ger, occasioning a wound or death, which might have been prevented by due vigilance.

45. Breaking Quarantine, &c.　By a Military Court of and fabricating false bills of Justice. health.

46. Actions prejudicial to　Condemnation to the public health, or nuisance, where the works, with or without fetters; necessary precautions prescribed either from 1 day to a month, by the laws of health are neg- or from 1 month to a year. lected in cases of dead animals, distempers among cattle, &c. &c.

Civil Offences that affect the Fortunes and Rights of Citizens.

47. Stealing to the value of　Confinement, corporal correc- 25 crowns of any moveable, tion, and the augmentation of when not accompanied with ag- the punishment if requisite. gravating circumstances: *Steal-*
ing　　　　　　　　　　　The

CRIMES.   PUNISHMENTS.

Civil Offences that affect the Fortunes and Rights of Citizens. (Cont.)

ing Wood in a forest—Poaching by an unqualified person—Stealing Fruit from Trees—or earth from open Fields—though beyond the value of 25 crowns. (See ante, No. 38, 39.)

48. Using frauds in playing at Games allowed by Law.

The pillory and condemnation to the public works, in atrocious cases; also imprisonment, from 1 day to a month, and restitution.—In cases of foreigners, the pillory and banishment.

49. *Accomplices* co-operating in such frauds.

Imprisonment from 1 day to a month.

50. *Playing at prohibited Games.*

A fine of 300 ducats, or imprisonment.

51. *Persons selling Merchandize* at higher prices than fixed by the Police, or by false weight or measure.

Imprisonment from 1 day to a month, which may be augmented.

52. *Adultery.*

Corporal correction, or imprisonment from 1 day to a month.

53. *Contracting illegal Marriage.* (See ante, No. 42.)

Imprisonment from 1 day to a month, and condemnation to the public works.

54. *Servants* receiving earnest and engaging to serve more masters than one, or otherwise misbehaving.

Corporal correction, or imprisonment from 1 day to a month

55. *Masters* giving servants a false character.

Imprisonment from 1 day to a month.

56. *Libels* on another by writings or disgraceful prints or drawings causing injury to another. (See ante, No. 28.)

Condemnation to the public works; reserving the right to recompence to the party wronged.

57. *Distributing* or publishing Libels.

Condemnation to the public works; reserving the right of recompence to the party wronged.

58. *Actions* by which danger by fire may be occasioned; such as smoaking tobacco in a stable, timber yard, &c.

Corporal correction.

59. *Acts* of hasty petulance, leading to quarrels, assaults, and damages.

Imprisonment various, or condemnation to the public works.

Civil

CRIMES.   PUNISHMENTS.

Civil Offences that tend to the Corruption of Morals.

60. Wickedly insulting the Supreme Being by words, deeds, or actions, in a public place, or in the presence of another person.

Detention in the hospital destined for madmen; where the offender is to be treated like a man out of his senses, until his amendment be perfect and assured.

61. Disturbing the exercise of Public Worship, &c.

Imprisonment from 1 day to a month; to be augmented by fasting and corporal correction.

62. Writing or preaching against the Christian Religion, and Catholic Faith, &c. &c. Heresies, &c.

Pillory and Imprisonment, from 1 day to a month, or to a year.

63. Committing indecencies in any public street or place.

Imprisonment from 1 day to a month, augmented by fasting.

64. Attempting to seduce or insult women of reputation, by shameful debauchery, and using gestures, or discourses, tending to that purpose.

Imprisonment from 1 day to a month.

65. Carnal Commerce by Man with Beast, or with a person of the same sex.—*Sodomy.*

Corporal Correction, and condemnation to the public works; and banishment from the place where the offence has been publicly scandalous.

66. Consenting to shameful debauchery in his house: Keeping a *Bawdy House.*

Condemnation to the public works, from 1 month to 1 year; to be augmented when an innocent person has been seduced; second offence, the pillory.

67. Any person, man or woman making a business of prostitution, and deriving profit from thence.

Imprisonment from 1 month to a year; second offence, punishment double, and augmented by fasting and corporal correction.

68. Dealing in Books, Pictures, or Prints which represent indecent actions.

Imprisonment from 1 day to a month.

69. Disguising in Masks, and obtaining admission into societies, and secret fraternities not notified to the Magistrate.

The same.

70. Harbouring in dwellings persons not known to have an honest mean of living.

The same.

71. Banished persons from the whole of the Austrian Dominions—returning, &c.

Corporal correction, to be doubled at each successive return; and the offender to be banished from the Hereditary Dominion

In contemplating the various component parts of this Code, it is easy to discover that although some features of it may be worthy of imitation, upon the whole it is not suited either to the English constitution or the genius of our people. It is, however, a curious and interesting document, from which considerable information may be drawn ; if ever that period shall arrive when a revision of our own criminal Code (in many respects more excellent than this) shall become an object of consideration with the Legislature.—At all events it strongly evinces the necessity of adapting the laws to the circumstances and situation of the Government ; and of the people whose vices are to be restrained.

The total abolition of the Punishment of death (excepting in military offences cognizable by Courts Martial) is a very prominent feature in this Code ; which appears to have been founded in a great measure on the principles laid down by the Marquis Beccaria, in his Essay on Crimes and Punishments : That able writer establishes it as a maxim, which indeed will scarcely be controverted—" That the " severity of Punishment should just be sufficient " to excite compassion in the spectators, as it is in- " tended more for them than the criminal.—A " punishment, to be just, should have only that de- " gree of severity which is sufficient to deter others, " and no more."—This author further asserts, " That " perpetual labour has in it all that is necessary to " deter the most hardened and determined, as much

" as

" as the punishment of death, *where every example*
" *supposes a new crime :*—perpetual labour on the
" other hand affords a frequent and lasting ex-
" ample*."

Doubtless, the fundamental principle of good legislation is, rather to prevent crimes than to punish.—
If a mathematical expression may be made use of,
relative to the good and evil of human life, it is the
art of conducting men to the *maximum* of happiness
and the *minimum* of misery.

But in spite of all the efforts of human wisdom,
aided by the lights of Philosophy, and freed from the
mist of prejudice or the bigotry of darker ages ;—In
spite of the best laws, and the most correct system of
Police which the most enlightened Legislature can

* The punishment of death is not authorized by any right.—
If it were so, how could it be reconciled to the maxim, that a
man has no right to kill himself?

The punishment of death is a war of a whole nation against a
citizen, whose destruction is considered as necessary or useful to
the public good.—If I can demonstrate that it is neither necessary
nor useful, I shall have gained the cause of humanity.—If the
experience of all ages be not sufficient to prove that the punishment of death has never prevented determined men from injuring
society—if the example of the Romans—if twenty years' reign
of Elizabeth, Empress of Russia, be not sufficient, let us consult
human nature in proof of my assertion.

The death of a criminal is a terrible, but momentary spectacle;
and therefore a less efficacious method of deterring others, than
the continued example of a man deprived of his liberty, and condemned to repair by his labour, the injury done to Society. A
condition so miserable is a much more powerful preventive than
the fear of death, which men always behold in distant obscurity.

BECCARIA, cap. 28.

form :

form: it will not be altogether possible, amid the various opposite attractions of pleasure and pain, to reduce the tumultuous activity of mankind to absolute regularity :—We can only hope for a considerable reduction of the evils that exist.—*Let the Laws be clear and simple;—let the entire force of the Nation be united in their defence; let the Laws be feared, and the Laws only.*

CHAPTER III.

The causes and progress of small Thefts in London ex-
plained and traced to the numerous Receivers of
stolen Goods, under the denominations of Dealers in
Rags, Old Iron, and other Metals.—The great in-
crease of these Dealers of late years.—Their evil
tendency, and the absolute necessity of Regulations,
to prevent the extensive Mischiefs arising from the
Encouragements they hold out, to persons of every age
and description, to become Thieves, by the purchase
of whatever is offered for sale.—A Remedy sug-
gested.—Petty Thefts in the country round the Me-
tropolis—Workhouses the causes of idleness—Com-
mons—Cottages—Gypsies—Labourers and Ser-
vants; their general bad character and propensity to
thieving small articles from their Masters, encouraged
by Receivers.—Thefts in Fields and Gardens—
Their extent and amount throughout England—
Frauds in the sale and adulteration of Milk in the
Metropolis.

IN a preceding Chapter the small thefts committed
by persons not known to belong to the fraternity of
Thieves, are estimated to amount to the enormous
sum of 700,000*l.* a year.

The

This discovery (except what relates to embezzled silk, cotton, and worsted) was originally made through the medium of a considerable Dealer in Rags and Old Iron, and other Metals, who communicated to the Author much interesting information, respecting Receivers of stolen Goods, confirmed afterwards through other channels, the substance of which has been already alluded to; and of which the following are more ample details :

" That there exists in this Metropolis, (and also in all the towns where his Majesty's Dock-Yards are established) a class of Dealers, of late years become extremely numerous, who keep open shops for the purchase of *Rags, Old Iron, and other Metals.*

" That these Dealers are universally, almost without a single exception, the Receivers of stolen Goods of every denomination ; from a nail, a skewer, a key, or a glass bottle, up to the most valuable article of portable household goods, merchandize, plate, or jewels, &c. &c.

" That they are divided into two classes :—*Wholesale* and *Retail Dealers.* That the Retail Dealers are generally (with some exceptions) the immediate purchasers in the first instance, from the pilferers or their agents ; and as soon as they collect a sufficient quantity of iron, copper, brass, lead, tin, pewter, or other metals, worthy the notice of a large Dealer, they dispose of the same for ready meney ;

money; by which they are enabled to continue the trade.

" That the increase of these old iron, rag, and store shops has been astonishing within the last twenty years.

" That, as the least trifle is received, the vigilance of the parties, from whom the articles are stolen, is generally eluded; by the prevailing practice of taking only a small quantity of any article at a time.

" That the articles thus received are generally pur-chased at about one third of the real value, and sel-dom at more than half;—glass bottles in particu-lar, are bought at one penny each, and no question asked:—they are afterwards sold to dealers in this particular branch, who assort and wash them, and again re-sell them to inferior wine-dealers at nearly the full value:—this has become, of late, an exten-sive line of trade.

" That further facilities are afforded by the dealers in old iron, in the collection of metals, rags, and other articles purloined and stolen in the Country; which are conveyed to town by means of *single-horse carts*, kept by itinerant Jews, and other doubtful characters; who travel to Portsmouth, Chatham, Woolwich, Deptford, and places in the vicinity of London, for the purpose of purchasing metals from persons who are in the habit of em-bezzling the King's stores, or from dealers on the

spot,

spot, who are the first receivers; from them, *copper-bolts, nails, spikes, iron, brass, lead, pewter,* and other ship articles of considerable value are procured.—These single-horse carts have increased greatly of late years, and have become very profitable to the proprietors.

" That some of these dealers in old metals, notoriously keep men employed in knocking the broad Arrow, or King's mark, out of the copper-bolts, nails, and bar iron, whereon it is impressed, and also in cutting such bar iron into portable lengths, after which it is sold to the great dealers, who supply the Public Boards; and who are in some instances supposed by this means to sell the same Article to these boards even *two* or *three* times over.

" That the trade thus carried on, is exceedingly productive both to the retail and wholesale dealers; many of whom are become extremely opulent, and carry on business to the extent of from ten to thirty, and in some few instances, fifty thousand a year in old metals alone.

" That the quantity of new nails, taken from the public repositories, and from private workshops, and disposed of at the old iron shops, exceeds all credibility.

" And finally, that the retail dealers in old iron, with some exceptions, are the principal purchasers of the pewter pots stolen from the Publicans, which they instantly melt down (if not previously done) to elude detection."

Thus

Thus are the lower ranks of Society assailed on all hands; and in a manner allured to be dishonest, by the ready means of disposing of property, unlawfully acquired, to satisfy *imaginary* and too frequently *criminal* wants, excited by the temptations which the amusements and dissipations of a great Capital, and the delusion of the Lottery, hold out.

The rapid growth of this Evil within the last twenty years, and the effect it has upon the morals of menial servants and others, who must in the nature of things have a certain trust committed to them, is a strong reason why some effectual remedy should be administered as speedily as possible.

It seems, under all circumstances, that the regulation of these Iron-shops, by licence, and by other restrictions connected with the public security, has become a matter of immediate necessity; for it is a dreadful thing to reflect that there should exist and grow up, in so short a period of time, such a body of criminal dealers, who are permitted to exercise all the mischievous part of the functions of Pawnbrokers; enjoying equal benefits, without any of the restrictions which have already been extended to this last class of dealers; who themselves also require further regulations, which will be hereafter discussed.

But beside the dealers in *old iron*, it will be necessary to extend the regulation proposed, to dealers in *second-hand wearing apparel*, whether *stationary* or *itinerant;* for through this medium also, a vast quantity of of bed and table linen, sheets, wearing apparel, and other articles, pilfered in private families, is disposed of; and money is obtained, without asking questions, with the same facility as at the iron shops.

To prevent metals from being melted by Receivers of stolen Goods, and other persons keeping crucibles and melting vessels, by which means the most infamous frauds are committed, to the evasion of justice, by immediately melting plate, pewter pots, and every kind of metal that can be identified; it may be also necessary to regulate, by licence, all *Founders of metal,* and also the horse and truck carts used for the purpose of conveying old metal from place to place: so as, upon the whole, to establish a *mild, but complete System of Prevention;* by limiting the dealers in old metals and second-hand wearing apparel, to the honest and fair part of their trade, and by restraining them with regard to that which is fraudulent and mischievous.

At present these respective dealers may truly be said to be complete pests of Society.—They are not, like Pawnbrokers, restrained, as to the hours of receiving or delivering goods.—Their dealings are often in the night time, by which means they enjoy every opportunity of encouraging fraud and dishonesty.

It is impossible to contemplate the consequences arising from the seduction of so many individuals, young and old, who must be implicated in the crimes which these abominable receptacles encourage, with-

out

out wishing to see so complicate and growing a mischief engage the immediate attention of the Legislature, that a remedy may be applied as early as
possible. *

This System of petty thievery and general depredation is, however, by no means confined to the precincts of the Metropolis : it is extended in a peculiar
manner through the different Counties in its Vicinity.—The following particulars, extracted from Mr.
Middleton's View of the Agriculture of *Middlesex*,
will enable the Reader to form some judgment of
the extent of the mischief, and the causes from which
it originates ; producing and increasing that band of
plunderers, of which the Metropolis itself has ultimately been at once the Nurse and the Victim.

" The funds raised for supporting the *Idle Poor of
this country* (says this intelligent writer) are so numerous, efficient and comfortable, as to operate
against the general industry of the *Labouring Poor.*

" Lodging and diet in the workhouses, in every
instance, are superior to what the industrious labourer can provide for his family. It is obvious that
this must have an influence over their minds, and become most injurious to the interests of society ; it
holds out encoaragement to prefer the workhouse to
labour ; and, by filling the poor houses with improper
inhabitants, it reduces the amount of industry."

* This remedy as it respects Receivers of stolen Goods, is specifically explained at the close of a subsequent Chapter which
relates entirely to that subject, and to which the Reader is particularly referred.

The

The annual expence of each pauper is calculated by the same Writer at about *Fifteen Guineas;* a stout healthy labourer in husbandry, with a wife and three children, earns only Thirty for the support of five persons.

" The want of prudence is encreased, and general industry lessened, on the part of the poor, by the facility with which voluntary contributions are raised during every temporary inconvenience, such as a few weeks' frost, or an extraordinary advance in the price of provisions.*   And also by the constantly cloathing

upwards

* This observation can only apply to such voluntary contributions as are liable to abuses, and where the poor are permitted to dispose of the benevolence of the opulent in their own way.—The *Soup-Charities* established in different parts of the Metropolis are a peculiar exception, inasmuch as they contribute only to the relief of those that are really objects of distress, while no Public Charity heretofore instituted has been found to be liable to fewer abuses. In a great Metropolis like London, it has been clearly established, that in spite of every regard to prudence and œconomy, decent families will be suddenly broke down, while the habits of life peculiar to the lower orders, and their want of the knowledge of frugal cookery, have proved a source of much real calamity; for where nothing is laid up, every pressure arising from sickness, child-birth, or death, throws many hundreds upon the Public, who have no legal parochial Settlement, and who but for some relief must absolutely perish :— While the Soup-Charities hold out immediate and constant relief to many families, who might otherwise perish with hunger;—while this species of relief may be said to be accessible to every indigent family in the Metropolis, no lure is held out to the idle or profligate It cannot be disposed of, as bread, meat, and coals, for gin and other articles. There is therefore scarcely any risque of deception, more especially as the applicants pay down half the original cost on re-ceiving it.—Thus establishing the means of discrimination between

upwards of ten thousand children of the labouring
Poor in this Country.

" Every institution which tends to make the poor
depend on any other support than their own industry
does them great disservice, and is highly injurious to
society, by diminishing the quantity of labour which
annually produces consumable goods, the only wealth
of a nation."

Although these suggestions may appear harsh, and

real and *pretended distress.* About 10,000 families, composed
chiefly of persons who had not the means of obtaining sufficient
food to support nature, consisting of 50,000 men, women, and children, were relieved by the daily distribution of Soups at *Spital-
Fields, Clerkenwell, St. George's Fields,* and *Westminster,* during the
last winter, at an expence to the Subscribers not exceeding One
Guinea for every 504 meals of rich nourishing Soup, which those
poor people received. But this is not the only advantage which
attends these Institutions, since there is every reason to believe,
that while the poor are thus frugally fed, they are taught by example, and by circulating among them printed friendly advices,
what they never knew before—*The means of making a little go far,*
by introducing the same beneficial mode of dressing food in their
own houses. And from a minute attention to this object, the Author
has great satisfaction in stating, that from the eagerness shewn to
obtain the Soup, and the thankfulness almost universally expressed
for the benefits it conferred, there is every reason to hope, that more
good has arisen to the industrious poor from these establishments
(which are now extending themselves in the Villages and Manufacturing Towns) than by any plan which has ever been resorted to
for relieving distress. Among the various classes of benevolent individuals, to whom the Public have been indebted for their pecuniary
and personal aid in promoting this design, the Society of *The Friends*
is peculiarly prominent. To the zeal and perseverance they have
manifested, and the valuable time they have bestowed, in giving
effect and utility to the System, is owing much of its success.

some

some of them may admit of more extended discussion, yet they certainly deserve very serious consideration, as do also the following observations on
the Commons and Waste Lands with which this
kingdom still abounds; and on the general character of Servants and Labourers ; the latter of which
afford but too melancholy a confirmation of many
opinions which the author of this treatise has thought
it his duty to bring forward to the Public eye.

" On estimating the value of the Commons in
Middlesex, including every advantage that can be
derived from them in pasturage, locality of situation,
and the barbarous custom of turbary, it appears that
*they do not produce to the Community, in their present
state, more than four shillings per Acre!* On the other
hand, they are, in many instances, of real injury to
the Public, by holding out a lure to the poor man ;
by affording him materials wherewith to build his
cottage, and ground to erect it upon ; together with
firing, and the run of his poultry and pigs for nothing.
This is, of course, temptation sufficient to induce a
great number of poor persons to settle upon the borders of such Commons.   But the mischief does not
end here; for having gained these trifling advan
tages, through the neglect or connivance of the Lord
of the Manor, it unfortunately gives their minds an
improper bias, and inculcates a desire to live, from
that time forward, without labour, or at least with as
little as possible.

" The animals kept by this description of persons,
                                                it

it is soon discovered by their owners, are not likely
to afford them much revenue, without better feed
than the scanty herbage on a Common ; hence they
are tempted to pilfer corn, &c. towards their support ;
and as they are still dependant on such a deceptious
supply, to answer the demands of their consumption,
they are in some measure constrained to resort to
various dishonest means, so as to make up the deficiency.

   " It is a notorious fact, that in all cases cottages
not having any ground belonging to them, promote
thieving to a great extent ; as their inhabitants constantly rob the neighbouring farms and gardens of
roots and pulse sufficient for their own consumption,"
and which they would have no temptation to do, if
they had the same articles growing of their own."
Hence Mr. Middleton suggests the evil admits of an
easy remedy, namely, the allotting to each cottager a
piece of ground.

   " Another very serious evil which the Public suffers from these Commons is, that they are the constant rendezvous of Gypsies, Strollers, and other loose
persons, living under tents which they carry with
them from place to place, according to their conve-
niency.   Most of these persons have asses, many of
them horses, nay, some of them have even covered
carts, which answer the double purpose of a caravan
for concealing and carrying off the property they
have stolen, and also of a house for sleeping in at
night.   They usually stay a week or two at a place ;
                                                    and

and the cattle which they keep serve to transport
their few articles of furniture from one place to another.   These, during the stay of their owners, are
turned adrift to procure what food they can find in
the neighbourhood of their tents, and the deficiency
is made up from the adjacent hay-stacks, barns, and
granaries.   They are known never to buy any hay
or corn, and yet their cattle are supplied with these
articles of good quality.   The women and children
beg and pilfer, and the men commit greater acts of
dishonesty. *In short, the Commons of this Country are
well known to be the constant resort of footpads and
highwaymen, and are literally and proverbially a public
nuisance.*"——

  "*The Labourers of this country are ruined in morals
and constitution by the public houses.*   It is a general
rule, that the higher their wages, the less they carry
home, and consequently the greater is the wretchedness of themselves and their families.   Comforts in a
cotttage are mostly found where the man's wages are
low, at least so low as to require him to labour six
days a week.   For instance, a good workman at nine
shillings per week, if advanced to twelve will spend
a day in the week at the alehouse, which reduces his
labour to five days, or ten shillings : and as he will
spend two shillings in the public house, it leaves but
eight for his family, which is one less than they had
when he earned only nine shillings.

  " If by any means he be put into a situation of
earning eighteen shillings in six days, he will get
                                                    drunk

drunk Sunday and Monday, and go to his work stupid on Tuesday; and should he be a mechanical journeyman of some genius, who by constant labour could earn twenty-four shillings or thirty shillings per week, as some of them can, he will be drunk half the week, insolent to his employer, and to every person about him.

" If his master has business in hand that requires particular dispatch, he will then, more than at any other time, be absent from his work, and his wife and children will experience the extreme of hunger, rags and cold.

" The low *Inns on the road sides* are, in general, receiving houses for the corn, hay, straw, poultry, eggs, &c. which the farmers' men pilfer from their masters.

" *Gentlemens' Servants* are mostly a bad set, and the great number kept in this country, is the means of the rural labourers acquiring a degree of idleness and insolence unknown in places more remote from the Metropolis.

" The poor children who are brought up on the borders of commons and copses, are accustomed to little labour, but to much idleness and pilfering. Having grown up, and these latter qualities having become a part of their nature, they are then introduced to the farmers as servants or labourers; and very bad ones they make.

" The children of small farmers, on the contrary, have the picture of industry, hard labour, and
honesty,

honesty, hourly before them, in the persons of their *parents*, and daily hear the complaints which *they* make against idle and pilfering servants, and comparisons drawn highly in favor of honesty. In this manner honesty and industry become, as it were, a part of the nature of such young folks. The father's property is small, and his means few; he is therefore unable to hire and stock a farm for each of his children; they consequently become servants on large farms, or in gentlemens' families, and in either situation are the most faithful part of such establishments."——

" One great hinderance to comfort in a life of agriculture, and which drives liberal minded men, who are always the best friends to improvement, out of the profession, is the want of laws to put a total stop to the Receivers of stolen goods. These are the wretches who encourage servants in agriculture, and others to pilfer, by holding out the lure of buying every article, which such servants can bring, without asking them any questions. Most things which are usually produced on a farm, from so small an article as an egg, to hay, straw and grain of all sorts, are daily stolen,* and sold on the sides of every principal road in this country. Among the Receivers are to

* These thefts are committed by degrees in a small way, seldom exceeding a truss of hay or a bushel of corn by one man at one time; and are generally of smaller articles. In some places the stealing of gate-hooks and iron fastnings is so common as to compel the farmer both to hang and fasten his gates with wood. *Middleton*.

be

be reckoned Millers, Cornchandlers, Dealers in eggs, butter and poultry, and the Keepers of Chandlers' shops.

" The Drivers of Gentlemens' carriages are in-trusted to buy hay, straw, and corn, for their horses; in the doing which, they generally cheat their masters of 5s. in each load of hay, of 2s. 6d. in each load of straw, and 1s. in every quarter of corn. This gives them an interest in the consumption, makes them extremely wasteful, and brings on habits of dis-honesty.

" The Ostlers at the Inns on the sides of the roads, purchase stolen hay, straw, corn, eggs, and poultry. A person who kept a horse several weeks at one of these inns, in attending occasionally to see the animal, discovered him to be fed with wheat, barley and oats mixed together, which could only happen by the farmers' servants robbing their Master, and selling the corn to the Ostler."——

" The fields near London are never free from men strolling about in pilfering pursuits by day, and com-mitting greater crimes by night. The depredations every Sunday are astonishingly great. There are not many gardens within five miles of London, that escape being visited in a marauding way, very early on a Sunday morning, and the farmers' fields are plundered all day long of fruit, roots, cabbages, pulse and corn. Even the ears of wheat are cut from the sheaves, and carried away in the most daring manner

in

in open day, in various ways, but mostly in bags containing about half a bushel each. It has been moderately estimated, that 20,000 bushels of all the various sorts are thus carried off every Sunday morning, and 10,000 more during the other six days of the week ; or one million and a half of bushels in a year, which, if valued at so small a sum as sixpence each, would amount to 37,500*l.*

" The occupiers of many thousand acres round London, lose annually in this manner to the amount of much more than 20s. an acre.

"A Miller near London being questioned as to small parcels of wheat brought to his mill to be ground, by a suspected person, soon after several barns had been robbed, answered, that any explanation on that head would put his mills in danger of being burnt. Well may the *farmers* say, ' Their ' *property is not protected like that of other men.*"

Mr. Middleton calculates that the depredations committed on the landed interest probably amount to 4s. an acre per annum, on all the cultivated lands, in England, or to eight millions of pounds sterling per annum : and including the injuries done by game and vermin, he supposes, that the farmers' property suffers to the amount of 10s. an acre, or nearly twenty millions annually.

The following curious circumstances relative to the adulteration of *Milk* in the Metropolis, ought to be added to the list of petty frauds, which not merely
affect

affect the pockets but the health of the inhabitants of London. The number of milch cows kept for the purpose of supplying the Metropolis with this article, is stated by Mr. Middleton, after very diligent inquiry, at 8,500; and each cow is supposed to afford on an average nine quarts of milk per day.—

" When the families of fashion are in London for the winter season, the consumption, and consequent deterioration of milk are at the highest; during the summer months, when such families are for the most part in the country, the milk may probably be of rather a better quality.

" The milk is always given in its genuine state to the retail dealers; and as it is sold to them by the Cow-keepers after the rate of two-pence and 1-8th of a penny per quart, and is retailed by them at threepence halfpenny a quart, the profit is surely so large as ought to prevent even the smallest adulteration. But when it is considered how greatly it is reduced *by water*, and impregnated with *worse* ingredients, it is much to be lamented that no method has yet been devised to put a stop to the many scandalous frauds and impositions in general practice, with regard to this very necessary article of human sustenance.

" It is certainly an object well deserving the particular consideration of the Legislature. It cannot be doubted, that many persons would be glad to make some addition to the price now paid for it (high
as

as that price is) provided they could, for such increased price, procure so useful an article in domestic œconomy perfectly genuine *.

"Five or six men only are employed in attending near three hundred cows. As one woman cannot milk above eight or nine cows twice a day, that part of the business would necessarily be attended with considerable expence to the Cow-keeper, were it not that the Retailer agrees for the produce of a certain number of cows, and takes the labour and expence of milking on himself.

"Every Cow-house is provided with a milk-room (where the milk is measured and served out by the Cow-keeper) and this room is mostly furnished with *a pump*, to which the Retail Dealers apply in rotation; not secretly, but openly before any person that may be standing by, from which they pump water into the milk vessels at their discretion. The pump is placed there expressly for that purpose, and indeed is very

* Not satisfied with the profit here stated, which, considering the difference of measures, is above 100 per cent. it is a common practice with the Retailers of this useful article to carry the milk first home to their own houses, where it is set up for half a day, when the cream is taken from it, at least all that comes up in that time, and it is then sold for new milk. By which means, what is delivered in the morning is no other than the milk of the preceding afternoon, deprived of the cream it throws up by standing during that time. By this means a farther considerable profit accrues to the Retailers, and the milk is greatly reduced in point of strength and quality. This cream, poor as it is, they again mix with flour, chalk, and perhaps other more baneful ingredients, and yet it finds a ready market in the Metropolis. *Middleton.*

seldom

seldom used for any other. A considerable Cow-keeper in Surrey has a pump of this kind, which goes by the name of the *Famous Black Cow* (from the circumstance of its being painted black), *and is said to yield more than all the rest put together.*

" Where such a pump is not provided for them things are much worse, for in that case the Retailers are not even careful to use *clean* water. Some of them have been seen to dip their pails in a common horse-trough. And what is still more disgusting, though equally true, one cow-house happens to stand close to the edge of a stream, into which runs much of the dung, and most of the urine of the cows, and even in this stream, so foully impregnated, they have been observed to dip their milk-pails.

" A Cow-keeper informs me, that the Retail Milk Dealers are for the most part the refuse of other employments, possessing neither character, decency of manners, nor cleanliness.

" No person could possibly drink of the milk, were they fully acquainted with the filthy manners of these dealers in it.

" The same person suggests, *as a remedy for these abuses, that it would be highly proper for every Retail Milk Dealer to be obliged to take out an Annual Licence from the Magistrates*; which licence should be granted only to such as could procure a certificate of good conduct, signed by the Cow-keeper and a certain number of their customers ; and also on their being sworn to sell the milk pure and unadulterated."

CHAP.

CHAP. IV.

General Reflections arising from the perpetration of the higher and more atrocious crimes of Burglary, Highway Robbery, &c.—These crimes more peculiar to England than to Holland and Flanders, &c.— The Reason explained.—A general View of the various classes of Criminals engaged in Robberies and Burglaries, and of those discharged from Prison and the Hulks.—Their miserable situation as Outcasts of Society, without the means of Support.— The necessity of some Antidote previous to the return of Peace.—The means used at present by Thieves in accomplishing their nefarious Purposes.—Observations on the stealing Cattle, Sheep, Corn, &c.— Receivers of Stolen Goods shewn to be the Nourishers of every description of Thieves.—Remedies suggested, by means of Detection and Prevention.

———————

Iᴛ is impossible to reflect upon the outrages and acts of violence continually committed, more particularly in and near the Metropolis, by lawless ravagers of property, and destroyers of lives, in disturbing the peaceful mansion, *the Castle of every Englishman*, and also in abridging the liberty of travelling upon the
Public

Public Highways, without asking—*Why are these enormities suffered in a Country where the Criminal Laws are supposed to have arrived at a greater degree of perfection than any other ?*

This is an important inquiry, interesting in the highest degree, to every member of the Body Politic.

If, in pursuing such an inquiry, the situation of Holland, Flanders, and several of the Northern States on the Continent, be examined, it will be found that this terrific evil had (alluding to these States previous to the present war) there scarcely an existence: and, that the precaution of bolting doors and windows during the night was even seldom used ; although in these Countries, from the opulence of many of the inhabitants, there were great temptations to plunder property.

This security did not proceed from *severer punishments,* for in very few Countries are they more sanguinary than in England. —It is to be attributed to a more correct and energetic system of Police, joined to an early and general attention to the employment, education, and morals of the lower orders of the people ; a habit of industry and sobriety is thus acquired, which, universally imbibed in early life, " grows with their growth, and strengthens with their strength."

Idleness is a never-failing road to criminality. It originates generally in the inattention and the bad example of profligate parents.—And when it has unfortunately taken hold of the human mind, unnecessary

sary wants and improper gratifications, not known or thought of by persons in a course of industry, are constantly generated : hence it is, that crimes are resorted to, and every kind of violence, hostile to the laws, and to peace and good order, is perpetrated.

The criminal aud unfortunate individuals, who compose the dismal catalogue of Highwaymen, Footpad-Robbers, Burglars, Pick-pockets, and common Thieves, in and about this Metropolis, may be divided into the three following classes :

1. Young men of some education, who having acquired idle habits of abandoning business, or by being bred to no profession, and having been seduced by this idleness to indulge in gambling and scenes of debauchery and dissipation, at length impoverished and unable to purchase their accustomed gratifications, have recourse to the highway to supply immediate wants.

2. Tradesmen and others, who having ruined their fortunes and business by gaming and dissipation, sometimes as a desperate remedy, go upon the road.

But these two classes are extremely few in number, and bear no proportion to the lower and more depraved part of the fraternity of thieves, who pursue the trade systematically ; who conduct their depredations under such circumstances of caution, as to render detection extremely difficult ; and whose knowledge of all the weak parts of the Criminal Law is generally so complete, as to enable them to elude justice, and obtain acquittals, when detected and put upon their trial :—*Namely*—

3. 1st Ser-

3. 1st. Servants, Ostlers, Stable and Post-Boys out of place; who, preferring what they consider as idleness, have studied the profession of Thieving.—2d. Persons who being imprisoned for debts, assaults, or petty offences, have learned habits of idleness and profligacy in gaols.—3d. Idle and disorderly mechanics and labourers, who having on this account lost the confidence of their masters or employers, resort to thieving, as a means of support; from all whom the notorious and hacknied thieves generally select the most trusty and daring to act as their associates.—4th. Criminals tried and acquitted of offences charged against them, of which class a vast number is annually let loose upon Society:—5th. Convicts discharged from Prison and the Hulks, after suffering the sentence of the Law: too often instructed by one another in all the arts and devices which attach to the most extreme degree of human depravity, and in the perfect knowledge of the means of perpetrating Crimes, and of eluding Justice.

To form some judgment of the number of persons in this great Metropolis who compose at least a part of the Criminal Phalanx engaged in depredations and acts of violence, it is only necessary to have recourse to the following Statement of the number of prisoners discharged, during a period of four years, from the eight different Gaols in the Metropolis, and within the Bills of Mortality.

1. Discharged by proclamation and gaol-deliveries; having been committed in consequence of being charged with various offences for which bills were not found by the Grand Jury, or where the prosecutors did not appear to maintain and support the charges   -   -   -   -   -   -   5593

2. Dis-

2. Discharged by acquittals, in the different Courts ;
  (frequently from having availed themselves of
  the defects of the Law,— from frauds in keeping
  back evidence, and other devices)   -   -   -   -   2962

3. Convicts discharged from the different goals,
  after suffering the punishment of imprisonment, &c. inflicted on them for the several
  offences   -   -   -   -   -   -   2484

Total   11038

The following is a Statement of the number of
these discharges from the year 1792 to 1799 inclusive :—

1. Discharged by Proclamations and Goal-
  deliveries   -   -   -   -   8650
2. Discharged by Acquittals   -   -   4935
3. Discharged after punishment :   or by
  being bailed or pardoned   -   -   6925

Total   20,510

If to this deplorable Catalogue shall be added the
Convicts which have been returned on the Public
from the Hulks within the same period, namely, from
1792 to 1799 inclusive, either from pardons, escapes,
or the expiration of their punishment, the numbers
will stand thus :

Enlarged

Enlarged in 1792	- -	303
—— —1793	-	435
—— —1794	-	62
—— —1795	-	67
—— —1796	-	38
—— —1797	-	39
—— —1798	-	93
—— —1799	-	346
		1383

Totals from Gaols and from the Hulks 21,893

Humanity shudders at the contemplation of this interesting part of the discussion, when it is considered, who these our miserable fellow-mortals are! and what is to be expected from the extreme depravity which attaches to the chief part of them!

And here a prominent feature of the imperfect state of the Police of the Metropolis and the Country is too evident to escape notice.

Without friends, without character, and without the means of subsistence, what are these unhappy mortals to do?—They are no sooner known or suspected, than they are avoided—No person will employ them, even if they were disposed to return to the paths of honesty; unless they make use of fraud and deception, by concealing that they have been the inhabitants of a *Prison,* or of the *Hulks.*

At

At large upon the world, without food or raiment, and with the constant calls of nature upon
them for both, without a home or any asylum to
shelter them from the inclemency of the weather,
what is to become of them?

The Police of the Country has provided no place
of industry, in which those who were disposed to reform might find subsistence in return for voluntary
labour; which, in their present situation, becomes useless to them, because no person will purchase it by
employing them.*   Under all these circumstances it
is to be feared, indeed it is known, that many Convicts,
from dire necessity, return to their old courses.—And
thus, through the medium of these miserable outcasts
of Society, crimes are increased and become a regular
trade, because many of them can make no other
election.

It is indeed true, that during the first three years
of the present war, many Convicts and idle disorderly persons were sent to the Army and Navy:
but still a vast number remained behind, who could
not be accepted on account of ruptures, fits, or some

---

* That man will deserve a statue to his memory who shall devise and carry into effect a plan for the employment of *Discharged
Prisoners and Convicts,* who may be desirous of labouring for their
subsistence in an honest way.—It is only necessary for some men of
weight and influence to make the attempt, in order to ensure the
assistance of the opulent and humane in so good and necessary
a work. See a future Chapter as to the present state of punishment
and the remedies proposed.

                                              other

other disability or infirmity, which, although they incapacitate them from serving his Majesty, do not prevent them from committing crimes.

While it must be evident, that the resource afforded by the present war gives employment, for a time only, to many depraved characters and mischievous members of the community; how necessary is it to be provided with antidotes, previous to the return of peace; when, to the multitude of thieves now at large, there will be added numbers of the same class, who may be discharged from the Navy and Army?— If some plan of employment is not speedily devised, to which all persons of this description may resort, who cannot otherwise subsist themselves in an honest way; and if the Police of the Metropolis is not greatly improved, by the introduction of more energy, and a greater degree of System and Method in its administration; it is much to be feared, that no existing power will be able to keep them within bounds.

It is in vain to say the Laws are sufficient. —They are indeed abundantly voluminous, and in many respects very excellent, but they require to be revised, consolidated, modernized, and adapted in a greater degree to the prevention of existing evils, with such regulations as would ensure their due execution not only *in every part of the Capital*, but also in all parts of the Kingdom.

The means these depredators at present use in accomplishing their nefarious purposes are complicated and various; and of late years have become as much diversified

diversified as it is possible for the ingenuity of men
to devise, who frequently join good natural abilities
to all the artifices of the finished villain.

It is no uncommon thing for the more daring and
strong-minded to form themselves into gangs or
societies; to the exclusion of those of their fraternity
whose hearts are likely to fail them, and who are supposed not to be sufficiently firm, so as to secure their
accomplices against the hazard of discovery in case
of detection.

Robbery and theft, as well in houses as on the
roads, have long been reduced to a regular System.
Opportunities are watched, and intelligence procured,
with a degree of vigilance similar to that which marks
the conduct of a skilful General, eager to obtain an
advantage over an enemy.

Houses intended to be entered during the night,
are previously reconnoitered and examined for days
preceding. If one or more of the servants are not already associated with the gang, the most artful means
are used to obtain their assistance; and when every
previous arrangement is made, the mere operation of
robbing a house becomes a matter of little difficulty.

By the connivance and assistance of immediate, or
former servants, they are led to the places where the
most valuable, as well as the most portable, articles
are deposited, and the object is speedily attained.

In this manner do the principal Burglars and
House-breakers proceed; and let this information
serve

serve as a caution to every person in the choice both
of their male and female servants; since the latter as
well as the former are not seldom accomplices in very
atrocious robberies.

The same *generalship* is manifested in the nocturnal expeditions of those criminal associates upon the
highways.

A perfect knowledge is obtained every evening of
the different routes and situations of the patroles :
—they are narrowly watched, and their vigilance
(wherever they are vigilant) is in too many instances
defeated.

Infinite pains are bestowed in procuring intelligence
of persons travelling upon the road with money,
bank-notes, or other valuable effects; and when discovered, the most masterly pains are concerted to way-
lay and rob them of their property : Nor have the
measures pursued by these atrocious villains, the
Footpads, exhibited less skill in the plans adopted;
while their outrages are too often marked with those
acts of cruelty and barbarity which justly render them
objects of peculiar terror.

The same adroitness also marks the conduct of
those who turn their attention chiefly to picking of
pockets, and other smaller robberies.

It would almost fill a volume to detail the various
artifices which are resorted to, in carrying on this
species of thieving; by which even the most cautious, and those who are generally upon their guard,
are

are not exempted from the ravages of these inferior pests of Society.

In addition to the injuries or losses arising from burglaries, highway-robberies, and lesser thefts, it is to be lamented that extensive and increasing depredations are made upon horses, cattle, and sheep, and also upon flour, corn, potatoes, provender, and poultry; stolen from the drovers, millers, corn-factors, and farmers in the vicinity of the Metropolis. These have been stated more at large in a preceding Chapter.

It cannot be too often repeated that the great facility experienced, in the immediate disposal of every article obtained by dishonesty, is one of the chief encouragements to all the acts of outrage and depredation enumerated in the course of this Work.

It frequently happens that the Burglars, the Highwaymen, and footpad robbers, make their contracts with the Receivers, on the evening before the plunder is obtained; so as to secure a ready admittance immediately afterwards, and before day-break, for the purpose of effectual concealment by melting plate, obliterating marks, and securing all other articles so as to place them out of the reach of discovery. This has long been reduced to a regular system which is understood and followed as a trade.

Nor do those Thieves who steal horses,* cattle, and sheep

* The frauds and felonies committed in the course of a year with respect to horses exceed all credibility. Above thirty thousand of these useful animals are said to be flayed and boiled in the Metropolis, at the Seventeen Licensed Houses, annually, of which about one

sheep experience more difficulty in finding purchasers immediately for whatever they can obtain :—they too,. generally, make a previous bargain with the Receivers, who are ready at an appointed hour to conceal the animals, at kill them immediately, and to destroy the skins for the purpose of eluding detection.

It sometimes happens also, that the persons who perpetrate these robberies are journeymen-Butchers, by trade; who kill whatever they steal, and often afterwards sell their plunder in the Public Markets.

If, by wise regulations, it were possible to embarrass and disturb the extensive trade carried on by all the *concealed Receivers,* who are the particular class having connection with the professed thieves, a very great check would be given to public depredations.

In suggesting Remedies, this of all others appears, at first view, to be the most difficult; because of the apparent impossibility of regulating any class of Dealers who have no shop, or visible trade, and who transact all their business under concealment:—but still the object is to be obtained by a combination of

one-fourth are brought there alive, supposed chiefly to be stolen horses. These establishments require many additional regulations to inforce and insure that purity of conduct, which the Legislature had in view when the Act of the 26th Geo. 3, cap. 71, was passed for licensing persons to slaughter horses. In the operation of this Act is strongly evinced the efficacy of the best laws, when measures are not pursued to insure an accurate and chaste execution. Wherever the vigilance of a General Police does not extend its influence in carrying into effect all regulations of a preventive nature, it is in vain to hope that the evil in the view of the Legislature will be diminished.

different

different legislative regulations, carried into execution by a consolidated, vigilant and well-regulated Police.

The detail, however, of the means of detecting Receivers will, of course, be discussed hereafter, in a subsequent Chapter; at present the following Hints will suffice.

A register of lodging-houses and lodgers in every parish, liberty, hamlet, and precinct, where the rent does not exceed a certain sum (suppose ten shillings) weekly, would prove one great means of embarrassment to Thieves of every class; and of course would tend, with other regulations, to the prevention of Crimes.

Night-Coaches also promote, in an eminent degree, the perpetration of burglaries and other felonies : Bribed by a high reward, many hackney coachmen eagerly enter into the pay of nocturnal depredators, and wait in the neighbourhood until the robbery is completed, and then draw up, at the moment the watchmen are going their rounds, or off their stands, for the purpose of conveying the plunder to the house of the Receiver, who is generally waiting the issue of the enterprise. Above one half of the present Hackney Coachmen, in London, are said to be (in the cant phrase) *Flashmen* designed to assist thieves.

It being certain that a vast deal of mischief is done which could not be effected, were it not for the assistance which night coaches afford to Thieves of every description, it would seem, upon the whole, advantageous

tageous to the Public, that no Hackney Coaches should be permitted to take fares after twelve o'clock at night; or, if this is impracticable, that the coach-hire for night service should be advanced, on condition that all coachmen going upon the stands after twelve o'clock, should be licensed by a Board of Police. By this means the night-coachmen, by being more select, would not be so open to improper influence; and they might even become useful to Public Justice in giving informations, and also in detecting Burglars and other Thieves.

Watchmen and Patroles, instead of being, as now comparatively of little use, from their *age, infirmity, inability, inattention,* or *corrupt practices,* might almost at the present expence, by a proper selection, and a more correct mode of discipline, by means of a general superintendance over the whole to regulate their conduct, and keep them to their duty, be rendered of great utility in preventing Crimes, and in detecting Offenders *.

At

---

* The depredations which are committed almost every evening in Cheapside, and the adjacent streets leading into it, affords strong proofs of the necessity of an improved system with regard to watchmen and patroles.

Allured to that particular part of the Metropolis, from the extensive and valuable property in *piece goods* and other portable articles which are constantly removing to and from the different shops and warehouses;—a multitude of thieves and pickpockets, exhibiting often in their dress and exterior, the appearance of gentlemen and men of bussiness, assemble every evening in gangs, watching at the corners of every street, ready to *hustle* and *rob,* or *to trip up the heels* of the *warehouse-porters and the servants of shopkeepers carrying*

At present the System of the nightly watch is
without energy, disjointed and governed by almost
as many different Acts of Parliament, as there are
Parishes, Hamlets, Liberties, and Precincts within
the Bills of Mortality ; and where the payment is as
various, running from 8½d. up to 2s. a night.

The Act of the 14th of George IIId. *(cap.* 90.*)*
entituled, *An Act for the better regulation of the Nightly
Watch within the City and Liberty of Westminster, and*

carrying goods; or at the doors of warehouses, at dusk and at the
time they are locked, to be ready to seize loose parcels when unperceived; by all which means, aided by a number of other tricks
and fraudulent pretences, they are but too successful in obtaining
considerable booty. In short, there is no device or artifice to
which these vigilant plunderers do not resort: of which an example appeared in an instance, where almost in the twinkling of
an eye, while the servants of an eminent silk-dyer had crossed a
narrow street, his horse and cart, containing raw silk to the value of
twelve hundred pounds, were driven clear off. Many of these atrocious villains, are also constantly in waiting at the inns, disguised
in different ways, personating *travellers, coach-office clerks, porters,
and coachmen,* for the purpose of plundering every thing that is
portable; which, with the assistance of two or three associates
if necessary, is carried to a coach called for the purpose, and
immediately conveyed to the receiver.

The most adroit thieves in this line are generally *convicts from
the hulks or returned transports,* who under pretence of having
some ostensible business, (while they carry on the trade of thieving) generally open a *chandler's shop,* set up a *green-stall,* or get
into a *public-house;* some of these old offenders are known also
to keep livery-stables for thieves, and horses for the use of highwaymen: thereby forming a connected chain by which these
criminal people extend and facilitate their trade; *nourishing,
accommodating,* and supporting one another.

parts

parts adjacent, contains many excellent Regulations, but they do not extend to the eastern part of the Metropolis; and for want of an active and superintending agency, superior to beadles, it is believed and felt that they are not, (even within the district included in the Act,) correctly carried into execution : and that no small portion of those very men who are paid for protecting the public, are not only instruments of oppression in many instances, by extorting money most unwarrantably; but are frequently accessaries in aiding, abetting or concealing the commission of crimes, which it is their duty to detect and suppress.

If as an improvement to the preventive System and as a check upon the improper conduct of parochial watchmen, a body of honest, able, and active Officers, in the character of Police Patroles, were attached to each Public Office, or to a General Police System with a sufficient fund to defray the expences, to follow up informations for the detection of negligent servants of the Public, and liberally to reward those who are active and useful in apprehending delinquents, and in making discoveries, tending either to the recovery of property stolen, or to the detection of the offenders, little doubt need be entertained, under the guidance of a Central Board and vigilant Police, aided by zealous and active Magistrates, that such a System would soon be established, as would go very far towards the prevention of many atrocious crimes.

Among

Among the various advantages which may thus be expected to result to the Community from the arrangements recommended in this work, would be *the suppression of Highway Robberies.* A desideratum impracticable in the present state of the Police, although easy and certain under a Police Board; having a general superintendance competent to look at every point of danger, and with pecuniary resources equal to an object so interesting to the inhabitants of this Metropolis *. Upon the adoption of this important measure, therefore, (a measure so strongly recommended by the Select Committee of the House of Commons on Finance †) depends in a great degree, that security to travellers on the highways in the vicinity of the Metropolis; the want of which, and of many other valuable regulations, for the prevention of crimes, has long been a reproach to the Criminal Jurisprudence, as well as the Police, of the Country.

---

* Hints have been submitted to the Author for establishing a plan of *Travelling Police*, to extend 20 miles round the Metropolis; by means of Patroles well armed and mounted, who should be on the road at all hours; the expence to be defrayed by the produce of a toll to be raised for the purpose. The scheme might in all probability be much improved under the sanction of a General Police Board, without the additional expence of the proposed toll.

† See the 28th Report of that Committee.

CHAP.

CHAP. V.

Reasons assigned why forgeries and frauds must prevail in a certain degree, wherever the interchange of property is extensive. A considerable check already given to the higher class of Forgeries, by shutting out all hopes of Royal Mercy.—Petty Forgeries have however increased:—The Reason assigned.—The qualifications of a Cheat, Swindler, and Gambler explained.—This mischievous class of men extremely numerous in the Metropolis.—The Common and Statute Law applicable to offences of this nature explained.—The different classes of Cheats and Swindlers, and the various tricks and devices they pursue, to enable them to live in idleness, by their wits.— Sharpers, Cheats, and Swindlers, divided into eighteen different Classes—1st. Sharpers who become Pawnbrokers.—2d. Sharpers who obtain Licence as Hawkers and Pedlars.—3d. Swindlers who open shops as Auctioneers.—4th. Swindlers who pretend to discount Bills.—5th. Itinerant Jews.—6th. Cheats who sell by false Weights and Measures.— 7th. Swindlers who defraud Tradesmen of Goods.— 8th. Cheats who take Genteel Lodgings with false Names, &c.—9th. Cheats, who personate former Masters to defraud their Tradesmen.—10th. Cheats who personate Footmen, and order Goods from Tradesmen.—11th. Cheats and Sharpers who deceive Persons from the Country.—12th. Cheats and Sharpers

*ers who trick Shopmen and Boys out of Parcels.—
13th. Sharpers who attend Inns to pick up Parcels by
various tricks and devices.—14th. Cheats who go
from door to door, begging on false pretences.—15th.
Sharpers selling smuggled Goods; known by the
name of Duffers.—16th. Female Sharpers, who attend Court and Public Places.—17th. Female Bankers who lend money to Barrow-Women at 6d. a day
for Five Shillings.—18th. Cheats who pretend to
tell Fortunes.—Various Remedies suggested.*

Iɴ a great Metropolis, like London, where trade
and commerce have arrived at such an astonishing
height, and where from the extensive transactions in
the Funds, and the opulence of the People, the
interchange of property is so expanded, it ceases to
be a matter of wonder that Forgeries and Frauds
should prevail, in a certain degree:—the question of
difficulty is, *why the Laws and the means of prevention, have not kept pace with the progressive ad-
vancement of the Country : so as to check and keep
within bounds these nefarious practices?*

Forgeries of the higher class, so dangerous in a
commercial country, have by the wise policy of the
Executive Government, in shutting out all hopes of
the extension of the Royal Mercy to the guilty, received a most severe check : beneficial in the highest
degree to the country, and clearly manifested by the
records

records of the Old Bailey, where trials for offences of this nature certainly do not increase in number.

But it is to be lamented, that, with regard to petty forgeries and frauds, this is by no means the case, for they seem to multiply and advance with the opulence and luxury of the country; and to branch out into innumerable different shades, varying as the fashions of the year, and as the resources for the perpetration of this species of fraud change their aspect.

When those depraved people who (to use a vulgar phrase) *live entirely by their wits*—find that any tricks which they have practised for a certain length of time become stale, (such as *pricking the belt for a wager, or dropping the ring*) they abandon these; and have recourse to other devices more novel, and more likely to be effectual in cheating and defrauding the unwary.

One of the most prevailing and successful of these, is the fraud practised upon shop-keepers, tradesmen, publicans, and others, by the circulation of forged copper-plate notes and bills for small sums, of 5*l*. and 10*l*. the latter purporting to be drawn, by bankers in the manufacturing and sea-port towns, on different banking-houses in London.

This species of forgery has been carried to a considerable extent, suggested no doubt by the confidence which is established from the extensive circulation of country bankers' notes and bills, now made payable in London; by which the deception is, in some

some degree covered, and detection rendered more difficult.

The great qualifications, or leading and indispensable attributes of a *Sharper*, a *Cheat*, a *Swindler*, or a *Gambler*, are, to possess a genteel exterior, a demeanor apparently artless, and a good address.

Like the more violent depredators upon the public, this class (who are extremely numerous) generally proceed upon a regular system, and study as a *trade* all those infamous tricks and devices by, which the thoughtless, the ignorant, and the honest are defrauded of their property.

The common law has defined the offence of cheating— to be a *deceitful practice in defrauding, or endeavouring to defraud, another of his own right, by means of some artful device, contrary to the plain rules of common honesty.*

The Statute of the 33d of Henry the Eighth, *cap.* 1. entered into a more specific explanation of what might constitute such an offence, and fixed the mode of punishment; by declaring, " *that if any person* " *shall falsely or deceitfully obtain, or get into his* " *hands or possession, any money, goods, &c. of any* " *other person,* by colour or means of any false privy " token, or counterfeit letter, *&c.—he shall, on con-* " *viction, be punished by imprisonment, the pillory, or* " *whipping—saving to the party aggrieved the same* " *power of recovering the property as he might have* " *had at Common Law, &c.*"

From this remote period, until the 30th of George the

the Second, the Legislature does not appear to have seen the necessity of enacting any new Law, applicable to this species of offence.

In the progress however of Society and Commerce, joined to the consequent influx of riches, producing luxury and extravagance, a larger field opened for cheats and sharpers of every description; insomuch, that the evil became so great, and the existing Laws were found so insufficient, as to render it necessary to provide a legislative remedy.

In applying this remedy, it seems that the great increase of a new species of cheating, practised by persons known in modern times by the name of *Swindlers*, had suggested the propriety of defining the offence, in a more applicable and specific manner, and of rendering the punishment more severe. By the act of 30 Geo. II. *cap.* 24. it is declared, " *that* " *all persons obtaining money, goods, wares, or mer-* " *chandize,* by false pretences, *shall be deemed offenders* " *against the Law and the public peace; and the* " *Court, before whom any such offender shall be tried,* " *shall on conviction, order them to be put in the* " *pillory, or publicly whipped, or transported for seven* " *years.*"

Thus stand the Laws at present with regard to Swindlers*. They ought certainly to embrace a wider field,

* There appears to be a deficiency in the Act of 30th George the Second, cap 24. in omitting to add *Bank Notes* after the word *Money,* and also *Horses, Cattle, Sheep, or other Animals,* after goods,

field, so as to reach those artifices by which sharpers and persons of depraved minds obtain money from the ignorant and unwary, by assuming false characters, taking genteel lodgings,- and cheating innocent tradesmen, who lose large sums annually by such depredations.

We shall next proceed to particularize the various classes of Sharpers who thus prey upon the public: reserving all that relates to those more immediately connected with *Gaming Houses* and *Lottery Insurances* to the subsequent chapter.

I. *Sharpers who obtain Licences to become Pawnbrobers,** and bring disgrace upon the reputable part of the trade, by every species of fraud which can add to the distresses of those who are compelled to raise money in this way: for which purpose there are abundance of opportunities.—Swindling Pawnbrokers, of this Class, are uniformly receivers of stolen

goods, wares, and merchandize; since(as has already been noticed, (*ante* page 9) it has been held that Bank Notes are not Money, nor are horses, cattle, &c. considered as goods, wares, or merchandize, according to the legal construction of any existing Statute.— An amendment of the Law with regard to these and other objects is the more necessary, as *Bank Notes* and *Horses* are, perhaps, more the objects of swindling, than other species of property.

	Persons	£.
* Number of Pawnbrokers within the Bills of Mortality, paying a licence of 10*l.* a year	213	2130
In the Country, paying 5*l.* a year	432	2160
Total	644	4290

goods;

goods; and under the cover of their licence do much mischief to the Public. The evil arising from them might, in a great measure, be prevented by placing the power of granting licences in a general Board of Police; and rendering it necessary for all persons to produce a Certificate of character, before they can obtain such licence; and also to enter into recognizance for good behaviour.*

II. *Sharpers and Swindlers who obtain Licences to be Hawkers and Pedlars;* under the cover of which every species of villainy is practised upon the country people, as well as upon the unwary in the Metropolis, and all the great towns in the kingdom.—The artifices by which they succeed, are various, as for example;—By fraudulent raffles, where plated goods are exhibited as silver, and where the chances are exceedingly against the adventurers;—By selling and uttering base money, and frequently forged Bank Notes, which make one of the most profitable branches of their trade;—By dealing in smuggled goods,

---

* A regulation of this kind is of great importance; as the property of the poorest and most distressed part of the community, to the amount of nearly one million sterling, is constantly in the hands of Pawnbrokers in the Metropolis alone! and although it is of the utmost consequence that they, above all others, should be *honest*, *correct*, and even *humane* characters, (and it is to be hoped many of them are of that description,) yet certain it is that any person, even the most notorious rogue or vagabond, who can raise ten pounds to pay for a licence, may at present set up the trade of Pawnbroker; and it is even said that some have got licences who have actually been on board the Hulks!—a thing unavoidable under the present circumstances.

thereby

thereby promoting the sale of articles injurious to the Revenue, besides cheating the ignorant with regard to the value;—By receiving stolen goods to be disposed of in the country, by which discoveries are prevented, and assistance afforded to common thieves and stationary receivers;—By purchasing stolen horses in one part of the country, and disposing of them in another, in the course of their journies, in accomplishing which, so as to elude detection, they have great opportunities;—By gambling with E O Tables at Fairs and Horse-races.

A number of other devices might be pointed out, which render this class of men great nuisances in Society; and shew the necessity of either suppressing them totally, (for in fact they are of little use to the Public;) or of limiting the licences only to men of good character; to be granted by a general Board of Police, under whose controul they should be placed, while they enter at the same time into a recognizance in a certain sum, with one surety for good behaviour; by which the honest part would be retained to the exclusion of the fraudulent.

III. *Swindlers who take out Licences as Auctioneers,* and open shops in different parts of the Metropolis, with persons at the doors, usually denominated *Barkers,* inviting strangers to walk in. In these places various articles of silver plate and household goods are exposed to sale, made up on a slight principle, and of little intrinsic value; associates, generally denominated *Puffers,* are in waiting to bid up the

the article to a sum greatly beyond its value, when, upon the first bidding of the stranger, it is knocked down to him, and the money instantly demanded; the goods, however, on being carried home and examined, are generally found to be very different in reality, from what their appearance exhibited, and upon a close examination the fraud is discovered.

Neither the common Law, nor the Act of the 30th George II. cap. 24, seem to be sufficiently *broad* and explanatory to include this species of offence; and hence it is, that this mode of selling goods continues with impunity, and seems to encrease. It is not, however, meant here to insinuate that all petty auctions are fraudulent.—It is to be hoped there may be some exceptions, although probably they are not numerous. A licence from a general Board of Police, and to be subject to certain restrictions only burdensome to the dishonest, and obliging the parties to find security, would, in a great measure, regulate this kind of business, in a proper manner.

IV. *Swindlers who raise money, by pretending to be Discounters of Bills, and Money Brokers*; These chiefly prey upon young men of property, who have lost their money at play, or spent it in expensive amusements, and are obliged to raise more upon any terms, until their rents or incomes become payable; or who have fortunes in prospect, as being heirs apparent to estates, but who require assistance in the mean time.

Availing themselves of the credit, or the ultimate responsibility, of such thoughtless and giddy young men,

men, in the eager pursuit of criminal pleasures, and under the influence of those allurements which the Faro Tables, and other places of fashionable resort hold out—these Swindlers seldom fail to obtain from them securities and obligations for large sums; upon the credit of which they are enabled, perhaps, at usurious interest, to borrow money, or discount bills; and thus supply their unfortunate customers upon the most extravagant terms.

Another class, having some capital, advance money upon bonds, title-deeds, and other specialties, or upon the bond of the parties having estates in reversion: by these and other devices too tedious to detail, large sums of money are, most unwarrantably and illegally wrested from the dissipated and thoughtless: and misery and distress are thus entailed upon them, as long as they live; or they are driven, by utter ruin, to acts of desperation or to crimes.

A law seems absolutely necessary to be pointed at this particular mischief, which is certainly an increasing evil.—Humanity pleads for it; and *Policy* points out the necessity of some effectual guard against those miseries which it generates; and which could not exist in so great a degree, were it not for the opportunities held out by these blood-suckers in affording money to the young and inexperienced, to be expended in scenes of gambling and debauchery.

V. *A Class of Cheats of the Society of Jews, who are to be found in every street, lane and alley in and near the Metropolis, under the pretence of purchasing old*

old cloaths, and metals of different sorts; Their chief business really is to prowl about the houses and stables of men of rank and fortune, for the purpose of holding out temptations to the servants to pilfer and steal small articles, not likely to be missed, which these Jews purchase at about one third of the real value.—It is supposed that upwards of fifteen hundred of these depraved people are employed in diurnal journies of this kind; by which, through the medium of bad money, and other fraudulent dealings, many of them acquire property, and then set up shops and become Receivers of stolen Goods.

It is estimated that there are from fifteen to twenty thousand Jews in the city of London, besides, perhaps, about five or six thousand more in the great provincial and sea-port towns; (where there are at least twenty synagogues, besides six in the Metropolis;) must of the lower classes of those distinguished by the name of German or Dutch Jews, live chiefly by their wits, and establish a system of mischievous intercourse all over the country, the better to carry on their fraudulent designs in the circulation of base money,—the sale of stolen goods, and in the purchase of metals of various kinds; as well as other articles pilfered from the Dock-Yards, and stolen in the provincial towns, which they bring to the Metropolis to elude detection,— and *vice versâ.*

Educated in idleness from their earliest infancy, they acquire every debauched and vicious principle which

which can fit them for the most complicated arts of fraud and deception; to which they seldom fail to add the crime of perjury, whenever it can be of use, in shielding themselves or their associates from the punishment of the law.—From the orange boy, and the retailer of seals, razors, glass, and other wares, in the public streets, to the shop-keeper, dealer in wearing apparel, or in silver and gold, the same principles of conduct too generally prevail.

The itinerants utter base money to enable them, by selling cheap, to dispose of their goods; while those that are stationary, with very few exceptions, receive and purchase, at an under-price, whatever is brought them, without asking questions.

VI. *Cheats, who sell provisions and other articles, by means of false weights and measures.* Nothing requires the assistance of the Legislature in a greater degree than this evil; to shield the Poor against the numerous tricks thus practised upon them, by low and inferior shop-keepers and itinerants.

The ancient System of regulating this useful branch of Police by the Juries of the Court-Leet, having been found ineffectual, and in many respects inapplicable to the present state of Society, an act passed the 35th of his present Majesty, (*cap.* 102,) to remedy the inconvenience with regard to fraudulent weights; but difficulties having occurred on account of the expence of carrying it into execution, certain amendments were made by another act, (37 Geo. III. *c.* 143,) and the Magistrates in Petty

Sessions

Sessions have now power to appoint Examiners of weights, and to authorise them to visit shops, seize false weights, &c.

This plan, if pursued as steadily as that which already prevails in regulating Bakers, promises to produce very valuable benefits to the lower ranks of people at a very small expence.

VII. *Cheats and Swindlers who associate together, and enter into a conspiracy for the purpose of defrauding Tradesmen of their goods.*—One of these sharpers generally assumes the character of a Merchant;—hires a genteel house, with a counting-house, and every appearance of business.—One or two associates take upon them the appearance of clerks, while others occasionally wear a livery: and sometimes a carriage is set up, in which the ladies of the party visit the shops, in the stile of persons of fashion, ordering goods to their apartments.—Thus circumstanced, goods are obtained on credit, which are immediately pawned or sold, and the produce used as a means of deception to obtain more, and procure recommendations, by offering to pay ready money, —or discount bills.

When confidence is once established in this way, notes and bills are fabricated by these conspirators, as if remitted from the country, or from foreign parts; and application is made to their newly acquired friends, the tradesmen, to assist in discounting them. Sometimes money and bills upon one another are lodged at the bankers for the purpose of extending
their

their credit, by referring to some respectable name for a character.

After circulating notes to a considerable amount, and completing their system of fraud by possessing as much of the property of others as is possible, without risk of detection, they move off; assume new characters; and when the bills and notes are due, the parties are not to be found.

Offences of this sort, where an actual conspiracy cannot be proved, which is generally very difficult, are not easily punished; and it seems of importance that frauds and impositions of this sort, and others of the same nature, where the confidence of tradesmen and manufacturers is abused by misrepresentation and falsehood, should be defined, so as to render it difficult for the parties to escape punishment.

VIII. *Cheats who take genteel Lodgings, dress elegantly, assume false names :*—pretend to be related to persons of credit and fashion—produce letters familiarly written to prove an intimacy,—enter into conversation, and shew these letters to tradesmen and others, upon whom they have a design—get into their good graces, purchase wearing apparel and other articles, and disappear with the booty.

This species of offence would be very difficult to reach by any existing Law, and yet it is practised in various shapes in the Metropolis, whereby tradesmen are defrauded to a very considerable extent.—Some legislative guards would certainly be very desirable to define and punish these offences also.

IX.

IX. *Cheats, who have been formerly in the service of Milliners, Mantua-Makers, Taylors, and other Traders, who have occasion to send to shop-keepers and warehousemen for goods;*—These, after being discharged from their service, getting into the company of sharpers and thieves, while out of place, teach them how to personate their former employers; in whose names they too frequently succeed in obtaining considerable quantities of goods before the fraud is discovered.

It would certainly be a good rule at no time to deliver goods upon a verbal message; and it would be useful if all persons discharging servants, would give notice of it to every tradesman with whom they deal.

X. *Cheats who personate Gentlemens' footmen;* These order goods to be sent to a genteel lodging, where the associate is waiting, who draws upon some banker in a distant part of the town for the money; or, if the check is refused, a country bank-note (the gentleman just being arrived in town) is offered to be changed, which, although a forgery, often succeeds: if this should also fail, this mischievous class of people, from habit and close attention to the means of deception, are seldom at a loss in finding out some other expedient; and before the fraud is discovered, the parties are off; and the master transformed into the livery-servant, to practise in his turn the same trick upon some other person.

XI. *Cheats who associate systematically together,*
                                                    for

for the purpose of finding out and making a prey of every person from the country, or any ignorant person who is supposed to have money, or who has come to London for the purpose of selling goods.—It is usual in such cases for one of them to assume the character of a young 'Squire, just come to his estate; to appear careless and prodigal, and to shew handfuls of bank-notes, all of which are false and fabricated for the purpose.

Another personates the guardian of the 'Squire, while a part of the associates pretend to sit down to play, and having won money of the young spend-thrift, who appears extremely ignorant and profuse, the stranger's avarice gets the better of his prudence, and he is induced at length to try his luck,—the result is that he is soon left without a penny.

XII. *Cheats who prowl about in all the streets and lanes of the trading part of the Metropolis, where shopmen and boys are carrying parcels:* These, by means of various stratagems, find out where the parcels are going, and regulating their measures accordingly, seldom fail by some trick or other, (such as giving the lad a shilling to run and call a coach,) to get hold of the property.—Porters and young men from the country should be particularly cautious never to quit any property intrusted to their care, until delivered (not at the door) but within the house to which it is directed.

XIII. *Cheats who attend Inns, at the time that coaches and waggons are loading or unloading.* These by personating *porters* with aprons and knots, or *clerks* with

with pens stuck in their wigs or hair, and by having recourse to a variety of stratagems, according to the peculiar circumstances of the case, aided by their having previously noticed the address of several of the parcels, seldom fail of success, in the general hurry and confusion which prevails at such places. This proves how necessary it is at all times to have one or two intelligent officers of Justice, who know the faces of thieves, in attendance, while goods are receiving and delivering.

XIV. *Cheats who go from door to door collecting money; under pretence of soliciting for a charitable establishment*, for the benefit of poor children, and other purposes. But the money, instead of being so applied, is generally spent in eating and drinking; and the most infamous imposition is thus practised upon the charitable and humane, who are the dupes of this species of fraud in too many instances.

XV. *Sharpers who are known by the name of Duffers.* These go about from house to house, and attend public houses, inns, and fairs, pretending to sell smuggled goods, such as India handkerchiefs, waistcoat patterns, muslins, &c. By offering their goods for sale, they are enabled to discover the proper objects, who may be successfully practised upon in various ways; and if they do not succeed in promoting some gambling scheme, by which the party is plundered of his money, they seldom fail passing forged country bank notes, or base silver and copper in the course of their dealings.

XVI.

XVI. *Female Sharpers who dress elegantly, perso-nate women of fashion, attend masquerades, and even go to St. James's.* These, from their effrontery, actually get into the circle; where their wits and hands are employed in obtaining diamonds, and whatever other articles of value, capable of being concealed, are found to be most accessible.

The wife of a well known sharper, lately upon the town, is said to have appeared at Court, dressed in a stile of peculiar elegance : while the sharper himself is supposed to have gone in the dress of a clergyman. —According to the information of a noted receiver, they pilfered to the value of 1700*l.* on the King's birth-day (1795,) without discovery or suspicion.

Houses are kept where female Cheats dress and undress for public places.—Thirty or forty of these sharpers generally attend all masquerades, in different characters, where they seldom fail to get clear off with a considerable booty.

XVII. *Among the classes of Cheats may be ranked a species of Female Bankers.* These accommodate barrow-women and others, who sell fish, fruit, ve-getables, &c. in the streets, with five shillings a day; (the usual diurnal stock in trade in such cases ;) for the use of which, for twelve hours, they obtain a premium of *six-pence,* when the money is returned in the evening, receiving thereby at this rate, about *seven pounds ten shillings a year* for every five shillings they lay out!

The Author, in the course of his Magisterial duty, having

having discovered this extraordinary species of fraud, attempted to explain to a barrow-woman on whom it was practised, that by saving up a single *five shillings*, and not laying any part of it out in gin, but keeping the whole, she would save 7*l.* 10*s.* a year, which seemed to astonish her, and to stagger her belief.—It is to be feared, however, that it had no effect upon her future conduct, since it is evident that this improvident and dissolute class of females have no other idea than that of making the day and the way alike long.—Their profits (which are often considerably augmented by dealing in base money, as well as fruit, vegetables, &c.) seldom last over the day, for they never fail to have a luxurious dinner and a hot supper, with abundance of gin and porter:—looking in general no farther than to keep whole the original stock, with the *six-pence* interest, which is paid over to the female banker in the evening: and a new loan obtained on the following morning, of the same number of shillings again to go to market.

In contemplating this curious system of Banking, (trifling as it seems to be) it is impossible not to be forcibly struck with the immense profits that arise from it. It is only necessary for one of these female sharpers to possess a capital of *seventy shillings*, or three pounds ten shillings, with fourteen steady and regular customers, in order to realize an income of ONE HUNDRED GUINEAS a year.

XVIII. *Cheats who pretend to tell fortunes.* These impose on the credulity of the public, by advertisements

ments and cards; pretending a power, from their knowledge of astrology, to foretel future events, to discover stolen property, lucky numbers in the Lottery, &c.

The extent to which this mischief goes in the Metropolis is almost beyond belief; particularly during the drawing of the Lottery. The folly and phrenzy which prevail in vulgar life, lead ignorant and deluded people into the snare of adding to the misfortunes which the Lottery occasions, by additional advances of money, (obtained generally by pawning goods or apparel) paid to pretended astrologers for suggesting *lucky numbers*, upon which they are advised to make insurances; and under the influence of this unaccountable delusion, they are too often induced to increase their risks, and ruin their families.

One of these impostors who lived long in the Curtain-Road, Shoreditch, is said, in conjunction with his associates, to have made near 300*l.* a year by practising upon the credulity of the lower orders of the people.—He stiled himself (in his circulating cards) an *Astronomer and Astrologer;* and stated, *That he gave advice to Gentlemen and Ladies on business, trade, contracts, removals, journies by land or water, marriages, children, law-suits, absent friends, &c.* and further, that *he calculated nativities accurately.*—His fee was half-a-crown.

An instance of mischievous credulity, occasioned by consulting this impostor, once fell under the review

view of the Author.   A person having property
stolen from him, went to consult the conjuror respecting the thief; who having described something like
the person of a man whom he suspected, his credulity and folly so far got the better of his reason
and reflection, as to induce him upon the authority
of this impostor *actually to charge his neighbour with
a felony*, and to cause him to be apprehended.   The
Magistrate settled the matter by discharging the prisoner; reprimanding the accuser severely, and ordering the conjuror to be taken into custody, according
to law, *as a Rogue and Vagabond.*

But the delusion with regard to Fortune-tellers is
not confined to vulgar life, since it is known, that
ladies of rank, fashion, and fortune, contribute to the
encouragement of this fraudulent profession in particular, by their visits to a pretended Astrologer of
their own sex in the neighbourhood of Tottenham-
Court Road : This woman, to the disgrace of her
votaries, whose education ought to have taught them
the folly and weakness of countenancing such gross
impositions, found the practice of it extremely productive*.

The act of the 9th George the Second, *cap. 5,
punishes all persons pretending skill in any crafty science
or telling fortunes, or where stolen goods may be found;*

---

* The encouragement which this impostor received from the
weaker part of the females of rank and fortune in the Metropolis,
raised up others; who had the effrontery to insult the understanding of the Public, by advertising in the News-papers.

with

with a year's imprisonment, and standing four times in the pillory, (once every quarter) *during the term of such imprisonment. The Act called the Vagrant Act, made the 17th year of the same reign, (cap. 5,) declares such persons to be rogues and vagabonds, and liable to be punished as such.*

It is sincerely to be hoped that those at least who are convinced from having suffered by the gross imposition practised upon the credulity of the people by these pests of society, will enable the civil Magistrate, by proper informations, to suppress so great an evil.

Innumerable almost are the other tricks and devices which are resorted to by the horde of Cheats, Swindlers, and Sharpers, who infest the Metropolis.

The great increase of commerce, and the confidence resulting from an intercourse so wide and extended, frequently lays men of property and tradesmen open to a variety of frauds ; credit is obtained by subterfuges and devices contrary to the plain rules of common honesty, against which, however, there is no remedy but by an action of common law.

If it were possible to look accurately at the different evils arising from fraudulent and swindling practices, so as to frame a statute that would generally reach all the cases that occur, whenever the barrier of common honesty is broken down ; it would certainly be productive of infinite benefit to the community ; for, in spite of the laudable exertions of the Society, established for prosecuting swindlers,

it

it is to be lamented that the evil has not diminished. On the contrary it has certainly encreased, and must continue to do so, until the Legislature, by applicable Laws and an improved System of Police, either directly or collaterally attached to these offences, shall find the means of suppressing them.

CHAP.

CHAP. VI.

The great anxiety of the Legislature to suppress the evils of Gaming :—The Misery and Wretchedness entailed on many respectable Families from this fatal propensity :—Often arising from the foolish vanity of mixing in what is stiled, Genteel Company; where Faro is introduced.—Games of Chance, though stigmatized by the Legislature, encouraged by high-sounding names, whose houses are opened for purposes odious and unlawful :—The Civil Magistrate called upon by his public duty, as well as by the feelings of humanity, to suppress such mischiefs.—The danger arising from such seminaries—No probability of any considerations of their illegality, or inhumanity, operating as a check, without the efforts of the Magistracy.—The evil tendency of such examples to servants in fashionable Families, who carry these vices into vulgar life; and many of whom, as well as persons of superior education, become Sharpers, Cheats, and Swindlers, from the habits they acquire.—A particular Statement of the proceedings of persons who have set up Gaming Houses as regular Partnership-Concerns; and of the Evils resulting therefrom.—Of Lottery Insurances of the Higher Class.—Of Lottery Offices opened for Insurance—Proposed Remedies. —Three Plans suggested to the Author by Correspondents.

GAMING

GAMING is the source from which has sprung up all that race of cheats, swindlers, and sharpers, some of whose nefarious practices have already been noticed, and the remainder of which it is the object of the Author to develope in this chapter.

Such has been the anxiety of the Legislature to suppress this evil, that so early as the reign of Queen Anne, this abandoned and mischievous race of men seems to have attracted its notice in a very particular degree; for the act of the 9th year of that reign (cap. 14. § 6, 7,) after reciting, " *that divers lewd and* " *dissolute persons live at great expences, having no* " *visible estate, profession, or calling, to maintain* " *themselves; but support these expences by Gaming* " *only;* Enacts, *that any two Justices may cause to be* " *brought before them, all persons within their limits* " *whom they shall have just cause to suspect to have* " *no visible estate, profession, or calling, to maintain* " *themselves by; but do for the most part support* " *themselves by Gaming; and if such persons shall not* " *make it appear to such Justices that the principal* " *part of their expences is not maintained by gaming,* " *they are to be bound to their good behaviour for a* " *twelvemonth; and in default of sufficient security,* " *to be committed to prison, until they can find the* " *same; and if security shall be given, it will be for-* " *feited on their playing or betting at any one time,* " *for more than the value of twenty shillings.*"

If, in conformity to the *spirit* of this wise statute,

sharpers

sharpers of every denomination, who support themselves by a variety of cheating and swindling practices, without having any visible means of living, were
in like manner to be called upon to find security for
their good behaviour, in all cases where they cannot
shew they have the means of subsisting themselves
honestly, the number of these Pests of Society, under
a general Police and an active and zealous Magistracy,
would soon be diminished, if not totally annihilated.

By the 12th of George the Second, (cap. 28. § 2, 3,)
" *the Games of Faro, Hazard, &c. are declared to be*
" *Lotteries, subjecting the persons who keep them to a*
" *penalty of two hundred pounds, and those who play to*
" *fifty pounds."—One* witness only is necessary to
prove the offence before any Justice of the Peace;
*and the Justice forfeits ten pounds if he neglects to
do his duty under the Act :*—and under this Act,
which is connected with the statute 8th of George I.
cap. 2, it seems that " *the keeper of a Faro Table*
" *may be prosecuted even for a penalty of five hun-*
" *dred pounds."*

Notwithstanding these salutary laws, to the reproach of the Police of the Metropolis, houses have
been opened, even under the sanction of high-sound-
g names, where an indiscriminate mixture of all
ranks was to be found, from the *finished sharper* to
the *raw inexperienced youth.* And where all those
evils existed in full force, which it was the object of
the Legislature to remove.

Though it is hoped that this iniquitous System
of plunder, has of late been somewhat restrained by
the

the wholesome administration of the Laws, under the excellent Chief Justice who presides in the High Criminal Department of the Country, in consequence of the detection of Criminals, through the merito-rious vigilance and attention of the Magistrates; to which the Author of this work, by bringing the evil so prominently under the view of the Public, may flatter himself in having been, in some small degree, instrumental: Still it is much to be feared, that the time is not yet arrived which would induce him to withhold the following narrative.

GAMING, although at all times an object highly deserving attention, and calling for the exertions of Magistrates, never appeared either to have assumed so alarming an aspect, or to have been conducted upon the methodized system of *Partnership-Con-cerns*, wherein pecuniary capitals were embarked, till about the years 1777 and 1778, when the vast licence which was given to those abominable engines of fraud, E O Tables, and the great length of time which elapsed before a check was given to them by the Police, afforded a number of dissolute and aban-doned characters, who resorted to these baneful sub-terfuges for support, an opportunity of acquiring pro-perty: This was afterwards increased in low Gaming Houses, and by following up the same system at Newmarket, and other places of fashionable resort, and in the Lottery; until at length, without any pro-perty at the outset, or any visible means of lawful support, a sum of money little short of *One Million Sterling*, is said to have been acquired by a class of individuals

individuals originally (with some few exceptions) of the lowest and most depraved order of Society. This enormous mass of wealth (acquired no doubt by entailing misery on many worthy and respectable Families, and driving the unhappy victims to acts of desperation and suicide,) is said to have been afterwards engaged as a great and an efficient capital for carrying on various illegal Establishments; particularly Gaming-Houses, and Shops for fraudulent Insurances in the Lottery; together with such objects of dissipation as the Races at Newmarket and other places of *fashionable* resort, held out: all which were employed as the means of increasing and improving the ill-gotten wealth of the parties engaged in these nefarious pursuits.

A System, grown to such an enormous height, had, of course, its rise by progressive advances. Several of those who now roll in their gaudy carriages, and associate with some men of high rank and fashion, may be found upon the Registers of the Old Bailey; or traced to the vagrant pursuit of turning, with their own hands, EO Tables in the open streets. These mischievous Members of Society, through the wealth obtained by a course of procedure diametrically opposite to Law, are, by a strange perversion, sheltered from the operation of that Justice, which every act of their lives has offended: they bask in the sun-shine of prosperity; while thousands, who owe their distress and ruin to the horrid designs thus *executed, invigorated* and *extended*, are pining in misery and want.

Certain it is, that the mischiefs arising from the rapid

rapid increase, and from the vast extent of capital employed in these Systems of ruin and depravity, have become great and alarming beyond calculation ; as will be evinced by developing the nature of the very dangerous Confederacy which systematically moves and directs this vast Machine of destruction—composed in general of men who have been reared and educated under the influence of every species of depravity which can debase the human character.

Wherever Interest or Resentment suggests to their minds a line of conduct calculated to gratify any base or illegal propensity ; it is immediately indulged. Some are taken into this iniquitous Partnership for their dexterity in securing the dice; or in dealing cards at Faro.—Informers are apprehended and imprisoned upon writs, obtained, by perjury, to deter others from similar attacks. Witnesses are suborned —officers of justice are bribed, wherever it can be done, by large sums of money*—ruffians and blud-

---

* An Affidavit, made not very long since in one of the superior Courts of Justice, illustrates this observation in a very striking degree. It is in these words—" That it is almost impossible to " convict persons keeping Gaming-Houses before the Magistrates, " by reason of the enormous wealth generally applied to the cor- " ruption of unwilling evidence brought forward to support the " charge—That on an information exhibited against one of the " Partners of a Gaming-House, he got himself discharged by " deterring some of the witnesses from appearing, and by the " perjury of another partner who was examined as a witness, " and for which he then stood indicted—That divers of these " Gaming-Houses were kept by practising attornies, who, by " threatening indictments for pretended Conspiracies, and other " infamous means, have deterred persons from prosecuting them.'*

geon-men

geon-men are employed to resist the Civil Power, where pecuniary gratuities fail—and houses are barricadoed and guarded by armed men : thereby offering defiance to the common exertions of the Laws, and opposing the regular authority of Magistrates.

It is impossible to contemplate a Confederacy thus circumstanced, so powerful from its immense pecuniary resources, and so mischievous and oppressive from the depravity which directs these resources, without feeling an anxiety to see the strong arm of the Law still further and unremittingly exerted for the purpose of effectually destroying it.

Whilst one part of the immense property by which this confederacy was so strongly fortified was employed in the establishment of *Gaming-Houses*, holding out the most fascinating allurements to giddy young *men of fortune*, and others, having access to money, by means of splendid entertainments,* and regular suppers, with abundance of the choicest wines, so as to form a genteel lounge for the dissipated and unwary : another part of the capital was said to form the stock which composes the various Faro-Banks which were to be found at the routes of *Ladies of Fashion :*   Thus drawing into this vortex of

---

* The expence of entertainments at a Gaming-House of the highest class, during eight months, has been said to exceed *Six Thousand Guineas !* what must the profits be to afford such a profusion ?

ini-

iniquity and ruin, not only the *males,* but also the *fe-males* of the thoughtless and opulent part of Society; who too easily became a prey to that idle vanity which frequently overpowers reason and reflection ; and the delusion of which is seldom terminated till it is too late.

Evil example, when thus sanctioned by apparent respectability, and by the dazzling blandishment of rank and fashion, is so intoxicating to those who have either suddenly acquired riches, or who are young and inexperienced, that it almost ceases to be a matter of wonder that the fatal propensity to Gaming should become universal; extending itself over all ranks in Society, in a degree scarcely to be credited, but by those who will attentively investigate the subject.

At the commencement of the troubles in France, and before this Country was visited by the hordes of Emigrants of all descriptions, who fixed a temporary or permanent residence in this Metropolis, the num-ber of Gaming-Houses (exclusive of those that are select, and have long been established by Subscrip-tion,) did not exceed above *four* or *five :* In the year 1797, not less than *thirty* were said to be actually open ; where, besides *Faro* and *Hazard,* the foreign games of *Roulet* and *Rouge et Noir,* were introduced, and where there existed a regular gradation of esta-blishment, accommodating to all ranks ; from the man of fashion, down to the thief, the burglar, and the pick-pocket—where immense sums of money
were

were played for every evening, for eight months in the year.*

In a commercial Country, and in a great Metropolis, where from the vast extent of its trade and manufactures, and from the periodical issue of above Twenty Millions annually, arising from dividends on funded security, there must be an immense circulation of property, the danger is not to be conceived, from the allurements which are thus held out to young men of business, having the command of money, as well as to the clerks of merchants, bankers, and others concerned in different branches of trade: In fact, it is well known, that too many of this class resort at present to these destructive scenes of vice, idleness, and misfortune.†

The

* The latter part of the Affidavit, already mentioned, also illustrates these assertions, and proves that they are but too well founded. It states——" That Gaming Houses have increased to
" such a degree, that there were lately not less than six in one street
" near the Hay-Market, at all which, persons stood at the door
" to entice passengers to play—That the generality of persons
" keeping these houses are *prize fighters*, and persons of a despe-
" rate description, who threaten assasination to any person who
" will molest them."

† " The same affidavit further states—That the principal Gam-
" ing-Houses at the West end of the Town have stated days on
" which they have luxurious dinners, (Sunday being the chief day,)
" to which they contrive to get invited merchants' and bankers'
" clerks, and other persons entrusted with money ; and that it has
" been calculated, (and the calculation was believed not to be over-
" rated,) that the expences attendant on such houses, amounted to
" 150,000*l*. yearly, and that the keepers of such houses, by means
" of their enormous wealth, bid defiance to all prosecutions, some

" of

The mind shrinks with horror at the existence of a System in the Metropolis, unknown to our ancestors, even in the worst periods of their dissipation; when a *Ward*, a *Waters*, and a *Chartres*, insulted public morals by their vices and their crimes: for then no regular Establishments—no systematic concerns for carrying on this nefarious trade, were known.—No Partnerships in Gaming-Houses were conducted with the regularity of Commercial Houses.

But these Partnerships have not been confined to Gaming-Houses alone. A considerable proportion of the immense capital which the conductors of the System possess, is employed periodically in the *two Lotteries*, in *Fraudulent Insurances*, where, like the Faro Bank, the chances are so calculated as to yield about 30 per cent. profit to the Gambling proprietors; and from the extent of which these transactions have been, and we fear still are carried, no doubt can be entertained that the annual gains must be immense.— It has, indeed, been stated, with an appearance of truth, that a single individual acquired no less than 60,000*l.* during one English Lottery!

Although it is impossible to be perfectly accurate in any estimate which can be formed; for in this, as in all other cases where calculations are introduced in this Work, accuracy to a point is not to be expected; yet when all circumstances are considered, there ap-

" of them having acquired from 50 to 100,000*l.* each; consider-
" able estates have been frequently won by them in the course
" of one sitting,"

pear

pear just grounds to suppose that the following Statement, placing the whole in one connected point of
view, may convey to the Reader no very imperfect
idea of the vast and unparalleled extent to which this
horrid mischief had arrived; and to which, if not
closely watched, it may yet rise once more.

GAMING.

	Persons attached.	Money played for nightly.	Yearly aggregate lost and won.
		£.	£.
1. 7 Subscription Houses open one third of the Year, or 100 nights *suppose*	1000	2000	1,400,000
2. 15 Houses of a superior class one-third of the Year, or 100 nights ———	3000	2000	3,000,000
3. 15 Houses of an inferior class one half of the Year, or 150 Nights ———	3000	1000	2,225,000
4. 6 Ladies Gaming Houses 50 Nights ———	1000	2000	600,000
			7,225,000

FRAUDULENT INSURANCES IN THE LOTTERY.

350 Insurance Offices at 100l. a day average, during the 33 days of the Irish Lottery	1,155,000
400 Insurance Offices at 150l. a day average, during the 33 days* of the English Lottery	1,980,000
	3,135,000
Total	10,460,000

* The longer the Lottery continues, the greater the evil. A Lottery of
60,000 Tickets is therefore a much greater evil than one of 50,000: and
that in a ratio more than proportionate to the numbers in each.

This aggregate is only to be considered as shewing
the mere interchange of property from one hand to
another; yet when it is recollected that the operation
must

must progressively produce a certain loss, with not many exceptions, to all the innocent and unsuspecting adventurers either at Faro or the Lottery, with an almost uniform gain to the proprietors; the result is shocking to reflect upon.—To individual families in easy circumstances where this unfortunate mania prevails, as well as to the mass of the people who are fascinated by the delusion of the Lottery Insurances, it is the worst of all misfortunes.—By seizing every opportunity to take advantage of this unhappy bias, it is no uncommon thing to see the pennyless miscreant of to-day become the opulent gambler of to-morrow : leaving the unhappy sufferers often no alternative but exile, beggary, or a prison; or perhaps, rendered desperate by reflecting on the folly of their conduct, to end their days by suicide,* while wives, children, and dependants are suddenly reduced from affluence to the lowest abyss of misery.

In contemplating these vast establishments of regular and systematic fraud and depredation upon the Public, in all the hideous forms which they assume, nothing is so much to be lamented as the unconquerable spirit which draws such a multitude of the lower ranks of Society into the vortex of the Lottery.

The agents in this iniquitous System, availing themselves of the existence of the delusion, spare no pains to keep it alive; so that the evil extends far and

* The Gambling and Lottery transactions of one individual in this great Metropolis, are said to be productive of from ten to fifteen suicides annually.

wide

wide, and the mischiefs, distresses, and calamities resulting from it, were it possible to detail them, would form a catalogue of sufferings of which the opulent and luxurious have no conception.

Of how much importance therefore is it to the Public at large, to see these evils suppressed; and above all, to have this novel System completely annihilated, by which Gambling establishments have been formed upon commercial principles of methodical arrangements, with vast capitals employed for the most infamous and diabolical purposes.

Let those who have acquired wealth in this way be satisfied with what they have gotten, and with the misery their gains have occasioned to ruined thousands: let them abstain from employing it in channels calculated to extend these evils. The Law is generally slow in its operations: but it seldom fails to overtake the guilty at last.

To this Confederacy, powerful in wealth, and unrestrained by those considerations of moral rectitude, which govern the conduct of other men engaged in the common pursuits of life, is to be attributed those vast additional hazards to which the young and inexperienced have been subjected—Hazards, which not only did not exist before these establishments were matured and moulded into System; but which were considerably increased, from its becoming a part of the general arrangements to employ men of genteel exterior, (and it is to be feared too, in many instances of good connections) who, having been ruined by the delusion,

delusion, descended as a means of subsistence, to accept the degrading office of seeking out those customers, whose access to money rendered them proper
objects to be ensnared.—For such was the nature of
this new System of destruction, that while a young
man entering upon life, conceived himself honoured
by the friendship and acquaintance of those who were
considered to be men of fashion, and of good connections, he was deluded by splendid entertainments
into the snare, which afterwards robbed him of his
property and peace of mind.

Such were the arrangements of this alarming and
mischievous Confederacy, for the purpose of plundering the thoughtless and unwary.—The evidence
given in the Court of King's Bench, in an action,
tried for Gaming, on the 29th November, 1796,
served pretty fully to develope the shocking System
of fraud pursued, after the inexperienced and unwary were entrapped into these receptacles of ruin
and destruction*.

While

* The following is the substance of the most striking parts of
the Evidence of John Shepherd, in the action alluded to.

" The witness saw Hazard played at the Gaming-House of the
defendant, in Leicester-street.—Every person who was three times
successful, paid the defendant a Silver Medal, which he purchased
from him on entering the house, at eight for a guinea, and he received six or seven of these in the course of an hour for the Box
Hands, as it was called. The people who frequented this house
always played for a considerable sum. Sometimes 20l. or 30l.
depended on a single throw of the Dice. The witness remembered
being once at the defendant's Gaming-House about three or four
o'clock in the morning, when a gentleman came in very much in
liquor.

While a vice, ruinous to the morals and to the fortunes of the younger part of the Community who move in the middle and higher ranks of life, is suffered to be pursued in direct opposition to *positive statutes*,—surely, blame must attach somewhere!

liquor.—He seemed to have a great deal of money about him.— The defendant said he had not intended to play, but now he would set to with this fellow.—He then scraped a little wax with his finger off one of the candles and put the Dice together, so that they came seven every way. After doing this, he dropped them into the box and threw them out, and afterwards drew all the money away, saying he had won it.—*Seven* was the main, and he could not throw any thing but *seven*. The young gentleman said he had not given him time to *bar*.—A dispute arose between the defendant and him. It was referred to two or three persons who were round the table, and they gave it in favour of the defendant. The gentleman said he had lost upwards of 70*l*. The defendant said, *we have cleared him*. The witness has seen a man pawn his watch and ring in several instances ; and once he saw a man pawn his coat and go away without it.

" After the Gaming Table was broken by the Bow-street Officers, the defendant said it was too good a thing to be given up, and instantly got another Table, large enough for twenty or thirty people. The frequenters of this house used to play till day-light : and on one or two occasions, they played all the next day. This is what the defendant called, *sticking to it rarely*. The guests were furnished with wine and suppers gratis, from the funds of the partnership, in abundance. Sunday was a grand day. The witness has seen more than forty people there at a time. The table not being sufficient for the whole, half-a-crown used on such occasions to be given for a seat, and those behind looked over the back of the others and betted."

The person above-mentioned (whose name was Smith) who pawned his coat, corroborated the above evidence ; and added, that he had seen a person after he had lost all his money, throw off his coat and go away, losing it also.

The

The idle vanity of being introduced into what is generally, but erroneously, termed genteel society, where a fashionable name announces an intention of seeing company, has been productive of more *domestic misery* and more *real distress, poverty*, and *wretchedness* to *families* in this great City (who but for their folly might have been easy and comfortable,) than many volumes could detail.

A mistaken sense of what constitutes human happiness, fatally leads the mass of the People who have the means of moving in any degree above the middle ranks of life, into circles where Faro Tables and other games at hazard are introduced in private families:—Where the least recommendation (and Sharpers spare no pains to obtain recommendations) is a passport to all who can exhibit a genteel exterior; and where the young and the inexperienced are initiated in every propensity tending to debase human character; while they are taught to view with contempt every acquirement, connected with the duties which lead to domestic happiness, or to those qualifications which can render either sex respectable in the world.

When such infamous practices are encouraged and sanctioned by high-sounding names,—when sharpers and black-legs find an easy introduction into the houses of persons of fashion, who assemble in multitudes together, for the purpose of playing at those most odious and detestable games of hazard, which the Legislature has stigmatized with such marks of reprobation,

reprobation, it is time for the Civil Magistrate to step forward :—It is time for him to feel, that, in doing that duty which the Laws of his Country impose on him, he is perhaps saving hundreds of families from ruin and destruction; and preserving to the infants of thoughtless and deluded parents that property which is their birth-right: but which, for want of an energetic Police in enforcing the Laws made for their protection, is now too frequently squandered.; and the mind is tortured with the sad reflection, that with the loss of fortune, all opportunities (in consequence of idle habits) are also lost, of fitting the unfortunate sufferer for any reputable pursuit in life, by which an honest livelihood could be obtained.

In this situation, the transition from the plain gamester to the fraudulent one, and from that to every other species of criminality, is easily conceived : and it is by no means an unfair conclusion, that this has been the fate of not a few who have been early introduced into these haunts of idleness and vice; and who, but for such an education, might have become useful members of the State.

The accumulated evils, arising from this source, are said to have been suffered to continue, from a prevailing idea, that Persons of Rank and their immediate associates were beyond the reach of being controlled, by laws made for the mass of the People; and that nothing but capital offences could attach to persons of this condition in life.

If these evils were, in fact, merely confined to Per-

sons

sons of rank and fortune, and did not extend beyond
that barrier where no general injury could accrue to
Society, there might be a shadow of excuse (and *it*
would be but a shadow) for not hazarding an attack
upon the amusements of the Great, where the energy
of the Laws to controul their œconomy may be
doubtful: but surely in the present case, where the
mischief spreads *broad* and *wide*, no good Magistrate
can or ought to be afraid to do his duty, because persons in high life may dare to sanction and promote
offences of a nature the most mischievous to Society
at large, as well as to the peace, comfort, and happiness of families.

If the exertions of the Magistracy are to be suspended until the Higher Ranks see the frivolity, the
shameful profligacy and the horrid waste of useful
time, as well as the cruel destruction of decent and
respectable families in that point of view which will
operate as an antidote to the evil, it is much to be
feared that it must, under such circumstances, become incurable.

But there are other inducements, more nearly al-
lied to the occurrences in humble life, which render
it in a particular degree incumbent on Magistrates
to make trial, at least, whether there is not sufficient
energy in the law to control the hurtful vices of the
higher, as well as the middling, and inferior ranks of
the People: The examples of the great and opulent,
operate most powerfully among the tribe of *menial
servants* they employ; and these carry with them

into

into the lower ranks that spirit of gambling and dissipation which they have practised in the course of their servitude; thus producing consequences of a most alarming nature to the general interests of the Community. To the contagion of such examples, is owing in a great measure the number of persons attached to pursuits of this kind, who become the Swindlers, Sharpers, and Cheats, of an inferior class, described in the preceding Chapter: and from the same course spring up those Pests of Society, *The Lottery Insurers*, whose iniquitous proceedings we shall in the next place lay before the Reader.

These, with some exceptions, are composed of persons, in general very depraved or distressed: the depredations committed on the Public by their means are so ruinous and extensive as to require a consideration peculiarly minute: in order to guard the ignorant and unwary, as much as possible, against the fatal effects of that fraud and delusion, which, if not soon checked, bidfair to destroy all remains of honesty and discretion.—These Classes consist of

Sharpers, who take Lottery Insurances, by which means gambling, among the higher and middling ranks, is carried on to an extent which exceeds all credibility; producing consequences to many private families, otherwise of great worth and respectability, of the most distressing nature; and implicating in this misery, the innocent and amiable branches of such families, whose sufferings, arising from this source, while they claim the tear of pity, would require

quire many volumes to recount; but silence and
shame throw a veil over the calamity : and, cherished
by the hopes of retrieving former losses, or acquiring
property, in an easy way, the evil goes on, and seems
even yet to increase, in spite of every guard which
the Legislature has repeatedly endeavoured to
establish.

With a very few exceptions all who are or have
been proprietors of the Gambling-Houses are also
concerned in the fraudulent Insurance Offices; and
have a number of Clerks employed during the drawing of the two Lotteries, who conduct the business
without risk in counting-houses, where no insurances
are taken, but to which books are carried, not only
from all the different Offices in every part of the
town, but also from the Morocco-Men; so called,
from their going from door to door with a book covered with red leather for the purpose of taking insurances, and enticing the poor and the middle ranks to
become adventurers.

*Several of the Keepers of Insurance Offices, during the
interval of the drawing of the English and Irish Lotteries* have invented and set up private Lotteries, or
Wheels, called by the nick-name of *Little Go's*, containing Blanks and Prizes, which are drawn for the purpose of establishing *a ground for Insurance*; the fever
in the minds of the lower order of the people is thus
kept up, in some measure, all the year round, and
produces incalculable mischiefs; and hence the spirit
of gambling becomes so rooted from habit, that no
domestic

domestic distress, no consideration, arising either with the frauds that are practised, or the number of chances that are against them, will operate as a check upon their minds.

In spite of the high price of provisions, and of the care and attention of the Legislature in establishing severe checks and punishments for the purpose of preventing the evil of Lottery Insurances, these criminal agents feel no want of customers; their houses and offices are not only extremely numerous all over the Metropolis, but in general *high-rented;* exhibiting the appearance of considerable expence, and barricadoed in such a manner, with iron doors and other contrivances, as in many instances to defy the arm of the Law to reach them.

In tracing all the circumstances connected with this interesting subject, with a view to the discovery of the cause of the great encouragement which these Lottery Insurers receive, it appears that a considerable proportion of their emolument is derived from *menial servants* in general, all over the Metropolis; but particularly from the pampered male and female domestics in the houses of men of fashion and fortune; who are said, almost without a single exception, to be in the constant habit of insuring in the English and Irish Lotteries.

This class of *menials,* being in many instances cloathed as well as fed by their masters, have not the same calls upon them as labourers and mechanics, who

who must appropriate at least a part of their earnings
to the purpose of obtaining both food and raiment.

With a spirit of gambling, rendered more ardent,
than prevails in vulgar life, from the example of their
superiors, and from their idle and dissipated habits,
these servants enter keenly into the Lottery business;
and when ill luck attends them, it is but too well
known that many are led, step by step, to that point
where they lose sight of all moral principle; impelled
by a desire to recover what they have lost, they are
induced to raise money for that purpose, by selling
or pawning the property of their masters, wherever
it can be pilfered in a little way, without detection;
till at length this species of peculation, by being
rendered familiar to their minds, generally terminates
in more atrocious crimes.

Upon a supposition that one hundred thousand
families in the Metropolis keep two servants upon
an average, and that one servant with another insures only to the extent of twenty-five shillings each,
in the English, and the same in the Irish Lottery,
the aggregate of the whole will amount to HALF A
MILLION STERLING.

Astonishing as this may appear at first view, it is
believed that those who will minutely examine into
the Lottery transactions of their servants, will find
the calculation by no means exaggerated; and when
to this are added the sums drawn from persons in the
middle ranks of life, as well as from the numerous
classes

classes of labourers and artisans who have caught the mania; it ceases to be a matter of wonder, that so many Sharpers, Swindlers. and Cheats, find encouragement in this particular department.

If servants in general, who are under the control of masters, were prevented from following this abominable species of gambling; and if other expedients were adopted, which will be hereafter detailed, a large proportion of the present race of rogues and vagabonds who follow this infamous trade, would be compelled to become honest; and the poor would be shielded from the delusion which impels them to resort to this deceitful and fraudulent expedient; at the expence sometimes of pledging every article of household goods, as well as the last rag of their own, and their childrens' wearing apparel, not leaving even a single change of raiment!

This view of a very prominent and alarming evil, known to exist from a variety of facts well established and evinced, among others, by the pawnbrokers' shops overflowing with the goods of the labouring poor, during the drawing of the three Lotteries, ought to create a strong desire on the part of all masters of families, to exert their utmost endeavours to check this destructive propensity; and to prevent, as far as possible, those distresses and mischiefs which every person of humanity must deplore. The misery and loss of property which springs from this delusive source of iniquity, is certainly very far beyond any

idea

idea that can be formed of it by the common observer.*

A general Association, or perhaps an Act of Parliament, establishing proper regulations, applicable to
this and other objects, with regard to menial servants,
would be of great utility.

* In consequence of a very accurate inquiry which has been made,
and of information derived from different sources, it appears that
fraudulent Lottery Insurances have not diminished. The Offices
are numerous all over the Metropolis, and are supposed to exceed
four hundred of all descriptions; to many of which there are persons
attached, called *Morocco Men*, who go about from house to house
among their former customers, and attend in the back parlours of
Public Houses, where they are met by customers who make insurances. It is calculated that at these offices (exclusive of what is done
at the *licensed* offices) premiums for insurance are received to the
amount of *eight hundred thousand pounds*, during the Irish Lottery,
and above *one million* during the English; upon which it is calculated
that they make from 15 to 25 per cent. profit.—This infamous confederacy was estimated, during the English Lottery of the year 1796,
to support about 2000 agents and clerks, and nearly 7500 Morocco
Men, including a considerable number of hired *armed Ruffians* and
Bludgeon Men: these were paid by a general association of the Principal Proprietors of these fraudulent Establishments; who regularly
met in Committee, in a well-known public house in Oxford Market, twice or thrice a week, during the drawing of the Lottery; for
the purpose of concerting measures to defeat the exertions of the
Magistrates, by alarming and terrifying, and even forcibly resisting,
the Officers of Justice in all instances where they could not be bribed
by pecuniary gratuities;—to effect which last purpose, neither money nor pains were spared; and the wretched agents of these unprincipled miscreants were, in many cases, prepared to commit murder,
had attempts been made to execute the Warrants of Magistrates; as
can be proved by incontestable evidence. It is greatly to be feared
that too much success attended these corrupt and fraudulent proceedings, in violation and defiance of the Laws of the Kingdom.

If

If a Legislative regulation could also be established, extending certain restrictions to the members of the different *Friendly Societies* situated within the Bills of Mortality with regard to Fraudulent Lottery Insurances, above *seventy thousand families* would be relieved from the consequences of this insinuating evil; which has been so fatal to the happiness and comfort of a vast number of tradesmen and artisans, as well as inferior classes of labourers. *

Such prohibitions and restraints would have a wonderful effect in lessening the profits of the Lottery-Office Keepers; which, perhaps, is the very best mode of suppressing the evil.—At present, the temptation to follow these fraudulent practices is so great, from the productive nature of the business, that unless some new expedient be resorted to, no well-grounded hope can be entertained of lessening the evil in any material degree.

In addition, therefore, to what has already been suggested on the subject, other expedients have occurred to the Author; and some have been suggested by persons well informed on this subject.

The Lottery in itself, if the poorer classes could be exempted from its mischiefs, has been considered by

---

* The regulation proposed, is this—that every member belonging to a Friendly Society should be *excluded* or *expelled*, and deprived of all future benefits from the funds of that Society on proof of his having insured in any Lottery whatsoever, contrary to law;—and that this rule should be general, wherever the Acts of Parliament, relative to Friendly Societies, have taken effect.

many

many good Writers and Reasoners as a fair resource of Revenue ; by taxing the vices or follies of the People, in a country where such a considerable proportion of the higher and middling ranks are possessed of large properties in money, and may be induced, through this medium, to contribute to the assistance of the State, what would (probably to the same extent) be otherwise squandered and dissipated, in idle amusements.

It is a means also of benefit to the Nation, by drawing considerable sums of money annually from foreign countries, which are laid out in the purchase of tickets.

In many respects therefore, it might be desirable to preserve this source of Revenue if it can be confined to the purchase of Tickets, and to persons of such opulence, as upon the abolition of the Lottery could not probably be restrained from squandering their money in another way, from which the State would derive no benefit.

The Lottery, on the plan upon which it is at present conducted, has not yet ceased to be an evil of the utmost magnitude, and perhaps one of the greatest nurseries of crimes that ever existed in any country.—At the close of the English Lottery drawn in 1796, the Civil Power was trampled upon and put to defiance in a most alarming and shameful manner, disgraceful to the Police of the Metropolis. The means used for this purpose have been already fully detailed ; *ante, p.* 156. *in the note.*

The

The profits of these Cheats and Swindlers were said to be immense beyond all former example, during the Lottery drawn in the spring both of 1796 and 1797; and of course, the Poor were never in a greater degree plundered.

In calculating the chances upon the whole numbers in the wheels, and the premiums which are paid, there is generally about 33 1-3d per cent. in favour of the Lottery Insurers; but when it is considered that the lower ranks, from not being able to recollect or comprehend high numbers, always fix on low ones, the chance in favour of the insurer is greatly increased, and the deluded Poor are plundered, to an extent which really exceeds all calculation.

At no period is there ever so much occasion for the exertions of the Magistracy, as during the drawing of the English and Irish Lotteries; but it is to be feared, that even by this energy, opposed as it always undoubtedly will be, by a System as well of corruption as of force unexampled in former times, no proper check can be given, until by new Legislative regulations, some more effectual remedy is applied.

The following expedients with the assisstance of a superintending, energetic, and well-regulated Police, it is to be hoped, might be the means of greatly abridging this enormous evil, and of securing to Government the same annual revenue, which is at present obtained, or nearly so.

" 1. That

" 1. That the numbers of the Tickets to be placed in the Lottery Wheels shall not be *running numbers ;* as heretofore used ; but shall be *intermediate* and *broken;* thereby preventing insurances from being made on specific numbers, from the impossibility of its being known, to any but the *holders of tickets, or the Commissioners,* what particular ticket at any time remains in the wheel.

" 2. That all persons taking out licences to sell Lottery Tickets, shall (instead of the bond with two sureties for one thousand pounds, now entered into under the act of the 22d George 3. cap. 47) enter into a bond, with two sureties also, for 50,000*l.* — which sum shall be forfeited, on due proof that any person, so licensed, shall have been, directly or indirectly, concerned in taking insurances contrary to law ; or in setting up, or being connected in the profit or loss arising from any illegal insurance-office ; or in employing itinerant Clerks, to take insurances on account of persons so licensed.

3. That besides the above-mentioned bond, all licensed Lottery Office Keepers shall, previous to the drawing of each Lottery, make oath before a Magistrate, that they will not, in the course of the ensuing Lottery, be concerned, either directly or indirectly, in setting up any illegal offices for the sale of tickets, or insurance of numbers, contrary to law : Which affidavit shall be recorded, and a certificate thereof shall be indorsed on the licence
                                                    without

without which it shall not be valid. And that the affidavit may be produced in evidence, against persons convicted of illegally insuring; who shall in that event be liable to the punishment attached to perjury, and, of course, to the ignominy of the pillory and imprisonment.

" 4. That all peace officers, constables, head-boroughs, or others, lawfully authorised to execute the warrants of Magistrates, who shall receive any gratuity, or sum of money from illegal Lottery Insurers, or from any person or persons, in consideration of any expected services in screening such offenders from detection or punishment, shall, on conviction, be rendered infamous, and incapable of ever serving any public office; and be punished by fines, imprisonment, or the pillory, as the Court, before whom the offence is tried, shall see proper.

" 5. That all persons who shall be convicted of *paying money* on any contract for the benefit arising from the drawing of any Lottery Ticket, insured upon any contingency (not being in possession of the original ticket, or a legal share thereof) shall forfeit 20*l.* for every offence, to be levied by distress, &c.

" 6. That an abstract of the penalties inflicted by law on persons insuring, or taking illegal insurances in the Lottery, shall be read every Sunday, in all churches, chapels, meeting-houses, and other places of public worship, during the drawing
of

of the Irish and English Lotteries respectively; with a short exhortation, warning the people of the consequences of offending against the law: And that a copy of the same shall be pasted up in different parts of Guildhall, and constantly replaced during the drawing of the Lottery; and also at all the licensed Lottery Offices within the Metropolis.

" 7. That a reward, not exceeding 50*l.* be paid to any person employed as a clerk or servant in any illegal Lottery Office, who shall be the means of convicting the actual or principal proprietor or proprietors of the said office, who shall not appear themselves in the management; also a sum not exceeding 40*l.* on conviction of a known and acting proprietor; and a sum not exceeding 10*l.* on conviction of any clerk or manager, not being partners.

" 8. That the punishment to be inflicted on offenders shall be fine, imprisonment, or the pillory; according to the atrocity of the offence, in the discretion of the Court before which such offenders shall be tried."

The following Plans have also been transmitted to the Author by Correspondents who appear to be well-wishers to Society. They are here made public, in hopes that from the whole of the suggestions thus offered, some regulations may ultimately be adopted by the Legislature towards effectually remedying this peculiarly dangerous and still-increasing evil.

PLAN

PLAN I.

" It is proposed, that the *Prizes only* should be drawn, and that Seven Hours and a Half per Day should be the time of drawing, instead of Five Hours, by which means a lottery of the same number of tickets now drawn in thirty-five days, would be drawn in seven days and a half; and each adventurer would have exactly the same chance as he has by the present mode of drawing; since it is evidently of no consequence to him whether all the blanks remain in the Number Wheel undrawn, or an equal number of Blanks are drawn from a Blank and Prize Wheel; the chance of blank and prize on *each ticket* being in either case exactly the same.

" According to the usual mode of drawing, 50,000 tickets take about thirty-five days in drawing, which is $1,420\frac{5}{7}$ per day.—By increasing the time of each day's drawing, from five hours to seven and a half, 2,131 tickets would be drawn each day; but as the reading prizes above 20*l. thrice*, causes some little delay, I reckon only 2000 per day; at which rate 15,000 tickets, the usual proportion of prizes in a Lottery of 50,000 tickets, would be drawn in seven days and a half. Thus the *Period* of Insurance would be nearly reduced to one-fifth part of its present duration, and the *daily* insurance on *Blanks*, and *Blank and Prize*, which opens the most extensive field for gambling,

gambling, would be *entirely abolished*. Reducing, therefore, the time of insurance to one-fifth, and the numbers drawn to less than one-third of what they have hitherto been, there could scarce remain in Lotteries thus drawn, one fifteenth part of the insurance as in former Lotteries of an equal number of Tickets. —It is also worthy of remark, that as all the late Lotteries have been thirty-five days at least in drawing, the Insurance Offices had thirty-four to one in their favour the first day, by which circumstance they were enabled to tempt chiefly that class of people who can only gamble on the lowest terms, and to whom gambling is most extensively pernicious, with a very moderate premium, (*e. g.* about twelve shillings to return twenty pounds) which increases daily by almost imperceptible degrees, and thus insensibly leads them on to misery, desperation, and guilt.

" But in the proposed Plan, the Insurance Offices would have only six days and a half to one in their favour the first day; so that they must begin with a much higher premium than the generality of the common people can advance, which premium must each day be very considerably increased.—These considerations would undoubtedly operate as an absolute prohibition, on far the greatest part of Lottery Insurers; beside which, the great probability of numbers insured being drawn each day, would deter even the Office Keepers from venturing to insure so deeply, or extensively, as they have been accustomed to do.

" Should it be objected, that if Insurance is thus
abridged,

abridged, or prohibited, tickets will not sell, and the
Lottery, as a source of Revenue, must be abandoned :
the following expedient may, it is apprehended, effectually obviate such an objection.—

" Let Tickets, which cannot now be legally divided
below a sixteenth, be divisible down to a *Sixty-fourth*
share, properly stamped ; which regulation, while it
would greatly benefit and encourage Licensed Offices,
would equally discountenance illegal Gamblers; and
whilst it permitted to the lower orders of the Community a fair chance of an adventure in the Lottery
on moderate terms, would co-operate with the restrictions on Insurance to advance the intrinsic value,
as well as the price of tickets, which every illegal
Scheme. evidently tends to depreciate."

The preceding Plan appeared in the Appendix to
the fifth edition of this Treatise ; in consequence of
which the Author received the following observations, and which therefore he presents as—

PLAN II.

" The Suggestions as far as they extend and relate
to the shortening the duration of the drawing are
highly useful, but they fall short of the object, and
the Plan, if executed, would nearly prevent the sale
of tickets, and totally so that of shares, and consequently abolish Lotteries altogether ;—a consumma-
tion devoutly to be wished by every friend to the
public, but under the pecuniary influences, which
perhaps

perhaps too much affect political considerations, little to be expected.

It will be necessary to exhibit only a plain Statement of the proportionate chances in the wheel during the 7½ days of drawing on the Scheme of 50,000 Tickets, viz.—

	Prizes.		*Blanks.*	
1st. Day	15,000	to	35,000	2⅓ to a Prize
2d. ————	13,000	—	35,000	
3d. ———	11,000	—	35,000	
4th. ———	9,000	—	35,000	
5th.———	7,000	—	35,000	
6th.———	5,000	—	35,000	
7th.———	3,000	—	35,000	
last.———	1,000	—	35,000	35 to a Prize.

" Hence it is evident, that on supposition the value of the Prizes diminish by an equal ratio, every day of drawing, still the actual value of the Prizes in proportion to the permanent number of the Blanks will be diminished by the relative proportion increasing at the rate of about 4666 Blanks every day after the first.   Consequently it must follow, that the premiums of insurance, as well as the price of Shares and Tickets, instead of acquiring in their value *a very considerable increase*, must be subject to a very considerable diminution.

" To maintain the foregoing Plan, No. I. which is a good ground-work for lessening the evil, I take the liberty (says my Correspondent) of suggesting the following improvement.

" After

" After the Prizes are drawn each day, let the proportion of the Blanks, namely 4665, be drawn also. Let there be a suspension likewise of five or seven days between each drawing for the sale of Tickets and Shares, and to give time for insurance. It may be objected, that the time being thus prolonged the inconvenience will remain the same; to avoid which, the blank numbers so drawn, must be done secretly and sealed up by the Commissioners, or, they may be drawn openly but not unfolded or declared, and if necessary, made public after the drawing; by which means the insurance against Blanks or Blank and Prize will be equally abolished."

PLAN III.

" The Evils of a Lottery are many.—The Advantages might, if well regulated, be as numerous. According to the Schemes that have hitherto prevailed the *principle* has been wrong. Since the bait held out has been the obtaining of an immense fortune, and the risk has been proportionably great—Insurance has reigned unchecked by all penalties and punishments that could be devised to the ruin and misery of thousands. The price of tickets has been fluctuating, and fortunes have been won and lost on the chance of the great Prizes keeping in the Wheel: the 20*l.* prizes have always proved dissatisfactory, as though there are only 2½ prizes *on an average* to a blank, yet such is the uncertainty, that many have

scores

scores of tickets without obtaining the proportionate
advantage even from these low prizes. It is thought,
therefore, that a scheme which fhould offer considerably more chances for prizes of and above 50l. and
which should ensure a return on all blanks, would
be acceptable: If also it could be made to prevent
insuring of tickets and capitals, it seems to be the
grand desideratum in this branch of financiering.

" The principle on which these benefits may be
obtained is this. There should be a considerable
number of moderate prizes, such as might be fortunes,
if obtained by the inferior ranks, and of consequence
sufficient to answer the risk of the rich. The tickets
to be drawn each day should be previously specified,
which may be done by appropriating a certain share
of the prizes to a certain number of tickets. All the
tickets not drawn prizes of 50l. or upwards, shall be
entitled to a certain return, which would be superior
to a chance for a 20l. prize.

SCHEME.

Number of Prizes.	Value of each. £.	Total Value. £
25	5,000	125,000
25	1,000	25,000
100	500	50,000
250	100	25,000
600	50	30,000
1,000		255,000
49,000—£.5 returned on each.		245,000
50,000 Tickets		500,000

" SCHEME

" SCHEME OF DRAWING.

" Let 2000 Tickets from No. 1, to 1999 inclusive (with Number 50) be put into a Wheel the first day, and proceed in the same manner numerically for 25 days. In the other Wheel, each day let there be put the following proportion of Prizes, viz.

	£.	£.
1	5000	5000
1	1000	1000
4	500	2000
10	100	1000
24	50	1200
40		10,200
1960—£. 5 to be returned on each.		9,800
2000 Tickets		20,000

" In Lotteries where the lowest prizes have been of 20l. the blanks have been in the proportion of 2½ to a prize. If therefore a person had seven tickets they were entitled to expect only two 20l. prizes or 40l. In this, however, they were frequently disappointed, and their chance for a prize of 50l. or upwards has been as about 200 to 50,000. By the above Scheme, if a person has seven tickets they are sure of a return of 35l. and have a chance of 40 to 2000, or 1000 to 50,000 for a superior prize. The certainty of the numbers and the prizes to be drawn each day would prevent insurance on those events, and every ticket being

being a prize, there could be no insurance against blanks.

" In fact, the Lottery might be drawn in one day,—thus : Let there be twenty-five bags containing each 2000 numbers, either promiscuously chosen or of stated thousands.   Let there be also 25 bags, each containing the 40 prizes above appropriated to each day's drawing.   Let the Commissioners empty one bag of numbers and one of prizes into two wheels. Let them draw 40 numbers out of the Number Wheel, and the 40 prizes out of the other.   The remaining 1960 numbers to be entitled to 5l. each.— Then let them proceed with other 2000 numbers in the same way."

———

At all events, whether these Plans for reforming this enormous evil, are or are not superior to others which have been devised, it is clear to demonstration that the present System is founded on a principle not less erroneous than mischievous ; and, therefore, it cannot too soon be abandoned ; especially since it would appear that the Revenue it produces might be preserved, with the incalculable advantage to the nation of preserving, at the same time, the morals of the people, and turning into a course of industry and usefulness the labour of many thousand individuals, who, instead of being, as at present, pests in Society, might be rendered useful members of the State.

CHAP.

CHAP. VII.

*The Frauds arising from the manufacture and circu-
lation of base Money :—The Causes of its enormous
increase of late years.—The different kinds of false
Coin detailed:—The Process in fabricating each
species explained :—The immense Profits arising
therefrom :—The extensive Trade in sending base
Coin to the Country.—Its universal Circulation in
the Metropolis.—The great Grievance arising from
it to Brewers, Distillers, Grocers, and Retail
Dealers, in particular, as well as the Labouring Poor
in general—The principal Channels through which it
is uttered in the Country and in the Metropolis.—
Counterfeit foreign Money extremely productive to
the dealers.—A summary View of the Causes of the
mifchief.—The Defects in the present Laws explained :—And a Detail of the Remedies proposed to be
provided by the Legislature.*

THE frauds committed by the fabrication of base
Money, and by the nefarious practices, in the introduction of almost every species of Counterfeit Coin
into the circulation of the Country, are next to be
discussed.

The great outlines of this enormous evil having
been stated in the first Chapter, it now remains to
elucidate

elucidate that part of the subject which is connected with *specific detail.*

One of the greatest sources of these multiplied and increasing frauds is be traced to the various ingenious improvements which have taken place of late years, at Birmingham, and other manufacturring towns, in mixing metals, and in stamping and *colouring* ornamental buttons.

The same ingenious process is so easily applied to the coining and colouring of false money, and also to the mixing of the metals of which it is composed, that it is not to be wondered at, that the avarice of man, urged by the prospect of immense profit, has occasioned that vast increase of counterfeit money of every description, with which the Country is at present deluged.

The false coinages which have been introduced into circulation, of late years, are *Guineas, Half-Guineas, and Seven Shilling Pieces, Crowns and Half-Crowns, Shillings, Sixpences, Pence, Halfpence, and Farthings,* of the similitude of the coin of the realm : of foreign coin, *Half Johannas, Louis d'ors, Spanish Dollars, French Half-Crowns, Shillings and Sixpences,* 30 *Sol pieces, Prussian and Danish Silver money, and other continental coins;* to which may be added, *Sequins of Turkey,* and *Pagodas of India.* These foreign coins, except in the instance of the *Spanish Dollars** issued

by

* The circulation of stamped Spanish Dollars, in 1797, gave rise to a very extensive coinage of counterfeit money of the same species,

which

by the Bank of England in 1797, have generally been sold as articles of commerce for the purpose of being fraudulently circulated in the British Colonies or in Foreign Countries.

So dexterous and skilful have Coiners now become, that by mixing a certain proportion of pure gold with a compound of base metal, they can fabricate guineas that shall be full weight, and of such perfect workmanship as to elude a discovery, except by persons of skill; while the intrinsic value does not exceed thirteen or fourteen shillings, and in some in-

which was generally executed in a very masterly manner, and before the fraud was discovered vast quantities were in the hands of many innocent members of the community. Several detections, however, having checked the circulation, and silver bullion having fallen greatly in price, those who were in the habit of dealing in base money availing themselves of this circumstance, purchased Dollars in great quantities at about 4s. 2d. which they instantly stamped and circulated at 4s. 9d. and by which species of villainy large sums of money were suddenly amassed.——One dealer in particular is said to have made above 5000l. in six weeks. The Laws attaching no punishment to this unforeseen offence, and the Author representing the circumstances of the case to the Bank Directors, the whole were called in, leaving, however, in the hands of the dealers a large surplus of actual counterfeits,—which appears to have suggested to them the expedient of finding a market in the British American Colonies and the United States, where, in general, frauds are less likely to be detected from the payments being made (particularly in the West India islands) in dollars put up in bags containing a certain value in each. However, they were fortunately defeated in this object by the timely notice given by the Author of this Treatise to his Majesty's Secretary of State, and the American Minister, and through these respectable mediums commercial people were put upon their guard before the intended fraud could be carried into effect.

stances

stances is not more than eight or nine. Of this coinage considerable quantities were circulated some years since, bearing the impression of George the Second : and another coinage of counterfeit guineas of the year 1793, bearing the impression of his present Majesty, has been for some years in circulation, finished in a masterly manner, and nearly full weight, although the intrinsic value is not above eight shillings : half guineas are also in circulation of the same coinage : and lately a good imitation of the seven-shilling pieces.   But as the fabrication of such coin requires a greater degree of skill and ingenuity than generally prevails, and also a greater capital than most coiners are able to command, it is to be hoped it has gone to no great extent ; for amidst all the abuses which have prevailed of late years, it is unquestionably true, that the guineas and half-guineas which have been counterfeited in a style to elude detection, have borne no proportion in point of extent to the coinage of base *Silver*.   Of this latter there are *five* different kinds at present counterfeited ; and which we shall proceed to enumerate.

The first of these are denominated Flats, from the circumstance of this species of money being cut out of flatted plates, composed of a mixture of silver and blanched copper.   The proportion of silver runs from one-fourth to one-third, and in some instances to even one-half : the metals are mixed by a chemical preparation, and afterwards rolled by flatting mills, into the thickness of *shillings, half-crowns*, or *crowns*, according

cording to the desire of the parties who bring the copper and silver, which last is generally stolen plate. It is not known that there are at present above one or two rolling mills in London, although there are several in the Country, where all the dealers and coiners of this species of base money resort, for the purpose of having these plates prepared; from which, when finished, *blanks* or round pieces are cut out, of the sizes of the money meant to be counterfeited.

The artisans who stamp or coin these blanks into base money are seldom interested themselves. They generally work as mechanics for the large dealers who employ a capital in the trade ;—and who furnish the plates, and pay about eight per cent. for the coinage, being at the rate of one penny for each shilling, and twopence-halfpenny for each half-crown.

This operation consists first in turning the blanks in a lathe;—then stamping them, by means of a press, with dies of the exact impression of the coin intended to be imitated :—they are afterwards rubbed with sandpaper and cork ; then put into aquafortis to bring the silver to the surface ; then rubbed with common salt; then with cream of tartar; then warmed in a shovel or similar machine before the fire ; and last of all rubbed with *blacking*, to give the money the appearance of having been in circulation.

All these operations are so quickly performed, that two persons (a man and his wife for instance,) can completely finish to the nominal amount of fifty
                                                          pounds

pounds in shillings and half-crowns in two days, by which they will earn each two guineas a day.

A shilling of this species, which exhibits nearly the appearance of what has been usually called a Birmingham shilling, is intrinsically worth from *two pence to fourpence*; and crowns and half-crowns are in the same proportion. The quantity made of this sort of counterfeit coinage is very considerable : it requires less ingenuity than any of the other methods of coining, though at the same time it is the most expensive, and of course the least profitable to the. Dealer ; who for the most part disposes of it to the utterers, vulgarly called *Smashers*, at from 28s. to 40s. for a guinea, according to the quality ; while these *Smashers* generally manage to utter it again to the full import value.

The Second Species of Counterfeit Silver money passes among the dealers by the denomination of Plated Goods; from the circumstance of the shillings and half-crowns being made of copper of a reduced size, and afterwards plated with silver, so extended as to form a rim round the edge. This coin is afterwards stamped with dies so as to resemble the real coin ; and, from the circumstance of the surface being pure silver, is not easily discovered except by ringing the money on a table : but as this species of base money requires a knowledge of *plating* as well as a great deal of ingenuity, it is of course confined to few hands. It is however extremely profitable to those who carry

it

it on, as it can generally be uttered, without detection, at its full import value.

The Third Species of base Silver-money is called Plain Goods, and is totally confined to shillings. These are made of copper blanks turned in a lathe, of the exact size of a Birmingham shilling, afterwards silvered over by a particular operation used in colouring metal buttons; they are then rubbed over with cream of tartar and blacking, after which they are fit for circulation.

These shillings do not cost the makers above one halfpenny each: they are sold very low to the *Smashers* or *Utterers*, who pass them where they can, at the full nominal value; and when the silver wears off, which is very soon the case, they are sold to the Jews as bad shillings, who generally resell them at a small profit to customers, by whom they are recoloured, and thus soon brought again into circulation. The profit is immense, owing to the trifling value of the materials; but the circulation, on account of the danger of discovery, it is to be hoped is not yet very extensive. It is, however, to be remarked, that it is a species of coinage not of a long standing.

The Fourth Class of counterfeit silver-money is known by the name of CASTINGS or CAST GOODS. This species of work requires great skill and ingenuity, and is therefore confined to few hands; for none but excellent artists can attempt it, with any prospect of great success.

The process is to melt blanched copper, and to

cast

cast it in moulds, having the impression, and being
of the size of a *crown*, a *half-crown*, a *shilling*, or a
sixpence, as the case may be; after being removed
from the moulds, the money thus formed is cleaned
off, and afterwards neatly silvered over by an operation similar to that which takes place in the manufacture of buttons.

The counterfeit money made in imitation of shillings by this process, is generally cast so as to have a
crooked appearance; and the deception is so admirable, that although intrinsically not worth *one halfpenny,* by exhibiting the appearance of a *thick crooked
shilling,* they enter into circulation without suspicion,
and are seldom refused while the surface exhibits no
part of the copper; and even after this the itinerant
Jews will purchase them at threepence each though
six times their intrinsic value, well knowing that they
can again be récoloured at the expence of half a farthing, so as to pass without difficulty for their nominal value of twelve pence.—A vast number of the
sixpences now in circulation is of this species of
coinage.

The profit in every view, whether to the original
maker, or to the subsequent purchasers (after having
lost their colour), is *immense.*

In fabricating Cast Money, the workmen are always
more secure than where presses and dies are used;
because upon the least alarm, and before any officer
of justice can have admission, the counterfeits are
thrown into the crucible; the moulds are destroyed;
and

and nothing is to be found that can convict, or even criminate the offender: on this account the present makers of cast money have reigned long, and were they careful and frugal, they might have become extremely rich; but prudence rarely falls to the lot of men who live by acts of criminality.

The *Fifth and last Species* of base coin made in imitation of silver-money of the realm is called Figs or Fig Things. It is a very inferior sort of counterfeit money, of which composition, however, a great part of the sixpences now in circulation are made. The proportion of silver is not, generally speaking, of the value of one farthing in half a crown, although there are certainly some exceptions, as counterfeit sixpences have been lately discovered, some with a mixture, and some wholly silver; but even these did not yield the makers less than from 50 to 80 per cent. while the profit on the former is not less than from five hundred to one thousand per cent. and sometimes more.

It is impossible to estimate the amount of this base money which has entered into the circulation of the Country during the last twenty years; but it must be very great, since one of the principal Coiners of stamped money, who some time since left off business, and made some important discoveries, acknowledged to the Author, that he had coined to the extent of *two hundred thousand pounds* sterling in counterfeit *half-crowns*, and other base silver money, in a period

of

of seven years. This is the less surprising, as two persons can stamp and finish to the amount of from 200*l.* to 300*l.* a week.*

Of the Copper Money made in imitation of the current coin of the realm, there are many different sorts sold at various prices, according to the size and weight; but in general they may be divided into two kinds, namely, the stamped and the plain halfpence, of both which kind immense quantities have been made in London; and also in Birmingham, Wedgbury, Bilston, and Wolverhampton, &c. †

The plain halfpence are generally made at Birmingham; and from their thickness, afford a wonderful deception. They are sold, however, by the coiners to the large dealers at about a farthing each, or 100 per cent. profit in the tale or aggregate number. These dealers are not the *utterers*; but sell

---

* A *Liquid Test* has been discovered by Mr. ALSTON, an eminent Manufacturer, in Birmingham, of great worth and respectability, which cannot fail to be of the greatest use in detecting every species of counterfeit Gold and Silver money, whether *plated* or *washed*. This discovery is mentioned with pleasure by the Author, as it is likely to be productive of much benefit to the Public, in protecting the fair dealers against the frauds daily practised upon them, in the circulation of base money.—The discovery is instantaneous by a single touch, and the expence of the Liquid and Apparatus is trifling.

† A species of counterfeit halfpence made *wholly of lead*, has been circulated in considerable quantities, coloured in such a manner as even to deceive the best judges. They are generally of the Reign of George II. and have the exact appearance of old Mint halfpence.

them

them again by retail in *pieces*, or *five shilling papers*, at the rate of from 28s. to 31s. for a guinea ; not only to the Smashers, but also to persons in different trades, as well in the Metropolis as in the Country Towns, who pass them in the course of their business at the full import value.

Farthings are also made in considerable quantities, chiefly in London, but so very thin that the profit upon this species of coinage is much greater than on the halfpence, though these counterfeits are not now, as formerly, made of base metal. The copper of which they are made is generally pure. The advantage lies in the weight alone, where the *coiners*, *sellers*, and *utterers*, do not obtain less than 200 per cent. A well known coiner has been said to finish from sixty to eighty pounds sterling a week. Of halfpence, two or three persons can stamp and finish to the nominal amount of at least two hundred pounds in six days.

When it is considered that there are seldom less than between forty and fifty coinages or private mints, almost constantly employed in London and in different country towns, in stamping and fabricating base silver and copper money, the evil may justly be said to have arrived at an enormous height. It is indeed true that these people have been a good deal interrupted and embarrassed from time to time, by detections and convictions ; but while the laws are so inapplicable to the new tricks and devices they have resorted to, these convictions are only *a drop in the bucket:*

bucket : while such encouragements are held out the execution of one rogue only makes room for another to take up his customers; and indeed as the offence of selling is only a misdemeanor, it is no unusual thing for the wife and family of a culprit, or convicted *seller* of *base money* to carry on the business, and to support him luxuriously in Newgate, until the expiration of the *year* and *day's* imprisonment, which is generally the punishment inflicted for this species of offence.

It has been already stated [*page* 16, &c.] that trading in base money has now become as regular and systematic as any fair branch of trade.

Certain it is, that immense quantities have been regularly sent from London to the Camps during the summer season; and to persons at the sea-ports and manufacturing towns, who again sell in retail to the different tradesmen and others, who pass them at the full *import* value.

In this nefarious traffic a number of the lower order of the German Jews in London assist the dealers in an eminent degree, particularly in the circulation of bad halfpence.

It has not been an unusual thing for several of these dealers to hold a kind of market every morning, where from forty to fifty of these German Jew boys are regularly supplied with counterfeit halfpence; which they dispose of in the course of the day in different streets and lanes of the Metropolis, for *bad shillings,* at about 3d. each.   Care is always taken that

the

the person who cries bad shillings shall have a companion near him who carries the halfpence, and takes charge of the purchased shillings (which are not cut:) so as to elude the detection of the Officers of the Police, in the event of being searched.

The bad shillings thus purchased are received in payment by the employers of the boys, for the bad halfpence supplied them, at the rate of four shillings a dozen; and are generally resold to *Smashers,* at a profit of two shillings a dozen; who speedily re-colour them, and introduce them again into circulation, at their full nominal value.

The boys will generally clear from five to seven shillings a day, by this fraudulent business; which they almost uniformly spend, during the evening, in riot and debauchery; returning pennyless in the morning to their old trade.

Thus it is that the frauds upon the Public multiply beyond all possible conception, while the tradesman, who unwarily at least if not improperly, sells his counterfeit shillings to Jew boys at three-pence each, little suspects that it is for the purpose of being returned upon him again at the rate of twelve-pence; or 300 per cent. profit to the purchasers and utterers.

But these are not the only criminal devices to which the coiners and dealers, as well as the utterers of base money, have had recourse, for answering their iniquitous purposes.

Previous to the Act of the 37 Geo. 3. cap. 126,
counterfeit

counterfeit French crowns, half-crowns, and shillings, of excellent workmanship, were introduced with a view to elude the punishment of the then deficient Laws relative to Foreign Coin.

Fraudulent die-sinkers are to be found both in the Metropolis and in Birmingham, who are excellent artists; able and willing to copy the exact similitude of any coin, from the British guinea to the sequin of Turkey, or to the Star Pagoda of Arcot. The delinquents have therefore every opportunity and assistance they can wish for: while their accurate knowledge of the deficiency of the laws, (particularly relative to British Coin) and where the point of danger lies, joined to the extreme difficulty of detection, operates as a great encouragement to this species of treason, felony, and fraud : and affords the most forcible reason why these pests of society still continue to afflict the honest part of the community.

An opinion prevails, founded on information obtained through the medium of the most intelligent of these coiners and dealers, that of the counterfeit money now in circulation, not above one third part is of the species of *Flats* or *composition money*; which has been mentioned as the most intrinsically valuable of counterfeit silver, and contains from one fourth to one third silver; the remainder being blanched copper.—The other two thirds of the counterfeit money being *cast* or *washed*, and intrinsically worth little or nothing, the imposition upon the public is obvious.

Taking

Taking the whole upon an average, the amount of the injury may be fairly calculated at within ten per cent. of a total loss upon the mass of the base silver money now in circulation; which, if a conclusion may be drawn from what passes under the review of any person who has occasion to receive silver in exchange, must considerably exceed *one million sterling !* To this we have the miserable prospect of an accession every year, until some effectual steps shall be taken to remedy the evil.

Of the Copper Coinage, the quantity of counterfeits at one time in circulation might be truly said to equal three fourth parts of the whole, and nothing is more certain than that a very great proportion of the actual counterfeits passed as Mint halfpence, from their size and appearance, although they yielded the coiners a large profit.

Even at present the state both of the silver and copper coinage of this kingdom (the copper pence only excepted) deserves very particular attention, for at no time can any person minutely examine either the one coin or the other, which may come into his possession, without finding a considerable proportion counterfeit.

Until, therefore, a new coinage of halfpence and farthings takes place upon the excellent plan adopted by Government, with respect to the pence now partially in circulation, what must be the situation of the retail dealers, the brewers, distillers, and many other classes of industrious traders, who in the course

of

of their business are compelled to receive depreciated counterfeit money ?*

The burden is not only grievous beyond expression, to those who have no alternative but to take such base money in payment; but extends indirectly to *the Poor :* in as much as the diminished value of such coin, arising from its reduced or base quality, taken in connection with the quantities thrown into circulation, tends to enhance the price of the first articles of necessity.

The labourer, the handicraftsman, and the working manufacturer, being generally paid their weekly wages, partly in copper money of depreciated value; —it is obvious that they must obtain less than they would otherwise receive, were the coin of a higher standard; for the retail dealers who furnish the poor with food, must shield themselves, at least in part,

* It is a curious fact, that although the number of Pence which have been supplied by that admirable Artist, Mr. Boulton, of Birmingham, and which have been actually circulated, amounts to Forty Million of Pieces, making 166,666*l*. 12*s*. 4*d*. sterling, and which is equal to 4*d*. for every inhabitant of this Island, according to the largest computation : yet the quantity of halfpence (chiefly counterfeits) which are found in actual circulation, are at least in the proportion of forty to one. This must ever be the case until some expedient, such as is hereafter recommended, shall be adopted for calling them in, and substituing in their place a new Coinage of the full standard weight: For it is evident that the Dealers and Tradesmen at present hoard up the penny pieces, and only circulate the counterfeit halfpence which they receive; the nuisance therefore remains, and the coiners are thus encouraged to continue their nefarious practices.

against

against the unavoidable losses arising from base money, by advancing the prices of their various commodities.

Nor are such advances made upon a principle which cannot be defended ; since it is evident that the relative value *even of the old copper coin of the Mint* to gold or silver, is nearly *twice its intrinsic value* ; and while such copper money cannot be paid into the receipt of his Majesty's Exchequer, or received in payment by the officers of the revenue, the burden and loss of a diminished coin fall entirely upon the traders, (who are compelled to receive such money,) and upon the labourers and mechanics through whose medium it is chiefly circulated.

While the disproportion thus stated between the denominative value of copper and silver money is so very great, it is evident that the legal coinage of copper must produce an immense profit ; as *one pound* of copper estimated at 15 *pence* * will make as many halfpence, of the legal coinage, as pass for *two shillings.*

This fact plainly shews the vast temptation which is held out to those who carry on the counterfeit coin-age, where the profit from the coiner to the dealers, and from these dealers to the utterers, at the full de-

---

* A few years ago sheet-copper was as low as 11½d. a pound, and will probably be again at the same price on the return of Peace. Indeed it has been even lower, although it has recently very much advanced in price.

nominative

nominate value, must be in many instances from two to three hundred per cent. When to this circumstance is added the security which the deficiencies in the present laws hold out, the whole operates as a kind of bounty to these fraudulent people, who cannot resist the prosecution of a trade where the profit is so immense, and where a coinage equally *pure and heavy* as the old mint standard would even be extremely productive.*

In every view the evil at present arising from base money of every denomination appears to be of the greatest magnitude—while its extent will scarce be credited by any but those who have turned their attention very minutely to the subject.

The trade of dealing in counterfeit coin acquires its greatest vigour towards the end of March; for then the Lotteries are over, when *Swindlers, Gamblers, Pretended Dealers in Horses, Travellers with E O Tables,* and *Hawkers,* and *Pedlars* go into the country, carrying with them considerable quantities of base silver and copper money; by which they are enabled, in a great degree, to extend the circulation, by cheating and defrauding ignorant country people.

---

* This observation does not apply to Mr. Boulton's New Copper Coinage; for although some feeble attempts have been made to counterfeit it, these can never go to a great extent, from its not being a sufficient object of profit; besides the fraud is easily detected, since each penny weighs an exact ounce: of course the halfpence should weigh half an ounce, and the farthings one quarter of an ounce, when these last two denominations are brought into circulation; as it is expected they will be.

In

In the spring season too, the dealers in counterfeit coin begin to make up their orders for the different country towns; and it is supposed, upon good grounds, that there is now scarcely a place of any consequence all over the kingdom where they have not their correspondents; it is also a fact well established, that many of these correspondents come regularly to the *Metropolis*, and also go to Birmingham and the neighbouring towns once or twice a year for the purpose of purchasing base money, where the evil is said to be increasing even more than in London.

It very seldom happens, on account of the great demand, (especially of late years) that the dealers have ever any considerable stock on hand. The base money is no sooner finished, than it is packed up and sent to customers in town and country; and with such rapidity has it been fabricated, on occasions of pressing emergency, that a single dealer has been known to procure from the coiners who worked for him, from 300l. to 500l. for country orders, in the course of the week!

The lower ranks among the Irish, and the German Jews, are the chief supporters of the trade of circulating base money in London;—there is said to be scarce an Irish labourer who does not exchange his week's wages for base money, taking a mixture of shillings, sixpences, and copper.

The Jews principally confine themselves to the
coinage

coinage and circulation of copper; while the Irish women are the chief utterers and colourers of base silver.   A vast number of these low females have acquired the mischievous art of colouring the bad shillings and sixpences, which they purchase from the employers of Jew-boys, who cry *bad shillings*.

It is somewhat singular that among the Jews, although many cases occur where they appear to be coiners of copper money and dealers to a great extent, yet scarce an instance can be adduced of their having any concern in the coinage of base silver: neither are they extensive dealers in any other base money than copper.

The Jews, however, deal largely in foreign coin, counterfeited in this country; having been the chief means by which *Louis d'Ors*, *Half Johannas*, as well as various silver coins, (particularly *Dollars*) made of base metal, have been sent out of this country. It is through the same channel that the Sequins of Turkey have been exported; and also the Pagodas of India.*

In contemplating and in developing the causes of the vast accumulation and increase of base money, which has thus deluged the country of late years, the evil will be found to have proceeded chiefly from the want of *a new coinage :—of laws, applicable to the new tricks and devices practised by the coiners :—of proper checks upon fraudulent Circulation :—of rewards for*

* See ante, p. 17, 18.

the

the detection and apprehension of Offenders ;—and of a sufficient fund to ensure the prompt execution of the law, by a vigorous and energetic Police, directed not only to the execution of apposite laws in the detection and punishment of offenders, but also to the means of prevention.

The vigor and energy requisite to put good and apposite laws in execution for the suppression of crimes of every kind, but particularly that of the coinage and circulation of bad money, depend much on the zeal and activity of the Magistrate : and on the affording an adequate pecuniary resource, to enable him to reward men who may undertake to risk their persons in the company of desperate and daring offenders, in order to obtain that species of evidence which will produce a conviction. Without such pecuniary resource, the law, as well as the exertions of the Magistrate, becomes a dead letter : and his efforts for the purpose of promoting the ends of public justice, are crippled and lost to the community.

In suppressing great evils, strong and adequate powers must be applied, and nothing can give force and activity to these powers, but the ability to reward liberally all persons engaged in the public service, either as police officers, or as temporary agents for the purpose of detecting atrocious offenders. The following ideas are therefore suggested with a view to the important subject at present under discussion.

The Coinage Laws (except those relating to copper

per money) which contain the most important regulations in the way of prevention, having been made a century ago, it is not to be wondered at, in consequence of the regular progress of the evil, and the new contrivances and artifices resorted to, in that period, that many obvious amendments have become necessary. A consolidation of the whole laws from the 25th of Edward the Third, to the 14th of his present Majesty, would, perhaps, be the most desirable object; as it would afford a better opportunity of correcting every deficiency, and of rendering this branch of the criminal code, *concise, clear, explicit,* —applicable to the existing evils, and to the means of prevention.

For the purpose, however, of more fully elucidating this proposition, it will be necessary to state the existing laws, and what are considered as the most apparent deficiences therein.

We will begin by giving a short *Summary* of the existing Laws.

25 Edw. III. *stat.* 5, *cap.* 2.	These acts make counterfeiting the gold and silver coin of the realm—counterfeiting foreign money, current within the realm— knowingly bringing false money into the realm counterfeit to the money of England; or bringing in *any* false and counterfeit money, current within the realm; in order to utter the same here;—diminishing
1 Mary, *stat.* 2, *c.* 6.	
1 & 2 Ph. & Mary, *cap.* 11.	
5 Eliz. *cap.* 11.	
14 Eliz. *cap.* 3.	
18 Eliz. *cap.* 1.	

ing or lightening any current (gold or silver) coin—*High Treason.*—Counterfeiting foreign money, not current in the kingdom—*Misprision of Treason.*

8 & 9 Will. III. *cap.* 26 *(made perpetual by 7* Anne, *c.* 25)—
9 & 10 Will. III. *c.* 21.

These Acts contain a detail of the principal offences and punishments, upon which prosecutions are founded at present.

7th of Queen Anne, *cap.* 24.

Allows 400l. a year for prosecuting offenders; increased by 15 Geo. II. *c.* 28. § 10, to 600l.

15th of George II. *cap.* 28.

Amends some of the above laws, and establishes new regulations relative to the Copper Coinage.

11th George III. *cap.* 40.

Makes further regulations respecting the Copper Coinage; which, however, have not been at all effectual.

Since the last edition of this work the following additions have been made to the Statute Law on this subject.

By 37 Geo. III. *c.* 126. so much of 15 Geo. II. *c.* 28, as relates to *halfpence and farthings,* and the statute 11 Geo. III. *c.* 40, and all other acts relating to the copper money of this realm, are extended to all such copper money as shall be coined and issued by the King's Proclamation.—This was for the purpose

pose of protecting the Coinage of *penny* and *twopenny* pieces made for Government by Mr. Boulton, of Birmingham ; and which it is believed have not yet been counterfeited, at least to any great extent.

By the same statute, 37 Geo. III. *c.* 126, persons counterfeiting any *foreign gold, or silver coin,* tho' not current in this realm, are made guilty of felony, punishable by seven years' transportation ; as are also persons bringing the same into the realm, with intent to utter it.—A penalty is imposed on persons tendering *such* counterfeit coin in payment, *or exchange ;* for the first offence, six month's imprisonment ; for the second, two years ; and on the third, they are declared guilty of felony without Clergy. —Persons having more than *five* pieces of such counterfeit coin in their possession, shall forfeit the same, and also a penalty of not more than 5*l.* nor less than 40*s.* for each piece ; or suffer three months' imprisonment.—Justices are impowered to grant warrants for searching suspected places, *for such counterfeit foreign coin*; which with the tools and materials may be seized and carried before a Justice, who shall secure the same as evidence : to be afterwards destroyed.

By statute 38 Geo. III. *c.* 59, the act 14 Geo. III. *c.* 42, prohibiting the importation of light silver coin of this realm, was revived and continued till June 1, 1799.—And by statute 39 Geo. III. *c.* 75, it was made perpetual.

By statute 38 Geo. III. *c.* 67, *Copper Coin* not being the legal Copper Coin of this realm, and *all counterfeit*

counterfeit gold or silver coin whatever, exported, or shipped for exportation, to Martinique or any of the British Colonies in the West Indies or America, is declared to be forfeited, and may be seized as under the laws respecting the Customs.—And a penalty is imposed on persons exporting it, of 200*l.* and double the value of the coin.

We next proceed to state the deficiencies which still remain unremedied.

1. The punishment inflicted on the different offences specified in the Coinage Laws, do not seem to be adequate to the degree of enormity, in some instances: while in others, from being too severe, the law is not always put in execution. The sale of base Money (for instance) under the value it imports, is only punishable by a year's imprisonment; although in point of fact, it is well known, that the Sellers are the *Employers of the Coiners*; that with them this high offence originates, and but for them it would not have been committed: while the actual Coiners, who work for these Dealers merely as Journeymen, subject themselves to the punishment of Death.

2. Prosecutions under the stat. 8 & 9 W. III. *c.* 26, are at present limited to commence within three months. This may often defeat justice, as offences committed in the country frequently cannot be tried in less than four, five, and in some cases nearly six months. ☞ *The limitation to twelve months would remove the difficulty.* [There

is

is no such limitation in the statutes of 37 & 38 of Geo. III. just alluded to.]

3. The words *Milled Money* seemed necessary, in the minds of the makers of the act of 8 & 9 William III. *cap.* 26, to form the description of coin similar to the current Coin of the Realm; and that Act declares it to be felony to take, receive, pay, or put off *counterfeit milled Money.*—A considerable portion of counterfeit Coin is *cast*, and *not milled.* ☞ *The words* counterfeit Money, Milled *or* not Milled, *would remove the ambiguity.*

4. It does not appear that any provision is clearly made, or punishment inflicted, for the offence of *uttering base silver Money in exchange*, as well as in payment: except under *stat.* 8 & 9 Will. III. *cap.* 26, where the expression of *counterfeit milled money* is used, the ambiguity of which has already been noticed. The words in the *stat.* 15 Geo. II. *c.* 28. are, "any person who shall utter or tender in payment," and it seems that the word *utter* cannot be detached from the subsequent words, " in payment." [The partial remedy applied in this particular in the instance of counterfeit *foreign gold and silver coin*, under 37 Geo. III. *c.* 126, should be extended to *all* cases of counterfeit money.

5. The laws peculiarly relating to the *Copper Coinage*, although more modern, have also been found to be extremely defective, and totally inadequate to their object. The Act of the 11th of his present Majesty,

Majesty, *cap.* 40, indeed, makes it felony to sell
Copper Money of the similitude *of the current
Money of the Realm* at a less value than the denomination doth import; but the benefit of Clergy
not being taken away, and no specific punishment
being mentioned, the offenders are generally
subjected only to a year's imprisonment, which
proves no check whatever, as their families carry
on business in the mean time; and if they sell
plain or evasive Halfpence, or what are called *Irish
Harps,* or mix them with *stamped Halfpence,*
similar to the current Coin of the Realm, so that
the stamped Coin does not exceed the value of
what the denomination imports, it is doubtful
whether the prosecution will not fail.

☞ It is submitted, that a statute ought to be
framed, declaring it *Felony,* punishable by seven years'
transportation: 1st. For any person to make or manufacture any piece of Copper or other metal, with
or without any device whatsoever, with an intent that
it shall pass as the *Copper Monies of the Kingdoms of
Great Britain or Ireland.* 2nd. For any smith, en-
graver, founder, &c. or any person, except those employed in the Mint, or authorized by the Treasury, to
make or mend, buy or sell, conceal or have in their
possession, without a lawful excuse, any puncheon,
stamp, die, mould, &c. on which shall be impressed,
or with intent that there shall be impressed on the
same, any resemblance whatever, in part or in the
whole, of such *Copper Monies.* 3d. For any person
to

to buy or sell, or offer to buy or sell, or to utter or tender in payment, or to give or offer to give in exchange, *thirty or more pieces of Copper* in any one day; such piece resembling or being intended to resemble, or passing or being intended to pass as the current Copper Money of the said kingdoms.

That such proposed statute should also make it a misdemeanor (punishable by a fine of 40*s.* for the first offence, 5*l.* for the second, and 10*l.* for every subsequent offence) for any person to buy, sell, utter, &c. any number *less than thirty* of such pieces of Copper, resembling or intended to resemble or pass, &c. as such current Copper Money. The fines to be recoverable in a summary way before one magistrate. This would reach Turnpike-men and others, who wilfully pass bad Halfpence at one gate which are refused at another: and would generally check the circulation of base Copper Money, which has become an evil of great magnitude.

6. The laws, as they now stand, are silent regarding Provincial Copper Coin, or what are called *Tokens*, representing an Halfpenny. It might perhaps be useful to legalize *Tokens* or *Provincial Coins* on three conditions. ☞ 1. *That the Copper of which they are made shall be pure.*—2. *That this Coin shall be at least* 10 *per cent. heavier than Mr. Boulton's new Coinage.*—3. *That the parties circulating such Coin be responsible to the holders, for the value in Gold or Silver, when demanded: and shall stamp their names and an obligation to that purpose*

purpose on the Coins, Tokens, or Medals so issued by them.—It would be necessary under such circumstances that every person, issuing Tokens or Medals, should take out a Licence for that purpose from the principal Officers of the Mint, as an authority for such Coinage : giving security at the same time to observe the above Conditions.

It may, however, be worthy consideration, whether these tokens should not be wholly suppressed, and the offence of fabricating any Copper pieces passing, or intended to pass " *as, for, or in lieu of*" the lawful Copper Coin, be made felony : and that such tokens should in all respects be considered as actual Counterfeit Coin, and treated accordingly : or, at all events, that persons issuing and circulating such tokens should be liable to a severe penalty ; and bound to pay the holder, on demand, the full denominated value.

7. The mischievous agents of the Dealers in base Money, *the persons who keep Flatting-mills and other machinery, for preparing, and rolling their metals, for being coined into base Money,* are not at present within the reach of punishment by any existing law. Although by preparing the metal for the subsequent process of stamping, they are in fact parties concerned, without whose aid the Coinage of what are called *Flats,* or milled money, could not be carried on.—The chief difficulty is in punishing persons for producing an article which may be

be turned into coach and harness ornaments, buttons, and many purposes as well as base Money.

☞ With respect to this whole tribe of dangerous manufacturers, whose trade and abilities are so liable to be converted to iniquitous purposes, it has been under consideration to regulate them, by legislative measures, to the following effect: viz. " That no person, except those employed in the mints, shall erect, set up, or use, or knowingly have in possession any *cutting engine for cutting round blanks by the force of a screw out of flatted bars or sheets of Copper, or other metal; or any stamping press, fly, rolling mill, flatting mill, or other instrument for stamping, flatting, or marking metals, or which, with the assistance of any matrix, stamp, or dye, will stamp or mark Copper or other metals, or prepare the same for stamping or marking,* without first giving notice thereof in writing to persons authorized to keep an entry and registry thereof, containing the Christian and Surnames of the owners of such instruments, and describing the use thereof, and the house or other place in which the same is intended to be erected, set up, used or kept; and to give the like notice on any removal, under a certain penalty, recoverable as in the case of Hair Powder, and other revenue laws."—It is believed, on the best authority, that the Licence here proposed (especially as it would subject the parties to no pecuniary burden) would meet the approbation of the principal manufacturers, on account of the facilities which it would

would afford in detecting and in embarrassing those who set up machinery for unlawful purposes.

8. No provision is made in any Act against, and consequently no punishment is inflicted on, the offence of *buying base money to recolour it.*—☞ This is a modern device, and may be remedied, as it seems, by enacting—" That every person who shall buy, take or receive any blank or round piece of blanched copper, mixed metal, or metal of any sort whatsoever, for the purpose of colouring the same, or causing the same to be coloured, or with intent or knowledge that the same shall or will be coloured, or which shall have been coloured, so as to pass for the current Gold or Silver Coins of Great Britain or Ireland, shall be punishable by a fine of 20*l.* and one month's imprisonment; and that any person who shall buy or sell, or offer to buy or sell any piece of blanched Copper, &c. which may formerly have passed as or for such current Gold or Silver Coin, shall be punishable by a fine of 40*s.* recoverable in a summary way; or by one month's imprisonment."—This last penalty will reach the Jew Boys, who cry bad shillings, and will prove, it is hoped, an effectual check by means of a very mild punishment upon shopkeepers, tradesmen, and others, who inadvertently sell defaced counterfeit shillings without reflecting that although they obtain 3*d.* in this traffick for what is not intrinsically worth one farthing, that the

same

same counterfeits are again coloured, and received by them at the full value of 12*d*.

9. No existing law gives any power to Magistrates upon information on oath, to search for, or seize Counterfeit Coin of this realm in the custody or possession of *known Dealers* or *reputed Utterers;* although these Dealers and Utterers are now the persons (and not the actual Coiners) who keep the base money : neither is there any power to seize base money conveying in coaches or waggons going into the country. Under this shelter the Dealers are enabled to hold markets for sale in their houses, where they frequently keep large stocks; and base money is also sent into the country without the least hazard of detection or seizure.

☞ Here again the partial remedy introduced by 37 Geo. III. c. 126, should be extended and applied.

10. No power is directly given by any existing law, (not even by the modern Act last mentioned) though upon the most pointed information, to search the houses or workshops of coiners *in the night time.* Hence it is that *detection* becomes so difficult, and the evil increases, because the law in some measure shields the offenders from discovery. Since in Lottery offences (which are certainly greatly inferior in their enormity to Coining) a power is granted to break open houses in the night-time, surely no reason can be assigned why treasonable

offences,

offences, in Coining base Money, should not in this respect be on the same footing. Unless a positive power is given to search in the night, and suddenly to force open doors or windows, it will be impossible to detect the Makers of Cast Money.

11. The act 11 Geo. III. cap. 40. gives a power to Magistrates to issue their warrants to search for tools and implements used in the *Copper Coinage,* (with regard to Silver or Gold Coinage of this realm no such power is given); but, what is very singular, *no punishment whatever can be inflicted by any existing law* on the owner or proprietor of such tools for making Copper Money, nor upon the person in whose house they are found; and if when such search is made, there should be found only *plain* Halfpence, or *Irish Harps,* or *evasive Halfpence* or *Farthings, varying in the Stamp* in any degree from the current Coin of the Realm, so as not to be of the exact similitude, (a practice which has now for some time very much prevailed) the act in question is defeated; inasmuch as the crime of felony does not attach to offences short of Coining *Copper Money of the similitude of the current Coin of the Realm.* The Coinage of base Copper therefore goes on with impunity; because it is owing to the carelessness of the parties themselves if ever they permit the law to reach them.

12. The laws now in being give no power to seize Counterfeit Halfpence; either in the hands of the Dealers, who keep a kind of open market at their

own

own houses every morning to supply Jew Boys, who cry bad Shillings, or in those of many others in various trades, who become the channels of circulation to a vast extent without risk or inconvenience. Neither does the statute law authorize the apprehension of Jew Boys, who go out every morning loaded with counterfeit Copper, which they exchange for bad shillings.

☞ To remedy this part of the evil, it is proposed " That on complaint made to any one Justice of Peace upon oath, that there is just cause to suspect that any person is concerned in making or using, or has in their custody any unlawful puncheon, stamp, die, mould, &c. made for the purpose, or which may be applied to the purpose, of counterfeiting the Gold, Silver, or Copper Coin of the Kingdoms of Great Britain or Ireland ; or of making or manufacturing any pieces of metal intended to pass as such coin, or any cutting engine for cutting round blanks by means of force applied to a screw, or flatted bars of metal, &c. or any wash or material which will produce the colour of Gold or Silver, or Copper, or any round blank of base metal or mixed metal, or of brass, copper, or lead, so as to resemble such coin ; or who hath been concerned in buying, selling, taking in exchange, receiving, or putting off any Gold, Silver or Copper Money, not melted or cut, at a lower rate or value than the same doth import, such Justice may, by a warrant under his hand, cause the house, out-house, and other places occupied by

such

such suspected persons to be searched, *either by night or by day;* and if any of the articles hereinbefore mentioned, or any counterfeit or pretended coin, blanks, or round pieces of metal be found, the parties to be seized, and, with the said articles, brought before a Justice, and such articles may be afterwards used in evidence, and then broken, defaced, and disposed of as the Court or Justices shall direct.

" That any Constable, Headborough, or Beadle, and every Watchman, while on duty, may apprehend and detain all and every person or persons who may be reasonably suspected of having and carrying, or any ways conveying for the purpose of selling or trafficking in the same, any counterfeited or forged Gold, Silver, or Copper Money, whether the same shall resemble or be intended to resemble, or shall pass or be intended to pass as and for the coin of the said kingdoms, or of any foreign Country or State; or having in their possession, without lawful excuse, any round blanks of base metal, or mixed metal, &c. or any pieces of Gold, Silver, Brass, Copper, or Lead, of a fit size and figure to be coined, coloured, or converted into Counterfeit Money; with power also to seize and detain the said Counterfeit Money, blanks, &c. and convey the same, with the person or persons apprehended, before one or more Justices; and if the party shall not give a satisfactory account how the same came into their possession, or shall not produce the party from whom it was received, he shall be deemed guilty of a misdemeanor, punishable

nishable by fine and mprisonment in a summary manner."

13. The statute 37 Geo. III. cap. 126. (see p. 194) has restrained the evil pointed out in former editions of this Treatise, respecting the counterfeiting of Foreign Gold and Silver Coin. It is to be wished, however, that the penalties imposed on the *exportation* of such counterfeit Coin by 38 Geo. III. cap. 67, could be further extended and enforced.

14. It must be here repeated, that the great cause of the defect in the execution of the Laws against Coiners, is the want of a proper fund for Prosecutions and Rewards, and other expences for detecting Offenders.—The acts 7 Anne, cap. 24, and 15 Geo. II. cap. 28, allow only 600*l.* for the expence of prosecutions, which has never been increased for above half a century; although the offences as well as the expence of detection and prosecutions, have increased, at least, six fold.

15. The reward of 40*l.* given under the acts 6 and 7 William III. cap. 17; 15 Geo. II. cap. 28, is construed to be limited only to the Conviction of actual Coiners and Clippers of Gold and Silver; and is not allowed to extend to colouring and finishing, as well as a number of other offences connected with *making, counterfeiting,* and *uttering base* Money :—the reward for Copper Coin is by the said Act of 15 Geo. II. cap. 28, limited to 10*l.* and is by no means a sufficient encouragement to

officers

officers to do their duty. *It would be a great improvement if a liberal sum were allowed by Parliament for detections, prosecutions, and rewards; to be paid on the report of the Judges who try the offenders, according to the merit and trouble of the apprehenders, prosecutors, and witnesses; whether there is a conviction or not.*

The following rewards have been suggested as proper to make part of a Bill now in a state of preparation, for the general Regulation of the Coinage: and which is meant to include all the remedies before hinted at and pointed out: a Legislative measure which must do honour to the Minister who will carry it into execution.

	£.	s.	d.
To persons contributing to the conviction of *Coiners of British or Foreign Coin*, or *persons plating with Gold or Silver*, or *persons colouring with wash* or *materials to produce the colour of Gold or Silver*, any blanks or flats of metal, base or mixed, to resemble the said current coin	40	0	0
Convicting, &c. persons guilty of counterfeiting Copper money of these Kingdoms or of Foreign States, or colouring such Copper money to resemble the same	20	0	0
Convicting, &c. persons guilty of uttering counterfeit Gold and Silver Coin, and selling it at a lower rate than it imports	10	0	0

Convicting,

Convicting, &c. persons guilty of buying
or selling Counterfeit Copper money of
Foreign States at a lower rate than it £. s. d.
imports 10   0   0
To be paid without deduction or fee, within one
month after such conviction, on tendering a certificate to the Sheriff.

It is also proposed that the Treasury shall have
power to issue out of the Duties of Customs a sufficient sum of money for prosecuting offenders
against the Mint laws.

Whatever might be the effect of these amendments in the Mint laws, and necessary as they appear to be, it is still to be feared that until a new
coinage of Silver money and Copper halfpence and
farthings shall take place, no legislative restrictions,
regulations, or punishments, can produce an effectual
cure to this enormous evil; although, from the many
deficiencies which have been detailed, it is evident
a great deal of good may be done immediately in this
way.

A coinage of Silver money is a great State question, which may require a fuller consideration; but
no doubt can be entertained of the indispensable necessity of such a measure, as soon as circumstances
will admit.

If to a new coinage of *shillings* and *sixpences*,
should be added an extensive coinage of silver money
of the value of *four pence* and *three pence*, according
to

to ancient usage, it would prove a great convenience to the public, and remedy much of the inconvenience which arises from the ponderous nature of Copper money; while a smaller quantity would be required for circulation.

No doubt can be entertained of the nation deriving considerable advantages from having increased the weight of copper coin, so as to bring it as near as possible to the *intrinsic* value of the metal of which it is composed.

This arrangement will, it is hoped, ultimately prove the means of effectually preventing counterfeits; and the copper, being a native article produced in the country, may in time, through the medium of *coined money*, become a profitable branch of commerce with foreign nations; where even an extensive circulation may be insured, in consequence of the *intrinsic* and *denominative* value being the same, or nearly so.

This is exemplified in the policy of Sweden, where the copper dollar being so heavy as to answer to sixpence sterling, has long been exported; and forms a considerable, and even a profitable branch of commerce to that nation.

In Russia the *Three Copee Piece* is very nearly of the weight of six English halfpence, yet its current value is only a small fraction above one penny sterling;—and thus by issuing no copper coin where the *denominative* is not in proportion to the *intrinsic* value, every class of dealers who vend the necessaries of life are shielded against loss; and every unnatural

unnatural rise in the price of provisions for the subsistence of the poor is of course prevented.

This principle seems to have been admitted by the
Legislature; for when the subject of Copper Money
was under the consideration of the House of Commons, at a period not very remote, the Journals shew
that an opinion then prevailed, " *that the most effec-*
" *tual means to secure the Copper Coin from being*
" *counterfeited, was, that the denominative value of*
" *such Coin should bear as near a proportion as possible*
" *to the intrinsic* value of the metal of which it was
" formed."*

In fine, it is a question worthy of attention, whether in order to prevent clamour, and to shut out at
once all pretence for circulating any of the old Copper money, *good or bad,* after the period when Mr.
Boulton shall be able to furnish a sufficient quantity
of halfpence and farthings for circulation, it might
not be proper to consider how far it would be practicable as a measure of State policy, to introduce a
clause into the proposed Bill, empowering the Treasury, within a given time, to receive all the old
Copper Coin, good and bad, at a certain price per
ton, allowing a *bonus* to the honest holders of it of
20 per cent. above the current price of Copper.—
This would at once clear the country of counterfeit
halfpence and farthings, and would reconcile the
holders to the loss; while the pecuniary sacrifice to

---

* Journal, House of Commons, Vol. xviii. p. 178.

Government

Government would be more than compensated an hundred-fold by a compleat and instant renovation of this species of coinage.—As the chief part of the bad halfpence are good copper, they could be re-coined, or sold, as might appear most beneficial.

It is earnestly to be hoped that the further regulations proposed will be adopted; and followed up, by an extensive coinage of Silver money, so as to shield the honest part of the community against a system of fraud, rapid beyond all example in its growth, and unparalleled as to its extent.*

Certain it is, that base money contributes more to the support as well as to the *increase* of the number of those mischievous and abandoned members of the community, who exist *wholly* by different kinds of fraud, than any other device which they pursue to enable them to live in their present state of idleness and debauchery, and to indulge in luxury and extravagance.

The increase is certainly astonishing, since it is known that in London and the Country, there were some time since, fifty-four actual Coiners, and fifty-six large Dealers, besides, at least, ten Die sinkers, whose *names, characters,* and pursuits, were perfectly known; but these bear no proportion to the horde

* It was suggested in a former edition of this work, that a coinage of *seven shilling* pieces of *gold* would be of great utility.— The expedient was adopted by Government at the end of the year 1797.

of

of smaller dealers and utterers of base money in the Metropolis, and in most of the commercial and manufacturing towns in the kingdom. Their numbers must amount to several thousands. From being at present nuisances to society, in the constant habit of defrauding the Public, they might be rendered (through the application of the remedies proposed) useful members of the State; by changing a life of idleness and crimes, for a course of useful labour and industry.

CHAP.

CHAP. VIII.

The magnitude of the Plunder of Merchandize and Naval Stores on the River Thames.—The wonderful extent and value of the Floating Property, laden and unladen in the Port of London in the course of a year. —Reasons assigned for the rise and progress of the excessive Pillage which had so long afflicted the Trade of the River Thames.—The modes pursued in committing Depredations as the result of a regular System, which had been established through the medium of various classes of Criminal Delinquents, denominated—River Pirates—Night Plunderers— Light Horsemen—Heavy Horsemen—Game Watermen—Game Lightermen—Mudlarks—Game Officers of the Revenue—And Copemen, or Receivers of Stolen Property.—The devices practised by each Class in carrying on their criminal designs.—General Observations on the extent of the Plunder and number of Individuals implicated in this species of Criminality.—The effects of the Marine Police in checking these Depredations.—The advantages which have resulted to Trade and Revenue from the partial experiment which has been made.—The further benefits to be expected when, by apposite Legislative Regulations, the System of Protection is extended to the whole Trade of the River.—General Reflections arising from the Subject.

THE.

THE immense depredations committed on every species of Commercial Property in the River Thames, but particularly on West India produce, had long been felt as a grievance of the greatest magnitude; exceedingly hurtful to the Commerce and Revenue of the port of London, and deeply affecting the interest of the Colonial Planters, as well as every description of Merchants and Ship-Owners concerned in the Trade of the River Thames.

The subject of this Chapter will therefore be chiefly confined to a detail of the causes, which produced these extraordinary and extensive depredations, and the various means by which they were perpetrated; and also to the remedies which have been successfully applied since the publication of the preceding editions of this Work, for the purpose of reducing within bounds, and keeping in check, this enormous and growing evil; for certain it is, that previous to the establishment of the Marine Police System, in the Month of July 1798, the increase had been regular and progressive, while the easy manner in which this species of property was obtained, generated an accession of plunderers every year.

To those whose habits of life afford no opportunities of attending to subjects of this nature, the details which are now to be given will appear no less novel than extraordinary; and with respect to the extent of the mischief in some instances perhaps incredible.

credible. The West India Planters alone have estimated their losses by depredations upon the River
and in the Warehouses at the enormous sum of
250,000*l.* a year. It cannot be unreasonable then
to suppose, that the extent of the plunder on the
other branches of Commerce, which form nearly
5-6th parts of the whole value of Imports and Exports, could not be less than 250,000*l.* more, mák-
ing an aggregate upon the whole of Half a Million
sterling* !

Surprising as this may appear at first view, yet
when, by a cool investigation of the subject, it comes
to be measured by the scale of the astonishing Commerce which centers in the port of London, (according to the annexed Abstract) and the vast extent of
Floating Property moving constantly upon the River
Thames, and the adjacent Wharfs and Quays subject to depredations ; when by calculation it is also
found, that the whole amount of the aggregate plunder, great and extensive as it appears to be, does not
much exceed *three quarters per cent.* on the value of
the whole property exposed to danger: the Reader
will be reconciled to an estimate, which from the
elucidations contained in this chapter, will ultimately
appear by no means to be exaggerated.

* For a specific Estimate of the plunder on all branches of
trade carried on to and from the port of London, see " A Treatise on the Commerce and Police of the River Thames: with a
summary View of the Laws of Shipping and Navigation:" by
the Author of this Work.

RECAPITULATION.

RECAPITULATION.

	Ships and Vessels.	Tonnage
Foreign and Coasting Trade as stated in the foregoing Table - - -	13,268	1,773,326
Value of Merchandize imported - -	30,957,421 8 2	
Value of Merchandize exported - -	29,640,568 4 6	
Total imported and exported	60,597,989 12 8	

To which add the Local Trade within the limits of the Port, in the Upper and Lower Thames, and the River Lea 235,000 0 0

With a view to give the mind of the Reader a competent idea of the whole of the property upon the River Thames, which is exposed to hazard, the following estimate is added, viz.—

1. Value of the Hull, Tackle, Apparel and Stores of 2144 British, and Coasting vessels, trading to the port of London, without including, as above, the repeated voyages - - - - -   8,825,000 0 0

2. Value of the Hull, Tackle, and Stores of 3507 Lighters, Barges, Punts, Hoys, Sloops, &c. employed in the Trade of the Thames, River Lea, &c. 350,000 0 0

3. Value of 3349 Wherries, Bumboats, and Police Boats employed on the River, &c. - - - - - - - -   25,000 0 0

70,032,989 12 8

4. Value of Goods, including Coals, exposed in Craft and upon the Quays, to the risque of pillage on an average each day in the year: (Exclusive of the Public Arsenals, Ships of War, Gunboats, Transports, and Hoys, for conveying Navy, Victualling, and Ordnance Stores, nearly equal to five Millions more) 235,000 0 0

General Total   70,267,989 12 8

Let

Let the mind only contemplate this proud view of the Commerce of a Single River, unparalleled in point of extent and magnitude in the whole world; where 13,444 ships and vessels discharge and receive in the course of a year above three *Millions of Packages*, many of which contain very valuable articles of merchandize, greatly exposed to depredations, not only from the criminal habits of many of the aquatic labourers and others who are employed, but from the temptations to plunder, arising from the confusion unavoidable in a crowded port, and the facilities afforded in the disposal of stolen property.—It will then be easily conceived, that the plunder must have been excessive, especially where from its analogy to smuggling, at least in the conceptions of those who are implicated: and from its gradual increase, the culprits seldom were restrained by a sense of the moral turpitude of the offence; and where for want of a *Marine Police* applicable to the object, no means existed whereby offenders could be detected on the River. *

The

* While every thing connected with the present state of Europe, and the whole Commercial world, appears favourable for the accomplishment of the aggrandisement of the port of London, by the establishment of Docks (already in part adopted by the Legislature) and by a general Warehousing System, there is no opinion more erroneous and delusive than that which supposes that arrangements of this kind will supercede the necessity of a Police for the protection of the trade, and for the preservation of the public peace within these extensive repositories.

In what manner are from two to three thousand labourers, who must be frequently employed at the same time within these Docks,

(and

The fact is, that the system of River depredations grew, and ramified as the Commerce of the Port of London advanced, until at length it assumed the different forms, and was conducted by the various classes of delinquents, whose nefarious practices are now to be explained under their respective heads.

1st. *River Pirates.*—This class was generally composed of the most desperate and depraved characters,

(and those too of a class that have been accustomed to plunder, and are not restrained by any sense of the turpitude of the action) to be over-awed and controlled, if no Police shall be conceived necessary?

The risk would be immense to commercial property and pillage, in spite of the gates, and every precaution which could be taken, would probably be as extensive as it has been from the Warehouses, or from his Majesty's Dock Yards, where the want of an appropriate Police has been the cause of many abuses.

Police as recently exemplified, is quite a new science in political œconomy, not yet perfectly understood; it operates as a restraint of the most powerful kind upon all delinquents who would be restrained by nothing else. To the system of vigilance which pervades the criminal actions of labourers upon the River, joined to the imminent danger of detection, is to be attributed the general success of the Marine Police, in preventing depredations.

Wherever a proper Police attaches, good order and security will prevail; where it does not, confusion, irregularity, outrages, and crimes must be expected; wherever great bodies of aquatic labourers are collected together, risk of danger from turbulent behaviour, will be greater in proportion to the number of depraved characters, who, from being collected in one spot, may hatch mischief, and carry it into effect much easier in Docks than on the River. A Police only can counteract this; and to the same preventive system will the commerce of the Port be indebted for securing both the Docks and the Pool againts Conflagration. In fine, under every circumstance where Property is exposed, a preventive Police must be resorted to, in order to be secure.

who

who followed aquatic pursuits. Their attention was principally directed to ships, vessels, and craft in the night, which appeared to be unprotected; and well authenticated instances of their audacity are recounted, which strongly prove the necessity of a vigorous and energetic Police. Among many other nefarious exploits performed by these miscreants, the following may suffice to shew to what extent their daring and impudent conduct carried them.

An American vessel lying at East-lane Tier was boarded in the night, while the Captain and crew were asleep, by a gang of River Pirates, who actually weighed the ship's anchor, and hoisted it into their boat with a complete new cable, with which they got clear off.—The Captain hearing a noise, came upon deck at the moment the villains had secured their booty, with which they actually rowed away in his presence, impudently telling him, they had taken away his anchor and cable, and bidding him good morning. Their resources afforded them means of immediate concealment. No Police then existed upon the River, and his property was never recovered.

A similar instance of atrocity occurred about the same time, where the bower anchor of a vessel from Guernsey was weighed, and, with the cable, plundered and carried off in the same manner.

Although only these two instances of extraordinary audacity are specified, others equally bold and daring could be adduced if the limits of this Work would admit of it. When vessels first arrive in the

river

river, particularly those from the West Indies, they are generally very much lumbered. Ships in this situation were considered as the harvest of the River Pirates, with whom it was a general practice to cut away bags of *Cotton, Cordage, Spars, Oars,* and other articles from the quarter of the vessels, and to get clear off, even in the day time as well as in the night. Before a Police existed upon the River all classes of aquatic labourers having been themselves more or less implicated in the same species of criminality generally connived at the delinquency of each other, and hence it followed, that few or none were detected while afloat, and the evil became so extensive.

It was frequently the practice of these River Pirates to go armed, and in sufficient force to resist, and even to act offensively if they met with opposition.— Their depredations were extensive among craft wherever valuable goods were to be found; but they diminished in number after the commencement of the war; and now since the establishment of the Marine Police they have almost totally disappeared.

On the return of peace, however, if a system of watchful energy is not maintained, these miscreants must be expected (as on former occasions on the termination of wars) to renew their iniquitous depredations in great force, as numbers of depraved characters may then be expected to be discharged from the Army and Navy.

2d. *Night Plunderers.*—These were composed chiefly of the most depraved class of watermen, who associated

associated together in gangs of four or five in number ; for the purpose of committing depredations on the cargoes of lighters and other craft employed in conveying goods to the quays and wharfs. Their practice was to associate themselves with one or more of the watchmen who were employed to guard these lighters while cargoes were on board, and by the connivance of these faithless guardians of the night, to convey away in lug boats every portable article of merchandize, to which, through this medium, they often had too easy access.

These corrupt watchmen did not always permit the lighters under their own charge to be pillaged.— Their general practice was, to point out to the leader of the gang those lighters that were without any guard, and lay near their own, and which, on this account, might be easily plundered. An hour was fixed on for effecting the object in view. The Receiver (generally a man of some property) was applied to, to be in readiness at a certain hour before day-light to warehouse the goods. A lug boat was seized on for the purpose. The articles were removed into it out of the lighter, and conveyed to a landing place nearest the warehouse of deposit. The watchmen in the streets leading to this warehouse were bribed to connive at the villainy, often under pretence that it was a smuggling transaction, and thus the object was effected.

In this precise manner was a quantity of ashes and hemp conveyed in 1798, to the house of an opulent Receiver.

Receiver.   Several other cargoes of hemp, obtained
in the same manner, were conveyed up the river, and
afterwards carted in the day time to the repositories
of the purchaser, till by the vigilance of the Police
Boats, a detection took place, and the whole scene
of mischief was laid open.

This species of depredation went to a great extent,
and when it was considered that the very men who
were appointed to guard property in this situation
were themselves associates in the criminality, and
participated in the profit arising from the booty; and
that matters were so arranged as to secure the connivance of all those who were appointed to situations,
with a view to detect and apprehend delinquents; it
ceases to be a matter of wonder, that the plunder
in this particular line was excessive.

In many instances where goods could not be plundered through the connivance of watchmen, it was
no uncommon thing to cut lighters adrift, and to
follow them to a situation calculated to elude discovery where the pillage commenced.   In this manner
have whole lighter loads even of coals been discharged at obscure landing places upon the river,
and carted away during the night.

Even the article of Tallow from Russia, which, from
the unwieldiness of the packages, appears little liable to
be an object of plunder, has not escaped the notice
of these offenders; large quantities have been stolen,
and an instance has been stated to the Author, where a
lighter loaded with this article was cut from a ship in
the

the Pool, and found next morning with six large casks of tallow stolen, and two more broken open, and the chief part plundered and carried away. In short, while the river remained unprotected nothing escaped these marauders.

3d. *Light-Horsemen*, or Nightly Plunderers of West India ships.—This class of depredators for a long period of time had carried on their nefarious practices with impunity, and to an extent in point of value, that almost exceeds credibility; by which the West India planters and merchants sustained very serious and extensive losses.

The practice seems to have originated in a connection which was formed between the Mates of West India ships * and the criminal Receivers, residing near the river, who were accustomed to assail them under the pretence of purchasing what is called *sweepings*, or in other words, the spillings or drainings of sugars, which remained in the hold and between the decks after the cargo was discharged. These sweepings were claimed as a perquisite by a certain proportion of the Mates, contrary to the repeated and express rules established by the Committee of Merchants, who early saw the evils to which such indulgences would lead, and in vain attempted to prevent it. The connivance, however, of the Revenue officers became necessary to get these sweepings on

---

* It is not here meant to criminate all the Mates of ships in this trade; for a large proportion are known to be men worthy of the trust reposed in them.

shore,

shore, and the quantity of spillings were gradually increased year after year by fraudulent means, for the
purpose of satisfying the rapacity of all whose assistance and collusion was found necessary to obtain
the object in view.

The connection thus formed, and the necessary
facilities obtained, from the sale of sweepings, recourse
was at length had to the disposal of as much of the
cargo as could be obtained by a licence to nightly
plunderers, composed of Receivers, Coopers, Watermen, and Aquatic Labourers, who having made a
previous agreement with the Mate and Revenue
Officers, were permitted, on paying from thirty to
fifty guineas, to come on board in the night,—to open
as many hogsheads of sugar as were accessible,—and
to plunder without controul. For this purpose, a
certain number of bags dyed black, and which went
under the appellation of *Black Strap*, were provided.
—The Receivers, Coopers, Watermen, and Lumpers,
went on board at the appointed time, for all these
classes were necessary. The hogsheads of sugar and
packages of coffee, &c. were opened ; the black bags
were filled with the utmost expedition and carried to
the Receivers, and again returned to be refilled until
daylight, or the approach of it, stopped the pillage
for a few hours. On the succeeding night the depredations were again renewed ; and thus, on many
occasions, from fifteen to twenty hogsheads of sugar
and a large quantity of coffee, and also in some instances rum (which was removed by means of a small
pump

pump called a Jigger, and filled into bladders with nozzels, were plundered in a single ship, in addition to the excessive depredations which were committed in the same ships by the Lumpers or labourers who were employed during the day in the discharge of the cargo.—Instances have been adduced, and judicially proved, of various specific ships having been plundered in an excessive degree in this manner; and it has been estimated upon credible authority, that previous to the establishment of the Marine Police, above one-fifth of the whole fleet suffered by nightly plunder.—The ships subject to this species of depredation were generally known from the characters of the Mates or Revenue Officers who were on board, and were denominated *Game Ships*, where the aquatic labourers, called Lumpers, would on every occasion agree to work without wages, and even solicit their employers to be preferred on these terms, trusting to a general licence to plunder for their remuneration.

This nefarious traffic had long been reduced to a regular system. The mode of negociation necessary to obtain all the requisite advantages for carrying into execution these iniquitous designs, was not only perfectly understood, but in most cases, where new Officers were to be practised upon, a plan of seduction was resorted to which seldom failed to succeed, when one or more of the old practitioners in this species of criminality happened to be stationed in the ship.—In this particular line of aquatic depredations (which certainly was the most mischievous,) scenes

of

of iniquity have been developed, which, from their extent and magnitude, could not have been credited had they stood on any other foundation than that of regular judicial proofs.

4th.—*Heavy Horsemen*, otherwise denominated Lumpers of the most criminal class, who generally selected ships where plunder was most accessible, either from the criminal connivance of the Mates and Revenue Officers, in permitting nightly plunder, or from the carelessness or inattention of these Officers.

This class, many of whom occasionally assisted in the depredations committed during the night, were exceedingly audacious and depraved. They generally went on board of West India ships, furnished with habiliments made on purpose to conceal sugar, coffee, cocoa, pimento, ginger, and other articles, which they conveyed on shore in great quantities, by means of an under waistcoat, containing pockets all round, denominated a *Jemie;* and also by providing long bags, pouches, and socks, which were tied to their legs and thighs under their trowsers.

It is a well-established fact, which does not admit even of the shadow of a doubt, that these miscreants during the discharge of what they called a *Game Ship*, have been accustomed to divide from three to four guineas a piece every night from the produce of their plunder, independent of the hush-money paid to Officers and others, for conniving at their nefarious practices.

Long habituated to this species of depredation, they

they became at length so audacious, that it was found extremely difficult to controul them where a disposition existed to protect the cargo from pillage, and where no seduction had taken place.—And indeed, so adroit had this class of Lumpers become, that no ship escaped plunder in a certain degree, wherever they were employed, in spite of the greatest vigilance and attention on the part of many of the ship-masters.

5th. *Game Watermen,* so denominated from the circumstance of their having been known to hang upon West India ships under discharge for the whole of the day, in readiness to receive and instantly convey on shore *bags of sugar, coffee,* and *other articles,* pillaged by the Lumpers and others in the progress of the delivery of the cargo, by which they acquired a considerable booty ; as they generally on such occasions were employed to dispose of the stolen articles, under pretence of their being a part of the private adventures of the crew, for which service they usually pocketed one moiety of the price obtained.—It was by such assistance that Mates, Boatswains, Carpenters, Seamen, and Ship Boys, have been seduced, and even taught to become plunderers and thieves, who would otherwise have remained honest and faithful to the trust reposed in them. Many of the watermen of this class were accustomed to live in a style of expence by no means warranted, from the fair earnings of honest industry in the line of their profession.—An instance has been known of an apprentice lad in this line having kept both a mistress and

and a riding horse out of the profits of his delinquency.

6th. *Game Lightermen.*—This class, which is composed of the working, or Journeymen Lightermen, who navigate the craft which convey West India produce and other merchandize from the ships to the quays are, with some exceptions, extremely loose in their morals, and are ever ready to forward depredations by the purchase or concealment of articles of considerable value, until an opportunity offers of conveying the property on shore. Many of these Lightermen, previous to the establishment of the Marine Police, were in the constant habit of concealing in the lockers of their lighters, *sugar, coffee, pimento, ginger,* &c. which they received from Mates, and other persons on board of West India ships.— These lockers are generally secured by a padlock ; they are calculated to hold and conceal considerable quantities of goods, whether stolen or smuggled, which were seldom taken out until after the discharge of the lighter, unless in certain instances where skiffs attended them.—When completely unladen, the practice has been to remove to the road where empty craft usually lies a-breast of the Custom-house quay, and then carry away the stolen or smuggled articles—and it has not seldom happened that many of these Lightermen have, under pretence of watching their own lighters while laden at the quays, or in connivance with the Watchmen selected by themselves, actually plundered the goods under their charge

charge to a very considerable amount, without detection.

Nor does it appear that the nefarious practices of these Lightermen have been confined to West Indian produce alone. Their criminal designs were directed to almost every species of merchandize placed under their charge; and the tricks and devices to which they were accustomed to resort, clearly evinced that their plans for obtaining pillage had long been sytematized, and that they seldom permitted any opportunity whereby they could profit by making free with property under their charge to escape their attention. As a proof that this assertion is well grounded, the following authenticated case, among others which could be detailed, is stated as an instance of the extreme rapacity of this class of men.— A Canada merchant, who had been accustomed to ship quantities of oil annually to the London market, finding (as indeed almost every merchant experiences) a constant and uniform deficiency in the quantity landed, greatly exceeding what could arise from common leekage, which his correspondents were quite unable to explain; having occasion to visit London, was resolved to see his cargo landed with his own eyes; so as, if possible, to develope a mystery heretofore inexplicable, and by which he had regularly lost a considerable sum for several years. Determined therefore to look sharp after his property, he was in attendance at the wharf in anxious expectation of a lighter which had been laden with his oil

on

on the preceding day ; and which, for reasons that he could not comprehend, did not get up for many hours after the usual time.

On her arrival at the wharf, the propietor was confounded to find the whole of his casks stowed in the lighter with their bungs downwards. Being convinced that this was the effect of design, he began now to discover one of the causes at least, of the great losses he had sustained ; he therefore attended the discharge of the lighter until the whole of the casks were removed, when he perceived a great quantity of oil leaked out, and in the hold of the vessel, which the Lightermen had the effrontery to insist was their perquisite. The proprietor ordered casks to be brought, and filled no less than nine of them with the oil that had thus leaked out. He then ordered the ceiling of the lighter to be pulled up, and found between her timbers as much as filled five casks more; thus recovering from a single lighter load of his property, no less than fourteen casks of oil, that, but for his attendance, would have been appropriated to the use of the Lightermen ; who, after attempting to rob him of so valuable a property, complained very bitterly of his ill usage in taking it from them.

7th. *Mud-Larks*, so called from their being accustomed to prowl about, at low water, under the quarters of West India ships ; (or at least that class which were denominated *Game*, these being mostly the objects of pillage;) under pretence of grubbing in the mud for *old ropes, iron,* and *coals,* &c. but whose chief

chief object, when in such situations, was to receive and conceal small bags of sugar, coffee, pimento, ginger and other articles, and sometimes bladders containing rum, which they conveyed to such houses as they were directed, and for which services they generally received a share of the booty.—These auxiliaries in this species of pillage were considered as the lowest cast of thieves; but from a general knowledge of the Receivers in the vicinity, they frequently afforded considerable assistance to the Lumpers, Coopers, and others, who collected plunder in the progress of the ships' delivery.

8th. *Revenue Officers.*—Notwithstanding the laudable severity of the Commissioners of his Majesty's Customs and Excise, in making examples of their inferior servants by immediate dismission, on proof made of any offence, or even neglect of duty; a certain class of these officers, who are denominated *Game,* have found means to promote pillage to a very extensive degree, not only in West India ships, but also in ships from the East Indies, and in every ship and vessel arriving and departing from the River Thames, of which it is to be lamented, that too many proofs have been adduced. This class of officers generally make a point of at least having the appearance of being punctual and regular in their attendance upon their duty, and by never being found absent by their superior officers obtain preferences, where such can be given, with respect to those particular

ticular ships which afford the best harvest, either from being under the charge of Mates or others, with whom they have had criminal transactions in former voyages, or from the cargo being of a nature calculated to afford a resource for plunder. They are also generally acquainted with the *Copemen* or Receivers, with whom and the other officers, after seducing the Mate, (if not already seduced) they negociate for the purchase of whatever can be plundered.

In those seasons of the year, when the crowded state of the port renders it necessary to have recourse to *extra* and *Glut Officers,* the general distress of this class of men, and the expectations most of them have formed of advantages by being placed on board ships of a certain description, render it an easy matter to seduce them; and by such means had every obstruction been removed to the perpetration of these excessive robberies, in all their ramifications, which had so long afflicted the port of London.*

9th. *Scuffle*

* In the throng season of the year at least 900 inferior Custom-house officers, and about 300 Excisemen, are stationed on board of ships in the Port of London, besides 82 Custom-house watermen and 36 superior Officers who do duty on the River Thames. The fair allowance of the established Tide officers may be from 50*l.* to 55*l.* a year. The preferable Officers having 3*s.* 6*d.* a day only when employed, are supposed to receive wages for 2-3ds of the year; while the extra Officers, who have only 3*s.* a day, are not supposed to be employed above half the year: and the Glutmen not more than two months in the throngest part of the season.

Men in such situations having a trust committed to them of great magnitude and importance, in the protection of a Revenue amounting

9th. *Scuffle-Hunters*—so denominated probably from their resorting in numbers to the quays and wharfs where goods are discharging, under pretence of finding employment as labourers upon the landing places, and in the warehouses, and from the circumstance of *disputes* and *scuffles* arising about who should secure most plunder from broken packages. This class of men, who may fairly be considered as the very scum of society, frequently prowl about with long aprons, not so much with a view to obtain employment, as for the purpose of availing themselves of the confusion which the crowded state of the quays often exhibits, and the opportunity of obtaining plunder; in which object they have too frequently been successful, particularly when admitted into the warehouses as labourers, where they have found means to pilfer and carry away considerable quantities of sugar and other articles, in which they were not a little countenanced, by similar offences committed by journeymen coopers and others, who, under the colour of

ing to more than Seven Millions, and receiving wages inferior to common labourers with pecuniary pressures upon them, arising from the wants in many instances of large families, assailed on all hands by temptations to connive at evil practices, as they relate both to the Revenue and the Individual—What can be expected from them?—Humanity, policy, and even justice pleads for an increase of salary, as the best means of preserving their morals and increasing the Revenue. Other Regulations through the medium of the Police System might be established, whereby their purity might be secured, and the Revenue eased of a considerable expence, by reducing the number employed at present, often in promoting mischievous instead of useful purposes.

sanctioned

sanctioned perquisites, abstract considerable quantities of sugar, thereby subjecting the proprietors to an accumulated loss : for, in addition to the first cost or price of the article, the duties which have been paid form no inconsiderable part of the ultimate value.   It is only necessary to resort to the Journals of the House of Commons, and the Appendix to the Report of the Dock Committee in 1796, in order to be satisfied, that the plunder in the warehouses has been excessive.   And if credit is to be given to the evidence then brought forward, and also to the affidavits of persons, who have worked for many years in the sugar warehouses, the loss sustained on an importation of 140,000* casks of sugar has not fallen much short of 100,000l. a year.†

* Sugar and Rum imported into the Port of London, from the 25th of March 1789 to the 25th of March 1799 :—

Islands.			Ships,	Casks, Sugar,	Casks, Rum.
Jamaica	-	-	151	64,108	17,279
Antigua	-	-	14	5,258	715
St. Kitt's	-	-	14	6,137	755
Barbadoes	-	-	17	7,961	65
Granadoes	-	-	18	6,806	443
Mountserat	-	-	6	2,742	568
Nevis	-	-	4	1,867	418
Dominica	-	-	14	4,152	400
St. Vincent	-	-	26	10,147	908
Tortola	-	-	3	789	109
Sundry Places, including captured Islands, &c.			106	32,739	2,271
			373	142,760	23,931

10th *Copemen*

10th. *Copemen or Receivers of Stolen Commercial Property.*—This mischievous class of men may be considered as the chief movers and supporters of the extensive scene of iniquity which has been developed and explained in the preceding pages of this Chapter. They were heretofore extremely numerous, and divided into various classes.* Those denominated *Copemen* formed the junto of wholesale dealers, who were accustomed to visit ships on their arrival, for the purpose of entering into contract with such Revenue Officers or Mates as they had formerly known or dealt with, and such others as they could by means of friendly officers seduce to their views.

Their negociations were carried on in a language and in terms peculiar to themselves; and commenced by settling the price of

Sand,	by which, in their cant language, was meant	*Sugar.*
Beans	-	-	or	-	-	*Coffee.*
Peas	-	-	—	-	*Pimento* or *Pepper.*
Vinegar	-	-	—	*Rum* and *other Liquors.*
Malt	-	-	—	-	-	*Tea.*

It was their custom to afford assistance wherever such articles were to be procured, by providing *Black*

---

† Independant of the excessive pillage by the labourers in the Warehouses, which has been rendered but too evident from the detections of offenders since the establishment of the Marine Police, the samples alone, which on an average are said to amount to 1 2*lb.* per hhd. (instead of 1½*lb.* per hhd. in conformity to the Regulations of the West India Merchants of the 12th of June 1789,) make a net aggregate of 1,470,000 pounds of sugar, which at 10*d.* per pound amount to 61,250*l.* a year!

* See the "Treatise on the Commerce and Police of the River Thames," for a particular account of these classes.

Straps,

Straps, (*i. e.* the long black bags already mentioned) to contain sugar, and calculated to stow easily in the bottom of boats without being discovered on account of the colour. They also procured bladders with wooden nozzels for the purpose of containing rum, brandy, geneva, and other liquors, and furnished boats to convey the plunder from the ships during the night.

Some of these Receivers had acquired considerable sums of money by their nefarious traffic, and were able to tempt and seduce those who would permit them to plunder the cargo, by administering to their wants by considerable advances of money which, however, rarely amounted to a moiety of the value of the goods obtained, and frequently not 1-4th part, particularly in the article of Coffee.

Other classes of Receivers purchased from the Lumpers, Coopers, &c. after the property was landed, and being generally engaged in business as small grocers or keepers of chandlers' shops, and old iron and junk warehouses, they were accustomed to protect it in its transit, from one criminal dealer to another, by means of false bills of parcels.

It would fill a volume to recount the various ramifications of this nefarious traffic, and the devices used to defeat Justice and elude the punishment of the Law.*

It

---

* For the purpose of defraying the expence of prosecutions for criminal offences upon the River Thames, and to raise a fund for suborning

It extended to almost every article imported into, and exported from the port of London. But the dealings in stolen West India produce were by far the most extensive; at the same time it appears from recent investigation, that the *East India Company* and the *Russian* and *American Merchants,* as well as the Importers of *Timber, Ashes, Furs, Skins, Oil, Provisions,* and *Corn,* were also considerable sufferers. The suborning evidence, and employing counsel for higher crimes, and of paying the penalties under the Act of the 2d Geo. III. cap. 28. commonly called the Bumboat Act; there existed a club composed of *River Plunderers,* and *Lumpers, Coopers, Watermen,* and *Receivers,* (denominated *Light-Horsemen, Heavy-Horsemen,* and *Copes*), from the funds of which the Law expences and the penalties incurred by members of the fraternity were paid. By these iniquitous means not a few notorious offenders escaped justice, while those who were convicted of penalties for misdemeanors escaped the punishment of imprisonment, and being thus screened from justice, the culprits (previous to the establishment of the Marine Police System) returned to their evil practices without the least apprehension of any other inconvenience than the payment of a fine of 40s. defrayed by the Club. The New System, however, affording means of detection in the ships where the offences were committed: what were formerly misdemeanors are now treated as larcenies, which has operated most powerfully in breaking up this atrocious confederacy, and in defeating all the nefarious designs of the criminal delinquents of which it was formed, some of whom, although apparently common labourers, resided in handsome houses furnished in a very superior style for the rank in life of the occupiers.

As a proof, among many others, of the enormous extent of the River Plunder, the convictions for misdemeanors under the Act of the 2d Geo. III. cap. 28. from August 1792 to August 1799, exceeded *two thousand two hundred*; of which number about 2000 culprits paid the penalty; partly from their own resources, but chiefly, it is believed, from the funds of the club, amounting in all to about 4000l. in the course of seven years.

Coal

Coal Merchants have likewise sustained losses to a great amount annually, while every species of goods imported have been more or less subject to depredations.

Nor has the Export Trade on the River Thames been in any respect secured against the rapacity of this phalanx of plunderers. Many well-authenticated cases have recently been developed, which prove that Hamburgh vessels outward bound, have been plundered to a considerable amount,* particularly those which were laden with sugar, coffee, and other West India produce. Outward-bound ships to every part of the world have also been more or less objects of plunder, to the numerous herds of delinquents who were employed upon the River, aided by their associates in iniquity, the Receivers.

To enter *into particulars,* or to detail specific instances, would far exceed the limits prescribed for this branch of the general catalogue of delinquency exhibited in this Work. Suffice it to say, that the most satisfactory evidence can be adduced, that the system of depredation which had so long prevailed, and which had advanced with the growing Commerce of the Port, had pervaded every species of Merchan-

* A Shipmaster in the trade a few months since was compelled to pay 40l. for deficient sugars plundered by Lumpers and others, who assisted in lading his vessel, notwithstanding his utmost personal vigilance and attention while the sugars were taking on board. A single Marine Police Officer would have prevented this. The effect of their power in overawing delinquents, from the nature of the system and the discipline peculiar to the institution, is not to be conceived.

dize

dize laden or discharged, as well as the Tackle, Apparel and Stores of almost every ship and vessel arriving in, and departing from, the River Thames.

Nor can it be a matter of wonder, that such pervading mischiefs should have prevailed when it is known, that above 5000 individuals, employed in various stationary situations upon the River, have, with a very few exceptions, been nursed from early life in acts of delinquency of this nature.

In a group so extensive there are unquestionably many different shades of turpitude; but certain it is, that long habit, and general example, had banished from the minds of the mass of the culprits implicated in these offences, that sense of the criminality of the action, which attaches to every other species of theft.

SUCH was the situation of things in the Port of London, in the month of July 1798, when the MARINE POLICE INSTITUTION, a wise and salutary measure of Government, arose from the meritorious exertions of the West India Merchants.

The object of this Establishment was to counteract these mischievous proceedings, and by salutary arrangements *in the Science of Police,* to prevent in future a repetition of those crimes which had so long contaminated the morals of the people, and operated as an evil of no small weight and magnitude on the Trade of the River Thames.

How

How far this System, *planned* and adapted to the exigencies of the case, and carried into effect by the Author of these pages, assisted by a very able and indefatigable Magistrate, and by many zealous and active Officers, has been productive of the benefits which were in contemplation, must be determined by an accurate examination of the state of delinquency, among the aquatic labourers and others, employed at present in ships and vessels in the River Thames; compared with what existed previous to this Establishment, as detailed in the preceding pages of this Chapter.

Although much yet remains to be done to prevent the renewal of those criminal proceedings, which have by great exertions been happily in many instances suppressed.—Although the Marine Police * has been unquestionably crippled by the want of those apposite *Legislative* Regulations, upon which its energy and utility, as a *permanent Establishment*, must in a great measure depend, yet the proofs of the advantages which have resulted from it, not only to the West India Trade † (for the protection of which it was

originally

* For a particular account of this Institution, see the " Treatise on the Commerce and Police of the River Thames," already alluded to.

† With respect to the advantages which have resulted in the aggregate, to the West India Planters and Merchants, from this New Institution, it is impossible to form any decided opinion; but

estimating

originally instituted) but also to the whole Commerce
and Navigation of the Port of London, are so decided
and irrefragable, that specific details are unnecessary,
especially since Deputations of the most respectable
Merchants from the whole Commercial Body, sensible of the benefits derived from the system, have soli-
cited the sanction of Government, for the purpose of

estimating the savings, on an average, at 28lbs. of sugar per hhd.
(which is only one half of what the Committee of West India
Merchants, in their Report to a General Meeting in 1798, supposed the plunderage might have been formerly) it appears,
upon this data, that the gain to the Planters, Merchants, and the
Revenue, on a very reduced estimate as to the actual importation, may be thus stated.—

	Saving to the Planters.	Saving to the Revenue.	TOTAL.
On 115,000 casks of sugar, at 28lbs. per cask - -	£.97,012	£.25,150	£.122,162
15,000 casks of rum, at three gallons each - -,	9,000	15,000	24,000
Coffee, pimento, and other arti- cles, suppose - -	5,000	10,000	15,000
Totals -	£.111,012	£.50.150	£.161,162

If credit is to be given to the general and specific proofs of the
depredations which took place before the establishment of the Marine Police, and to the numerous documents which demonstrate the
saving of property, which has been the effect of this system of prevention, the above estimate will not appear to be over-rated. In
an importation amounting to above £.8,000,000 sterling a-year, it
is not too much to say that $1\frac{1}{2}$ per cent. on this sum may have been
saved under a system of such extreme vigilance, where every class
of depredators were defeated in their iniquitous designs, and deprived in a great measure of the powers they formerly possessed,
of doing mischief. The probability is, that it has amounted to
more, though the fact never can be accurately ascertained.

passing

passing a Bill to extend the design, so as to afford the same protection to the general Trade of the Port, which has been experienced by the West India Planters and Merchants; * and requesting to be permitted to defray the expence by an annual assessment upon the Trade.

It may only be necessary in this place to state, that under all the disadvantages and difficulties attending the execution of this design, it may truly be said to have worked wonders in reforming the shocking abuses which prevailed.—*The River Pirates do not now exist in any shape.—The Nightly Plunderers, denominated Light Horsemen, have not dared in a single instance to pursue their criminal designs.—The Working Lumpers, denominated Heavy Horse, are no longer to be found loaded with Plunder.*—Watermen are

---

* At a meeting of the Committee of the West India Merchants appointed to manage the general concerns of the Trade, held on the 4th of January 1799, It was

" RESOLVED,

" That this Committee are deeply impressed with a high sense of the singular advantages, which appear to have resulted to the Commerce of the Port of London in general, but particularly to the West India Planters and Merchants, in the protection afforded to their property by the exertions of *The Marine Police Institution,* as well as by the General System established for the prevention of pillage and plunder arising out of the measures for detection pursued by the Magistrates presiding at the Marine Police Office, by which, in the opinion of this Committee, great and extensive benefits have also resulted to his Majesty's Revenue."

not now as *formerly to be recognized in clusters hanging upon the bows and quarters of West India ships under discharge to receive plunder.*—Lightermen, *finding nothing to be procured by attending their craft, are accustomed to desert them until the period when they are completely laden.*—*Journeymen Coopers do not wilfully demolish casks and packages as heretofore, since no advantage is to be reaped from the spillings of sugar, coffee, or other articles.*—*The Mud-Larks find it no longer an object to prowl about ships at low water while under discharge, since the resource for that species of iniquitous employment, which they were accustomed to solicit, is no longer in existence.*—*The criminal class of Revenue Officers, who had long profited (in many instances to an enormous extent) by the nefarious practices which prevailed, have not been able to suppress their rage against the New Police, by the vigilance of which they feel themselves deprived of the means of profiting by the system of plunder, which they had so perfectly organized, and which, in collusion with the Revenue Watermen, they were so well able to cover by availing themselves of their official situations, on many occasions, in protecting to the houses of the Receivers articles which were both stolen and smuggled.*

By means of a Police Guard upon the Quays, which forms a collateral branch of the General System, *the Scuffle-hunters and Long-apron-men, who were accustomed to prowl about for the purpose of pillage, have in a great measure deserted the quays and landing-places; while the Copemen and Receivers, finding*

ing from several examples which have been made, that their former infamous pursuits cannot be continued without the most imminent hazard, have, in many instances, declined business, while not a few of these mischievous members of society have quitted their former residences, and disappeared.

Such has been the effect of the remedy which has been applied towards the cure of the enormous evil of River Plunder.

It is not, however, to be understood that this System has entirely eradicated the pillage which prevailed, a circumstance not to be expected, since the design was partial and limited in its nature, and only intended for the protection of West India property, although very extensive benefits have unquestionably arisen from its collateral influence, and its energy, in terrifying thieves of every description upon the River, and diminishing their depredations, which, but for the dread of detection by means of the Police Boats in the night, would unquestionably have been committed.

But while it is readily admitted that amidst the opposite attractions of pleasure and pain, it is impossible to reduce the tumultuous activity of such a phalanx of individuals to absolute order and purity, who have been in many instances reared up in habits of delinquency. And while it is a vain hope to expect that crimes can be totally annihilated, where temptations assail the idle and the dissolute, and religion and morality, or even in many instances, the

fear

fear of punishment, does not operate as a restraint;
—yet is it, notwithstanding, clear to demonstration,
from the effects produced by the limited experiment
which has been made, that the General Police for the
River Thames which is in contemplation, aided by
the apposite Legislative regulations which experience
has suggested to be necessary,* must in its operation,
under the guidance of an able and active Magistracy, so far diminish and keep down the depredations which were committed, as to prove scarce a
drop in the bucket, when compared to the extensive
and enormous evils which it has been the object of
the promoters of this new System to suppress.

Although in this arduous pursuit, the Author of
this work has experienced infinite difficulties and
discouragements, yet is he rewarded by the consciousness that he was engaged in an undertaking in
which the best interests of Society were involved :—
that independent of the pecuniary benefits derived
by the State, and the Proprietors of Commercial
Property (which already have unquestionably been
very extensive,) he has been instrumental in bringing
forward a great preventive System, and by administering the Laws in conjunction with a very zealous,

---

* For the specific provisions of *the Marine Police Bill*, see
the " Treatise on the Commerce Navigation Police of the River
Thames."—The object of this Bill is rather to prevent crimes
than to punish; and where punishments on conviction are to be
inflicted, they are of a nature which, it is to be hoped, will
operate sufficiently as an example to diminish the evil, without
the exercise of any great degree of severity.

able,

able, and humane magistrate,* in a manner rather
calculated to *restrain* than to *punish*,† a multitude
of individuals, together with a numerous offspring,
are likely to be rendered useful members of the
Body Politic, instead of nuisances in Society.—The
advantages thus gained (although his labours have
been in other respects gratuitous,) will abundantly
compensate the *dangers*, the *toils* and the anxieties
which have been experienced. In the accomplishment of this object, both the interests of *humanity*
and *morality* have been in no small degree promoted: unquestionably, there cannot be a greater
act of benevolence to mankind, in a course of *criminal
delinquency*, than that which tends to *civilize their
manners;—to teach them obedience to the* Laws*;—to
screen themselves and their families from the evils and
distress attendant on punishment, by preventing the
commission of crimes;* and *to lead them into the paths
of honest industry, as the only means of securing that
real comfort and happiness which a life of criminality,
however productive of occasional supplies of money, can
never bestow*.—If it shall be considered (as it certainly is) a glorious atchievement to subdue a powerful Army or Navy, and thereby secure the tranquillity
of a State—is not the triumph in some degree

* John Harriott, Esq. the Resident Magistrate.

† So powerful was the effect of the preventive System, where-
ever it was permitted to be applied, that no instance has occurred
in the course of more than fifteen months, since the Marine Police
was established, of sufficient grounds for a criminal prosecution
having taken place by the commission of any Larceny or Felony in
ships or craft under the immediate protection of the Institution.

analogous,

analogous, where a numerous army of delinquents, carrying on a species of warfare no less noxious, if not equally hostile, shall not only be subdued by a mild and systematic direction of the powers of the Law; but that the conquered enemy shall be converted into an useful friend, adding strength instead of weakness to the Government of the country?

Such has been, at least, the result of the partial operations of the Marine Police; and such will unquestionably be the issue of the general measures which have been planned and arranged, when the *Key-stone* shall be finally laid to the fabric, by passing into a Law the Bill which has been prepared for the extension of this design to the protection of the whole trade of the port of London *.

---

* As a proof of the approbation of the whole body of the West India Planters at the General Meeting, not only of the System of the Marine Police, but also of the Bill which has been prepared to extend its influence to the general Trade of the River Thames, the following extracts are inserted:

Extract from the Minutes of a Meeting of a Committee of the West India Planters and Merchants—London, June 7, 1799.

" Resolved,

" That this Committee is fully convinced that considerable advantages have been derived from the institution of the Marine Police in checking the depredations on West India produce on board ships in the River Thames; and consequently approves of the Bill for constituting the said *Marine Police*, with powers enlarged and more effective, and on a more extended plan, provided the Act for that purpose be in the first instance limited to the duration of three years, and that the whole expence of the Institution does not exceed Ten Thousand Pounds annually."

Extract

Extract from the Minutes of a General Meeting of the West India Planters, held by public Advertisement at Wright's Coffee-house, Soho-square, London, June 13, 1799.

The Right Honourable Lord PENRHYN in the Chair.

" Resolved,

" That this Meeting confirms the Report of its Committee, and approves of the project of a Bill for the purposes, and within the limitations stated in that Report.

" Resolved,

" That Lord Penrhyn be requested to present to the Chancellor of the Exchequer the Report of a Committee of this Meeting, on the subject of the Marine Police Institution, and the Resolution of this meeting approving the said Report,

" Resolved,

" That Lord Penrhyn be requested to communicate the thanks of this Meeting to Mr. Colquhoun for the zeal, ability, and perseverance with which he has endeavoured to form an effectual check to the system of depredation which prevailed on the River Thames."

CHAP.

CHAP. IX.

Reflections on the Causes of the Existence and Conti-
nuance of the Frauds, Embezzlements, Peculation,
and Plunder in his Majesty's Dock Yards and other
Public Repositories, and in the Naval Department
in general——Reasons why the Evil has not been sup-
pressed.—A summary View of the Means employed
in committing Offences of this Nature.—Reasons
assigned why the Defalcation of this Species of Pro-
perty must be extensive.—Illustrated by the immense
Value, and by an Estimate, and general View, of
the Public Property exposed to Hazard.—A sum-
mary View of the Laws which relate to Offences
on Public Property; Proofs adduced of their Defi-
ciency.—Remedies proposed and detailed under the
respective Heads of——1st. A Central Board of Po-
lice—2d, A Local Police for the Dock Yards—3d.
Legislative Regulations proposed in Aid of the Po-
lice System—4th. Regulations respecting the Sale of
Old Stores—5th. The Abolition of the Perquisites
of Chips—6th. The Abolition of Fees and Perqui-
sites, and liberal Salaries in lieu thereof—7th. An
improved Mode of keeping Accounts—8th. An an-
nual Inventory of Stores in Hand—Concluding Ob-
servations.

Under the pressure of those accumulated wrongs, which constitute the extensive frauds, embezzlements, pillage, and plunder, known and acknowledged to exist in the Dock-Yards and other Public Repositories, it is not easy, at first view, to assign a reason for that apparent supineness, on the part of men of known honour and integrity, who have heretofore presided, and who now preside at the Public Boards, in not using the means necessary to remedy so great an evil.

This may possibly be accounted for, by the extreme difficulty which men, constantly occupied in a laborious business, find in pursuing inquiries, or forming arrangements, out of their particular sphere; more especially when such arrangements require those powers of business, and that species of legal and general information, which do not usually attach to men whose education and habits of life have run in a different channel.

Under such circumstances, it is scarcely to be wondered at, that greater efforts have not been used (for great efforts are unquestionably necessary,) to correct those abuses, which have long existed, and which have been progressively increasing; by means of which, not only the property of the Public suffers a vast annual diminution by frauds and embezzlements, but the foundation of all morals is sapped; and the most baneful practices extend even to men

in

in the upper and middle ranks of Society, who are too seldom restrained by any correct principle of rectitude in transactions, where the interest of Government only is concerned; either in the supplying, or afterwards in the taking charge of the custody of Public Stores.

When the object in view is to acquire money, the power of example, sanctioned by usage and custom, will reconcile men, by degrees, to enormities and frauds which at first could not have been endured. —Acting under this influence, it too often happens that a distinction is made, as regards moral rectitude, in the minds of many individuals, between *the Property of the Nation*, and *private property*.—While the most scrupulous attention to the rules of honour prevails in the latter case, principles, the most relaxed, are yielded to in the former.

And thus it is, that in such situations, inferior agents also, induced by example, become insensibly reconciled to every species of fraud, embezzlement, and peculation.

It is no inconsiderable source of the evil, that large gratuities are given, under the colour of fees,* to those who can assist in promoting the views of the fraudulent, or in guarding them against detec-

* Since the publication of the last edition of this work, the Select Committee on Finance in the House of Commons, who have derived immortal honour from their various and useful Reports, have recommended the abolition of fees; and the Lords of the Admiralty, and the Commissioners of the subordinate Boards, are entitled to the thanks of their country, from the exertions they are using to carry this measure into effect.

tion.

tion.—What was at first considered as the wages of turpitude, at length assumes the form, and is viewed in the light of a fair perquisite of office.

In this manner abuses multiply, and the ingenuity of man is ever fertile in finding some palliative.— Custom and example sanction the greatest enormities: which at length become fortified by immemorial and progressive usage: it is no wonder, therefore, that the superior Officers find it an Herculean labour to cleanse the Augean stable.

A host of interested individuals opposes them. The task is irksome and ungracious. The research involves in it matter of deep concern, affecting the peace, comfort, and happiness of old servants of the Crown or the Public, and their families; who have not perhaps been sufficiently rewarded for their services; and who, but for such perquisites, could not have acquired property, or even supported themselves with decency.

It is an invidious task to make inquiries, or to impose regulations which may ultimately affect the interests or the character of dependants, who have heretofore, perhaps, been regarded as objects of partiality or affection. Those whose duty it is to superintend the departments, knowing their own purity, are unwilling to believe that the same principle of rectitude does not regulate the conduct of others in inferior situations: and matters, of apparently greater importance, constantly forcing themselves upon their attention, the consideration of such

abuses

abuses is generally postponed: while those who detect or complain of their existence, seldom meet with much encouragement; unless some specific act of criminality is stated, and then it is referred, as a matter of course, to the proper Law Officers.

These circumstances, however, only prove the necessity of some other and more effectual agency to remove an evil, which (if the assertions of those whose efficient situations give them access to the very best information as to its extent and enormity are correct) *is of the greatest magnitude,* and calls aloud for immediate attention.

To understand how this is to be accomplished, it will be necessary in the first instance to develope the means which are employed to commit these *abuses, frauds,* and *embezzlements.*—Then to take a general view of the property exposed to depredation, and afterwards to examine the nature and effect of the laws and regulations now in being for the purpose of preventing these evils ; and last of all, to suggest remedies.

The abuses, frauds, and embezzlements, are multifarious, and are perpetrated through the medium of a vast variety of agencies, which naturally divide themselves into two distinct branches.

The first relates to frauds committed by the connivance and assistance of Clerks, Store-keepers, and inferior officers in the Dock-yards, and other repositories, and in ships of war and transports, in *receiving and delivering Naval, Victualling, and Ordnance stores ;*—

stores ;—in surveys ;—in returns of unserviceable stores ;—in what is called *solving off stores ;—in fraudulent certificates ;—in the sale of old stores ;* and innumerable other devices; by which a number of individuals are enriched at the Public expence; and a system of plunder is supported by fraudulent documents and vouchers of articles which have no existence but upon paper.

The second branch relates to the actual pillage of *new and old Cordage, Bolts of Canvas, Sails, Bunting, Twine of all sorts, Fearnought and Kersey Leather and Hides, old and new Coppers, Locks, Hinges and Bolts, Copper Bolts and Nails in immense quantities, Bar-Iron, old Iron, Lead and Solder, Ship's-Plank, Oars, Timber of small sizes, Blocks, Quarterstuff, Candles, Tallow, Oil, Paint, Pitch, Tar, Turpentine, Varnish, Rosin, Beer and Water Casks, Iron Hoops, Biscuit Bags, Beer, Bread, Wine, Brandy, Rum, Oil, Vinegar, Butter, Cheese, Beef, Pork, &c.*—All these articles suffer a vast annual diminution, by means of that plunder which has become habitual to a number of the inferior servants of the Crown; who have in their respective situations, access to such stores. *

This species of plunder is much encouraged by the difficulty of detection : Vast quantities are con-

---

* It is by no means to be inferred from what is here stated, that there are not, both among the furnishers and contractors for Public Stores, as well as the Officers and Clerks employed in the departments here alluded to, many individuals of great honour and integrity.—It is to be hoped, the fraudulent are the smallest in point of number, or that they will soon be so.

stantly

stantly provided, and the storehouses are generally
full; it happens therefore as a matter of course, that
the articles which were recently deposited are issued
first; and hence many valuable stores, it is said, have
remained untouched and unseen for forty or fifty
years, until a number of articles perish or become
unserviceable from length of time.—An annual inventory upon the plan suggested at the close of this
Chapter, rendered practicable by more extensive
store-houses, would remove this obvious inconvenience.

All stores being delivered under the authority of
warrants signed by the Commissioners and proper
officers, the clerks, or in their absence the foreman of
the warehouses, where the articles stated in the warrants are deposited, deliver the stores; and, if opportunities offer, large additional quantities are said to
be frequently sent out, by the connivance of the inferior officers: sometimes stores are even delivered
two or three times over, under colour of the same
warrant without discovery.

A similar System prevails with regard to stores sent
to the public repositories from dismantled ships of
war and transports.

Many vessels in the coasting trade, and even ships
of foreign nations, it is said, touch at Portsmouth and
Plymouth, merely for the purpose of purchasing *cheap
stores* :—and it is well known, that many dealers in
naval stores in the neighbourhood of the Dock Yards
are chiefly supplied in this way.

The

The plan which prevails at present with regard to the sale of old stores, not only proves a kind of safeguard to these fraudulent dealers; but is also in itself subject to great abuses, from the delivery of larger quantities than are actually included in the public sales, by which the parties concerned are said frequently to pocket considerable sums of money.*

The artificers in the Dock-yards, availing themselves of their perquisite of Chips, not only commit great frauds, by often cutting up useful timber, and wasting time in doing so; but also in frequently concealing, within their bundles of chips, copper bolts, and other valuable articles, which are removed by their wives and children, (and, as has appeared in judicial evidence, by boys retained for the purpose) and afterwards sold to itinerant Jews, or to the dealers in old iron and stores, who are always to be found in abundance wherever the Dock-yards are situated. †

The

---

* See a plan for disposing of old stores with a view to remedy the evil, in a subsequent part of this chapter.

† It seems evident, that the abolition of the perquisite of Chips would be great improvement, and prove the means of correcting many gross abuses which at present prevail. In this suggestion the Author is supported by the very able and decided evidence of Brigadier-General Bentham, before the Select Committee of the House of Commons on Finance, in 1798. [*See the* 31*st Report of that Committee.*] On a supposition that 3000 shipwrights are employed in the several Dock-yards at the wages of 2*s*. 1*d*. with the privilege of one bundle of chips each day, which, though not worth more than 6*d*. to each shipwright, actually costs Goverment 1*s*. 6*d*.

because

The Naval, Victualling, and Ordnance Stores pillaged in the Dock-yards and other public Repositories, and also from ships of war, transports, and navyand victualling hoys, in the River Thames, and Medway, must amount to a very large sum annually. The detections, particularly in the victualling hoys and transports, since the establishment of the Marine Police, prove the existence of the evil, and the wide field which it embraces.

The vicinity of the Metropolis;—the assistance afforded by old iron and store shops on the spot;— by carts employed *in this trade alone*, constantly going and coming from and to the Capital;—by the advantage of an easy and safe conveyance for ponderous and heavy articles, in lighters and other craft pas-

because good and valuable timber is often cut down to make these ships.—The following estimate will elucidate what has been stated : and shew the benefits which Government would probably derive from the abolition of this perquisite, even if the wages should be raised, which are perhaps too low at present.

3000 men, working 300 days in a year, entitled to
900,000 bundles of chips at 1s. 6d. - £.67,5000
Time lost to Government in making up these chips,
equal to 6d. per day - - - 22,500
Articles purloined and stolen, by being concealed within these bundles, and by women and children, who resort to the yards on pretence of carrying them away, supposed - - - 50,000

£.140,000
Deduct 6d. a day additional wages in lieu of the perquisite of chips; which, it is understood, the shipwrights would consider an ample remuneration 22,500

Presumed gain by this arrangement £.117,500
sing

sing up and down the River; and the extensive
chain of criminal connection, at every town and
village on the Thames and Medway, which a course
of many years has formed, joined to the ease with
which frauds are committed, have combined to render this nefarious traffic a very serious and alarming evil.

Among the multitude of persons concerned in it,
some are said to keep men constantly employed in
untwisting the cordage, for the purpose of removing
the King's mark, or coloured stran, which is introduced into it as a check against fraud; while others
(as has been already noticed) are, in like manner, employed in knocking the Broad Arrow out of copper
bolts, nails, bar iron, and other articles, on which it
is impressed, so as to elude detection.

It is scarcely to be credited, to what an extent the
sale of the cordage, sail-cloth, and other Naval
articles, including victualling stores, thus plundered,
is carried, in suplying coasting vessels and smaller
craft upon the River Thames, at a cheap rate.*

If the actual value of stores deposited at the different Dock-yards and public Repositories in the
course of a year, is to be considered as a rule whereby
a judgment may be formed of the extent of the losses
sustained by frauds, plunder, and embezzlement, it

* When it is recollected, that 9176 coasting vessels, and also
4268 traders to foreign parts, enter and clear in the Custom-house
of London, in the course of a year, independent of small craft in
the River; an inexhautible resource for the sale of cheap cordage,
sail-cloth, and every other material, must be obvious at first view.

will

will be found to be very erroneous, since a large proportion of what forms the great aggregate loss sustained annually by Government, does not arise from the actual stealing of stores, but from frauds committed in fabricating documents both at home and abroad.

Reasons have already been assigned, why many individuals reconcile their minds to devices, whereby they may be suddenly enriched at the Public expence, who would be shocked at the idea of overreaching an individual. For the purpose, therefore, of estimating truly the probable extent of the evil, a general view must not only be taken of the Naval, Victualling, Ordnance, and other Stores at all times deposited in the Public Arsenals, but also the stores and provisions on board of the numerous ships of war, and transports, constantly consuming and replacing in all quarters of the Globe ; and to measure the whole by the great annual expence, which is incurred in this necessary service, *The Bulwark of Britain, and the Glory and Pride of the Nation.*

Looking at the subject in this point of view, where the ramifications are so extensive, and the opportunities so numerous, whereby in the hurry and confusion of carrying on a most important public service, frauds and embezzlements may be committed with impunity, the question is, Whether measures are not practicable, whereby the public loss, by the rapacity of individuals, may not be greatly diminished, and what system would be best adapted to the attainment of this object ?

To

To illustrate this proposition it may be necessary to form an estimate, in the first instance, of the stationary and floating property belonging to his Majesty, in the different Public Arsenals and ships of War.— The following statement is hazarded with this particular view, not as an accurate detail of facts ; for accuracy to a point under the present circumstances is neither practicable nor absolutely necessary.   It is sufficient if it tends to elucidate and explain an important point, on the subject of the frauds and depredations committed on the public stores, which would not be otherwise intelligible or useful to the public, to the extent which the Author contemplates.—

Estimate of Floating Naval, Victualling, and Ordnance Stores, in the different Repositories and Ships of War.

Naval, Victualing and Ordnance Stores } at Deptford and Red House	£.1,800,000
- - - - - - - Woolwich - - -	150,000
- - - - - - - Sheerness - - -	100,000
- - - - - - - Chatham - - -	200,000
- - - - - - - Portsmouth - - -	1,300,000
- - - - - - - Plymouth - - -	900,000
- - - - - - - Ireland, Leith, and other parts	50,000
- - - - - - - { in the Arsenals at Halifax, and the East and West Indies }	150,000
- - - - - - - Gibraltar, Minorca, &c. -	50,000
- - - - - - - { in 900 Ships of War and Transports in Commission }	2,300,000
Total -	£.7,000,000

The

The annual pecuniary Supplies for the Navy may be estimated at *Thirteen Millions a year* during war ; of which sum about *Six Millions* may be applicable to the pay of the Officers and seamen, and *Seven Millions* to *Ship-Stores, Provisions, &c.* The last two, namely, the stores and provisions being in a constant state of movement, both at home and abroad, furnish abundant resource for frauds and depredations, which may certainly be greatly diminished, though perhaps impracticable to be eradicated entirely.

The object, therefore, is to devise means whereby this *diminution* may be accomplished : and in pursuing this important inquiry, it will be necessary to precede it by the following general view of the Laws now in being, which relate to offences committed in the Naval and other Public Departments.

The Acts of the 31st of Elizabeth, (cap. 4.) and the 22d of Charles II. (cap. 5.) made it felony, without Benefit of Clergy, to steal or embezzle any of his Majesty's Military or Naval Stores or Provisions, above the value of Twenty Shillings.

By the 9 and 10 of William III. (cap. 41.) the Receivers of embezzled stores, or such as should have the same in their custody, are subject to a penalty of 200*l.*

From this period, till the 1st of George the First, the attention of the Legislature does not seem to have been directed to this object; when by the statute

statute, 1st Geo. I. stat. 2. cap. 25, the principal
Officers or Commissioners of the Navy were au-
thorized to issue warrants to search for Public
Property stolen or embezzled, and to punish the
Offenders by fine or imprisonment.

A succeeding Act, (9 Geo. I. cap. 8.) empowered
the Judges to mitigate the fine of 200*l.* imposed
on persons having in their possession public stores,
and to punish the offenders corporally, by causing
them to be publicly whipped, or kept at hard
labour for six months in the House of Correction;
which certainly was a great improvement.

By the Act 17 Geo. II. c. 40. jurisdiction was given
to the Judges of Assize, and the General Quarter
Sessions, to try the Offenders, and punish them
by a fine not exceeding 200*l.* imprisonment for
three months, and other corporal punishment.

The Laws on this subject were further amended by
the 9th of his present Majesty, cap. 35; by which
the *Treasurer, Comptroller, Surveyor, Clerk of the
Acts*, or any Commissioner of the Navy, are empowered to act as Justices, in causing Offenders
to be apprehended and prosecuted. These powers
were given with a view to establish a greater degree of energy in detections; but experience has
shewn that the purpose has not been answered.

The last Act which relates to the protection of the
Public Stores, was made the 12th year of his present Majesty's reign (cap. 24.) and related solely
to

to burning ships, warehouses, and naval, military, or victualling stores, in any of the dominions of the Crown ; which offence is made felony without Benefit of Clergy.

A very superficial view of the above laws will demonstrate their insufficiency to the object of *Prevention*. And even if they were complete, the task imposed on the public officers, who are on every occasion to act as Justices, has proved from experience to be a measure ill calculated to attain the object in view, namely, the detection of offenders ; otherwise the evil would not have increased.—Other *remedies* must therefore be applied. It is not, however, by any single act of the Legislature, that the enormous frauds and depredations in the Navy and Victualling Departments of his Majesty's Service, which the Commissioners and chief Officers, under whose management they are placed, are so anxious to suppress,* can be remedied : This important object must

* Much to the honour of the present Commissioners, both of the Navy and Victualing, a most laudable zeal has been manifested to suppress the frauds, embezzlements, and pillage, which have so long afflicted these departments of the public service. The following copy of a letter from the Solicitor to the Navy Board to the Author of this Work, is a strong proof, not only of the sense they entertain of the evils which are felt to exist, but of the necessity of a speedy and effectual remedy being applied.—

" Sir, 　　　　　　　　　　 *Norfolk Street*, 19 *May*, 1799.

" The Commissioners of the Navy having an intention of applying to Parliament, to extend and amend the Laws, for preventing the

must be obtained by a combination of various salutary measures, calculated to afford collateral aid to specific Legislative Regulations, and to secure their effectual execution, by means which are now to be explained under their respective heads.—

I.　A General Police System.

By the Establishment of a Central Board of Police, on the plan strongly recommended by the Select Committee of the House of Commons on Finance, in their 28th Report, ordered to be printed in June 1798:—It is there proposed to bring under regulations by licences, all those classes of dealers in *old and second-hand ship's stores—old iron and other metals,* and several other dangerous and suspicious trades, the uncontrolled exercise of which, by persons of loose conduct, is known to contribute to the concealment and multiplication of crimes—Infinite embarrassments would, through this collateral medium,

the emmbezzlement and stealing of his Majesty's Naval Stores: and having directed me, in preparing the intended Bill, to attend to the suggestions and recommendations on the subject, in your excellent and valuable publication, I shall consider myself much obliged to you, as I am sure the Commissioners will, if you will, at your leisure, have the goodness to furnish me with any hints on the subject, which may have occurred to you, since the publication of your Treatise, and which you think may be worthy the attention of the Legislature.

"I am, Sir, with respect,
"Your most obedient humble Servant,

P. *Colquhoun, Esq.*　　　CHA. BICKNELL."

dium,

dium, be placed in the way of those particular
Dealers, who reside in the vicinity of the Dock-
yards, and who, by a variety of criminal devices,
while they are instrumental in doing much mischief,
have been able, in many instances, to elude Justice,
and to carry on their nefarious practices with impunity.

A Board of Police so organized, by means of Licences and subordinate Officers, as to keep the conduct of these classes of delinquents in view who, by
giving facilities to the embezzlers and stealers of
naval and other stores, are the chief sources from
whence the evil springs; and with power to refuse
Licences to those who are known to have been guilty
of criminal conduct; would operate very powerfully
in limiting these classes of dealers to the honest part
of their trade, by which infinite mischief would be
prevented.

II. A LOCAL POLICE FOR THE DOCK-YARDS.

SALUTARY as the Central Board, recommended by
the Select Committee on Finance, must certainly be
in controlling and checking the Naval plunder, in
common with the general delinquency of the whole
country, it would seem indispensably necessary,
under circumstances where the moving property is
so extensive, and where there exists so many resources and temptations leading to the commission
of crimes, to fix on some one person the responsibility

bility of carrying the Laws into effect, and of controlling and overawing the various classes of Delinquents, whose attention is directed to the Dockyards, as a means of obtaining plunder: That for this purpose, one able and intelligent Magistrate should preside in a Police Office, to be established by Law, at or near the Dock-yards, at *Chatham*, *Portsmouth*, and *Plymouth*, with an establishment consisting of *one Clerk, two House, and four Boat Constables*, with *two Police Boats* attached to each Office. One Magistrate would be sufficient at each Office, as assistance from the neighbouring Justices could always be procured in case of sickness, or absence, or where any judicial proceeding would require two Magistrates.

No establishment would be necessary for the Dock-yards, and Public Arsenal, at Deptford and Woolwich, as the great civil force, and the number of boats attached to the Marine Police Office at Wapping, when strengthened, extended, and improved in the manner which is proposed, would be competent to carry into effect the Laws now in being, and such as may hereafter be enacted, for the prevention and detection of offences in every part of the River Thames, from London Bridge to the Hope Point.

The Magistrate proposed to be established at Chatham, could occasionally administer justice at Sheerness, while the Boat Officers belonging to the Institution, might be employed advantageously in traversing the River Medway, and in keeping a watchful

watchful eye on the various Receivers of stolen goods, who reside in the vicinity of that River, between the two Dock-yards.

At Portsmouth and Plymouth there would be regular employment for the respective Magistrates, and the Boat and other Officers on these establishments.

These three Institutions may be conducted at an expence not exceeding one thousand pounds a year each, viz:—

	£.	s.	d.
To the responsible resident Magistrate -	300	0	0
To his Clerk - - - - -	100	0	0
To the Constables, 6 in number, 50l. each	300	0	0
To House Rent, Coals, Candles, Stationary, tear and wear of Boats, and Rewards for meritorious Services - -	300	0	0
Total -	1000	0	0

Towards defraying this expence, the fees which would be received, and the penalties inflicted for minor offences, under the Legislative regulations hereafter to be proposed, would go a certain length in reducing the expences of the three Police Institutions. But considering the advantages likely to result from those Establishments, were the expence to be incurred even *fifty times* the amount of what is estimated, it would in all probability be much more than compensated by the savings to the Public, which will result from the preservation of the Public property, independent of the advantages which

which must arise from an improvement in the morals
of a numerous class of delinquents, who have long
been in a course of criminal turpitude.

A Police System thus organized under the direction of a Magistrate in each situation, whose attention would be solely confined *to this one object*, could
not fail to be productive of the greatest good, especially when aided by officers, well selected and encouraged to be *vigilant* and *pure* in their conduct,
from the advantages they would derive from a moiety
of the pecuniary penalties, when offenders were
convicted, in addition to their salaries, thereby rendering their situations comfortable and desirable,
and fortifying them against seduction and connivance with Receivers and Thieves, as too often has
been discovered to take place, with respect to parochial Constables resident near the Dock-yards, by
which Public Justice has been frequently defeated.
The terror which such a System would excite, and
the extensive evils a Boat Police are likely to prevent,
can only be conceived by those who have witnessed
the effect of the Marine Police on the River Thames.

But still apposite Legislative regulations will be
necessary to give full effect to this design, and the
following heads are suggested as likely to be productive of infinite public advantage, when passed
into a Law.

III. Le-

III. Legislative Regulations proposed in aid
of the general and local Police System.

1st. That persons having possession of *New Naval
Stores;* or *Naval Stores not more than one-third
worn,* with the King's mark thereon, shall be
deemed guilty of receiving goods, knowing them
to have been stolen, and on conviction may be
transported for 14 years ; with power, however, to
the Court to reduce it to seven years, or to
impose a fine, or punish the offender corporally
at its discretion.

2d. Defacing the King's Mark, on any of his Majesty's Stores, to be deemed felony, and punished
by transportation for 7 or 14 years.

3d. The powers and provisions of the Act of 2 Geo.
3. cap. 28. *commonly called, The Bumboat Act;*
and also, the general powers and provisions of the
Thames Police Act, when it shall pass into a Law,
to be extended to all his Majesty's Dock-yards,
and to the Rivers and Creeks leading thereto,
within the distance of 20 miles.

4th. In all cases where the Crown or its Agents
shall decline to prosecute persons, in whose possession the King's Stores shall be found, any one Justice before whom the offender is carried, may proceed as for an offence under the *Bumboat Act ;* or
the *Thames Police Act* (by which maritime offences
are to be more minutely explained) and if the
party shall not give an account to the satisfaction

of

of the Justice, how the said goods came into his possession, to be convicted of a misdemeanor, and subject to a fine of 40*s.* or such other minor punishment as these Acts direct.

5th. That all Marine Police Constables (whether the *Thames Police,* the *Medway Police,* or the *Police Offices* at Portsmouth and Plymouth) shall have power to board all hoys and craft in the service of his Majesty, while employed in conveying stores, or in returning after such stores are delivered, for the purpose of searching the same; and in all cases, where stores are found which appear to have been abstracted from the cargo, or otherwise unlawfully obtained, to seize and convey the same, with the offender or offenders, (without prejudice to the service) before a Justice; and in case the Solicitor for the Crown, (on due notice given) shall decline to prosecute for the major offence, the parties in whose custody the stores were found, not giving a satisfactory account of obtaining the same, shall be convicted of a misdemeanor, and punished by fine or imprisonment.

6th. The act of having *jiggers or small pumps, or bladders with or without nozzles, or casks for drawing off liquor in hoys or craft; of throwing goods over board when pursued to elude detection; of fabricating false bills of parcels, to cover suspected goods, and defeat the ends of Justice; of having goods in possession, suspected to be King's stores, and not giving a good account of the same; of officers*

to

to assist Marine Police Constables in the execution of their duty; of obstructing the said Officers; of damaging Police Boats, to be punished as misdemeanors, under the authority of the said Bumboat Act, and the proposed Thames Police Act; namely, by fine or imprisonment.

7th. *Boats, craft, carts, carriages*, or *horses*, &c. from which stolen or embezzled King's stores shall be seized, to be forfeited, and disposed of as directed by the said Marine Police Bill.

8th. In all cases where, in seizing stores, articles not having the King's mark shall be found intermixed with stores having such mark, the party in whose possession they are found shall be obliged to give an account, to the satisfaction of the Justice, by what means he obtained the unmarked stores, otherwise the same to be forfeited, and sent to his Majesty's Repositories.

9th. Power to be granted to the Commissioners of the Navy, or any one Justice, to issue warrants, on proper information upon oath to Peace Officers, to search for King's stores, *without any proof of such stores being actually stolen, taken*, or *carried away*. The power of the Commissioners in this case to extend to all Counties in England.

10th. The Laws relating to falsifying, erasing, or fabricating *documents, vouchers, books, accounts*, or *writings*, of any kind, with an intent to defraud his Majesty, to be revised and amended, so as to apply more pointedly to offences of this nature.

11th. Persons

11th. Persons in his Majesty's service in any of the Dock-yards or Public Arsenals, having King's stores in their possession, to the amount of 5*l.* value, and not being authorised to keep such stores, to be conclusive evidence of embezzlement, and to be punished by transportation.

12th. As an encouragement to excite vigilance in Officers of Justice, it is humbly proposed, that the Commissioners of his Majesty's *Navy, Victualing, and other Departments*, should be authorised, and required by Law, to pay the following rewards for the conviction of offenders, on the certificate of Judges and Magistrates, before whom such convictions took place—

40*l.* on Conviction for any Capital Offence.

20*l.* on Conviction for Felony, punished—Transportation, Fine or Imprisonment, or Whipping, before a Superior Court.

10*l.* for Misdemeanors, by Indictment before the Quarter or General Sessions of the Peace.

2*l.* for Convictions before Justices for Minor Offences.

From such *Legislative Regulations* infinite would be the advantages which might reasonably be expected, when by the establishment of a Naval Police System, their due and proper execution would be rendered certain; and also, in all cases, where the evidence against offenders, although perfectly conclusive as to the fact, may be deficient in some points of legal nicety, by putting the *onus probandi* on the offender,

offender, and treating it as a minor offence: the ends of Public Justice will, in a great measure, be answered by inflicting some punishment on the offender, and however inferior it may be to what he deserves, it will still have an excellent effect, since it is not so much by severe punishments, as by the certainty of *some punishment* being inflicted, and the obloquy of a conviction when offences are committed, that Delinquents of this class are deterred from the commission of crimes.

Having thus traced the outlines of such remedies, for the protection of his Majesty's *Naval, Victualling,* Ordnance and other stores, as certainly require Legislative Regulations; it remains now to consider, what other measures may appear necessary, within the limits of the authority with which the Lords Commissioners of the Admiralty are invested, for the purpose of rendering the Preventive System complete.

Those which have occurred to the Author of this Work will be classed under the following Heads:

IV. *Regulations respecting the Sale of Old Stores.*

V. *The Abolition of the Perquisite of Chips.*

VI. *The Abolition of Fees and Perquisites of every description; to be recompensed by a liberal increase of Salaries.*

VII. *An improved Mode of keeping Accounts.*

VIII. *An annual Inventory of Stores on hand.*

IV.˙ OLD

IV. Old Stores.

THE mode at present practised in disposing of
unserviceable Naval and Victualling Stores by Auction, in the Public Arsenals and Repositories, is
productive of infinite evils, independent of the cover
which is thereby afforded to many purchasers, of
loose conduct, in protecting them, by means of the
certificates they obtain against the penalties of the
Law, as Receivers of stolen and embezzled goods
of the same species and quality; thereby not only
defeating the ends of Public Justice, but operating
as an encouragement to these criminal dealers to
extend the iniquitous part of their trade, by holding
out facilities and incitements to those who have
access to commit depredations on the Public Property, which possibly would never have otherwise
taken place.

The Public Sales at the Dock-yards and other
Repositories, draw together men of loose and depraved morals; who, in order to obtain bargains, do
not hesitate (wherever it can be done) to seduce, by
means of pecuniary gratuities, the inferior officers
and labourers into the evil practice of mixing superior stores with unserviceable articles, ordered to be
made up in lots, so as to elude discovery. New
and valuable cordage has been detected coiled
within

within old cables,* while frauds also are practised
as to the weight, and in the delivery of greater
quantities than are actually sold.—Such practices
have taken place in spite of the vigilance and attention of the superior officers, by which a two-fold
mischief arises,—in the immediate loss which is sustained by the frauds thus practised, and in the cover
which is thus afforded for the protection of additional
stores purchased clandestinely; perhaps from the
persons who have been thus corrupted.—An evil so
prominent, in the view of a very able and penetrating
Judge now upon the bench, as to induce him to declare publicly in Court, immediately after a trial,
where a notorious offender (as many notorious offenders do) escaped Justice, under the cover of his
certificates: " That *Government had better burn their*
" *old Stores than suffer them to be the means of ge-*
" *nerating so many offences*"—or to the same effect.

It is however humbly presumed that a remedy
may be applied without the destruction of such valuable materials; and the following suggestions are
offered with a view to this object.

---

* An instance of this kind occurred about two years ago in one
of the principal yards, where a large quantity of new and
valuable Cordage was found concealed within the coils of a large
unserviceable Cable; which composed one of the lots in the
Catalogue of the Sale.—And thus a connection was discovered
between the Criminal Purchaser and the Labourers employed
in making up the Lots.

Plan

Plan for an improved mode of disposing of unservice-able Naval and Victualling Stores.

1st. That instead of selling those stores upon the spot where the criminal connections are formed, the Naval articles shall be made up in assorted lots suitable to the *London, Bristol, Liverpool, White-haven, Glasgow, Newcastle, and Hull* Markets. That a responsible Agent should be appointed to conduct the sales at each of these *Ports.*—That they shall be men of the first respectability in the commercial line, who can give ample security for their fidelity in the execution of the trust reposed in them.—That they shall receive the stores at the yards or repositories where they are made up, and convey them to their respective Warehouses at their own expence : on having an allowance of *6 per Cent. for Freight-charges, Warehouse-rent, Insurance* against *Sea-risk and Fire,* and all other expences ; *and 4 per Cent. for commission on the amount of the Sales.*

That the said stores shall not on any pretence be sold to dealers, but only to the *actual consumers,* or Rope Spinners, to convert into small cordage ; *nor shall any certificate be granted to purchasers on any pretence whatsoever.*

That accounts of sales shall be furnished monthly, and such sales shall be accompanied by *a full remit-tance*

tance for the amount, it being always understood that no credit is to be allowed.

That at the end of each year, an inventory shall be transmitted on a specific day to be fixed, of the whole stores on hand, and a general account current shall be then furnished; in which shall be exhibited, agreeable to a form to be prescribed, a complete view of the whole transactions, which have occurred during the preceding year, with a full remittance for the balance due on the said account.

2d. That the *Metallic Stores* which are deemed unserviceable shall be deposited in a commodious Magazine in London, under the charge of a responsible Agent, competent to such a trust.— That it shall be his duty to employ proper Artificers to convert all that are capable of being converted into serviceable Stores, and when so renovated, to be returned to Deptford Yard.—And such Metallic Stores as are incapable of being converted into useful purposes at a moderate expence, so as clearly to demonstrate a saving to Government, shall be disposed of to founders and others, at the best price that can be obtained.

The Agent for Metallic Stores to be allowed 10 per Cent. on the value as ascertained, by the original Invoice, founded on a survey and valuation upon oath, and this to be in full of *Freight, Carriage, Warehouse-rent, Insurance from fire, and all other expences,*

including

including Commission for his trouble, on all Stores that are again converted to useful purposes; and 7½ per cent. on the value of such as are sold; in consequence of their being incapable of being rendered useful; so as to make it the interest of the Agent to render as large a portion useful as possible.

It is presumed that by an arrangement of this kind, an immense sum will be saved to the Public annually; who would retain the Contractor's profit in all cases where Old Stores are received back at the price of old Metal, and again returned at the full contract price, after a small expence is incurred in converting them into serviceable Stores.

3d. That in consequence of the superior resource for the consumption of *Provisions, Casks,* &c. in London, the whole of the unserviceable Victualling Stores (except sucn as from their small value and bulky nature will not defray the expences of conveyance) shall be collected in a large repository in London, under the charge of an able and intelligent Agent, who shall give proper security for his faithful management; and conduct the sales upon the principles already explained *for ready money only,* rendering an account *and making his payments monthly,* and a final Account and Inventory at the end of the year; to be at the whole expence of removing the goods from the different Repositories to the Magazine in London; to be allowed 4 per Cent. Commission on the sales, and 6 per Cent. in lieu of all charges.

4th. That

4th. That the attention of the respective Boards may not be diverted from other objects by attending to the details, which will arise in the management of those establishments, a superintending Agent shall be appointed, who shall receive the directions of the different Boards, and correspond with the local Agents.—He shall moreover be the *Receiver General of the monthly remittances*, and shall immediately pay the same as directed by the Lords Commissioners of the Admiralty.—It will be his duty to arrange the shipping of Old Stores from the different Yards, in conformity to the wants or demands of the respective Agents, so as to keep up their several assortments, by conveying to each not only such articles, (as far as it can be done) as are most in demand, but also such as comparatively fetch the best price.—He shall receive the monthly and yearly accounts, and lay an abstract of the same before the Lords of the Admiralty, and the Navy and Victualling Board respectively, as they apply to their different departments, and shall be the general medium of communication from the respective Boards to the local Agents.— The superintending Agent shall transmit a regular invoice to the local Agents of all goods shipped;— Shall keep regular books and accounts of all transactions under his charge, and shall receive for his trouble 1 *per cent.* on the Remittances or Payments which he may make, under the directions of the Lords of the Admiralty.

By

By this arrangement it will be the interest of all the parties concerned, to render the sale as productive as possible; and as the stores in question will constantly be exposed to sale, where the demand for such articles is most extensive, the probability is, that higher prices will be obtained than at present; and that upon the whole, after paying all expences, a larger aggregate sum will be received annually by Government, since, as the sales are only to be made to the actual Consumers, the Dealer's profit will make a part of the Sale Price, and will be thereby secured to the Public. As men of the first character and respectability may be expected to solicit for such Commissions, no doubt can be entertained, either of the purity of their conduct, or their exertions to sell to the best advantage. Their credit and interest, and also the emulation between one Agent and another, as to who shall make the best sales, will prove a powerful stimulus and a strong ground of security.—Above all, the plan is easy and practicable:—It imposes no trouble upon the superior or inferior officers in the different Naval Departments, and no doubt can be entertained, that while it shuts up all the avenues to fraud and peculation, which at present operate so powerfully in facilitating the stealing and embezzling of Naval and Victualling Stores, in the result it will prove highly beneficial to Government.

V. The

V. THE PERQUISITES OF CHIPS.

THE extensive evils arising from the permission granted to Artificers in the Dock-yards, to convert chips to their own use, and to remove them in bundles from the Dock-yards, having already been noticed, it may only be necessary to add, that on the abolition of this perquisite, which the Author has reason to believe is now in contemplation, a liberal increase of wages should be made to the Artificers in lieu thereof; and that hereafter Chips should not be sold in the Yards by Public Auction, but removed to a place of deposit at some small distance, and disposed of, not to the highest bidder, but at such price as should be offered above the estimated value, and by no means by contract.

By adopting this mode, the saving of *useful Timber, Time, and Property,* which through the medium of the existing practice, is *purloined, lost, and stolen,* would probably exceed any estimate that has been formed from a view of the present abuses.

This measure, while it forms an important Link in the preventive Chain, would appear to be easy and practicable.

If necessary the superintending Agent for unserviceable stores, whose functions have already been explained, could take upon him the sole management of the disposal of the chips at the different Yards, by
which

which a handsome sum might be obtained annually
in aid of the resources of the State, perhaps more than
would be sufficient to pay the additional wages of the
Artificers, while no existing arrangement in the Yards
would be disturbed, nor any trouble given to the
Officers, who at present fill the respective Departments in those Arsenals.

VI. The Abolition of Fees and Perquisites, and an Increase of Salaries.

The total Abolition of Fees guarded by the se-
verest penalties, is an important object in the preventive System: Until this is effected, it will be in
vain to expect purity of conduct. Under this pretext,
men of loose principles, in transactions with Government, seldom fail to seduce from the strict line of
their duty, *avaricious, extravagant, or indigent Officers,*
whose business it is to check and controul the receipt
and delivery of property, and to *arrange, settle, and
adjust Accounts, to form Public Documents.* The
delusion and seduction of these Officers is not seldom
effected by the supposed liberality of those whose
business must pass through their hands ; and they
are not at all times perfectly aware of the injury that
is done to the Public.

It has already been observed, and it is a circumstance much to be lamented, that in too many instances, where individuals have pecuniary transactions with any of the Departments of Government, a
dere-

dereliction of principle is apparent which does not extend to the general intercourse of society, and hence arises the necessity of *stronger guards*, where the Public interest is concerned; and nothing appears to be better calculated to counteract this baneful propensity in the human mind than *the total abolition of fees and perquisites.*

It is said to be no uncommon thing to pay 300*l.* for a Clerk's situation in the Dock-yards, where the salary does not exceed 30*l.* or 40*l.* a year; and it is known that some who hold such situations live very expensively. It may be fairly asked, in what manner a person so situated is to reimburse himself? the conclusion is obvious, and the result has been already explained, which may perhaps be still farther elucidated by stating the following fact :—

An Officer of Justice having discovered some instances of pillage and peculation going forward in the course of the removal of old copper and other articles, from a dismantled ship of war, complained to the Store-keeper in the Dock-yard, whose province it was to have received those articles into his charge, which were conveyed elsewhere.—He replied thus: " D—n " it, mind your own business—Such things have al- " ways been done, and will continue in spite of you " and me; it will, at any rate, last our time."

While the resources of Government are fully commensurate to the liberal remuneration of its servants, so as to place them above all temptations to
abuse

abuse the trust reposed in them: and while such remuneration is in itself no less politic than just, the
object and view of the Author of these pages differs
widely from this faithless servant of the Crown. The
suggestions now offered, lead to measures, which he
now trusts, to the honour and credit of those respectable characters, at the head of the different departments, are in the best train of being adopted, by the
total abolition of Fees and Perquisites, and a liberal
Increase of Salary in lieu of the reduction of income,
which such an arrangement will occasion : Such salaries as will secure to the Nation those inestimable
advantages which always result from *rectitude of conduct, zeal, accuracy*, and *fidelity*, in the discharge of
Public trusts committed to subordinate Officers. It
is by this and other wise and practicable arrangements, that a confidence is to be established, " that
" the resources of the State *will not only last our
" time,"* but extend to many generations ; while the
improvement of public morals will contribute, in an
eminent degree, to the happiness and prosperity of the
country.

VII. An improved Mode of Keeping Accounts.

Under an impression, that very few improvements
have been introduced, since the establishment of the
original System, for keeping the Navy and Victualling Accounts, brought forward by King James II.
when Duke of York ; while the frauds which have
been

been committed by various devices, prove some imperfections in the mode of accomptantship as now
practised, since no means appear to exist, whereby
deficiencies can be checked and discovered ; it may
be worthy of inquiry, whether many of the modern
improvements, which the vast extent of our Commerce
has introduced, might not be rendered useful in establishing new Checks, by means of a System of Book-
keeping, which would have the same effect in detecting frauds, and discovering inaccuracies, as prevails in
arranging and closing the accounts of well-regulated
Commercial Establishments ; adopting at the same
time in the general detail, particularly in the transit of
stores, some of these excellent regulations, which have
been found so salutary and useful in the system of the
Excise. Of the practicability of improvements of
this nature there can be little doubt, since it merely
depends on the exercise of that *knowledge, attention,*
and *assiduity,* which, when properly exerted, has generally accomplished objects, which have often appeared impracticable to minds uninformed, or not enlarged by an extensive intercourse with the world, or
a knowledge of the general affairs of life :—But as
this observation can in no respect apply to the respectable and intelligent Individuals, who superintend
the Great Public Concerns, which have been subject
to the various abuses, which they feel so anxious to
remedy, sanguine hopes are entertained, that an improvement in the mode of keeping the Official Accounts may be speedily carried into effect.

VIII. A x

VIII. An Annual Inventory of Stores.

Supposing an accurate System of Book-keeping to be adopted, and to be followed as a part of the proposed System of Accuracy, indispensably necessary, *by an annual account of Stores;* the advantages resulting from it are not to be estimated by the most sanguine mind. Independant of the benefits which would arise from the general accuracy, which would thus encircle the whole œconomy of the design, discoveries would be made wherever frauds or embezzlements took place, while the labour and expence; which such a task might impose, would be compensated one hundred fold, in the National advantages which it would produce.

———

THUS has the Author briefly gone over the whole ground, which he had assigned to himself, as comprehending every object on the subject of the depredations on his Majesty's Stores, which appeared likely to render his suggestions useful to his country, whether they relate to improved Legislative Regulations requiring the aid of Parliament, or to Measures competent for the Lords Commissioners of the Admiralty to carry into effect. In the prosecution of this task he has been stimulated in a particular degree, by the laudable and patriotic disposition, which has been manifested to promote improvements in Naval Police,

and

and the honourable proofs he has received of a desire to render his suggestions useful.

If the period should indeed arrive (and it is to be hoped it may soon arrive) when these suggestions, or even a part of them, shall be acted upon, in a manner calculated to promote the National Interest, the Author of these pages will then feel himself gratified, and rewarded by the pleasing reflection, that his well-meant labours, in placing an important branch of the political œconomy of the country in this particular point of view, have not been in vain.

CHAP.

CHAP. X.

Receivers of stolen Goods, more mischievous than Thieves;
—the latter could not exist without the assistance of
the former :—the Suppression therefore of Receivers
would restore to Society, and to honest Industry, a
great number who at present live by crimes.—The
increase of Receivers of stolen Goods to be attributed
to the imperfection of the Laws, and to the disjointed
state of the Police of the Metropolis.—The number
of common Receivers does not exceed sixty : of whom
not above ten are persons of property able to purchase
valuable articles.—Thieves, in many instances, settle
with receivers before they commit robberies :—Re-
ceivers always benefit more than Thieves :—Their
profit immense :—They are divided into two classes.
—The immediate Receivers connected with Thieves,
and those who keep shops and purchase from Pil-
ferers in the way of trade :—The latter are ex-
tremely numerous.—The laws are insufficient effec-
tually to reach either class.—The existing statutes
examined and briefly detailed, namely, the 3d and 4th
of William and Mary, cap. 9; the 1st Anne, cap. 9;
the 5th of Anne, cap. 31; 4 George I. cap. 11; 29
George II. cap. 30 30; George II. cap. 24; 2 George
III. cap 28; 10 George III. cap. 48; 21 George III.
cap. 69 ; 22 George III. cap. 58.—Observations on
these respective statutes.—Amendments and improve-
ments suggested.—Means proposed to ensure the due
execution of these improvements.

HAVING

Having in the preceding Chapters completed the proposed explanation of the various depredations and frauds upon the Public: It remains now, in the order of the plan, to examine and follow up the progress of this property, from the hands of *Thieves, Robbers, Cheats,* and *Swindlers,* to that of *Receivers,* or first Purchasers of Goods stolen or fraudulently obtained.

In contemplating the characters of all these different classes of delinquents, there can be little hesitation in pronouncing the *Receivers* to be the most *mischievous of the whole;* inasmuch as without the aid they afford, in purchasing and concealing every species of property stolen or fraudulently obtained, Thieves, Robbers, and Swindlers, as has already been frequently observed, must quit the trade, as unproductive and hazardous in the extreme.

Nothing therefore can be more just than the old observation, " *that if there were no Receivers there would be no Thieves.*"—Deprive a thief of a sale and ready market for his goods, and he is undone.

Let the strong arm of the law, and the vigour and energy of the Police be directed in a particular manner against *Receivers;* and the chief part of those robberies and burglaries, which are so much dreaded, on account of the acts of violence which attend them, *would absolutely cease to exist :*—and the resource for plunder being thus narrowed in so great a degree, robberies on the highway would *alone* seldom answer the purpose of the adventurer ; where the risk would

be

be so exceedingly multiplied, while the advantages were in the same proportion diminished;—the result therefore would be, that in *the suppression of the Receivers*, the encouragement to become Thieves and Robbers would be taken away : and the present Depredators upon the Public must either return to honest labour as useful members of the State, or submit to be starved.

Obvious and desirable however as a measure of this sort would be, it has never hitherto been put in practice. This has proceeded from a variety of causes; one of the principal of which is the disjointed state of the Police of the Metropolis, occasioned by a number of jurisdictions clashing with each other, and preventing the full operation of a proper system of vigilance and energy; which, with the aid of apposite and improved laws and a superintending agency, could not fail, either to root out all the Receivers of stolen Goods of any consequence, or compel them to abandon their mischievous trade.

These observations apply to that class of Receivers alone, who are in immediate connection with the thieves, burglars, and highway robbers;—and who aid and assist them in the purchase and concealment of whatever is stolen.—From the best information that can be obtained, their number does not exceed *fifty* or *sixty in all;* of whom not more than ten, (whose names and places of abode are well known) can be said to be persons of property who can raise money to purchase articles of considerable value.

Aided

Aided by a well-regulated and energetic system of Police that might pervade the whole Metropolis, how easy would it be to compel these large dealers to abandon the trade? The measure of watching their houses day and night would cost no great sum, and would embarrass the thieves and burglars, more than any other system that could be pursued.

It rarely happens that thieves go upon the highway, or commit burglaries, until the money they have previously acquired is exhausted. Having laid their plans for new depredations, negociation is frequently entered upon with the most favourite Receiver, who (to use their own language) is likely to be *staunch*, and to keep their secrets.—The plan is explained.—Some liquor is drunk to the good luck of the enterprize, and the hour fixed when they are to return with the booty: if plate is expected, the crucible is ready in a small furnace, built for the purpose, instantly to melt it, and arrangements are made for the immediate concealment of the other articles.— Of the nature of these previous arrangements, something has already been said in Chap. IV. on Burglary and Highway Robbery.

There are, however, exceptions to this rule, where the Receivers are not trusted till the booty is acquired: and where it is in the first instance removed to the houses of the thieves, or to those of some of their friends; but it seldom remains longer than may be necessary to obliterate the marks: for money must be procured. Most thieves are improvident; their

wants

wants are therefore pressing—they *must* sell—the Receiver knows this and makes his own terms ;—and he of course enjoys by far the largest share of the profit.

The plunder thus purchased, finds a ready vent through the extensive connections of the Jew dealers, both in this Country and upon the Continent : and from the facts already stated in the course of this Work, it may easily be conceived that the trade is not only extensive, but that the profit is immense, since it rarely happens (except in the articles of plate,) that thieves receive to the amount of above one-third or one-fourth of the value of what is stolen.

The mass of the Receivers of stolen property in and near the Metropolis (exclusive of those more immediately concerned in River-plunder, as stated in Chapter VIII. on that subject,) may be classed in two divisions :

" 1. The Dealers already mentioned, as immediately connected with professed and notorious thieves, and who are their principal supporters, especially when apprehended and under prosecution. Many of these have themselves been originally thieves upon the town, *acquitted, pardoned, or discharged from the hulks :* who prefer the trade of a Receiver as less hazardous and more profitable, than that of a thief ; and to conceal the fraud frequently set up *Chandlers-Shops, Coal-Sheds, Potatoe-Warehouses,* or *Old Iron-Shops,* and not seldom become *Masters of Public Houses,* that they may appear to have some *visible*

means

means of obtaining a livelihood. Those who have not been originally thieves generally keep shops in different branches of trade, some of whom are very opulent.

" 2. The Dealers in *Old Iron and other Metal—Rags —Old Wearing Apparel—Buyers, Refiners, and Workers of Gold and Silver—Dealers in Second-hand Furniture, and Building Materials, and that Class of Sharping Pawnbrokers who have connections with criminal people.*

" The Dealers last mentioned are extremely numerous, and amount to several thousands in the Metropolis alone, some of whom are *innocent Receivers,* not aware that they are purchasing stolen articles;—others, *careless Receivers,* asking no questions, and purchasing every thing that is offered;—but a large proportion of *criminal Receivers,* who purchase every thing that is offered *in the way of trade*; well knowing, from the price and other circumstances, that the property was originally stolen."

As the Laws now stand, (numerous, and pointed as they appear to be) it has been found from experience, that neither of these classes can be easily reached; and hence it is that they have multiplied in so great a degree, (particularly the small Receivers) within the last twenty years, and may even be said to have reigned with impunity.

For the purpose of suggesting an effectual legislative

tive Remedy, it will be necessary to examine shortly the laws now in being, which are applicable to this peculiar offence. —

By the Statute of the 3d and 4th of William and Mary, cap. 9, it is enacted, " *that Receivers of stolen Goods, knowing them to be stolen, shall be deemed Accessaries after the fact.*"

But this offence being dependent on the fate of the Principal—a Receiver, thus circumstanced, could not be tried till after the conviction of such Principal; so that, however strong and conclusive the evidence might be, the Receiver was still safe, unless the Thief could be apprehended—and even if apprehended and put upon his trial, if acquitted through any defect of evidence, the Receiver, (although he had actually confessed the crime, and the goods found in his possession, could be proved to have been stolen,) must be acquitted;—this offence also, even if completely proved, applied only to capital felonies, and *not to petty larceny.*

These defects were discovered, and partly remedied by the Statutes 1 Anne, cap. 9; and 5 Anne, cap. 31, which enact, " *That Buyers and Receivers of stolen Goods, knowing them to be stolen, may be prosecuted for a misdemeanor, and punished by fine and imprisonment; though the Principal be not previously convicted of felony.*"

This Act, 5 Anne, c. 31, also greatly improved the Laws applicable to this species of offence by *empowering the Court to substitute a corporal punish-*

ment

*ment instead of fine and imprisonment; and by de-
claring, that if the felony shall be proved against the
Thief, then the Receiver shall be taken as Accessary,
and shall receive judgment of death; but the benefit
of Clergy is reserved.*

The Laws being still found insufficient, the Statute
of the fourth of George the First, cap. 11, enacted,
" *That Receivers of stolen Goods, knowing them to be
stolen, should, on conviction, be transported for fourteen
years; and that buying at an under value should be pre-
sumptive evidence of such knowledge :*—and the same
statute *makes it felony (according to the nature of the
felony committed in stealing the Goods) for any person
directly or indirectly to take a reward for helping any
person to stolen Goods; unless such person bring the
felon to his trial, and give evidence against him.*"

But these amendments also proving ineffectual,
and not being found to apply immediately to persons
receiving stolen *lead, iron, copper, brass, bell-metal or
solder* taken from buildings, or from ships, vessels,
wharfs, or quays—It was enacted by the 29th of
George the Second, cap. 30, " *That every person
who shall buy or Receive such articles, knowing the
same to be stolen, or who shall privately purchase these
respective metals by suffering any door, window, or
shutter, to be left open between sun-setting and sun-
rising, or shall buy or receive any of the said metals in
any clandestine manner, shall, on conviction, be transported for fourteen years, although the principal felon
has not been convicted.*" Sec. 1.

The

The same Act *empowers one Justice to grant a warrant to search in the day time for such metals. suspected to be stolen, as by the oath of one witness may appear to be deposited or concealed in any house or place;* and if Goods are found, the Act goes so far as *to empower two Justices to adjudge the person having the custody of the same, guilty of a misdemeanor, if he cannot produce the party from whom he purchased, or give a satisfactory account how they came into his possession; and the offender shall, for the first offence forfeit* 40s. *for the second* 4l. *and for every subsequent offence* 6l. Sec. 2; 6.

This Act also *empowers officers of justice (and watchmen while on duty) to apprehend all persons suspected of conveying any stolen metals, as already described, after sun-set or before sun-rise; and if such persons cannot give a good account of the manner in which they were obtained, two Magistrates are in like manner authorized to adjudge them guilty of a misdemeanor, and they forfeit forty shillings,* &c. Sec. 3; 6.

The persons also to whom such articles are offered for sale or to be pawned, where there is reasonable ground to suppose they were stolen, are empowered to apprehend and secure the parties and the materials, to be dealt with according to law. And if it shall appear even on the evidence of the thief, corroborated by other testimony, that there was cause to suspect the goods were stolen, and that the person to whom they were offered, did not do his duty in apprehending the person offering the same, he shall be adjudged guilty of a misdemeanor,

demeanor, and forfeit twenty shillings for the first of-
fence: forty shillings for the second, and four pounds
for every subsequent offence, Sec. 5, 6. And so anxious has the Legislature been to suppress the evil of
stealing and receiving metals, that the 8th Section
entitles the actual Thief to a pardon, on the discovery
and conviction of two or more of the Receivers. And
the 9th Section *screens from prosecution any person*
stealing such metals, who shall discover the Receiver to
whom the same were delivered, so as a conviction may
follow.—In spite, however, of these numerous and
apparently effectual checks, it is to be lamented that
the evil has continued to increase.

In the following year it was provided by the Act
30th of George the Second, cap. 24, *that it shall be*
lawful for any Pawnbroker, or any other dealer, their
servants or agents, to whom any goods shall be offered to
be pawned, exchanged, or sold, which shall be sus-
pected to be stolen, to seize and detain the person
offering the same, for the purpose of being examined by a
Justice; who is empowered, if he sees any grounds to
apprehend that the goods have been illegally obtained,
to commit the persons, offering the same, to prison for a
period not exceeding six days: and if on further exami-
nation, the Justice shall be satisfied that the goods were
stolen, he shall commit the offender to prison, to be
dealt with according to Law; and although it may,
under such circumstances, afterwards appear that the
goods in question were fairly obtained, yet the parties
who seized the supposed offender shall be indemnified.—
Sec. 7, 8.

It

It would have been useful if the principles of the first of these excellent Acts had extended to every kind of goods and chattels, *horses, cattle, money,* and *Bank-notes,** as well as to the metals therein described. Indeed it is to be lamented, that the System has not been to look at great features of abuse in *the gross,* so as to meet every existing evil at once. Thus another partial Statute was made, 2 George III. *c.* 28, extending the provisions of the 29th Geo. II. *c.* 30, to goods, stores, or materials taken from ships in the River Thames, by enacting, *" that all persons purchasing such goods, knowing them to be stolen, or receiving the same in a concealed or clandestine manner between sun-setting and sun-rising, shall be transported for fourteen years, although the principal felon be not convicted:"* but by the wording of this Act it is doubtful if it applies to receiving goods stolen from vessels not afloat in the river.†

The next Statute applicable to the Receivers of stolen goods, is the 10th of George III. cap. 48, by which it is enacted, *" that every person who shall buy or receive any jewels, gold, silver, plate, or watches, knowing the same to be stolen, where such stealing was accompanied by a burglary or highway robbery, may be*

* Vide Page 9.

† It was held in the trial of Moses Pike, at the Old Bailey, in May, 1784, that to steal from a Barge aground in Limehouse-Dock, was not within the meaning of the Act of 24th of George the Second, cap. 45, which makes it felony to steal from any vessel or craft upon a Navigable River, &c.

tried

tried as well before as after the principal felon is con-
victed; and whether he be in, or out of custody; and
if found guilty, shall be transported for fourteen
years."

Eleven years after passing of the above mentioned
Statute, the Legislature, appearing to be impressed
with the great extent of the depredations committed
by persons stealing *pewter pots,* and desirous to punish the Receivers, the Statute of the 21st of George
the Third, cap. 69, enacts, " *that every person who*
shall buy or receive any pewter pot or other vessel, or
any pewter in any form or shape whatsoever, knowing
the same to be stolen, or who shall privately buy or re-
ceive stolen pewter, in a clandestine manner, between sun-
setting and sun-rising, shall, on conviction, be transport-
ed for seven years, or detained in the House of Correc-
tion, at hard labour for a term not exceeding three
years, nor less than one; and may be whipped not more
than three times; although the principal felon has not
been convicted."

In the following Session of Parliament, the Statute
22 George III. c. 28 (said to have been framed by
an able and experienced Lawyer and Magistrate),*
removed many of the imperfections of former Statutes, and particularly that which respected Petty
Larceny; by enacting, " *that where any goods (ex-*
cept lead, iron, copper, brass, bell-metal, or solder, the
Receivers of which are punishable under the 29th

* Mr. Serjeant ADAIR, then Recorder of London.

George

George II. c. 30. *noticed before, p. 295) have been stolen, whether the Offence amount to Grand Larceny, or some greater offence, or to Petty Larceny only ; (except where the offender* has *been convicted of Grand Larceny, or some greater offence ; when the Receiver must be prosecuted as an Accessary, and under the 4th* George I. c. 11. *may be transported for fourteen years;* see page 295.)—*Every person who shall buy or receive the same, knowing them to be stolen, shall be guilty of a misdemeanor, and punished by fine, imprisonment, or whipping, as the Quarter Sessions, who are empowered to try offenders, or any other Court before whom they shall be tried, shall think fit, although the Principal be not convicted; and if the felony amounts to Grand Larceny, or some greater offence, and the person committing such felony has not been before convicted, such offender shall be exempted from being punished as Accessary, if the principal shall be afterwards convicted.*"—Sec. 1.

This Act also empowers *one Justice to grant a warrant to search for stolen goods in the day time, on oath being made that there are just grounds of suspicion; and the person concealing the said goods, or in whose custody they are found, shall in like manner be guilty of a misdemeanor, and punished in the manner beforementioned.*—Sec. 9.

The same Act extended the powers granted by former Acts relative to metals, *to any other kind of goods: by authorizing peace officers (and also watchmen while on duty) to apprehend all persons suspected of of carrying stolen goods after sun-setting and before sun-rising, who shall, on conviction, be adjudged guilty of a misdemeanor, and imprisoned, not exceeding six, nor less than three months.*—Sec. 3.

Power is also given by this Act *to any person to whom goods, suspected to be stolen, shall be offered to be sold or pawned, to apprehend the person offering the same, and to carry him before a Justice.*—Sec. 4.

And as an encouragement to young Thieves to discover the Receivers, the same Act provides, *That if any person or persons being out of custody, or in custody, if under the age of 15 years, upon any charge of felony within benefit of Clergy, shall have committed any felony, and shall discover two Receivers, so as that they shall be convicted, such Discoverer shall have pardon for all felonies by him committed before such discovery.*

These various Acts of Parliament prove how very prominent the evil of receiving stolen goods has been in the view of the Legislature.—It is to be lamented, however, that a more general and comprehensive view has not been taken of the subject, by substituting, instead of the piece-meal System which has been from time to time adopted, on suggestions applicable only to particular cases, *one general law that should have embraced every object,* and remedied every defect in the existing Statutes, on this important subject of criminal jurisprudence.

That these Laws, numerous as they are, and applicable as many of them appear to be, have not been

in

in any degree effectual, is clearly manifested by the
unquestionable increase of the evil, even to an extent
beyond all calculation.

Under such circumstances, where the Receiver is
in reality the greatest offender, and even the source
from whence most of the burglaries and highway
robberies have their origin, the Thief being not seldom his pupil—*Why should not the Receipt of Stolen
Goods be made an original offence ?*—Why should not
the rewards for detection, and the punishment on
conviction, be the same, in the case both of the
Receiver and the Thief?*

In contemplating the best means of preventing
depredations upon the public, the simplest and perhaps the most effectual mode would be to *make a
stand at this particular point ;* by bending the attention *wholly* to the means of destroying effectually *the
trade of receiving stolen goods ;* under the fullest conviction that by accomplishing so valuable a purpose,
thieving and swindling in all its branches would also
be, in a great measure, destroyed.

It is believed, that this object (difficult as it may
appear) is attainable, by well digested applicable
laws, containing and enforcing such regulations as
would ensure a full and energetic execution.

---

* The general rule of the ancient Law is this :—that Accessaries
shall suffer the same punishment as Principals. If one be liable
to death, the other is also liable. BLACKSTONE.

In France, (before the Revolution) the offence of receiving
stolen goods was punished with death.

The

The importance of a measure of this kind is so immense, that if even a considerable part of one Session of Parliament were employed in devising and legalizing a proper System, it would be time well and usefully spent for the benefit of the Country.

The obvious means of remedy seem to lie within a narrow compass. The first point to be obtained is the *Licensing* all those dealers (some of them already particularized in pages 292, 293), whose various branches of trade are friendly to the encouragement of depredations; and the putting them under the control of the *Central Board of Police*, in the manner stated more fully in the concluding part of this Work.

The next step must be to consolidate and improve the Laws now in being, relative to *Receivers of stolen goods;* by an arrangement which shall render the whole *clear* and *explicit*, and applicable to all the evils which have been felt to exist.

And lastly to make the following additions to these Laws :

" 1. To make the receiving stolen goods an *original offence;* punishable in the same manner, in all cases, as the principal felony is punishable by Law.

" 2. The offence of receiving *money, bank notes, horses, cattle, poultry*, or *any matter* or thing whatsoever, to be the same as receiving goods and chattels.

" 3. The persons committing any felony or larceny to be competent to give evidence against the Receiver,

ceiver, and *vice versa ;* Provided that the testimony and evidence of such principal Felon against the Receiver, or the evidence of the Receiver against the principal Felon, shall not be of itself sufficient to convict, without other concurrent evidence: and that the offenders so giving evidence shall be entitled to his Majesty's pardon, and also to a reward of from 10*l.* to 50*l.* as hereafter mentioned ; unless they shall be found guilty of wilful and corrupt perjury.—*By this means the Thief will be set against the Receiver, and the Receiver against the Thief.*

" 4. That rewards be paid for the detection and apprehension of Receivers as well as Thieves, in all cases whatsoever, according to the discretion of the Judge; *whether there shall be a conviction or not ;* which reward shall not be less than *ten* and may extend to *fifty pounds.*

" 5. That the various classes of dealers to be licensed shall enter into recognizance for their good behaviour: and that no licences be granted to persons having been convicted of felony or perjury, nor to any but such as can obtain and produce a certificate of good character.

" 6. That all such licensed dealers, as also *Publicans, Pawnbrokers,* &c. shall be subject to a penalty for concealing any stolen goods which may come into their possession, after the same are advertised ;— or punished with transportation, if it can be made appear that such goods were purchased at an under value, being known to be stolen.

" 7. That

7. " That all drivers of Hackney-Coaches, employed to take fares after twelve o'clock at night, shall
be licensed by the Magistrates of the division;
and shall enter into recognizance for their good
behaviour, themselves and one surety in 50*l.* at
least; and that every such coachman shall be
obliged, whenever he carries any goods or valu-
ables, to make a report of the same, on the following morning, to the Magistrate of his district, if
no suspicion arises as to any improper or felonious
intention; but in all cases where a felonious intention shall appear, the coachman to be authorized and required to call the assistance of the
watchmen and patroles, and to seize and apprehend the parties, and lodge them and the goods
in the nearest watch-house; there to be kept until
brought before a justice, at the Public Office
of the district on the following morning: And
although it may ultimately appear that the coachman was mistaken and the parties innocent, yet
where it shall be manifest to the Justice that he
hath acted *bona fide*, he shall not be liable to any
prosecution :* and if it shall appear that the
goods so conveyed *were* stolen property, then the
coachman shall be entitled, whether a conviction
shall follow or not, to a reward of *two guineas*;
and in all cases where a prosecution shall follow,
he shall be entitled to such further reward as the
Court shall think proper.

* Vide Act 30 Geo. II. cap, 24.

8. " That

8. " That all watchmen or patroles who shall appear
upon proper proof to connive at the commission of
felonies* in the night time, or while they are on
duty.; or shall knowingly conceal any felonious
removal of stolen goods, or goods suspected to be
stolen, and conveying to Receivers' houses, shall
be deemed guilty of a misdemeanor, and liable to
be *imprisoned, whipt,* or *put in the pillory.*—And in
all cases where such watchmen or patroles shall
observe any goods or other articles conveyed in
Hackney-coaches, or in any other manner, while
they are upon duty, from one place to another,
they shall report the same to the Justices at the
nearest Public Office, in the morning : But if
they shall have good grounds to suspect a felonious intention, and that the property is stolen, the
goods and all the parties concerned shall be conveyed to the nearest watch-house, for the purpose
of being brought before a magistrate ; and such
watchmen (acting *bona fide*) shall not be liable to
any prosecution in case of a mistake ; and if a
felony shall have been actually committed, they
shall each be entitled to one guinea, besides their
proportion of any future reward which may be

---

* An Officer of Police who was watching the house of a noted
Receiver in St. James's parish, being taken for a Thief by the
watchman, the latter entered into conversation with him, and
naming the Receiver, he told the officer that he being very liberal
and kind to them, they did not disturb any person going to his
house ; and if he had any thing to carry there, he would step out
of sight, so as to be able to say he had seen nothing.

ordered

ordered by the Court who shall try the offenders."*

In the formation of such a System, it is absolutely
necessary that care should be taken to secure a *regular* and perfect *execution*, by means of a proper
superintendance and inspection ;—without this, the
best laws will remain a *dead letter*.—Such has, in
fact, been the case in a great measure with respect to
several of the very excellent Statutes, now, in force,
relative to Receivers of stolen Goods; and such also
would be the case with regard to the laws relative to
the *Revenue*, if a System had not been established to
secure their execution.

If it be allowed that the prevention of crimes is at
least of as much importance to Society, as any consideration connected with partial revenue :—if experience has shewn that, after the skill and ingenuity
of the ablest lawyers and the most profound thinkers
have been exhausted in framing laws to meet offences,
which are daily committed, these offences are progressively increasing :—Is it not clear to demonstration, that some *active principle* is wanting, which
does not at present exist, for the purpose of rendering these laws effectual ?

This principle of activity is, (it is humbly apprehended,) only to be established by the introduction
of such a System of *regulation*, as shall attach to all
classes of dealers, who, in their intercourse with

* Vide Act 30 Geo. II. cap. 24.

Society,

Society, are in the train of encouraging either directly or collaterally, transactions of *an immoral*, *a fraudulent*, or a *mischievous nature*.

The idea is not new in the System of jurisprudence of the country;—Publicans have long been under regulations prescribed by Magistrates; Pawnbrokers also have been of late years regulated to a certain extent by Statute.—Let the same principle be extended to the other dealers alluded to; and let the Legislature, profiting by that experience which has manifested the cause of the inefficacy of a vast number of penal Statutes, establish such a system of *regulation, inspection*, and *superintendance*, as will insure to the Public the full benefits arising from good laws, administered with activity, purity, and discretion.

Nothing can evince in a greater degree the necessity of *inspecting* the execution of all *laws of regulation* where the well-being of Society is concerned, than the abuses which occur with regard to the two classes just mentioned, namely, Public-houses and Pawnbrokers.—Many excellent rules are established by the Legislature, and the Magistrates; but while it is seldom the interest of the depraved or dishonest part of these two classes to adhere to such rules, by what means is the execution to be insured, so as to operate as a complete protection to the Public?—surely not by the operation of the law through the medium of common informers; since independent of the invidious nature of the office, experience has
shewn

shewn that the public good rarely enters into the consideration of persons, of this description; who look merely to their own emolument, frequently holding up the penalties as a rod by which money is privately extorted, and the parties laid under contribution, for the purpose of allowing them to continue in the practice of those abuses, which the engine used for this nefarious purpose was meant to prevent.

The System of Inspection, thus strongly and repeatedly recommended, while it remedied these corrupt practices, by preventing the existence of the evil, could only be disagreeable to *Fraudulent Dealers*.

The honest and fair Tradesmen, as things are at present circumstanced, are by no means on an equal footing with men who carry on business by fraudulent devices.—Such fair traders who have nothing to dread, would therefore rejoice at the System of inspection which is proposed, and would submit to it cheerfully; as having an immediate tendency to shield them from fraudulent competition, and to protect the Public against knavery and dishonesty.

CHAP.

CHAP. XI.

The prominent Causes of the increase of Crimes reviewed and considered.—Imputable in the first instance to deficient Laws and an ill-regulated Police:—To the unfortunate habits of the lower orders of the People in feeding their families in Ale-houses.—To the bad and immoral Education of Apprentices.—To the number of individuals broke down by misfortunes arising from want of Industry. —To idle and profligate Menial Servants out of place.—To the deplorable state of the lower orders of the Jews of the Dutch and German Synagogue. —To the depraved morals of Aquatic Labourers.— To the Dealers in old Metals—Second-hand Ships' Stores—Rags—Old Furniture—Old Building Materials—Old Apparel: and Cart-keepers for removing these articles.—To disreputable Pawn-brokers.—And finally to ill-regulated Public-houses, and to the Superabundance of these receptacles of idleness and vice.—Concluding Reflections on the evils to the State and the Individual, which arise from the excesses of the Labouring People.

In contemplating the mass of turpitude which is developed in the preceding Chapters, and which exhibit afflicted Society, groaning under a pressure of evils and Public wrongs, which, but for the

different

different views which have been taken of the subject, could not have been conceived to exist; it may
be truly affirmed in the first instance, that much is
to be imputed to deficient and ill-executed Laws,
arising chiefly from the want of a proper System of
Police.

Offences of every description have their origin
in the vicious and immoral habits of the people, and
in the facilities which the state of manners and society,
particularly in vulgar life, afford in generating vicious
and bad habits.

In tracing the progress of those habits which are
peculiar to the lower orders of the Community in
this great Metropolis, from infancy to the adult state,
the cause will be at once discovered, why that *almost
universal* profligacy prevails, which, by being productive of so much evil to the unfortunate Individuals
as well as the Community at large, cannot be sufficiently deplored.

Before a child is perhaps able to lisp a sentence,
it is carried by its ill-fated mother to the tap-room
of an ale-house;* in which are assembled multitudes of low company, many of whom have been
perhaps reared in the same manner. The vilest and
most profane and polluted language, accompanied by
oaths and imprecations, is uttered in these haunts
of idleness and dissipation.—Children follow their
parents during their progress to maturity, and are al-

---

* It is even a practice with not a few of the labouring families
in the Eastern part of the Town, to take lodgings in Ale-houses.

most

most the constant witnesses of their besotted cour[...].
—Reduced, from their unfortunate habits, to the
necessity of occupying a miserable half furnished
lodging from week to week, there is no comfort at
home—No knowledge of frugal cookery exists, by
which a nourishing and palatable meal can be provided, and frequently a sufficiency of fuel for that
purpose is not accessible.—A succedaneum is found
in the ale-house at three times the expence.—A common fire is provided for the guests, calculated to
convey that warmth which could not be obtained at
home; and food * and liquor is furnished at an expence which too seldom leaves any part of the weekly
earning for cloathing, and none at all for education.—
In this manner is a large proportion of what may be
denominated the lowest classes of the people reared
in the Metropolis; † and the result is, that while
many

* Such is the thoughtless improvidence of this class of the
labouring people, that they are generally the first who indulge
themselves by eating Oysters, Lobsters, and Pickled Salmon,
&c. when first in Season, and long before these luxuries are considered as accessible to the middle ranks of the Community;
whose manners are generally as virtuous as the others are depraved.

† It is not to be inferred from this statement, that there are not
to be found even among the lower classes of the labouring People
in the Metropolis, many instances of honest and virtuous Poor,
whose distresses are to be attributed to the calamity of a failure of
employment, bad health, death of Parents or Children, and other
causes which human prudence cannot prevent; and particularly
where the want of opulent Inhabitants in several of the Eastern
Parishes, renders it necessary to assess *Indigence* for the support of
Poverty.—To these Parishes and Hamlets the Poor resort, both from
the

many of the adults are lost to the state by prematura death, from sottishness and irregularity, not a few of their offspring are never raised to manhood: But this is not all:—when by means of strong constitutions, they survive the shocks which nature has sustained in its progress to maturity under the influence of habits so exceedingly depraved, they are restrained by no principle of morality or religion,* (for

the nature of their employments, and the impossibility of finding habitations any where else.—They have perhaps no legal settlement where they reside, or the funds of the Parish can afford but a very scanty and inadequate relief. Depressed with sickness, and broke down and dispirited by extreme poverty, the little furniture and apparel of Man, Woman, and Child, is carried to the Pawn-broker's to obtain a scanty pittance for the immediate support of life, until at length there does not remain what is sufficient to cover nakedness. —In these miserable mansions the Author has himself frequently witnessed scenes of distress, which would rend the heart of the most unfeeling of the human species.—A temporary and partial expedient has, through the benevolence of the Publick, been administered in the excellent institutions of *Soup-houses :* but until the funds of the different Parishes can be made *one Common Purse,* and an intelligent management substituted in the place of an ignorant and incompetent superintendance, the evil will not diminish.— To the opulent part of the Community the burden would never be felt.—At present, where the most indigent are assessed, the rates are double and treble those in the rich Parishes.—It is principally to this cause, that Poverty is no where to be found in so great a degree, cloathed in the garb of the extremest misery and wretchedness, as in the Metropolis.—And it is to this cause also, joined to various others explained in this Chapter, *that above Twenty Thousand miserable Individuals of various classes, rise up every morning without knowing how, or by what means they are to be supported, during the passing day ; or where, in many instances, they are to lodge on the succeeding night.*

 * The Author has often had occasion to witness the extreme ignorance

they know nothing of either), and only wait for opportunities, to plunge into every excess and every crime.

Profligate and depraved as the lower orders of the People appear to have been for several centuries in this great Metropolis, it would seem that the practice of married females resorting to Public-houses, and mixing generally in tap-rooms with the idle and dissolute, is an evil habit of a very modern date; for the period is not even too remote to be recollected, since it was considered as disgraceful for Females who pretended to any degree of modesty to be seen in a Public-house. —It is however now to be lamented that the obloquy of thus exposing themselves has as little influence, as the rude and obscene language they uniformly hear uttered.

Another cause of the increase of crimes, may be traced to the bad and immoral education of Apprentices to Mechanical employments.

Although many of their Masters may not be, and certainly are not, composed of the class whose manners have just been depicted, yet their habits lead them too generally to Public-houses, where no inconsiderable proportion of their earnings are expended; —where low gaming is introduced, producing ruin and distress to many families even among the inferior

rance of the younger part of this class, when called upon to give evidence in judicial proceedings.—Of the nature of an oath they had not the least conception,—nor even of the existence of a Supreme Being.

ranks,

ranks, who might otherwise have moved through life with credit and reputation.

The force of such an example on young minds is obvious.—No sooner does an apprentice advance towards the last year of his time than he thinks it incumbent upon him to follow the example of his master, by learning to *smoke*.—This accomplishment acquired (according to his conception) he is a fit associate for those who frequent Public-houses. He resorts at first to those of a lower class, to avoid his master or his relations.—There he meets with depraved company; while he conceives he is following only the example of those whose manners and habits he has been taught, by example, to imitate, he is insensibly ensnared.—Having arrived at the age of puberty, and meeting profligate females in those haunts of idleness, his passions become inflamed.—The force of evil example overpowers him.—He too becomes depraved.—Money must be procured to administer to the new wants which are generated by depravity.— Aided by the facilities held out by Old Iron Shops, he pilfers from his master to supply those wants, or associates himself with Thieves, whose acquaintance he made in progress of his seduction.*

* In the course of the Author's investigations, in his official situation as a Magistrate, he actually discovered that clubs of apprentice boys were harboured in Public-houses, for the purpose of supporting their fellow apprentices who ran away from their masters. The means of thus indulging themselves in lewdness and debauchery was obtained by pilfering from their Masters, and disposing of the property at Old Iron Shops.

Under

Under the circumstances thus stated, where so many temptations assail the young and inexperienced, the transition from innocence to guilt is easy to be conceived.—And in a Metropolis where there are seldom fewer than 150,000 apprentices bound to mechanical employments, the crimes which spring from this source must be very extensive.—That there are, however, many good and virtuous young men among the class of apprentices, who, from a better education, or being under the controul of reputable masters, and attentive parents, escape the snare, or resist these temptations, is *certain;* and fortunate too for the best interests of Society. It is to be lamented, however, that the major part, and particularly parish apprentices, have not always these advantages ; and hence it is that so many become disorderly, and require the interference of legal authority and punishment for the purpose of compelling obedience and good conduct.*

Another

* It is to be feared that much evil arises from the want of attention on the part of Masters among the superior classes of Tradesmen with respect to their apprentices, who too seldom consider the morals of their apprentices as a matter in which they have any concern.—It is even the practice to allow apprentices a certain sum of money weekly, for the purpose of enabling them to provide themselves out of doors, and to prevent the trouble of boarding them in the house. If it were possible for a Master, after exerting all his ingenuity, to invent one mode more likely than another to ruin his apprentices, it is by adopting this plan. If he means to subject himself to great risques with respect to the security of his property, he will permit his apprentice, at the age of puberty when open to seduction, to be at large in this great Town, where he is liable to be

assailed

Another cause of the increase of crimes, arises from the number of individuals in various occupations among the lower and middling ranks of life, (and which must naturally be expected in a large Metropolis) who from their own mismanagement and want of industry, or attention to their business, are suddenly broke down, and in some degree excluded from the regular intercourse with society. Unable to find employment, for want of character, or want of friends, with constant demands upon them for the means of subsistence to themselves and families, they resort to Public-houses, under the influence of despondency, or to kill time which hangs heavy upon them.

In these haunts of depravity they meet persons who perhaps have been in the like circumstances; but who have resorted to illegal Lottery Insurances,

assailed by swindlers, cheats, and sharpers, who availing themselves of the inexperience of youth, may corrupt the mind, and give it a wrong bias. The dangers arising from allowing apprentices to victual out of doors, extend much farther than masters are generally aware of: and they who suffer it do great injury to themselves, and even great injustice to their apprentices, whose morals they are virtually, at least, bound to preserve pure. This is not to be expected where apprentices are not under the eye of the master at meal times. Their Sundays, in such cases, are their own, which they waste in idleness, not seldom in water-parties on the River, where they are introduced into low and bad company, which gives frequently a taint to their manners of the most injurious nature. The result is, that their master, without reflecting that he himself was the cause of their idleness, withdraws his confidence, and turns them adrift after their time expires, if not before; and in the end ruin, as might well be expected, inevitably ensues.

and

and other swindling devices for subsistence, under whose banners they enlist; and thus strengthen the phalanx of low gamblers, swindlers, and cheats, whose various pursuits have been developed in this Work.— From one vice to another the transition is easy when the mind becomes depraved, and the pursuits which are ultimately followed, depend in a considerable degree on the person with whom this class of men associate.—If at the low gaming-houses, to which from idle habits they are led to resort, they meet with highwaymen and footpads, they are easily persuaded to become associates in their iniquitous pursuits; or if in the wide range of their acquaintance, by living chiefly in Public-houses, they become acquainted with venders of base money, they enter with equal facility into their views, as means of supplying their pecuniary wants.

In cases where they have been bred to ingenious mechanical employments, they embrace, wherever a proper opportunity offers, such propositions as may be made them, to become forgers of Bank Bills and Notes, and Coiners of Counterfeit Money.

Such is the lamentable progress of vice in the human mind, that by degrees it embraces eagerly what could not have been endured at the commencement of the career.

Another cause of the increase of Crimes in the Metropolis and its environs, may be traced to the situation of idle and profligate menial servants out of place, and destitute of the means of obtaining situations

tions from the loss of character.—These too, seek
for resources in Public-houses, where they soon become the associates of Thieves, Pickpockets, Burglars, and Highwaymen; and it is believed to be
chiefly from this class, particularly *Riding Footmen*,
and *Postillions*, that the corps of Highway Robbers is
constantly recruited.—While others less skilled in
horsemanship become Footpads, Burglars, and Pick-
pockets.

With the major part of this class the transition is
easy—depravity had previously taken hold of their
minds—every other resource has failed them, and
to this they resort, as soon as they can find means, to
exist in any gang that will receive them, where, to
those who confine themselves chiefly to burglaries,
their knowledge of the interior of the houses of their
former masters, and their probable acquaintance with
some of the female servants, will be a considerable recommendation, and even a ground of seduction.

Another cause, and no inconsiderable one, of the
progress and increase of crimes may be developed,
by contemplating the deplorable state and condition
of the lower order of the Jews in the Metropolis,
who are of the Society of the Dutch Synagogue.*—
Totally

---

* Another class of Jews which belong to the Portuguese Synagogue are generally opulent and respectable, and hold no community
with the others: they use a different Liturgy, and their language is
even different; their number does not exceed three thousand; they
never intermarry with the Jews of the Dutch Synagogue.—They
generally pride themselves on their Ancestry, and give their Children
the best education which can be obtained in the countries where
they

Totally without education, and very seldom trained
to any trade or occupation by which they can earn

they reside.—While the Dutch Jews (or rather *the German Dutch
Jews)* get no education at all. Even the most affluent of them are
said to be generally unable either to read or write the language
of the country that gave them birth.—They confine themselves
to a Bastard or vulgar Hebrew which has little analogy to the
original. The Portuguese Synagoguge has been established in England ever since the Usurpation—Their place of worship is in Bevis
Marks.—The Members of it being mostly wealthy are extremely
attentive to their poor, among whom there is said not to be a single
beggar or itinerant.—The Brokers upon the Exchange of the
Jewish Persuasion, are all or chiefly of the Portuguese Synagogue.
Their number is limited to *Twelve* by a particular Act of Parliament.
—Originally this privilege was given gratis by the Lord Mayor,
but afterwards 100l. was required, which has gradually increased
to *One Thousand Guineas for each Broker.*

The schism between the two classes of Jews prevails all over the
world, though the rational Jews treat the distinction as absurd.

The German Dutch Jews, who may amount to from twelve to
fifteen thousand, have Six Synagogues, the principal of which are in
Duke's Place, Leadenhall Street, and *Church Row, Fenchurch Street.*
They observe the particular ritual of the German Synagogue, and
also include the *Polish, Russian,* and *Turkish Jews,* established in
London.—With the exception of three or four wealthy individuals,
and as many Families who are in trade on the Royal Exchange,
they are in general a very indigent class of people, through whose
medium crimes are generated to a considerable extent.—Their
Community is too poor to afford them adequate relief, whence
they have resorted to the expedient of lending them small sums
of money at interest to trade upon, which is required to be repaid
monthly or weekly, as the case may be, otherwise they forfeit all
claim to this aid.—The reproach arising from their evil practices
and idleness, is said to have engaged the attention of the respectable part of both Synagogues with a view to a remedy, but all
their attempts have been heretofore unsuccessful.

their

their livelihood by manual labour :—their youths excluded from becoming apprentices, and their females
from hiring themselves generally as servants, on account of the superstitious adherence to the mere
ceremonial of their persuasion, as it respects meat not
killed by Jews, nothing can exceed their melancholy condition, both with regard to themselves and
Society. Thus excluded from these resources, which
other classes of the Community possess, they seem
to have no alternative but to resort to those tricks
and devices, which ingenuity suggests to enable
persons without an honest means of subsistence to
live in idleness.

The habits they thus acquire are the most mischievous and noxious to the Community that can be
conceived.—Having connexions wherever the Dock-
yards are situated, as well as in several other large
trading towns in the Kingdom, they become in many
respects the medium through which stolen goods are
conveyed to and from the Metropolis ; and as their
existence depends on this nefarious traffick, they keep
alive a System of Fraud and Depredation which,
perhaps, is generated in a greater degree by their
peculiar situation in respect to Society; than by any
actual disposition on their parts to pursue these nefarious practices.

Even the system of supporting the poor of this
Community, by lending them small sums of money
by which they may support themselves by a species
of petty traffick, contributes in no small degree to
the

the commission of crimes; since in order to render it productive to an extent equal to the wants of families who do not acquire any material aid by manual labour, they are induced to resort to unlawful means by dealing in stolen goods and in counterfeit money, by which they become public nuisances in the Countries where they receive an asylum.

As there appears in reality to be no distinction made by the rational part of the Jewish persuasion between the Portuguese and the Dutch Synagogues, it is earnestly to be hoped that the opulent and respectable of the former Community will lend a helping hand in devising some means of rescuing this part of the Nation of the Jews who reside in England, from the reproach, which it is to be feared, has been too justly cast upon them. Policy dictates the measure, while humanity ardently pleads for it. In so good a work every man of feeling, be his religious persuasion what it may, will join in promoting and carrying into effect a measure so beneficial to the Community at large, by devising some means to render their labour productive: since it is clear to demonstration that to the idle habits of this numerous class of people, is to be ascribed a considerable proportion of the petty crimes, as well as some of the more atrocious offences by which the Metropolis and the Country is afflicted.

Another cause of the increase and multiplication of crimes has arisen from the deprave dmorals of the Aquatic labourers and others employed on the wharfs and quays, and in ships, vessels, and craft,
upon

upon the River Thames ; and from the want, *until lately*, of an appropriate Preventive System to check these depredations.

The analogy between actual pillage and smuggling in the conception of nautical labourers, and the uncontrolled habit of plunder which too long existed, trained up myriads of delinquents who affixed in their minds no degree of moral turpitude to the offence; which of course extended itself both with respect to Commercial and Public Property beyond all bounds, until a remedy was imperiously called for, and at length applied by means of an experimental System of Police applicable to that object.

Another cause, and certainly none of the least, which has tended to facilitate the commission of crimes, has been the want of a proper control over persons of loose conduct and dishonest habits, who have opened shops for the purchase and sale of *Old Iron*, and *other metals—Old stores—Rags—Old furniture—Old building-ing materials, and second hand wearing apparel, and other goods ;* and *also cart-keepers* for the collection and removal of these articles from place to place.

The easy and concealed mode of disposing of pilfered articles, through the medium of these receptacles, has tended more to the corruption of the morals of youth, and to the multiplication of crimes, than it is possible to conceive ; nor has the mode of Licensing *Pawnbrokers*, without a due regard to character and a more effectual control, been in many respects less mischievous to the Community.—To the

the reputable part of this class of dealers it is degrading and even cruel that the reproach and stigma, arising from the nefarious practices of the fraudulent, should unavoidably in the public mind, attach upon those that are blameless, and fair in their dealings.—While the law admits of no power of discrimination, and no means of excluding improper characters exist, the evil must continue ; and while it remains on the present footing, it must also be considered as no inconsiderable medium, by which both petty and more atrocious crimes are produced.

But perhaps the greatest source of delinquency and crimes is to be ascribed to ill-regulated Public Houses, conducted by men of loose conduct and depraved morals—Since it is in these receptacles that the corruption of morals originates.—It is here that the minds of youth are contaminated, and the conspiracies for the purpose of committing frauds and depredations on the Public formed and facilitated.

A disorderly and ill-regulated Public-house, therefore, is one of the greatest nuisances that can exist in civil Society.—Innumerable are the temptations which are to be found in these haunts of idleness to seduce the innocent, and to increase the resources of the evil-disposed to do mischief.

Whatever tends to promote vice and dissipation, whether arising from low gaming, by means of cards, dice, dominos, shuffleboard, and other sedentary games; or fraudulent insurances in the lottery, calculated to fascinate and seduce the unwary, and to

poison

poison the mind of all ranks in the humble walks of
vulgar life, is here to be found ; in spite of every laudable precaution, exercised by Magistrates, under the
present System of Police applicable to this object.—
Even Prostitutes of the lowest cast are not seldom
introduced, where the gains of the landlord are
thereby to be promoted.

It is in these receptacles that Thieves and Robbers
of every description hold their orgies, and concert
and mature their plans of depredation on the peaceful Subject; and here too it not unfrequently happens, that their booty is deposited and concealed.

It is here also that markets are held for the sale of
Base Money, where every facility is afforded for the
purpose of concealment, and assistance in escaping
justice.

In fact, there is scarce any moral evil by which
*Society is afflicted—the mind debauched—the virtuous
parent* and *master distressed,* and the *ruin of families
and individuals effected,* which is not generated in
Public-houses.

At present, in the Metropolis and its environs,
there are at least five thousand of these receptacles,
of which it is computed that about one thousand
change tenants from once to three times a year.—
Hence it follows that not less than two thousand individuals are in a floating state, either from one
Public-house to another, or perhaps, more frequently,
from the Alehouse to a Goal.

When a depraved character loses his licence in
one division of the Metropolis, he generally finds
means

means to obtain admission in another where he is not known. The separation of jurisdictions without a centre point, and the numerous changes which are constantly taking place, preclude the possibility of detection ; while the facility, with which the worst characters obtain the certificates required by law, (which are too often signed, without the least previous inquiry, by the Clergyman and Parish Officers as a matter of course,) enable them to effect their purpose ; and such houses being generally of the inferior class in point of trade, every species of disorder is permitted for the purpose of obtaining custom. This is soon discovered by those who have criminal objects in view; and to such houses they generally resort, where it has sometimes been discovered that the Landlord himself belongs to the gang; *and* that he has become a Publican, the better to facilitate its designs. That the Ale-houses are yet by far too numerous, is incontestibly proved by the frequent changes which take place in so large a proportion in the course of a year, while the irregularities which prevail render it equally clear that a more general controul is necessary to prevent the mischiefs which have been detailed.

It is chiefly in houses where the trade is inadequate to the support of the establishment that the greatest disorders prevail, as in such cases every lure is held out to invite customers, and to entice them to expend money.—And in return for this, where the Landlord is not himself of the fraternity of Thieves or Receivers, he is induced at least to afford them his assistance, as a medium of concealment.

If

If a plan could be devised, with equal advantage
to the Revenue, by the introduction of more innocent and less noxious gratifications, whereby the
lower ranks of the people could be gradually led into
better habits ; much benefit would arise to the State,
both with respect to health and morals.

The quantity of Beer, Porter, Gin, and compounds, which is sold in Public-houses in the Metropolis and its environs, has been estimated, after
bestowing considerable pains in forming a calculation, at nearly 3,300,000*l*, a year*.

This immense sum, equal to double the Revenue
of some of the Kingdoms and States of Europe,
independant of other evil consequences in producing indigence and promoting crimes, must in a
certain degree debilitate manhood—in lessening
the powers of animal life, and in shortening its
duration long before the period arrives, when an

---

* In a Tract entitled ' Observations and Facts relative to Public-
Houses,' by the Author of this Work, the mode of conducting Alehouses in the Metropolis, and the evils arising from this source of
iniquity and idleness is very fully explained. By this publication
it is discovered, after much investigation, that there is consumed
and sold in the 5000 Public-houses in and round the Metropolis,
158,400,580 pots of Porter, Ale, and Two-
    penny — — — —   £.2,311,466 15 10
Gin and Compounds from the Distillers and
    Rectifiers — — — —   975,000   0   0
                                   3,286,466 15 10
To which add Pipes, Tobacco, &c, at least—113,533   4   2
                    Total — — £. 3,310,000   0   0

adult

adult ceases to contribute by his labours to the resources of the state. In this point of view, independent of considerations of a moral tendency, and of all the other train of evils which have been detailed, it would seem of importance, as a political measure, to check the growing propensity to consume a greater quantity of Porter, Beer, and ardent Spirits, than is necessary to health.—To the State, indeed, it creates a Revenue; but it is a Revenue too dearly purchased if it wastes the human species—if it deprives the nation, prematurely, of the benefit of their labour, and occasions infinitely greater pecuniary pressures in the support of an indigent and helpless offspring, who must be reared again to manhood at the expence of the Public; not to speak of the grain, labour, fuel, &c. unnecessarily consumed in creating this poison to the health, the morals, and comforts of the poor*.—However unpopular it may appear in the view

* It is a curious and important fact, that during the period when Distillers were stopped in 1796 and 1797, although Bread, and every necessary of life was considerably higher than during the preceding year, the Poor in that quarter of the Town where the chief part reside were apparently more comfortable, paid their rents more regularly, and were better fed than at any period for some years before;—even although they had not the benefit of the extensive charities which were distributed in 1795. This can only be accounted for by their being denied the indulgence of Gin, which had become in a great measure inaccessible from its very high price. It may fairly be concluded, that the money formerly spent in this imprudent manner had been applied in the purchase of provisions and other necessaries to the amount of some hundred thousand pounds.—The effects of their being deprived of this

baneful

view of those who have not fully considered the subject, it may be clearly demonstrated that a triple duty on Malt Spirits, and a much higher duty on Strong Beer and Porter would be an act of the greatest humanity on the part of the Legislature.—The present Revenue might thus be secured, while that which is even of more importance to a State than any other consideration would be preserved—*the health and morals of the labouring people.* It is a mistaken notion, that a very large quantity of Malt Liquor is necessary to support labourers of any description.— After a certain moderate quantity is drank, it enervates the body, and stupefies the senses.—A Coalheaver who drinks from 12 to 16 pots of Porter in the course of a day, would receive more nourishment, and perform his labour with more ease and a greater portion of athletic strength, if only one-third of the quantity were consumed. He would also enjoy better health, and be fitter for his labour the following day. On a supposition that the excesses in which perhaps 200,000 of the labouring people in the Metropolis *indulge,* shortens the natural period of their existence only five years each on an average, the labour of one million of years is lost in the lives

baneful Liquor were also evident in their more orderly conduct.— Quarrels and assaults were less frequent, and they resorted seldomer to the Pawnbrokers' shops: and yet during the chief part of this period Bread was 15*d.* the Quartern Loaf, and Meat higher than the preceding year, particularly Pork, which arose in part from the stoppage of the Distilleries; but chiefly from the scarcity of Grain.

of this class of men, after the expence is incurred in rearing them to maturity, which, during a period of 36 years of adult labour, at 25*l.* a year, establishes a deficiency to the Community of *Twenty-five Millions sterling:* independant of the numerous other train of evils, which arise to a nation from idle, dissolute and immoral habits, by which the rising generation is contaminated, and great inconvenience imposed on the innocent and peaceful subject, from the increase of crimes which are generated through this medium.

It is to be lamented, that in pursuing this subject, new sources giving origin and progress to crimes press upon the mind in the course of the inquiry. To the catalogue already detailed may be added, *Gaming-Houses* of every description, particularly *houses of the lower cast;* but as this subject has been very fully handled in a preceding Chapter, it will be unnecessary to do more than place it in the general list of causes, which have contributed exceedingly to the evils, which have afflicted Society in this Metropolis, and which can only be remedied by a *Responsible Police,* attaching particularly upon this baneful propensity by appropriate regulations.

Next to Gaming, Illicit Trade or Smuggling may be mentioned as a very productive source of criminality. The vast extent of the trade and Revenues of the country; its insular situation, and the temptations arising from the magnitude of the duties, contribute exceedingly to the corruption of morals, not only of these engaged in illicit pursuits, but it is to
be

be lamented also of the inferior officers themselves, whose duty it is to prevent this evil.

Severe and pointed as the laws unquestionably are with an immediate view to the prevention of this evil, experience proves how ineffectual they have been, since every idle and profligate character becomes a smuggler. But it is not merely the offence of smuggling as it relates to the revenue, which is to be deplored as a grievance to the Public, since those on the Sea Coasts of the kingdom, concerned in such pursuits, are generally of ferocious habits, which produce such excesses and depredations upon the unfortunate, when suffering the calamity of shipwreck, as would disgrace the rudest savages.

With contaminated minds, depraved hearts, men given up to such warfare upon helpless humanity, become fit instruments for every species of criminality.—*Vagabonds by trade*, the transition from one offence to another is easy, and hence through this medium many culprits are added to the general catalogue of delinquency, which nothing can check or prevent but a System of Police, attaching responsibility *some-where instead of no-where as at present.*

Crimes are also generated in no inconsiderable degree, by the evil examples exhibited in *Prisons*, and by the length of time persons charged with offences are suffered to remain in gaols previous to their trial, particularly in the counties adjoining the Metropolis, where they frequently are in confinement five or six months before the assizes.—If they were novices in villainy

villainy before, the education they receive in these seminaries, in the event of their escaping justice, returns them upon Society completely proselyted and instructed in the arts of mischief and depredation.

Nor have the unequal scale of punishments, and the ultimate unconditional pardo s, dictated no doubt by the purest motives of humanity, a less tendency to generate new crimes.   Encouraged by the chances of escaping free, *even after conviction*, many delinquents pursue their evil courses, trusting ultimately to this resource, if other devices shall fail.

To shew mankind that crimes are sometimes wholly pardoned, and that punishment is not the necessary consequence, is to nourish the flattering hope of impunity, and is the cause of their considering every punishment which is actually inflicted, as an act of injustice and oppression.

Let the Legislator be *tender*, *indulgent*, and *humane;* but let the Executors of the Laws be inexorable in punishing;—at least to a certain extent.

CHAP.

CHAP. XII.

The Consideration of the causes of the progress and increase of Crimes pursued.—The condition of the unhappy Females, who support themselves by Prostitution—Their pitiable Case.—The progress from Innocence to Profligacy explained.—The morals of Youth corrupted by the multitudes of Prostitutes in the streets.—These temptations excite desires which suggest undue means of obtaining money.—Apprentices and Clerks are seduced—Masters are robbed—Parents are afflicted.—The miserable consequences of Prostitution explained.—The impossibility of preventing its existence in a great Metropolis.—The propriety of lessening the Evil:—By stripping it of its indecency and much of its immoral tendency.—The shocking indecency which has lately been suffered by Prostitutes at the Theatres.—The number of Prostitutes in the Metropolis estimated—Suggestions for rendering the consequences arising from Female Prostitution less noxious to Society.—The advantages of the measure in reducing the mass of turpitude.—Reasons offered why the interests of morality and Religion will be promoted by prescribing Rules with respect to Prostitutes.—The example of Holland, Italy, and the East Indies quoted.—Strictures on the offensive manners of the Company who frequent Public Gardens:—Imputable to the want of a proper Police.—Tea Gardens under a
proper

*proper Police might be rendered beneficial to the
State.—The Ballad Singers might also be rendered
instruments in giving a right turn to the minds of
the Vulgar.—Crimes generated by immoral Books
and Songs.—Responsibility as it relates to the execution of the Laws rests no where at present.—The
nature and advantages of the Police System explained.*

In addition to the prominent causes, which contribute to the origin and the increase of crimes, which
have been developed in the preceding Chapter, there
are other sources of a minor nature still to be traced,
from which infinite evils to the Community spring.

Among these the most important is, the state and
condition of the unhappy Females, who support
themselves by Prostitution in this great Metropolis.

In contemplating their case, it is impossible to
avoid dropping a tear of pity.—Many of them perhaps originally seduced from a state of innocence,
while they were the joy and comfort of their unhappy
parents. Many of them born and educated to expect a better fate, until deceived by falsehood and
villainy, they see their error when it is too late to
recede. In this situation, abandoned by their relations and friends; deserted by their seducers, and
at large upon the world; loathed and avoided by
those who formerly held them in estimation, what are
they

they to do? In the present unhappy state of things they seem to have no alternative, but to become the miserable instruments of promoting and practising that species of seduction and immorality, of which they themselves were the victims.* And what is the result?—It is pitiable to relate.—They are compelled of necessity to mingle with the abandoned herd, who have long been practised in the walks of infamy, and they too become speedily polluted and depraved.— Oaths, imprecations, and obscene language, by degrees, become familiar to their ears, and necessity compels them to endure, and at length to imitate, and practise in their turn, upon the unwary youth, who too easily falls into the snare.

Thus it is from the multitudes of those unhappy Females, that assemble now in all parts of the Town, that the morals of the youth are corrupted. That unnecessary expences are incurred; and undue, and too often criminal, means are resorted to, for the purpose of gratifying passions, which but for these temptations, which constantly assail them in almost every street in the Metropolis, would not have been thought of. Through this medium *Apprentices, Clerks, and other persons in trust,* are seduced from the

* It is in the first stage of Seduction, before the female mind becomes vitiated and depraved, that Asylums are most useful. If persons in this unhappy situation had it in their power to resort to a medium, whereby they might be reconciled to their relations, while uncontaminated by the vices attached to *General Prostitution,* numbers, who are now lost, might be saved to Society.

paths

paths of honesty—Masters are plundered, and Parents are afflicted; while many a youth, who might have become the pride of his family—a comfort to the declining years of his Parents, and an ornament to Society, exchanges a life of Virtue and Industry, for the pursuits of the Gambler, the Swindler, and the Vagabond. Nor is the lot of these poor deluded females less deplorable. Although some few of them may obtain settlements, while others bask for a while in the temporary sun-shine of ease and splendour, the major part end a short life in misery and wretchedness.

What has become of the multitudes of unfortunate females, elegant in their persons, and sumptuous in their attire, who were seen in the streets of the Metropolis, and at places of public Amusement twenty years ago? Alas! could their progress be developed, and their ultimate situations or exit from the world disclosed, it would lay open a catalogue of sufferings and affliction, beyond what the most romantic fancy could depict or exhibit to the feeling mind.

Exposed to the rude insults of the inebriated and the vulgar :—the impositions of brutal officers and watchmen, and to the chilling blasts of the night, during the most inclement weather, in thin apparel, partly in compliance with the fashion of the day, but more frequently from the pawnbroker's shop rendering their necessary garments inaccessible—diseases, where their unhappy vocation does not produce them, are generated. No pitying hand appears to help
them

them in such situations.   The feeling parent or relation is far off.   An abandoned monster of the same
sex, inured in the practice of infamy and seduction,
instead of the consolation which sickness requires,
threatens to turn the unhappy victim out of doors,
when the means of subsistence are cut off, and the
premium for shelter is no longer forth-coming; or
perhaps the unfeeling landlord of a miserable half-fur-
nished lodging afflicts the poor unhappy female, by
declarations equally hostile to the feelings of humanity, till at length turned out into the streets, she
languishes and ends her miserable days in an hospital
or a workhouse, or perhaps perishes in some inhos-
pitable hovel alone, without a friend to console her,
or a fellow mortal to close her eyes in the pangs of
dissolution.

If no other argument could be adduced in favour
of some arrangements, calculated to stop the progress of Female Prostitution, Compassion for the sufferings of the unhappy victims would be sufficient;
but other reasons occur equally powerful, why this
evil should be controlled.

To prevent its existence, even to a considerable
extent, in so great a Metropolis as London, is as impossible as to resist the torrent of the tides.   It is an
evil therefore which must be endured while human
passions exist: but it is at the same time an evil
which may not only be lessened, but rendered less
noxious and dangerous to the peace and good order
of society; it may be stript of its indecency, and
                                                    also

also of a considerable portion of the danger attached to it, to the youth of both sexes.

The lures for the seduction of youth passing along the streets in the course of their ordinary business, may be prevented by a Police, applicable to this object, without either infringing upon the feelings of humanity or insulting distress : and still more is it practicable to remove the noxious irregularities, which are occasioned by the indiscreet conduct, and the shocking behaviour of Women of the Town, and their still more blameable paramours, in openly insulting Public Morals; and rendering the situation of modest women at once irksome and unsafe, either in places of Public Entertainment, or while passing along the most public streets of the Metropolis, particularly in the evening.

This unrestrained licence given to males and females, in the Walks of Prostitution, was not known in former times at places of public resort, where there was at least an affectation of decency. To the disgrace, however, of the Police the evil has been suffered to increase; and the Boxes in the Theatres often exhibit scenes, which are certainly extremely offensive to modesty, and contrary to that decorum which ought to be maintained, and that protection to which the respectable part of the Community are entitled, against indecency and indecorum, when their families, often composed of young females, visit places of public resort.

In this instance, the enduring such impropriety of con-

conduct, so contrary to good morals, marks strongly
the growing depravity of the age. To familiarize the
eyes and ears of the innocent part of the sex to the
scenes which are often exhibited in the Theatres, is
tantamount to carrying them to a school of vice and
debauchery—

> Vice is a monster of such frightful mien,
> That to be hated needs but to be seen ;
> Yet seen too oft—familiar with her face,
> We first endure—then pity—then embrace.

For the purpose of understanding more clearly,
by what means it is possible to lessen the evils arising
from Female Prostitution in the Metropolis, it may
be necessary to view it in all its ramifications.

In point of extent it certainly exceeds credibility : but although there are many exceptions,—
the great mass, (whatever their exterior may be), are
mostly composed of women who have been in a state
of menial servitude, and of whom not a few, from the
love of idleness and dress, with (in this case) *the misfortune of good looks,* have partly from inclination,
not seldom from previous seduction and loss of character, resorted to Prostitution as a livelihood.

They are still, however, objects of compassion, al·
though under the circumstances incident to their
situation they cannot be supposed to experience those
poignant feelings of distress, which are peculiar to
women who have moved in a higher sphere, and who
have been better educated.

The

The whole may be estimated as follows :

1. Of the class of Well Educated women it is earnestly hoped the number does not exceed - - 2,000

2. Of the class composed of persons above the rank of Menial Servants perhaps - - - - - - 3,000

3. Of the class who may have been employed as Menial Servants, or seduced in very early life, it is conjectured in all parts of the town, including Wapping, and the streets adjoining the River, there may not be less, who live wholly by Prostitution, than - - - - - - - - - - - 20,000

                                                    _____
                                                    25,000

4. Of those in different ranks in Society, who live partly by Prostitution, including the multitudes of low females, who cohabit with labourers and others without matrimony, there may be in all, in the Metropolis, about - - - - - *r* - - 25,000
                                                    _____
                              Total   50,000
                                                    _____

When a general survey is taken of the Metropolis—The great numbers among the higher and middle classes of life, who live unmarried—The multitudes of young men yearly arriving at the age of puberty—the strangers who resort to the Metropolis—The seamen and nautical labourers employed in the Trade of the River Thames, who amount at least to 40,000—And the profligate state of Society in vulgar life, the intelligent mind will soon be reconciled to the statement, which at first view would seem to excite doubts, and require investigation.

                                                    But

But whether the numbers of these truly unfortunate women are a few thousands less or more is of no
consequence in the present discussion, since it is beyond all doubt, that the evil is of a magnitude that is
excessive, and imperiously calls for a remedy.—Not
certainly a remedy against the possibility of Female
Prostitution, for it has already been stated, that it is a
misfortune that must be endured in large societies.—
All that can be attempted is, to divest it of the faculty
of extending its noxious influence beyond certain
bounds, and restrain those excesses and indecencies
which have already been shewn to be so extremely
noxious to society, and unavoidably productive of
depravity and crimes.

The Author is well aware, that he treads on tender
ground, when in suggesting any measure, however
salutary it may be in lessening the Calendars of Delinquency, *it* shall have the appearance of giving a
Public sanction to Female Prostitution.

Under the influence of strong prejudices long
rooted in the human mind, it may be in vain to plead
plus apud me ratio valebit quàm vulgi Opinio.

If however the political maxim be true—*Qui non
vetat peccare, cum possit, jubet*—it certainly follows,
that by suffering an evil to continue, when we have it
in our power, in a great measure, to lessen or prevent
it, we do *violence to reason* and *to humanity.*—That
a prudent and discreet regulation of Prostitutes in
this great Metropolis, would operate powerfully, not
only in gradually diminishing their numbers, but also

in

in securing public morals against the insults to which they are exposed, both in the open streets and at places of public entertainment, cannot be denied.

That young men in pursuit of their lawful business in the streets of this Metropolis, would be secured against that ruin and infamy, which temptations thus calculated to inflame the passions, have brought upon many, who might otherwise have passed through life as useful and respectable members of Society, is equally true:—While *frauds, peculations,* and *robbery,* often perpetrated for the purpose of supporting those unhappy women, with whom connections have been at first formed in the public streets (and in which they themselves are not seldom the chief instruments) would be prevented,

Were such proper regulations once adopted, the ears and eyes of the wives and daughters of the modest and unoffending citizens, who cannot afford to travel in carriages, would no longer be insulted by gross and polluted language, and great indecency of behaviour, while walking the streets.   Indeed it is to be feared, that the force of evil example, in unavoidably witness-ing such scenes, may have debauched many females, who might otherwise have lived a virtuous and use-ful life.

Whatever consequences might be derived from a total removal of Prostitutes (if such a measure could be conceived practicable) with respect to the wives and daughters, who compose the decent and respect-able families in the Metropolis, this apprehension is
                                                       allayed

allayed by the proposed measure. While virtue is secured against seduction, the misery of these unhappy females will also be lessened. Their numbers will be decreased, and a check will be given, not only to female seduction by the force of evil example, but to the extreme degree of depravity, which arises from the unbounded latitude which is at present permitted to take place, from the unavailing application of the laws, made for the purpose of checking this evil. If it were either politic or humane to carry them into effect, the state of society where such members are congregated together render it impossible.

Although by the arrangement proposed, a kind of sanction would, in appearance, be given to the existence of Prostitution, no ground of alarm ought to be excited, if it shall be proved, that it is to lessen the mass of turpitude which exists; that it is to produce a solid and substantial good to the Community, which it is not possible to obtain by any other means.

What therefore can rationally be opposed to such an arrangement? Not surely Religion, for it will tend to advance it: Not Morality, for the effect of the measure will increase and promote it; not that it will sanction and encourage what will prove offensive and noxious in society, since all that is noxious and offensive is by this arrangement to be removed.—Where then lies the objection?—*In vulgar prejudice only.*— By those of inferior education, whose peculiar habits and pursuits have generated strong prejudices, this excuse may be pleaded; but by the intelligent and well-

z 4   in formed

informed it will be viewed through a more correct medium.

Ingenuous minds are ever open to conviction; and it is the true characteristic of virtuous minds, where they cannot overcome or destroy, to lessen as much as possible the evils of human life.

To the numerous unhappy females in the Metropolis who live by Prostitution, this observation peculiarly applies.—The evil is such as must be endured to a certain extent—because by no human power can it be overcome; but it can certainly be very much diminished—perhaps only in one way—namely, *by prescribing rules*—" Thus far shall you go, and no farther"—the rules of decorum shall be strictly preserved in the streets and in public places. In such situations Women of the Town shall no longer become instruments of seduction and debauchery.

It may be asked, will not all this promote the cause of religion and morality?—admitted; but could not this be done without giving the sanction of the Legislature to pursuits of infamy? The answer is obvious:—the Legislature has done every thing already short of this, to effect the object; but instead of promoting good, the evil has increased; and it is to be lamented *that it is daily increasing.*— Instead of the walks of Prostitutes being confined as formerly, to one or two leading streets in Westminster, they are now to be found in every part of the Metropolis—even within the jurisdiction of the city of London; where the dangers arising from seduction

tion are the greatest, they abound the most of all of late years.

In adopting the proposed measure, the example of Holland may be quoted, where, under its former Government, the morals of the people in general were supposed the purest of any in Europe, while the Police System was considered as among the best. Italy has also long shown an example, where Prostitutes were actually Licensed, with a view to secure Chastity against the inroads of violence, and to prevent the Public eye from being insulted by scenes of lewdness and indecorum.

Female Chastity, which is highly regarded by the natives of India, is preserved by rearing up a certain class of females, who are under the conduct of discreet Matrons, in every town and village; and with whom, under certain circumstances, an indiscriminate intercourse is permitted—a measure of political necessity. Their morals, however, in other respects, are strictly guarded, and their minds are not susceptible of that degree of depravity which prevails in Europe. They are taught the accomplishments of singing and dancing—they exhibit at public entertainments, and are even called upon to assist at religious ceremonies.

The unrestrained latitude which is permitted to unfortunate females in this Metropolis, is certainly an inlet to many crimes.

The places of resort in Summer, and particularly the Public Gardens, which were formerly an innocent relaxation to sober and discreet families, can now no longer

longer be attended with comfort or satisfaction, from the offensive manners of the company who frequent such places.

It is not that the Gardens are in themselves a nuisance, or that to the inferior exhibitions any blame is to be imputed; for both might be rendered the medium of that rational recreation so necessary both for the health and comfort of the middling or lower ranks of the people, to whom *policy* and *reason* must admit occasional amusements are necessary.—If so, what can be more innocent, or better calculated for health and occasional recreation than the assemblage of decent people in a Tea Garden!—

Many of them, however, have been shut up, and this recreation denied to the people, because Prostitutes resorted to those places; insulted public morals,—promoted lewdness and debauchery, and banished modest and decent families.

This, if the true cause was developed, is not to be imputed to the place, which in itself was favourable to the innocent amusement of the people, but to a deficiency in the Police System.—It was not the Gardens nor their Keepers that offended.—The evil arose from the want of proper regulations, to restrain these excesses and to keep them within bounds.

Such places of resort under appropriate Police regulations, might be rendered a considerable source of revenue to the State, while they added greatly to the comfort and innocent recreation of the People.—By shutting up the Gardens the People are driven to the

Ale-

Ale houses, where both air and exercise, so necessary to health, are denied them, and where the same excesses often prevail, tending in a still greater degree to the corruption of morals.

Wherever multitudes of people are collected together, as in a great Metropolis like London, amusements become indispensably necessary.—And it is no inconsiderable feature in the science of Police to encourage, protect, and controul such as tend to innocent recreation, to preserve the good humour of the Public, and to give the minds of the People a right bias.

This is only attainable through the medium of a well-regulated Police.—It is perfectly practicable to render Public Gardens as innocent and decorous as a Private Assembly: although under the present deficient System they are the greatest of all nuisances.— Decent and respectable families are compelled to deny themselves the privilege of visiting them, because no restraint is put upon indecency, and vice reigns triumphant.

It is because things are either done by halves, or nothing is done at all to secure the privileges of innocence, that the sober and harmless part of the community are compelled to forego those recreations which contributed to their comfort: while the young and thoughtless, heedless of the consequences and inexperienced as to the effect, rush into the vortex of dissipation, and, unable to discriminate, become victims to the licentiousness which is suffered to prevail.

Since

Since recreation is necessary to Civilized Society, all Public Exhibitions should be rendered subservient to the improvement of morals, and to the means of infusing into the mind a love of the Constitution, and a reverence and respect for the Laws.—How easy would it be, under the guidance of an appropriate Police, to give a right bias through the medium of Public amusements to the dispositions of the People.—How superior this to the odious practice of besotting themselves in Ale-houses, hatching seditious and treasonable designs, or engaged in pursuits of the vilest profligacy, destructive to health and morals.

Even the common Ballad-singers in the streets might be rendered instruments useful under the controul of a well-regulated Police, in giving a better turn to the minds of the lowest classes of the People. —They too must be amused, and why not, if they can be amused innocently ?—If through this medium they can be taught loyalty to the Sovereign, love to their Country, and obedience to the Laws, would it not be wise and politic to sanction it?

If in addition to this, moral lessons could occasionally be conveyed, shewing in language familiar to their habits, the advantages of *Industry and Frugality* —The pleasure of living independent of the Pawn-broker and the Publican—The disgrace and ruin attached to drunkenness and dishonesty, and the glory and happiness of a *good Husband,* a *good Father,* and *an honest Man,* might it not reasonably be expected, that in a religious as well as a moral point of view,

view, advantages would be gained, while the people were both instructed and amused?

Crimes have been generated in considerable degree both by immoral and seditious books and songs. —It is true the laws are open to punishment. The road however to justice, with respect to the former, is circuitous and difficult, while in the latter case their execution is felt to be *harsh, severe,* and *ultimately ineffectual :* hence licentious and mischievous Publications prevail, and Ballad-singers are suffered often to insult decency, and to disseminate poison in every street in the Metropolis.

Like many other evils they remain in spite of the statutes made to prevent them.—They were evils suffered centuries ago where the laws proved equally unavailing: but the state of society and manners rendered them less dangerous.

In the Machine of Government there are many component parts where responsibility attaches;—*but with respect to objects of Police, it would seem at present to rest no where,* and hence is explained at once, the want of energy in the execution of our laws, and why so many excellent Statutes remain a dead letter.— To live encircled by *fears* arising from uncontrolled excesses of the human passions, either leading to turpitude or terminating in the commission of crimes, *is to live in misery.*—Police is an improved state of Society, which counteracts these excesses by giving energy and effect to the law. It is like the Mechanical power applied to an useful Machine, devoid of

which,

which, it remains without motion, or action, and without benefit.

" Government," *says the benevolent Hanway,* " ori-
" ginates from the love of order.—Watered by Police
" it grows up to maturity, and in course of time
" spreads a luxuriant comfort and security.—Cut off
" its branches, and the mere trunk, however strong
" it may appear, can afford no shelter."

CHAP.

CHAP. XIII.

Indigence a cause of the increase of Crimes.—The Sys-
tem with respect to the Casual Poor erroneous—The
miserable condition of many who seek for an Asylum
in the Metropolis.—The unhappy State of broken-
down Families, who have seen better days.—The
effect of Indigence on the Offspring of the Sufferers.
—The discovery of the Children of unfortunate
Families applying for Soup at the Establishments.—
The unparalleled Philanthropy of the opulent Part
of the Community.—Estimate of the Private and
Public Benevolence amounting to 850,000l. a
year.—The noble Munificence of the Merchants.—
An Appeal to the exalted virtue of the Opulent,
who have come forward in acts of Humanity.—The
deplorable State of the Lower Ranks attributed to
the present System of the Poor Laws.—An Insti-
tution to inquire into the Causes of Mendicity in
the Metropolis explained.—The State of the Casual
Poor resumed.—The abuses and inefficacy of the
Relief received.—A new System proposed with
respect to them and Vagrants in the Metropolis.
—Its Advantages explained.—The distinction be-
tween Poverty and Indigence explained.—The
Poor divided into five Classes, with suggestions
applicable to each.—The evil Examples in Work-
houses a great cause of the Corruption of Mo-
rals.—The Statute of 43 Elizabeth considered.—
The

The defective System of Execution exposed—Confirmed by the opinion of Lord Hale.—A partial Remedy proposed in respect to Vagrant and Casual Poor.—A Public Institution recommended for the care of this class of Poor, under the direction of three Commissioners.—Their Functions explained.—A Proposition for raising a Fund of 5230l. from the Parishes for the support of the Institution, and to relieve them from the Casual Poor.—Reasons why the Experiment should be tried.—The assistance of Sir Frederick Eden, and other Gentlemen of talents, who have turned their thoughts to the Poor, attainable.—The advantages which would result to the Community, from the united Efforts of men of investigation and judgment, previous to any final Legislative Regulation.—Conclusion.

INDIGENCE, in the present state of Society, may be considered as a principal cause of the increase of Crimes.

The System which prevails in the Metropolis, with respect to these unfortunate individuals who are denominated the *Casual Poor*, will be found on minute inquiry to be none of the least considerable of the causes, which lead to the corruption of morals, and to the multiplication of minor offences in particular.

The

The number of persons, who with their families, find their way to the Metropolis, from the most remote quarters of Great Britain and Ireland, is inconceivable. In hopes of finding employment they incur an immediate and constant expence, for lodging and subsistence, until at length their little all is in the Pawnbrokers' shops, or sold to raise money for the necessaries of life. If they have been virtuously brought up in the country, despondency seizes upon their minds, in consequence of the disappointments and hardships, their adventurous or incautious conduct has doomed them to suffer; which, as it applies to the most deserving of this class, who will not steal and are ashamed to beg, often exceeds any thing that the human mind can conceive.

Their Parochial Settlements are either at a great distance, or perhaps as natives of Scotland or Ireland, they are without even this resource. The expence of removing, as the Law directs, is too serious a charge to be incurred by the parish where accident has fixed them. They are treated with neglect and contumely by the Parochial Officers; and even occasionally driven to despair. Willing to labour, but bereft of any channel or medium through which the means of subsistence might be procured. It is assigned to no person to hear their mournful tale, who might be able to place them in a situation, where they might gain a subsistence; and under such circumstances it is much to be feared, that not a few of them either actually perish for want, or contract diseases

diseases which ultimately terminate in premature death.

Such is frequently the situation of the more decent and virtuous class of the labouring people, who come to seek employment in the Metropolis. The more profligate who pursue the same course have generally other resources. Where honest labour is not to be procured, they connect themselves with those who live by petty or more atrocious offences, and contribute in no small degree to the increase of the general phalanx of delinquents. The young female part of such families too often become prostitutes, while the males pursue acts of depredation upon the Public, by availing themselves of the various resources, which the defects in the Police system allow.

In addition to the families who thus resort to the Capital, young men frequently wander up who have become liable to the penalties of the laws, in consequence of being unable to find security for the support of a natural Child in their own parish; or who perhaps have incurred the punishment due to some other offence.—Without money, without recommendations, and bereft of friends, and perhaps afraid of being known, they resort to low public houses, where they meet with thieves and rogues, who not unfrequently in this way recruit their gangs, as often as the arm of Justice diminishes their numbers.

But it is to be lamented, that in contemplating the mass of indigence, which, in its various ramifications,

produces

produces distresses more extensive and more poignant than perhaps in any other spot in the world,
(Paris excepted) its origin is to be traced in almost
every rank of society; and though sometimes the
result of unavoidable misfortune, is perhaps more frequently generated by idleness, inattention to business, and indiscretion.   But at all events, the tear of
pity is due to the helpless and forlorn offspring of
the criminal or indolent, who become objects of compassion, not only as it relates to their immediate subsistence; but much more with respect to their future
situations in life.   It is in the progress to the adult
state, that the infants of parents, broken down by
misfortunes, almost unavoidably learn, from the pressure of extreme poverty, to resort to devices which
early corrupt their morals, and mar their future success and utility in life.   Under the influence of these
sad examples, and their necessary consequences, do
many females become Prostitutes, who in other circumstances, might have been an ornament to their
sex, while the males, by contracting early in life habits
that are pernicious, become, in many instances, no
less noxious to Society.   Familiarized in infancy to
the Pawnbroker's shop, and to other even less reputable means of obtaining temporary subsistence, they
too soon become adepts in falsehood and deceit.   Im-
perious necessity has given an early spring to their
ingenuity. They are generally full of resource, which
in good pursuits might render them useful and valuable members of the community; but unhappily
                                                    their

their minds have acquired a wrong bias, and they are reared insensibly in the walks of vice, without knowing, in many instances that they are at all engaged in evil pursuits.

In all these points of view, from indigence is to be traced the great Origin and the Progress of Crimes.

In attending the different *Soup Establishments* (where 50,000 indigent families, at the expence of one halfpenny per head, have a meal furnished every day during the winter)* the Author has observed, with a mixture of pain and satisfaction, particularly at one of them, the children of unfortunate and reduced families, who, from their appearance, have moved in a higher sphere, the humble suitors for this frugal and nourishing aliment.

To have contributed in any degree to the relief of distress rendered painful in the extreme, from the recollection of better days, is an ample reward to those benevolent individuals, who have joined in the support and conduct of an undertaking, of all others the most beneficial that perhaps was ever devised, for the purpose of assisting and relieving suffering humanity.

While the wretchedness, misery, and crimes, which have been developed, and detailed in this work, cannot be sufficiently deplored, it is a matter of no little exultation, that in no country or nation in the world, and certainly in no other Metropolis, does there exist

---

* See pages 81 and 82 for an account of this Charity.

among

among the higher and middle ranks of Society, an equal portion of Philanthropy and Benevolence.— Here are to be discovered the extremes of vice and virtue, strongly marked by the existing turpitude on one hand, and the noble instances of charitable munificence, displayed by the opulent part of the community, on the other.

Nothing can place this in a stronger point of view, and perhaps nothing will astonish strangers more than the following summary Estimate of the various Institutions, supported chiefly by Voluntary Contributions, in addition to the legal Assessments, all tending to ameliorate and better the condition of human life, under the afflicting circumstances of indigence and disease.*

ESTIMATE.

1. Asylums for the Relief of Objects of Charity £.
   and Humanity   -   -   -   -   - 30,000
2. Asylums and Hospitals, for the Sick, Lame, and
   Diseased   -   -   -   -   -   - 50,000
3. Institutions for Benevolent, Charitable, and
   Humane Purposes   -   -   -   -   - 205,000
4. Private Charities   -   -   -   -   - 150,000
5. Charity Schools for Educating the Poor   -   - 10,000
6. To which add the annual Assessments for the
   Poor Rates, paid by the Inhabitants of the
   Metropolis and its Environs   -   -   - 255,000

   Total estimated amount of the annual Sums paid
      for the support and benefit of the Poor in the ———
      Metropolis, &c.   -   -   *(carried over)* £. 700,000

* For a specific account of these Institutions, see the Chapter on Municipal Police.

7. Besides

Brought over   £.700,000
7. Besides the endowed Establishments for which
    the Poor are chiefly indebted to our Ancestors   150,000

Total   -   -   - £.850,000

In addition to this, it is highly proper to mention the noble benevolence, which has been displayed by the Opulent of all ranks, but particularly the Merchants, in the very large sums which have been, at various times, subscribed for the relief of the brave men, who have been maimed and wounded, and for the support of the widows, orphans, and relations of those who have meritoriously lost their lives in fighting the battles of their country.

Such exalted examples of unbounded munificence the history of no other nation records.

It is to this source of elevated virtue, and nobleness of mind, that an appeal is made, on the present occasion, in behalf of those unhappy fellow-mortals, who, in spite of the unexampled liberality which has been displayed, still require the fostering hand of Philanthropy.

The cause of these distresses has been explained; and also the evils which such a condition in human life entails upon Society. It is not pecuniary aid that will heal this *gangrene:* this *Corruption of Morals.* There must be the application of a correct System of Police calculated to reach the root and origin of the evil.—Without *System, Intelligence, Talents,* and *Industry,* united in all that relates

lates to the affairs of the Poor, millions may be wasted
as millions have already been wasted, without bettering their condition. In all the branches of the
Science of Political Economy, there is none which
requires so much skill and knowledge of men and
manners, as that which relates to this particular
object : and yet, important as it is to the best interests
of the Community, the management of a concern, in
which the very foundation of the national prosperity
is involved, is suffered to remain, as in the rude ages,
when Society had not assumed the bold features of
the present period,—in the hands of changeable,
and in many instances, unlettered agents; wholly
incompetent to a task at all times nice and difficult
in the execution, and often irksome and incon-
venient.

One great feature of this evil, on which it is deplorable to reflect, is, that nearly one million of the
inhabitants of a country, the utmost population of
which is supposed to be short of nine millions, should
be supported in part or in whole by the remaining
eight.

In spite of all the ingenious arguments which have
been used in favour of a System admitted to be wisely
conceived in its origin, the effects it has produced
incontestably prove, that with respect to the mass of
the Poor, there is something radically wrong in the
execution.

If it were not so, it is impossible that there could
exist in the Metropolis such an inconceivable portion

of

of human misery, amidst examples of munificence and benevolence unparalleled in any age or country in the world.

Impressed with these sentiments, so far as they apply to the state of indigence in the Metropolis, a design has been sanctioned by the *Benevolent Society for bettering the Condition of the Poor*, the object of which is to establish a department for inquiring into the history, life, and the causes of the distress of every person who asks relief in any part of the Metropolis: not with a view to support these unfortunate persons in idleness and vice; but to use those means which talents, attention, and humanity can accomplish——(means which are beyond the reach of parochial officers), for the purpose of enabling them to assist themselves. *

* An office has for some time past been instituted under the direction of *Mathew Martin, Esq.* assisted by one or two philanthropic individuals, for inquiring into cases and causes of distress.—— The generality of the poor persons have been invited to the office by the distribution of tickets, directing them when and where they are to apply. On such occasions a small relief has been afforded, arising from a fund constituted by private benevolence;—but the chief advantage which these poor people have derived has been from the consolatory advice given them, and still more from the assistance afforded by the indefatigable industry, and laudable zeal of Mr. Martin, in getting those into workhouses who have parochial settlements in the Metropolis, or assisting in procuring the means of passing them to their parishes, where such settlements are in the country. Seasonable pecuniary relief has been also extended in certain cases, and small loans of money, made to enable those who are able to work to redeem their apparel, and tools to rescue them from despondence, and to help themselves by their own labour, in such employments as they could either themselves obtain, or as could be procured for them.

From

In the Metropolis the Magistrates interfere very little in parochial relief, except when appeals are made to them in particular cases, or when called upon to sign orders of removal, which is generally done as a matter of course. Hence it is that the poor are left almost entirely to the management of the Parochial Officers for the time being, who frequently act under the influence of ignorance or caprice, or are irritated by the impudent importunity of the profligate Gin-drinking poor. These Officers also, it is to be remembered, have private affairs which necessarily engage the chief part of

From the beginning of the year 1796 to the end of the year 1797, Mr. Martin investigated the cases of 120 poor persons, who attended him in consequence of the tickets which were distributed.— Of these 21 were men; the greater part maimed or disabled by age or sickness, only two of whom had any legal settlement in London. Of the women, 99 in number, 48 were widows, about one-third were aged—some crippled, and others distressed for want of work, while many were embarrassed by ignorance of the mode of obtaining parochial relief, or by the fear of applying for it:—of the wives, in most cases, the difficulty arose from want of work or incapacity of doing it, on account of a child in arms. There were cases of very great distress. Above half had two or more children. Some of them infants, and the chief part too young to work. Of the women 24 claimed settlements in London and Westminster—33 in different parts of England—22 belonged to Scotland and Ireland, and the remaining 20 said they could give no account of their place of settlement. In most instances by an application to their parishes, and in some to their friends, Mr. Martin was enabled to obtain effectual relief to all of them; the gift of a little food, and hearing their melancholy story, afforded some comfort; and had a small fund been appropriated to this object, it might have been possible to have enabled those who were in health to have earned a livelihood. See 12th Report of the *Society for bettering the Condition of the Poor.*

their

their attention, and are frequently no less incapable
than unwilling to enter on those investigations which
might enable them to make the proper discrimina-
tions; the modest and shamefaced poor are thus
frequently shut out from relief, while the vociferous
and idle succeed in obtaining pecuniary assistance,
which is soon improvidently dissipated.

The distress which is thus shewn to prevail, by
no means arises from the want of competent funds :
—the misfortune is, that from the nature of the present mode of management it is not possible to apply
these funds beneficially for the proper relief of those
for whom they were intended.   A much more moderate assessment, under a regular and proper management, would remove great part of the evil.

The expence of the class of persons denominated
Casual Poor, who have no settlement in any parish in
the Metropolis, amounts to a large sum annually.—
In the united parishes of St. Giles in the Fields, and
St. George, Bloomsbury, this expence amounted to
2000l. in the year 1796.   It arose from the support
of about 1200 poor natives of Ireland, who but for
this aid must have become vagrants.   The shocking
abuse of the vagrant passes previous to the year 1792,
produced the Act of the 32 Geo. III. cap. 45. which
requires that Rogues and Vagabonds should be first
publicly whipt, or confined seven days in the House
of Correction, (females to be imprisoned only, and
in no case whipped) before they are passed as directed by the Act of the 17 Geo. II. c. 5.   Hence it
is that so many who are either on the brink of vagrancy

grancy, or have actually received alms, are permitted
to remain a burden on the parishes; the Magistrates
being loth to incur the charge of inhumanity, by
strictly following the letter of the Act, in whipping
or imprisoning poor miserable wretches, whose indigence have rendered relief necessary.

In all the 146 parishes within and without the
walls, including the Bills of Mortality, &c. it is not
improbable that the casual charity given in this way,
may amount to 10,000l. a year.

The loose manner in which it is given, and the
impossibility either of a proper discrimination, or
of finding in the distributing these resources, that
time for investigation which might lead to the solid
benefit of the Pauper, by restoring him to a capacity
of earning his own livelihood, makes it highly probable that instead of being useful, this large sum is
perhaps hurtful, to the major part of the poor who
receive it. The trifle they receive, from being inju-
diciously given, and frequently to get rid of the
clamour and importunity of the most profligate, is
too often spent immediately in the Gin-shop.—No
inquiry is made into the circumstances of the family
—No measures are pursued to redeem the apparel
locked up in the Pawnbroker's shop, although a
small sum would frequently recover the habiliments
of a naked and starving family—no questions are
asked respecting the means they employ to subsist
themselves by labour; and no efforts are used to
procure

procure employment for those who are willing to labour, but have not the means of obtaining work.

Hence it is that poverty, under such circumstances, contributes in no small degree to the multiplication of crimes. The profligate thus partly supported, too often resorts to pilfering pursuits to fill up the chasm, and habits of idleness being once obtained, labour soon becomes irksome.

Why should not the whole nation, but particularly the Metropolis, be considered, so far at least as regards the vagrant and casual Poor, as one family, and be placed under the review of certain persons who might be considered as worthy of the trust, and might devote their time sedulously to that object?—Were such an establishment instituted, and supported in the first instance by a sum from each parish, equal to the casual relief they have each given on an average of the five preceding years, with power to employ this fund in establishing Houses of Industry, or Work-rooms, in various parts of the Metropolis, where the Poor should receive the whole of their earnings and a comfortable meal besides:—it is highly probable that while the expence to the parishes would gradually diminish, beggary would be annihilated in the Metropolis—the modest and deserving Poor would be discovered and relieved, while the idle and profligate, who resorted to begging as a trade, would be compelled to apply to honest labour for their subsistence.

This

This is a point in the political œconomy of the Nation highly important, whether it relates to the cause of humanity or to the morals of the people, upon which all good Governments are founded.— That such an institution is practicable is already proved from the partial experiments that have been made.   That the advantages resulting from it would be great beyond all calculation, is too obvious to require elucidation.

While it operated beneficially to the lower classes of the people and to the State, it would relieve Parochial Officers of a very irksome and laborious task, perhaps the most disagreeable that is attached to the office of an Overseer in the Metropolis.

To give this branch of Police vigor and effect, the aid of the Legislature would be necessary; which would be easily obtained when the measure itself was once thoroughly understood, and it could not then fail to be as popular as it would unquestionably be useful.

They who from their habits of life have few opportunities of considering the state of the Poor, are apt to form very erroneous opinions on the subject.

By *the Poor* we are not to understand the whole mass of the people who support themselves by labour; for those whose necessity compels them to exercise their industry, become by their poverty the actual pillars of the State.

Labour is absolutely requisite to the existence of all Governments; and as it is from the Poor only that labour can be expected, so far from being an evil,

evil, they become, under proper regulations, an advantage to every Country, and highly deserve the fostering care of every Government. It is not *Poverty*, therefore, that is in itself an evil, while health, strength, and inclination, afford the means of subsistence, and while work is to be had by all who seek it.—The evil is to be found only in *Indigence*, where the strength fails, where disease, age, or infancy deprives the individual of the means of subsistence, or where he knows not how to find employment when willing and able to work.

In this view *the Poor* may be divided into five Classes :—

The first Class comprehends what may be denominated *the useful Poor*, who are able and willing to work—who have already been represented as the pillars of the State, and who merit the utmost attention of all governments, with a direct and immediate view of preventing their *poverty* from descending unnecessarily into *indigence*. As often as this evil is permitted to happen, the State not only loses an useful subject, but the expence of his maintenance must be borne by the Public.— The great art, therefore, in managing the affairs of the Poor, is to establish Systems whereby the poor man, verging upon indigence, may be propped up and kept in his station.   Whenever this can be effected, it is done upon an average at one-tenth of the expence at most that must be incurred by

permitting

permitting a family to retrograde into a state of indigence, where they must be wholly maintained
by the Public, and where their own exertions cease
in a great measure to be useful to the Country.

The second Class comprehends the *vagrant Poor;* who
are able but not willing to work, or who cannot
obtain employment in consequence of their bad
character. This class may be said to have descended from poverty into beggary, in which state
they become objects of peculiar attention, since
the State suffers not only the loss of their labour,
but also of the money which they obtain by the
present ill-judged mode of giving charity. Many
of them, however, having become mendicants,
more from necessity than choice, deserve commiseration and attention, and nothing can promote in a greater degree the cause of humanity,
and the real interest of the Metropolis, than an
establishment for the employment of this class of
indigent Poor, who may be said at present to be
in a very deplorable state, those only excepted
who make begging a profession. It is only by a
plan, such as has been recommended, that the
real indigent can be discovered from the vagrant,
and in no other way is it possible to have that
distinct and collected view of the whole class of
beggars in the Metropolis, or to provide the means
of rendering their labour (where they are able to
labour) productive to themselves and the State.—
And it may be further added with great truth, that
in

in no other way is it possible to prevei t the offspring of such mendicants from becoming *Prostitutes* and *Thieves*.

If, therefore, it is of importance to diminish
crimes, and to obstruct the progress of immorality,
this part of the Community ought to be the peculiar objects of a branch of the National Police,
where responsibility would secure an accurate execution of the System. This measure ought to begin
in the Metropolis as an experiment, and when fully
matured might be extended with every advantage
to the Country.

The third Class may be considered under the denomination of the *Indigent Poor*, who from want of
employment, *sickness, losses,* insanity or disease,
are unable to maintain themselves.

In attending to this description of Poor, the first
consideration ought to be to select those who are
in a state to re-occupy their former station among
the labouring Poor; and to restore them to the
first class as soon as possible, by such relief as
should enable them to resume their former employments, and to help themselves and families.

Where insanity, or temporary disease, or infirmity actually exist, such a course must then be
pursued as will enable such weak and indigent
persons, while they are supported at the expence
of the Public, to perform such species of labour,
as may be suited to their peculiar situations,
without operating as a hardship, but rather as an
                                            amuse-

amusement. In this manner it is wonderful how productive the exertions of even the most infirm might be rendered.—But it must be accomplished under a management very different, indeed, from any thing which prevails at present.

The fourth Class comprehends the *aged and infirm,* who are entirely past labour, and have no means of support.—Where an honest industrious man has wasted his strength in labour and endeavours to rear a family, he is well entitled to an asylum to render the evening of his life comfortable. For this class the gratitude and the humanity of the Community ought to provide a retreat separate from the profligate and vagrant Poor. But, alas! the present System admits of no such blessing.— The most deserving must submit to an indiscriminate intercourse in Workhouses with the most worthless: whose polluted language and irregular conduct, render not a few of those asylums as great a punishment to the decent part of the indigent and infirm as a common prison.

The Fifth Class comprizes the *Infant Poor,* who from extreme indigence, or the death of parents, are cast upon the public for nurture. One fifth part of the gross number in a London Workhouse is generally composed of this class. Their moral and religious education is of the last importance to the Community. They are the children of the Public, and if not introduced into life, under circumstances favourable to the interest of the State,

the

the error in the System becomes flagrant.—Profligate or distressed parents may educate their children ill; but when those under the charge of Public Institutions are suffered to become depraved in their progress to maturity, it is a dreadful reproach on the Police of the Country.—And yet what is to be expected from children reared in Workhouses, with the evil examples before them of the multitudes of depraved characters who are constantly admitted into those receptacles? Young minds are generally more susceptible of evil than of good impressions; and hence it is that the rising generation enter upon life with those wicked and dangerous propensities, which are visible to the attentive observer in all the walks of vulgar life in this great Metropolis.

The limits of this Treatise will not permit the Author to attempt more than a mere outline on the general subject of the Poor; a System of all others the most difficult to manage and arrange with advantage to the Community; but which is at present unhappily entrusted to the care of those least competent to the task.

The principle of the Statute of the 43d of Elizabeth is certainly unobjectionable; but the execution, it must be repeated, is defective. In short, no part of it has been effectually executed, but that which relates to raising the assessments. It is easy to make Statutes; but omniponent as Parliament is said to be,

it

it cannot give *knowledge, education, public spirit, integrity,* and *time,* to those changeable Agents whom it has charged with the execution of the Poor Laws.

In the management of the affairs of the State, the Sovereign wisely selects men eminent for their talents and integrity.—Were the choice to be made on the principle established by the Poor Laws, the Nation could not exist even a single year.

In the private affairs of life, the success of every difficult undertaking depends on the degree of abilities employed in the management. In the affairs of the Poor, the most arduous and intricate that it is possible to conceive, and where the greatest talents and knowledge are required, the least portion of either is supplied. How then can we expect success?—The error is not in the original design, which is wise and judicious. The 43d of Elizabeth authorizes an assessment to be made for three purposes.

1st. To purchase Raw Materials to set the Poor to work, who could not otherwise dispose of their labour.

2d. To usher into the world, advantageously, the Children of poor people, by binding them apprentices to some useful employment.

3d. To provide for the lame, impotent and blind, and others, being poor and not able to work.

Nothing can be better imagined than the measures in the view of the very able framers of this act: but they did not discover that to execute such a

design

design required powers diametrically opposite to those which the law provided. The last two centuries have afforded a series of proof of the total inefficacy of the application of these powers, not only by the effects which this erroneous superintendance has produced; but also from the testimony of the most enlightened men who have written on the subject, from the venerable Lord Hale to the patriotic and indefatigable Sir Frederick Eden. But the strongest evidence of the mischiefs arising from this defective execution of a valuable System, is to be found in the Statute Books themselves.*

" The want of a due provision," says Lord Hale, " for the relief and education of the Poor in the " way of *industry*, is what fills the gaols with Male-" factors, the Country with idle and unprofitable " persons, that consume the stock of the Kingdom " without improving it; and that will daily increase " even to a desolation in time—and this error, in " the first concoction, is never remediable but by " gibbets and whipping."

That this will continue to be the case under any species of changeable management, however apparently correct in theory the System may be, must

---

* In the Preamble of the Statute on 3 & 4 *William* and *Mary*, *cap.* 11. and particularly § 11 of that Act, in which the sense entertained by Parliament, of the shocking abuses of the Statute of Elizabeth, " through the unlimited power of Parish Officers," is very forcibly expressed—the truths there stated are found to have full force, even at the distance of more than a Century.

appear

appear self-evident to every man of business and observation, whose attention has been practically directed to the general operation of the present mode
in various parishes, and who has reflected deeply on
the subject.

But to return to the immediate object of inquiry,
namely, the means of more effectually preventing
the numerous evils which arise from indigence and
mendicity in the Metropolis, whether excited by idleness or extreme and unforeseen pressures : Under
every circumstance it would seem impracticable without any burthen upon the Public, to provide for all
such at least as are denominated Casual Poor (from
whom the greatest part of this calamity springs) by
adopting the following or some similar plan, under
the sanction of Government, and the authority of
the Legislature.

THAT a Public Institution shall be established in
the Metropolis, with *three Chief Officers*, who shall
be charged with the execution of that branch of the
Police, which relates to STREET BEGGARS, and those
classes of Poor who have no legal settlements in the
Metropolis, and who now receive casual relief from
the different Parishes, where they have fixed their residence for the time ;—and that these principal Officers, (who may be stiled *Commissioners for inquiring
into the Cases and Causes of the Distress of the Poor
in the Metropolis*) should exercise the following

FUNCTIONS :

FUNCTIONS:—

1st. To charge themselves with the relief and management of the whole of the *Casual Poor*, who at present receive temporary aid from the different Parishes, or who ask alms in any part of the Metropolis or its Suburbs.

2d. To provide Work-rooms in various central and convenient situations in the Metropolis, where persons destitute of employment may receive a temporary subsistence for labour. To superintend these work-houses, and become responsible for the proper management.

3d. To be empowered to give temporary relief to prop up sinking families, and to prevent their descending from poverty to indigence, by arresting the influence of despondency, and keeping the spirit of industry alive.

4th. To assist in binding out the Children of the Poor, or the Unfortunate, who have seen better days, and preventing the females from the danger of becoming Prostitutes, or the males from contracting loose and immoral habits, so as if possible to save them to their parents, and to the state.

5th. To open Offices of inquiry in different parts of the Metropolis, where all classes of indigent persons, who are not entitled to parochial relief, will be invited to resort, for the purpose of being examined

mined, and relieved according to the peculiar circumstance of the case.

6th. To exercise the legal powers, through the medium of Constables, for the purpose of compelling all Mendicants, and idle destitute Boys and Girls who appear in the streets, to come before the Commissioners for examination ; that those whose industry cannot be made productive, or who cannot be put in a way to support themselves without alms, may be passed to their Parishes, while means are employed to bind out destitute Children to some useful occupation.

7th. To keep a distinct Register of the cases of all Mendicants or distressed individuals, who may seek advice and assistance, and to employ such means for alleviating misery, as the peculiar circumstances may suggest—never losing sight of indigence, until an asylum is provided for the helpless and infirm, and also until the indigent, who are able to labour, are placed in a situation to render it productive.

8th. That these Commissioners shall report their proceedings annually, to his Majesty in Council, and to Parliament ; with abstracts shewing the numbers who have been examined—How disposed of—The earning of the persons at the different Work-rooms—The annual expence of the Establishment ; together with a general view of the advantages resulting from it; with the proofs of these advantages.

Towards

Towards defraying the whole expence of this Establishment it is proposed, that (in lieu of the Casual Charity, paid at present by all the Parishes in the Metropolis which under this System will cease, together with the immense trouble attached to it,) each Parish in the Metropolis shall pay into the hands of the Receiver of the Funds of this *Pauper Police Institution*, a sum equal to what was formerly disbursed in casual relief, which for the purpose of elucidation, is estimated as follows:—

	£.	s.	d.
97 Parishes within the Walls, average 10*l*. each	970	0	0
16 Parishes without the Walls, in London and			
Southwark, average 60*l*. each - -	960	0	0
	£.1,930	0	0
3 Out-parishes in Middlesex and Surrey, average 10*l*. each - - - -	2,300	0	0
10 Parishes in Westminster, average 100*l*. each	1,000,	0	0
146	£.5,230	0	0

This sum (which is supposed to be not much above one half of the average Annual disbursements of the 146 Parishes above mentioned, especially since it has been shewn, that the expence in St. Giles' and St. George Bloomsbury alone, has been 2600*l*. in one year) will probably, with œconomy and good management, be found sufficient for all the relief that is required; more especially as the object is not to

maintain

maintain the indigent, but to put them in a way of supporting themselves by occasional pecuniary aids well and judiciously applied.

The experiment is certainly worth trying. In its execution some of the most respectable and intelligent individuals in the Metropolis, would gratuitously assist the Commissioners, who as taking responsibility upon them, in the direction of a most important branch of Police, ought undoubtedly to be remunerated by Government, especially as it is scarcely possible to conceive any mode in which the Public money could be applied, that would be productive of such benefit to the State.

If that utility resulted from the design, which may reasonably be expected, it would of course extend to other great towns, as the private *Soup Establishments* have done, and the condition of the poor would undergo a rapid change. The destitute and forlorn would then have some means of communicating their distress, while information and facts of the greatest importance, to the best interests of Society, would spring from this source.

With respect to the general affairs of the poor, much good would arise from consolidating the funds of all the parishes in the Metropolis.

The poor, for instance, who are supported from the parochial funds of Bethnal Green, and other distressed parishes in the eastern parts of the Metropolis, are the labourers of the citizens and inhabitants of the 97 Parishes within the Walls, who, although opulent,

opulent, pay little or nothing to the Poor, since the city affords no cottages to lodge them.

Why, therefore, should not the inhabitants of the rich parishes contribute to the relief of the distresses of those who waste their strength in contributing to their *ease, comfort,* and *profit ?* In several of the most populous Parishes and Hamlets in the eastern part of the Town, the Poor may actually be said to be assessed to support the indigent. In the very populous Hamlet of Mile-End New Town, where there is scarcely an inhabitant who does not derive his subsistence from some kind of labour, the rates are treble the assessments in Mary-le-bone, where opulence abounds. Nothing can exceed the inequality of the weight for the support of the Poor in the Metropolis; since where the demand is greatest, the means of supply are always most deficient and inadequate.

Certain it is that the whole system admits of much improvement, and perhaps at no period, since the Poor Laws have attracted attention, did there exist so many able and intelligent individuals as at present, who have been excited by motives of patriotism and philanthropy, to devote their time to the subject.

At the head of this most Respectable Group stands Sir FREDERICK EDEN ; a gentleman, whose entrance into life, has been marked by a display of the most useful talents, manifested by an extent of labour and perseverance, in his elaborate work on the Poor, which may be said to be unparalleled in point of information,

formation, while it unquestionably exhibits the respectable Author as a character in whose patriotism and abilities the State will find a considerable resource, in whatever tends to assist his Country, or to improve the condition of Human Life.

To the Lord Bishop of Durham, the Earl of Winchelsea, Count Rumford, Sir William Young, Thos. Ruggles, Esq. William Morton Pitt, Esq. Jeremy Bentham, Esq. Robert Saunders, Esq. Thomas Bernard, Esq. William Wilberforce, Esq. Rowland Burdon, Esq. the Rev. Dr. Glasse, the Rev. Thomas Gisbourn, the Rev. Mr. Howlet, Mr. Davis, Mr. Townsend, Arthur Young, Esq. and William Sabatier, Esq. as well as several other respectable living characters, who have particularly turned their thoughts to the subject of the Poor, the Public are not only already much indebted, but from this prolific resource of judgment, talents, and knowledge, much good might be expected, if ever the period shall arrive when the revision of the Poor Laws shall engage the attention of the Legislature.

The measure is too complicated to be adjusted by men, who have not opportunities or leisure to contemplate its infinite ramifications.

It is a task which can only be executed with accuracy by those, who completely understand the subject as well in practice as in theory, and who can bestow the time requisite for those laborious investigations, which must be absolutely necessary to form

a final

a final opinion, and to report to Parliament what is most expedient, under all circumstances, to be done in this important National Concern.

Happy is it for the country, that a resource exists for the attainment of this object, than which nothing can contribute, in a greater degree, to the prevention of Crimes, and to the general improvement of Civil Society.

CHAP.

C H A P. XIV.

The state of the Police, with regard to the detection of different classes of offenders, explained.—The necessity, under the present circumstances, of having recourse to the known Receivers of stolen Goods, for the purpose of discovering Offenders, as well as the property stolen.—The great utility of Officers of Justice as safeguards of the Community.—The advantages to be derived from rendering them respectable in the opinion of the Public. Their powers, by the common and statute law, are extensive.—The great antiquity of the Office of Constable, exemplified by different Ancient Statutes.—The authority of Officers and others explained, in apprehending persons accused of felony.—Rewards granted in certain cases as encouragements to Officers to be vigilant :——The statutes quoted, applicable to such rewards, shewing that they apply to ten different offences. The utility of parochial Constables, under a well-organized Police, explained.—A fund for this purpose would arise from the reduction of the expences of the Police by the diminution of Crimes.—The necessity of a competent fund explained.—The deficiency of the present System exemplified in the effect of the presentments by Constables to the Grand Inquest.—A new System proposed.—The functions of the different classes of Officers, explained.—Salaries necessary to all.—The System of rewards, as now established, shewn to be

radically

radically deficient; exemplified by the circumstance,
that in 1088 *prisoners, charged at the Old Bailey in*
one year, with 36 *different offences, only* 9 *offences*
entitled the apprehenders to any gratuity:—Improve-
ments suggested for the greater encouragement of
*Officers of Justice.—*1043 *Peace Officers in the*
Metropolis and its vicinity, of whom only 90 *are*
stipendiary Constables.—Little assistance to be ex-
pected from Parochial Officers, while there exists no
fund for rewarding extraordinary services.—Great
advantages likely to result from rewarding all Officers
for useful services actually performed.—The utility
of extending the same gratuities to Watchmen and
Patroles.—Defects and abuses in the System of the
Watch explained.—The number of Watchmen and
Patroles in the Metropolis estimated at 2044 :—*A*
general System of superintendance suggested.—A
view of the Magistracy of the Metropolis.—The
efficient duty shewn to rest with the City and Police
Magistrates.—The inconvenience of the present
System.—Concluding Observations.

As it must be admitted, that the evils arising from
the multiplied crimes detailed in the preceding Chapters, render a correct and energetic System of Police
with regard to the *detection, discovery,* and *apprehension*
of offenders, indispensably necessary for the safety and
well-being of Society; it follows of course, in the
order

order of this Work, to explain *how this branch of the public service is conducted at present, the defects which are apparent,—and the means of improving the System.*

When robberies or burglaries have been committed in or near the Metropolis, where the property is of considerable value, the usual method at present, is to apply to the City Magistrates, if in London; or otherwise, to the Justices at one of the Public Offices,* and to publish an Advertisement offering a reward on the recovery of the articles stolen, and the conviction of the offenders.†

* It is a well-known fact, that many persons who suffer by means of small Robberies, afraid of the trouble and expence of a prosecution, submit to the loss without inquiry; while others from being strangers to the laws, and to the proper mode of application, fall into the same mistake; this, by proving a great encouragement to thieves of every class, is of course an injury to the Public.—In all cases where robberies are committed, the parties sustaining the loss have only to inquire for the nearest Public Office, and apply there, and state the case to the sitting Magistrates, who will point out the proper mode of detection; every assistance through the medium of constables, will then be given for the purpose of recovering the property and apprehending the offenders.—The same assistance will be afforded by the Lord Mayor and Aldermen, sitting at the Mansion-house and Guildhall, whenever the offence is committed within the limits of the City of London.

† It had been usual for many years previous to 1752, when robberies were committed, to make a composition of the felony, by advertising a reward to any person who would bring the property stolen, to be paid without asking any questions; but the pernicious consequences of recovering goods in this way from the encouragement such advertisements held out to thieves and robbers of every description, became so glaring and obvious, that an Act passed the 25th year of George II. cap. 36. *inflicting a penalty of 50l. on any*
person

In many cases of importance, to the reproach of the Police, resource is had to noted and known Receivers of stolen Goods for their assistance in discovering such offenders, and of pointing out the means by which the property may be recovered : this has on many occasions been productive of success to the parties who have been robbed ; as well as to the ends of public justice; for however lamentable it is to think that Magistrates are compelled to have recource to such expedients, yet while the present System continues, and while robberies and burglaries are so frequent, without the means of prevention, there is no alternative on many occasions *but to employ a thief to catch a thief.*

It is indeed so far fortunate, that when the influence of Magistrates is judiciously and zealously employed in this way, it is productive in many instances of considerable success, not only in the recovery of property stolen, but also in the detection and punishment of atrocious offenders.

Wherever activity and zeal are manifested on the part of the Magistrates, the Peace Officers, under their immediate direction, seldom fail to exhibit a similar desire to promote the ends of public justice. And when it is considered that these Officers, while

person (including the printer and publisher) *who shall publicly advertise a reward for the return of stolen goods with " no questions asked," without seizing the person producing the goods stolen :—or who shall offer to return to any pawnbroker, or other person, the money lent thereon, or any other reward for the return of the articles stolen.*

they

they conduct themselves with purity, are truly *the safeguards of the Community*, destined to protect the Public against the outrages and lawless depredations of a set of miscreants, who are the declared enemies of the State, by making war upon all ranks of the body politic, who have property to lose;—they have a fair claim, while they act properly, to be esteemed as " *the civil defenders of the lives and* " *properties of the People.*"

Every thing that can heighten in any degree the respectability of the office of *Constable*, adds to the security of the State, and the safety of the life and property of every individual.

Under such circumstances, it cannot be sufficiently regretted that these useful constitutional officers, destined for the protection of the Public, have been (with a very few exceptions) so little regarded, so carelessly selected, and so ill supported and rewarded for the imminent risques which they run, and the services they perform in the execution of their duty.

The common Law, as well as the ancient Statutes of the kingdom, having placed extensive powers in the hands of *Constables* and *Peace Officers;*—they are, in this point of view, to be considered as *respectable;*—and it is the interest of the Community, that they should support that rank and character in society, which corresponds with the authority with which they are invested.—If this were attended to, men of credit and discretion would not be so averse to

fill

fill such situations; and those pernicious prejudices, which have prevailed in vulgar life, and in some degree among the higher ranks in Society, with regard to *thief-takers*, would no longer operate; for it is plain to demonstration, *that the best laws that ever were made can avail nothing, if the Public Mind is impressed with an idea, that it is a matter of infamy, to become the casual or professional agents to carry them into execution.*

This absurd prejudice against the office of Constable, and the small encouragement which the major part receive, is one of the chief reasons why unworthy characters have filled such situations; and why the public interest has suffered by the increase of crimes.

The office of Constable is as old as the Monarchy of England;—and certainly existed in the time of the Saxons.*—The law requires that he should be *idoneus homo :* or in other words, *to have honesty to execute the office without malice, affection, or partiality; knowledge to understand what he ought to do ; and ability, as well in substance or estate, as in body,* to enable him to conduct himself with utility to the public.

The Statute of Winchester, made in the 13th year of Edward the First (anno 1285) appoints two Constables to be chosen in every Hundred; and such seems to have been the attention of the Legislature to the Police of the Country at that early period of

* Fineux.

qur

our history, "*that suspicious night-walkers are ordered to be arrested and detained by the watch.*"*

The Statute of 5 Edward III. *cap.* 44, (anno 1332) empowers Constables "*to arrest persons suspected of man-slaughter, felonies, and robberies, and to deliver them to the Sheriff, to be kept in prison till the coming of the Justices:*" and another Act of the 34th of the same reign, *cap.* 1, (made anno 1361,) empowers Justices, *(inter alia,)* "*to inquire after wanderers, to arrest and imprison suspicious persons, and to oblige persons of evil fame to give security for good behaviour; so that the People may not be troubled by rioters, nor the peace blemished, nor Merchants and others travelling on the highways be disturbed or put in peril by such offenders.*"

By the common law, every person committing a felony may be arrested by any person whomsoever present at the fact, who may secure the prisoner in gaol, or carry him before a Magistrate;†—and if a prisoner thus circumstanced, resists and refuses to yield, those who arrest will be justified in the beating him,‡ or, in case of absolute necessity, even killing him. §

In arresting persons on suspicion of a felony, actually committed, *common fame* has been adjudged to be a reasonable cause. ||

There are four methods, known in law, by which

---

* Winton, chap. 4.   † Hale.   ‡ Pult. 10, a.
        § Hale. || Dalton.

Officers

Officers of Justice, as well as private individuals, may arrest persons charged with felony.—1. *By the warrant of a Magistrate.*—2. *By an Officer without a warrant.*—3. *By a Private Person without a warrant.*—And 4. *By Hue-and-Cry.**

When a warrant is received by an Officer, he is bound to execute it, so far as the jurisdiction of the Magistrate and himself extends.—But the *Constable* having great original and inherent authority, may, *without warrant,* apprehend any person for a breach of the Peace: and in case of felony, *actually committed,* he may, on probable suspicion, arrest the felon: and for that purpose (as upon the warrant of a Magistrate,) he is authorized to break open doors, and even justified in killing the felon, if he cannot otherwise be taken.†

All persons present, when a felony is committed, are bound to arrest the felon, on pain of fine and imprisonment, if he escapes through negligence of the by-standers; who will (the same as a constable) in such case be justified in breaking open doors, to follow such felon, and even to kill him if he cannot be taken otherwise. ‡

The other species of arrest is called *Hue-and-Cry,* which is an *alarm raised in the country* upon any felony being committed. This was an ancient practice in use as far back as the reign of Edward the First, (1285) by which, in the then infant state of society,

---

* Blackstone.　　† Blackstone.　　‡ Blackstone.

it

it became easy to discover criminal persons flying from justice.

However doubtful the utility of this ancient method of detecting offenders may be, in a great Metropolis, in the present extended state of Society, it is plain, that it has been considered as an important regulation of Police so late as the 8th George II. (1735;) since it was enacted in that year, (stat. 8 George II. cap. 16.) that the Constable who neglects making *hue-and-cry*, shall forfeit five pounds; and even the district is liable to be fined (according to the law of Alfred) if the felony be committed therein, and the felon escapes*. This, however, applies more particularly to the country, and where the practice cannot fail to be useful in a certain degree.

When a *hue-and-cry* is raised, every person, by command of the Constable, must pursue the felon, on pain of fine and imprisonment.

In this pursuit also, Constables may search suspected houses if the doors be open : *but unless the felon is actually in the house,* it will not be justifiable to use force; nor even then, except where admittance has been demanded and refused.

A Constable, even without a warrant, may break open a door for the purpose of apprehending a felon; but to justify this measure, he must not only shew that the felon was in the house, but also that access was denied after giving notice that he was a Con-

---

* Blackstone.

stable,

stable, and demanding admittance in that capacity.*
In the execution of the warrant of a Magistrate, the
Officer is certainly authorized to break open the
doors of the felon, or of the house of any person where
he is concealed.—The first is lawful under all circumstances: but forcibly entering the house of a
stranger may be considered as a trespass, if the felon
should not be there.†

Such are the powers with which Constables are
invested,—and which are, in many instances, enforced by penal ties; that public justice may not be
defeated‡.

In addition to this, the wisdom of the Legislature,
as an encouragement to officers and others to do
their duty in apprehending and prosecuting offenders, has granted rewards in certain cases; *Namely,*

4 Will. & Mary, c. 8; and 6 Geo. I. c. 23.

1. For apprehending, and prosecut- *£.*
ing to conviction, every robber, on the
highway, including the streets of the
Metropolis, and all other towns, a reward of 40l. besides the *horse, furniture, arms,* and *money,* of the said robber if not stolen property: to be paid
to the person apprehending, or if killed
in the endeavour, to his Executors,   40
    And the Stat. 8 Geo. II. c. 16. su-
peradds 10l. to be paid by the Hundred
indemnified by such taking.

* Hale.   † Hale.

‡ It may not be improper in this place to hint, that there is a deficiency in the present state of the Law, which calls aloud for a
remedy. None can be arrested on a Sunday, but for felony or
breach of the peace (except in certain cases, where their guilt
has been previously decided on, as in *Escape,* &c.) By this means
Lottery-Vagrants, Gamblers, Sharpers, and Swindlers, bid defiance to the Civil Power on that day; while a person guilty of
pushing or striking another in an accidental squabble, may be
arrested and confined.

                                                2. For

6 & 7 Will. and Mary, c.17; and 15 & 16 Geo. II. c. 28.

2. For apprehending and prosecut- £. ing to conviction, every person who shall have counterfeited, clipped, washed,* filed, or diminished the current coin; or who shall gild silver to make it pass as gold, or copper, as silver,— or who shall utter false money, (being the third offence) or after being once convicted of being a common utterer, &c. a reward of   40

3. For apprehending and prosecuting to conviction, every person counterfeiting copper money, a reward of   10

10 and 11 Will. III. c. 23.

4. For apprehending and prosecuting to conviction, every person privately stealing to the value of 5s. from any *Shop*, *Warehouse*, or *Stable*, a Tyburn ticket,† average value, about   20

10 and 11 Will. III. c. 23.
5 Ann, c. 32.

5. For apprehending and prosecuting to conviction, every person charged with a burglary, a reward of 40l. (to the apprehender, or if killed, to his executors) in money, and a Tyburn ticket, 20l.   60

6. For apprehending, and prosecuting to conviction, every person charged with house-breaking in the day-time, 40l. in money, and a Tyburn ticket   60

7. For apprehending, and prosecuting to conviction, any person charged with horse stealing, a Tyburn ticket   20

6 Geo. I. c. 23.

8. For apprehending and prosecuting with effect, a person charged with the offence of compounding a felony, by taking money to help a person to stolen goods, without prosecuting and giving evidence against the felon   40

* In consequence of some doubts which have been started relative to washed money, the reward in this case is not paid; it is confined entirely to the conviction of *Coiners*.

† This is a Certificate which may be assigned once, exempting the person who receives it, or his immediate assignee, from all offices within the parish or ward where the felony was committed. In some parishes it will sell from 25l. to 30l. In others it is not worth above 15l. to 18l. according to local situation.

9. For

14 Geo. II. c. 6. 15 Geo. II. c. 34.	9. For apprehending and prosecut- £. ing with effect, a person charged with stealing, or killing to steal, any sheep, lamb, bull, cow, ox, steer, bullock, heifer, or calf, 10
16 Geo. II. c. 15. 8 Geo. III. c. 15.	10. For apprehending, and prosecuting with effect, persons returning from transportation 20

These rewards apply to ten different offences, and ought, no doubt, to be a considerable spur to Officers to do their duty ; but it may be doubted whether this measure has not, in some degree, tended to the increase of a multitude of smaller crimes which are pregnant with the greatest mischiefs to Society.—It is by deterring men from the commission of *smaller* crimes (says the Marquis Beccaria) that *greater* ones are prevented.

If small rewards were given in cases of *Grand Larceny*, (now very numerous,) as well as of several other felonies, frauds, and misdemeanors, a species of activity would enter into the system of detection, which has not heretofore been experienced.

While rewards are limited to higher offences, and CONVICTION *is the indispensible condition upon which they are granted,* it is much to be feared that lesser crimes are overlooked ; and the Public subjected, in many instances, to the intermediate depredations of a rogue, from his first starting upon the town until he shall be worth 40*l.*

This system of giving high rewards only on conviction, also tends to weaken evidence : since it is obvious that the Counsel for all Prisoners, whose offences entitle the Prosecutors and Officers to a reward,

ward, generally endeavour to impress upon the minds of the Jury an idea that witnesses, who have a pecuniary interest in the conviction of any offender standing on trial, are not, on all occasions, deserving of full credit, unless strongly corroborated by other evidence; and thus many notorious offenders often escape justice.

By altering the system entirely, and leaving it in the breast of the Judge who tries the offence, to determine what reward shall be allowed, with a power to *grant* or *withhold,* or to *limit* and *increase the same,* according to circumstances connected with the trouble and risk of the parties, *whether there is a conviction or not,* a fairer measure of recompence would be dealt out;—the public money would be more beneficially distributed,* so as to excite general activity in checking every species of criminality;—and the objections, now urged against Officers and Prosecutors as interested witnesses, would, by this arrangement, be completely obviated.

For the purpose of elucidating these suggestions, it may be useful to examine the different offences

---

* The expence to the Public for rewards paid by the Sheriffs of the different Counties for 12 years, from 1786 to 1797 inclusive, appears from the Appendix of the 28th Report of the Select Committee on Finance, page 104 to stand thus :

1786	£.10,840	1792	£.7,330	
1787	15,060	1793	8,160	
1788	6,500	1794	7,140	
1789	7,340	1795	3,290	Total in 12 years,
1790	8,970	1796	4,010	£.94,430.
1791	6,050	1797	9,650	
	£. 54,850		39,580	

which

which constitute the aggregate of the charges made against criminals arraigned at the Old Bailey, in the courseof a year.

With this view the following statement is offered to the consideration of the Reader.—It refers to a period of profound peace (as most likely to exhibit a true average) and contains a register of the trials, published by authority, including eight sessions from September 1790 to 1791. From this it appears that 1088 prisoners were tried for different offences in that year, and that 711 were *discharged!* and yet, striking as this may appear, it may be asserted on good grounds, that the following melancholy Catalogue (extensive as it seems to be) does not probably contain even *one-tenth part* of the offences which are actually committed.

		£.
6	For Treason in making false money	
	A reward in money on conviction amounting for each to	40
81	Highway Robberies	
	A reward (besides the highwayman's property) for each	40
41	Burglaries	
	A reward 40l. besides a Tyburn ticket worth 20l.	60
10	House Breaking in the day time	
	A reward 40l. besides a Tyburn ticket worth 20l.	60
23	Stealing goods to the value of 5s. from a shop, &c.	
	A Tyburn ticket value as above, average	20
3	Coining Copper Money	
	A reward in money	10
17	Horse Stealing	
	A reward in a Tyburn ticket, average value	20

181 Carried forward   181 Brought

181 Brought over

10 For Stealing Cattle and Sheep   £.

  A reward in money - - - 10

2 Returning from Transportation

  A reward in money - - - 20

---

193 Prisoners tried for offences entitling the apprehenders to
—— rewards on conviction; and 895 also tried, for which
no rewards are allowed, *viz.*

	791 Prisoners brought forward
10 for Murders	9 for Dealing in and utter-
4 Arson	ing base Money
10 Forgeries	1 Sodomy
2 Piracies	7 Bigamy
4 Rapes	6 Perjuries
642* Grand Larcenies	6 Conspiracies
32 Stealing privately from	3 Fraudulent Bankrupts
persons	15 Frauds
13 Shop-lifting under 5s.	9 Misdemeanors
16 Ripping and stealing	1 Assaulting, and cutting
Lead	Clothes
12 Stealing Pewter Pots	1 Smuggling
22 Stealing from furnished	7 Obstructing Revenue
Lodgings	Officers
1 Stealing Letters	1 Wounding a Horse ma-
1 Stealing a Child	liciously
22 Receiving Stolen Goods	38 Assaults
791 Carried forward	895 Total
	193 For which rewards were paid.
	445 Prisoners from the late —— Sheriffs.

Aggregate number - - - 1533   *Dis-*

---

* Grand Larceny is defined to be a felonious and fraudulent
taking away by any person, of the mere personal goods of another,
above the value of *twelve pence.*—1 Hawk. P. C. c. 33. § 1.

Disposed of as follows, viz.

Executed - - - -	82
Died - - - - -	25
Sent to the Hulks - - -	2
Transported - - - -	517
Removed to other Prisons - -	95
Transferred to the new Sheriffs -	151
Discharged upon the town - -	711

Total 1583

Thus it appears that murders, as well as several other very atrocious crimes, are committed, where officers of justice are not entitled to any reward for their trouble and risque in apprehending the offenders.

Receivers of stolen Goods in particular, who, as has been repeatedly stated, are *the nourishers and supporters of thieves,* and who, of all other offenders, are of that class where the greatest benefit to the public is to arise from their discovery and apprehension, seem to be totally overlooked.

If it should be thought too loose a system to allow rewards *not exceeding a certain sum in any one case,* to be distributed according to the discretion of the Judges who try the offence; perhaps it might be possible *to form a scale of premiums* from *one guinea up to fifty pounds;* which, by holding out certain encouragement *in all cases whatsoever,* might not only excite a desire on the part of men of some property and respectability to become Officers of Justice: but would create that species of *constant vigilance and attention* to the means of apprehending every class of offenders,

offenders, which cannot be expected at present, while the rewards are so limited.

The *Officers of Justice*, (parochial and stipendiary) who are appointed to watch over the Police of the Metropolis and its environs, in keeping the peace, and in detecting and apprehending offenders, amount at present (as near as possible) to 1040 individuals, under five separate jurisdictions, *and are arranged as follows:*

OFFICERS, &c.

London, 1st.	The City of London in 25 Wards, exclusive of Bridge Without.	City Marshals 2 Marshals' Men 6 Beadles 36	
	Parochial Constables	Principals 98 Substitutes 145 ——243 Extra Officers 32	
			—— 319
Westminster, 2d.	The City and Liberty of Westminster, 9 parishes and 2 precincts	High Constable 1 Parochial Constables 70	
			—— 71
Middlesex, 3d.	The Division of Holborn in Middlesex, joining the Metropolis, in 13 parishes, liberties, and manors	High Constable 1 Parochial Constables 78 & Headboroughs	—— 79
	The Division of Finsbury, in Middlesex, joining the Metropolis, 4 parishes, and 1 liberty	High Constable 1 Parochial Constables 68 & Headboroughs	—— 69
	The Division called the Tower Hamlets, including the eastern part of the Metropolis, and comprehending 10 parishes, 4 hamlets, 1 liberty, and 2 precincts	High Constable 1 Parochial Constables 217 & Headboroughs	—— 218

Parochial Officers carried over   756

		Brought over	756
Tower Liberthy, 4th	The liberty of the Tower of London, being a seperate judiction	High Constable 1 Conftables 16 & Headboroughs	17
	The Division of Kenfington, Chelsea, &c. comprehending 2 parishes and 3 hamlets	High Constable 1 Parochial Conftables 21 & Headboroughs	22
Surrey, 5th.	The Borough of Southwark, &c. comprehending 9 parishes.	High Constable 1 Constables 87	88

Total Parochial Officers - 883

To which are to be added the stated Officers of Police, specially appointed for the purpose of preventing crimes, and of detecting and apprehending offenders.

1. The establishment at Bow-Street, under the direction of the three Magistrates presiding at that Office, viz. Constables . . . 6
and (under the direction of Sir W. ADDINGTON, Knt., Patroles for the Road . . 68
— 74

2. The establishment of seven Public Offices by the Act of the 32d of his present Majesty, cap. 53, under the direction of three Magistrates at each Office, viz.

Constables at the Public Office, Queen-Square 6
. . . . Marlborough-St. 6
. . . . Hatton Garden 6

18

Carried over   957

Brought over   957
Constables brought over   18.
Constables at the Public Office, Worship-Street   6
. . . . Whitechapel   6
. . . . Shadwell   6
. . . . Union Hall, Southw. 6

48

Total Civil Force in the Metropolis   999
To which add the Civil Force of the Thames Police Establishment,* established in July 1798,
under the sanction of Government   -   -   -   -   41

Total   1040

Of these 1040 officers the 'Reader will observe,
that only 89 (exclusive of the thirty-two extra officers
in the City of London ; and the sixty-eight patroles
at Bow-street ; making in the whole no more than
189,) *are Stipendiary Officers*, particularly pledged to
devote their whole time to the service of the Public :
—and hence a question arises, whether so small a
number are sufficient for the purpose of watching and
detecting the hordes of villains who infest the Metropolis, and who must be considerably increased on
the return of peace ?

* The Thames Police Establishment fluctuates according to
the Season of the year, and the number of West India ships on
the River.——

The permanent force in House Constables, Boat Surveyors, and Water Officers, &c. is   -   -   -   41
The fluctuating Civil Force in { Ship Constables   -   150
                                 { Quay Guards   -.   30

Total Civil Force of the Marine Police Establishment }
when the West India Fleets are in port - - - - - }   221.

1

Little assistance can be expected under the present System from parochial Officers : who, depending on their daily labour principally for their support, can afford to devote no more time than is absolutely necessary for their indispensable duties, during the 12 months they are in office: and more especially since Magistrates have no power, or funds, to remunerate such parochial officers for extraordinary exertions in the Public service, however meritorious they may be;—hence it is, that their zeal and activity are checked in many instances ; when under proper regulations (such as are hereafter suggested) and subject to a certain degree of control and discipline, and properly remunerated for their services, they might be rendered extremely useful. These facts, joined to the further elucidation of this particular branch of the subject, it is earnestly to be hoped, may produce an arrangement of more *energy* and *effect* than exists under the present system.

Officers of Justice, who are subjected not only to considerable risks, but also to want of rest, and to the inconvenience of being exposed much in the night time, ought certainly to be liberally paid; so as to make it an object to *good* and *able men* even to look up to such situations.

It having been thus shewn that the Stipendiary Constables are so inconsiderable in point of numbers, and their duty confined to particular objects, it follows that on the parochial officers the Public ought, in a considerable degree, to depend for the general prevention of offences, and particularly for defeating the

the crafty and iniquitous devices which are resorted to for the purpose of evading the operation of justice. —These men also from their local knowledge are, or ought to be, best qualified to procure accurate information, and to supply what may be necessary to enable Magistrates to discharge their duty with advantage to the Community, and by this means they might be rendered useful auxiliaries to the existing Police.

It would seem, therefore, of the highest importance that arrangements should be formed, calculated to give to these constitutional safe-guards of the peaceful subject, that utility, energy, and effect, which originally resulted from the exercise of their functions,—which the present state of Society imperiously calls for, and without which the preventive System of Police can never be effectual.

On looking accurately into the nature and effect of the institution of Constables, it will be found that the vigor and efficacy of the Civil Power, the security of innocence,—the preservation of good order, and the attainment of justice, depend in a great measure on the accuracy of the System, with respect to these Officers assigned to keep the peace in the respective parishes of the Metropolis; and it is because the original spirit of the design has been in so many instances abandoned, that crimes have multiplied, and that the public are so insecure.

The evil, however, admits of practicable remedies; which the Superintending Board of Police, recommended

mended by the Select Committee of the House of Commons, might considerably facilitate, by methodizing the general design, and giving strength, intelligence, and uniformity to the whole.

Preparatory to this object, however, the System in the respective parishes must be greatly improved, before a co-operation can be expected that will prove extensively beneficial to the Public.

The first step to be pursued, is to establish a fund for the remuneration of Constables of every description. It will not be difficult to demonstrate that a resource may be found for this purpose, which will not impose any new burden on the Country, provided these Officers do their duty.

The enormous expence at present incurred, and which is either defrayed from the County Rates, or the general Revenue of the Country, arises chiefly after offenders are detected and punished. Out of 234,153l. a year stated by the Committee on Finance, to be the annual amount of the Police expences, only 26,183l. is incurred previous to detection.—By diminishing crimes therefore, the chief part of the burden upon the Country will be taken away; and hence in this saving will be established a resource for the remuneration of those who may contribute to so important an object.

The present expenditure of the County Rates for criminal offences, is estimated to amount to 50,000l. a year. In proportion as offences diminish, through the medium of a well-organized and energetic Police,

lice, will this burden upon the Poor Rates also be diminished.

Independent, therefore, of the policy of improving the system with respect to parochial Constables, by attaching a greater degree of responsibility to their situation, and introducing that discipline and systematic activity, which can alone render their services effectual—the plan may even be recommended as a proper arrangement in point of œconomy.

It is in vain to expect energy or attention in the execution of any Public duty, unless there be that personal responsibility which is not to be obtained without emolument. To render Officers of Justice, therefore, useful to the Public, they must be stimulated by interest:—they must, in fact, be paid for devoting a portion of their time to the comfort and security of others. The Law may inflict, and, indeed, has inflicted, penalties for the neglect of specific duties; but this will not establish that sort of Police which the present state of Society requires.— This is strongly exemplified in what may not be improperly called the *Mockery of Police*, which is exhibited in the periodical presentments by Constables, of public grievances and nuisances, before the Grand Inquest, four times a year at Westminster-hall, and twice before the Magistrates of the Sessions held at Guildhall in the City of Westminster. These presentments, although in themselves of the highest importance, have degenerated into what may now be considered as an useless and burden-

burdensome formality; at best it is a tedious, expensive, and circuitous mode of removing nuisances and inconveniences, and so ill-suited to the present state of Society, that several modern parochial Acts have given relief in a summary way before Magistrates.

The fact is, that in a great majority of instances where presentments are made, the evils they describe, though often highly prejudicial, are suffered to accumulate with increasing malignity, at the same time frequently generating other mischiefs and pressures of a tendency equally pernicious to the Community.

It is admitted, that the proper Officer of the Crown notifies to the parties implicated in the presentment, the determination of the Inquest; but a prosecution seldom ensues. The Constable has neither money nor time to follow it up, and the matter is discharged when the customary term expires, on the payment of a Fee of 16s. 9d. or more, according to the length of the presentment; and thus the business terminates in the emolument of an individual, and in the continuance of the abuse.

The same system prevails at the Sessions at Westminster. When Juries make presentments of nuisances or evils in their respective districts, the Constables have general orders to prosecute, which is not done; and, indeed, to compel an Officer serving gratuitously, to incur an expence for the Public interest which he cannot afford, would be an act of

manifest

manifest injustice; and unless a fund be provided in numerous cases, he must be under the necessity of declining such prosecutions.

But would it not be far better to bring such minor offences at once under the cognizance of Magistrates, with the power of appeal to the Quarter Sessions?—This is already the case in Spitalfields, under a parochial Act, where nuisances and annoyances are in consequence instantly removed. Matters of much greater importance are submitted to the same authority. The advantage in this case would be, that justice would be promptly administered at a small expence, and the evil would be put an end to, instead of remaining as at present a reproach to the Police, arming at the same time every noxious and bad member of Society, with a kind of licence to do offensive acts to the neighbourhood, and the Public at large, with impunity.

To render parochial Constables useful, rules must be established to compel every qualified person to serve in his turn, or pay a fine. No person should be empowered to offer a Substitute. It is of the highest importance that an Office invested with so much power should be executed by reputable men, if possible of pure morals, and not with hands open to receive bribes.—This important office in the Metropolis at least, has too long been degraded by the introduction, in many instances, of men of loose principles, undeserving of public confidence. The reason is obvious:—A man in the more reputable classes on

whom

whom the lot may fall, surrenders his functions to a Substitute who probably makes the office a trade ;— performs the service of the year for four or five Guineas, trusting to other emoluments, many of which are obtained by corruption, to enable him to subsist.

To render this branch of Police pure and efficient, an Act of Parliament should enforce the following or similar regulations :

1st. To assign a competent number of local Constables to each parish, in proportion to the number of inhabited houses; to be chosen by the whole number of qualified inhabitants paying parish Rates—to be presented to the Court Leet, or to the Magistrates of the Division, according to a prescribed rule, which shall preclude the possibility of exemptions or preferences ; for which purposes the qualifications shall be clearly defined in the Act.—Thus might the abuses which at present prevail, in the selection and choice of Constables, cease to be felt and complained of: an equal distribution of the burden would take place, and the duty be confined to men sufficiently respectable, to establish in the Public mind a confidence that it would be executed with fidelity, and an attention to the Public interest.

2d. That with a view to that necessary discipline, and knowledge of the duty to be performed, without which Officers of Justice can be of little use,

and

and may often be converted into instruments of oppression by an abuse of power; the High-Constable of the Division shall become *a responsible permanent Officer*, with a competent Salary; and shall have under his direction certain subordinate Officers, not exceeding *one for a large Parish*, and *one for every 25 Constables in any number of smaller Parishes, Hamlets, Precincts, and Liberties*, who shall be stiled *the Parochial Chief Constable*, whose situation shall also *be permanent*, with a moderate Salary, and who shall each be *responsible* for the execution of the regular duty which may be assigned to the petty Constables, either by the Act of Parliament, or by the Commissioners of Police, having powers for that purpose granted by law.—That a certain stipend or gratuity for trouble, shall also be paid to each of the petty Constables, in consideration of the ordinary duty they are bound to perform, besides 5s. a day for all extraordinary duty. That among other things it shall be the business of the parochial Chief Constable to instruct the petty Constables in their duty —to attend them in their perambulations, and to marshal them on receiving a precept from the High-Constable, or an order from two Magistrates, in case of any tumult or disorder requiring their interference—to impress upon their minds the necessity of purity, vigilance, and attention to orders—and of being humane, prudent, and vigorous, in the execution of such duties as belong to

their

their functions.—That they shall instantly assemble on any alarm of Fire.—That the Public-houses, in the parish or district, shall be visited regularly; and also the Watchmen while upon duty, and regular returns made to the Police Magistrates of the District, stating the occurrences of the night. That wherever suspicious characters reside in the parish, who have no visible means of supporting themselves, the utmost vigilance shall be exercised in watching their conduct, to prevent as much as possible the commission of crimes, and to preserve peace and good order in the parish; and wherever the execution of any specific law depends on Constables, the utmost attention to be manifested in giving it effect, and preventing it from remaining a dead Letter.—That care be taken to make regular, impartial, and accurate returns of Jurors; and of persons eligible to serve in the Militia;— and that immediate cognizance be also taken of all nuisances and annoyances, and timely notice given to Magistrates of all occurrences threatening to disturb the Public peace, or to overturn the established Government of the Country.

2d. That the different High Constables should return to the Commissioners of Police annually, after a change of Officers has taken place, a list of the number of persons who compose the Civil Force, under their direction in their respective divisions; and regularly, every quarter, a list of the Publicans, with such facts as have occurred, respecting

specting their orderly or disorderly conduct in the management of their Houses.—The state of the Division with respect to Prostitutes—to the situation of the Poor for the preceding quarter, and their resource for employment.—The number and nature of the offences committed in the District during the preceding quarter, and the detections of the delinquents, shewing how many offenders have been discovered, and how many have escaped justice, and stating the means used and using to detect such as are at large, charged with specific offences within the division : so as to bring under the review of the Central Board a clear statement of the criminal Police in every part of the Metropolis on the first day of each quarter, with such other information as the Commissioners may require.

4th. It is humbly suggested, that the Salaries and Allowances to be paid to the *High Constables* and *parochial Chief Constables* should be paid out of the General Police Fund, under the Management of the Board, and the gratuities and allowances to the petty Constables out of the County Rate.

It might be expedient that the Stipend of the petty Constables should be very moderate, and that their remunerations should, partly at least, arise from *premiums* and *gratuities*, granted by the Judges and Magistrates, for meritorious services to the Public,

actually

actually performed; for which there would so many opportunities occur, that no fit man, acting as a Constable under such a system, and doing his duty conscientiously, need be under any apprehension of obtaining a very comfortable livelihood.

The invariable rule of rewarding, in every case where it can be made appear that any useful Public service has been performed, would have a most wonderful effect in preventing crimes: The expence, if judiciously and œconomically managed, need not exceed, in any material degree, *the present aggregate* of what is disbursed in different ways, in all the branches of the Police and Criminal Establishment; it might, in fact, be defrayed, as well as every other charge, *by the Police itself,* under the direction of the *Central Board,* hereafter more particularly alluded to, from the produce of the *Licences* proposed to be granted for regulating particular classes of Dealers, by whose aid and assistance, in supporting Thieves and Pilferers, such a system is rendered necessary.

Nor should the reward be wholly confined to Officers of Justice, either *parochial or stipendiary.* The Public Good requires, that they should extend also to Watchmen and Patroles, who should have every reasonable encouragement held out to them to be honest and vigilant, by small premiums paid down immediately, for every service they may render the Public; either in detecting or apprehending persons who are guilty of felonies, or other offences against the public peace.

At

At present, the watchmen destined to guard the lives and properties of the inhabitants residing in near *eight thousand* streets, lanes, courts, and alleys, and about 160,000 houses, composing the whole of the Metropolis and its environs, are under the direction of no less than above seventy different Trusts ; regulated by perhaps double the number of local acts of Parliament, (varying in many particulars from one another,) under which the *directors*, *guardians*, *governors*, *trustees*, or *vestries*, according to the title they assume, are authorised to act,—each attending only to their own particular *Ward*, *Parish*, *Hamlet*, *Liberty*, or *Precinct ;* and varying the payment according to local circumstances, and the opulence of the particular district, from $8\frac{1}{2}d$. up to 2*s.* each night.*

The encouragement being, in many instances, so

* There is, in some respect, an exception to this rule, with regard *to the City and Liberty of Westminster*, and the parishes of *St. Clement Danes*,—*St. Mary le Strand*,—*The Savoy*,—The united parishes of *St. Giles* and *St. George, Bloomsbury*,—The united parishes of *St. Andrew Holborn, above the Bars*, and *St. George the Martyr*, and the liberty of *Saffron Hill, Hatton Garden,* and *Ely Rents*.—The Act of the 14th George III, cap. 90, contains regulations applicable to the whole of these Parishes and Liberties, fixing the *minimum* of watchmen at 523, and patroles at 56 men, for the *whole ;* but leaving the management still to the inhabitants of each respective Parish or Liberty. The same act fixes the *minimum* of wages at 1s. a night, and patroles 15d. In the City of London, the salaries given to watchmen vary in each Ward, from 13l. to 18l. 19l. 20l. 21l. 7s. 23l. 8s, up to 26l. and patroles allowed from 13l. to 35l. and 40l. a year.

small

small, few candidates appear for such situations who are really, in point of character and age, fit for the duty which ought to beperformed; the managers have therefore no alternative but to accept of such aged, and often superannuated, men, living in their respective districts, as may offer their services; this they are frequently induced to do from motives of humanity, to assist old inhabitants who are unable to labour at any mechanical employment, or perhaps with a view to keep them out of the workhouse, and to save the expence of maintaining them.

Thus circumstanced, and thus encouraged, what can be expected from such watchmen?—

Aged in general;—often feeble; and almost, on every occasion, half starved, from the limited allowance they receive; without any claim upon the Public, or the least hope of reward held out, even if they perform any meritorious service, by the *detection of Thieves and Receivers of stolen Goods,* or idle and disorderly persons : and above all, *making so many separate parts of an immense system, without any general superintendance, disjoined from the nature of its organization,* it is only a matter of wonder, that the protection afforded is what *it really is.**—Not only is

---

* This proves how highly meritorious the conduct of the *Managers* and *Trustees* of this branch of the Police of the Metropolis must, in many instances, be. There can indeed be no manner of doubt, but that great advantages arise from dividing the labour, where all the benefits of local knowledge enter into the system.— So far as this goes, it ought not to be disturbed. But it is also necessary to consider the Metropolis as a *great Whole,* and to combine

there small encouragement offered for the purpose of insuring fidelity, but, as has been already shewn, innumerable temptations are held out to dishonesty, by Receivers of stolen Goods, to the watchmen and patroles in their vicinity; as well as by thieves and housebreakers in all situations where they contemplate the commission of a burglary.

Money is also received from disorderly persons in the night, to permit them to escape from the just punishment of the Laws; while on the other hand, unfortunate females are often cruelly oppressed and laid under contribution, for permission to infringe the very laws, which it is the duty of these nocturnal guardians of the Police to put in execution.

Excepting in the city of London, under the jurisdiction of the Lord Mayor and Aldermen, (where there are, in the 25 wards, 765 watchmen, and 38 patroles) and the parishes and liberties combined by the act of the 14th Geo. III. cap. 90, it will not be easy to ascertain the exact number of watchmen, &c. employed by the great variety of different Trusts, in every part of the Metropolis; more especially, as in several instances they vary in their numbers according to the season of the year, and other circumstances; but the following statement is believed to be very near truth :—

bine the organs of Police which at present exist, in such a manner, by a general superintendance, as to give equal encouragement, and to instil one principle of universal energy into all its parts.

25 Wards

1

Beadles, Watchmen,
and Patroles.

25 Wards in the City of London   -   -   803
11 Parishes, &c. in the City and Liberty of
    Westminster   -   -   -   -   -   302
13 Parishes &c. in the Division of Holborn   377
 5 Parishes, &c. in that part of the Division of
    Finsbury which joins the Metropolis   -   135
 7 Parishes, &c. in the Division of the Tower
    Hamlets   -   -   -   -   -   -   268
 1 Liberty of the Tower of London   -   14
 5 Parishes and Hamlets, being part of the Divi-
    sion of Kensington, near the Metropolis   66
 9 Parishes in the Borough of Southwark   -   -   79

Total Beadles, Watchmen, and Patroles   2044*

Nothing can certainly be better calculated for *complete protection* against acts of violence in the streets, than *the System of a well-regulated Stationary Watch;*

---

* Watch-houses are now placed at convenient distances all over the Metropolis; where a parochial constable attends, in rotation, every night, to receive disorderly and criminal persons, and to carry them before a Magistrate next morning.—In each watch-house also (in case of fire) the names of the turn-cocks, and the places where engines are kept, are to be found. This circumstance is mentioned for the information of strangers unacquainted with the Police of the Metropolis; to whom it is recommended, in case of fire, or any accident or disturbance requiring the assistance of the Civil Power, to apply immediately to the Officer of the night, at the nearest watch-house, or to the watchmen on the beat.

8 composed

composed of fit and able bodied men, properly controlled and superintended: and from the number of
persons already employed, independent of private
Watchmen, it would seem only to be necessary to lay
down apposite legislative rules, with respect to *age
or ability, character, wages, rewards for useful services,* and *general superintendance,* in order to establish
that species of additional security which would operate as a more effectual means of preventing crimes
within the Metropolis.

Let the same system of moderate rewards also be
extended to beadles, * for useful public service *actually
performed,* as is proposed with regard to officers of
justice, watchmen, and patroles; and much good
will arise to the community, without any great additional expence.

It is in vain to expect that the Public can be well
served, unless the emolument becomes an object to
good and able men; but these extraordinary rewards
(as has already been observed) should always depend
upon the vigilance and exertion of the parties themselves, in detecting offenders of every description:
and should be paid, on its appearing to the Magistrate, that no *impropriety* or *indiscretion* has marked
their conduct. If, on the contrary, they should be
proved to have acted oppressively or improperly, a
power of immediate dismission and punishment

* Beadles are, in many instances, employed at present as local
superintendants of the watch, within their respective Parishes.

should,

should, in all instances, be lodged in Justices of the Peace, to be exercised according to the nature of the offence.

Having thus stated the civil force of the Metropolis, in peace officers, watchmen and patroles, making an aggregate of 3084 men—it may be neceeasary and useful to give such information relative to the Magistracy, as may tend to shew the present state of the Police, and to illustrate what remains to be further suggested on the subject of its improvement; for the preservation of the Public peace, and the *detection* and *apprehension* of every class of offenders.

There exist at present no less than *five* separate jurisdictions within the limits of the Metropolis—namely,—

Magistrates.

1. The City of London, where there are, including the Lord Mayor, 26 Aldermen, who have an exclusive jurisdiction within the ancient limits,   -   -   26

2. The City and Liberty of Westminster—where there are upwards of 100 Justices of the Peace, who have jurisdiction only in that particular District; but where the Magistrates of the County of Middlesex have an equal jurisdiction.—The number resident, of those who are not Magistrates of Middlesex, is supposed to be about   50

3. That part of the Metropolis, which is situated in the county of Middlesex, where there are about 800 Justices, including the Princes of the Royal Family—many

Carried over   76
_____
of

Brought óver   76

of the Nobility—Great Officers of State—Members
of Parliament—and other Gentlemen of respectability ;—of those in the commission about 200 have
qualified ; and of these who have taken out their *De-
dimus Potestatem* only about 150 reside in or near the
Metropolis   -   -   -   -   150

4. That district of the Metropolis lying near, or particularly belonging anciently to the Tower of London,
comprehending about 750 houses—where the Magistrates (52 in number) have an exclusive jurisdiction,
and hold separate Sessions of the Peace.—The number
who are not Magistrates in Middlesex, is   -   31

5. The Borough of Southwark, and that part of the Metropolis adjoining thereto, within the Bills of Mortality
—where the City Magistrates have jurisdiction, besides
the whole of the Magistrates of the County of Surry,—
namely—132, but of whom not more than 28 reside
in Southwark, and 15 in London, &c.   (in all)   43

Total about   300

But, notwithstanding the great number of respectable names, which are in the different commissions in and near the Metropolis ; and although all
who have qualified have equal jurisdiction with the
Police Justices within their respective districts ; yet
the efficient duty for the whole of the Metropolis,
so far as it relates to the detection of offenders, is
principally limited to two classes of Magistrates—
namely,—

E E   1. The

1. The 26 Aldermen of London, whose jurisdiction is confined to the ancient limits of the City, comprehending 25 Wards, in which are 21,642 houses on the London side, and Bridge Ward without, in the Borough   26

2. The 24 established Magistrates, three of whom preside at each of the seven Publick Offices, appointed by the Act of the 32d of his present Majesty, cap. 53, viz.—

1. Public Office, Queen-Square, Westminster   3
2. Public Office, Marlborough-Street   -   3
3. Public Office, Hatton-Garden   -   3
4. Public Office, Worship-Street, Shoreditch   3
5. Public Office, Whitechapel   -   -   3
6. Public Office, Shadwell   -   -   3
7. Public Office, Union-Street, Southwark   3

    21

8. Existing (previous to the Act) at the Public Office, Bow-Street   -   -   -   3

    24

9. The Thames Police Institution at Wapping, for the River only   -   -   2

    26

Total efficient Magistrates who sit in rotation, daily, in the Metropolis   -   -   52

The jurisdiction of the Magistrates presiding at the seven Public Offices, not only extends to Westminster and Middlesex; (and, in most instances, lately, to the liberty of the Tower:) but also to the counties of Surry, Kent, and Essex, from which considerable advantages in the prompt detection and apprehension.

prehension of offenders have accrued to the Public :
The only difficulty that now remains to be removed,
with respect to the clashing of jurisdictions, is that
which regards the city of London ; where, from its
contiguity, and immediate and close connection with
every other part of the Metropolis, considerable inconveniences and injuries to the public are felt, not
only from the circumstance of the jurisdiction of the
City Magistrates not being extended over the *whole*
of the Metropolis, as well as the four adjoining coun ·
ties ; but also from the Police Magistrates having no
authority quickly to follow up informations, by issuing warrants to search for property, and to apprehend
persons charged with offences in the City. The
whole difficulty resolves itself into a mere matter of
punctilio, founded perhaps on ill-grounded jealousy,
or misapprehension, which a little explanation would
probably remove.

Where the object is to do good ;—and where not
even the shadow of harm can arise, no limits should
be set to local jurisdictions, especially where privileges are proposed to be given ; (as in this case, to
the city of London ;) and where none are to be
taken away.

For the purpose of establishing a complete and well-
connected System of *detection*, some means ought
certainly to be adopted, more closely to unite the
City and Police Magistrates,* that they may, in a
greater

* The Select Committee of the House of Commons, in their 28th
Report, 1798, on Finance, have strongly recommended a Concurrent

greater degree, go hand in hand in all matters regarding the general interest of the Metropolis and its
environs; making the suppression of crimes one
common 'cause, and permitting no punctilio, regarding jurisdiction, to prevent the operation of their
uited energy in, the prompt detection of offenders.
This, from the extended state of Commerce and
Society, and the great increase of property, is now
rendered a measure in which the inhabitants of the
whole Metropolis, as well as the adjacent villages,
have a common interest. It is an evil which affects
all ranks, and calls aloud for the speedy adoption of
some effectual remedy.

rent Jurisdiction; and also, that two Police Offices should be
established in London, upon the plan of the others, with Magistrates to be appointed by the Lord Mayor and Aldermen.

CHAP.

CHAP. XV.

*The prevailing practice explained, when offenders are
brought before Magistrates.—The necessary caution,
as well as the duty of Magistrates in such cases explained.—Professed thieves seldom intimidated when
put upon their trial, from the many chances they have
of escaping.—These chances shortly detailed.—Reflections on the false humanity exercised by prosecutors towards prisoners.—Their rudeness and cruelty,
when engaged in acts of criminality.—The delays and
expences of prosecutions, a great discouragement, inducing sufferers to put up with their loss, in silence.—
How the inconvenience may be remedied.—An account of the different Courts of Justice, appointed for
the trial of offences committed in the Metropolis.—
Five inferior and two superior Courts.—A statement, shewing the number of prisoners convicted and
discharged during the last year.—Reflections on this
sad catalogue of depravity.—A radical defect somewhere.—The great purity of the Judges of England.
—The propriety of a co-operation with them, in
whatever shall tend to promote the ends of Public
Justice.—This object to be attained, in the greatest
possible degree, by means of an authorised Public
Prosecutor.—The advantages of such an institution,
in remedying many abuses which prevail in the trial
of offenders.—From 2500 to 3000 persons committed*

E e 3　　　　　　　*for*

*for trial, by Magistrates, in the Metropolis, in the
course of a Year.—The chief part afterwards returned upon Society.*

ARRIVING at that *point* in the progress of this
Work, where persons accused of offences are detected and brought before Magistrates for examination, ultimately to be committed for trial, if the
evidence shall be sufficient;—it is proper to explain
the prevailing practice under such circumstances.

The task, in this case imposed upon the Magistrate, is arduous and important; requiring not only
great purity of conduct, a profound knowledge of
mankind, and of the common affairs of life; but in a
more peculiar manner those powers of discrimination
which may enable him to discover how far criminality attaches to the party accused; and whether there
are grounds sufficient to abridge for a time, or ultimately to deprive the prisoner of his liberty, until a
Jury of his country shall decide upon his fate.

It frequently happens that persons accused of
crimes are apprehended under circumstances where
no doubt can rest on the mind of the Magistrates as
to the guilt of the prisoner; but where the legal evidence is nevertheless insufficient to authorize an immediate commitment for trial.

In these instances, (while he commits *pro tempore,*)
he is called upon in a particular manner to exert the
whole

whole powers of his mind, by adopting such judicious measures as shall be the means of detecting the offenders; by discovering the goods or property stolen, or by admitting such evidence for the Crown as may, with other corroborating testimony, prevent the ends of justice from being defeated.

Where a Magistrate proceeds with indefatigable zeal and attention, and at the same time exercises good judgment, he will seldom fail of success: for in this case a similar spirit will animate the officers under his controul, whose activity and industry are generally in proportion to that manifested by their superiors.

Much as every active Magistrate must regret that deficiency of pecuniary resource, which, under the present system, prevents him from rewarding those who must occasionally be employed to detect notorious offenders, this circumstance ought not to abate his zeal in any respect; since by perseverance it generally happens, that every good and proper arrangement for the immediate advantage of the Public, may be ultimately obtained.

The Magistrate having done his duty by committing an offender for trial, satisfied of his guilt and the sufficiency of the evidence to convict him: and having also bound over the prosecutor and the witnesses as the Law directs, to attend the Grand Jury, and (if a bill be found) to prosecute and give evidence upon the indictment; it might appear to the common observer, that the culprit's case becomes hopeless and forlorn.

This,

This, however, is by no means a stage in the progress that intimidates a professed thief; he feels and knows that, although guilty of the crime laid to his charge, he has many chances of escaping; and these chances unquestionably operate as encouragements to the commission of crimes.

His first hope is, that he shall intimidate the Prosecutor and Witnesses, by the threatenings of the gang with whom he is connected;—his next, that he may compound the matter; or bribe or frighten material witnesses, so as to keep back evidence; or induce them to speak doubtfully at the trial, though positive evidence was given before the Magistrate; or if all should fail, recourse is had to perjury, by bringing the Receiver, or some other associate, to swear an *alibi.*

Various other considerations, also, operate in strengthening the hopes of acquittal; partly arising from the vast numbers who are discharged or acquitted at every Session of gaol-delivery; and partly from the carelessness and inattention of Prosecutors, who are either unable or unwilling to sustain the expence of Counsel to oppose the arguments and objections which will be offered in behalf of the prisoner: or are soured by loss of valuable time, experienced, perhaps in former prosecutions;*—or ultimately

* It is true, that by the Acts of 25th Geo. II. cap. 36, and 18th Geo. III. cap. 13, the expences of the prosecutors and witnesses are to be paid; and also (if the parties shall appear to be in poor circumstances) a reasonable allowance made for trouble and loss
of

ultimately from a dread entertained by timid persons, who foolishly and weakly consider themselves as taking away the life of a fellow-creature, merely because they prosecute or give evidence; not reflecting that it is the *Law* only that can punish offenders, and *not* the individual prosecutor or witnesses.

False Humanity, exercised in this manner, is always cruelty to the public, and not seldom to the prisoners themselves.—All depredations upon property are *public wrongs,* in the suppression and punishment of which it is the duty of every good man to lend his assistance; a duty more particularly incumbent upon those who are the immediate sufferers: through their means only can Public Justice operate in punishing those miscreants, by whom the innocent are *put in fear, alarmed, and threatened with horrid imprecations—with loss of life by means of loaded*

of time; but this is connected with the regulations of the Justices, confirmed by one of the Judges of Assize, which vary according to local circumstances, and it is also necessary to plead poverty in order to be remunerated for loss of time; *but as the poor seldom suffer by thieves,* these Acts appear to have had little effect in encouraging prosecutors to come forward; and it is believed few applications are made excepting in cases of real poverty.—In the county of Middlesex there is an exception; where witnesses are directed to be paid by the Overseers of the Poor of the Parish where the person was apprehended; but this mode of payment is seldom if ever adopted.—The fund, however, which the Legislature has thus provided, if œconomically and judiciously applied by a Public Prosecutor, would remove many difficulties, without any material addition to the county rates.

pistols;

pistols; or bodily injury, from being hacked with cutlasses, or beaten with bludgeons—under circumstances where neither age nor sex is spared.

Yet experience has shewn that these arguments, powerful as they are, are insufficient to awaken in the mind of men that species of public spirit which shall induce sufferers in general, by robberies of different kinds, to become willing prosecutors, under the various trying delays of Courts of Justice; and frequently with the trouble of bringing a number of witnesses from the country, who are kept in attendance on the court perhaps several days together, at a very considerable expence.

Such a burden imposed upon the subject, in addition to the losses already sustained, in a case too where the offence is of a public nature, is certainly not easily reconcileable with that spirit of justice, and attention to the rights of individuals, which forms so strong a general feature in the Jurisprudence of the Country.

From all these circumstances it happens that innumerable felonies are concealed, and the loss is suffered in silence as the least of two evils; by which means thieves are allowed to reign with impunity, undisturbed, and encouraged to persevere in their evil practices.

Nothing, it is to be feared, can cure this evil, and establish a general system of protection, but a vigorous Police: strengthened and improved by the appointment of Deputy-Prosecutors for the Crown,

acting

acting under the Attorney-General for the time being. An establishment of this sort, even at a very small salary, would be considered as an honourable *entré* to many young Counsel; who, in protecting the Public against the frauds, tricks, and devices of old and professed thieves, by which at present they escape punishment, might keep the stream of justice pure, and yet allow no advantage to be taken of the prisoner*.

As it must be admitted on all hands, that it is the interest of the Public that no guilty offender should escape punishment;—it seems to be a position equally clear and incontrovertible, that wherever, from a defect in the system of prosecutions, or any other cause, a prisoner escapes the punishment due to his crimes, substantial justice is wounded, and public wrongs are increased.

It has been already stated in the preceding Chapter, that there are five separate Jurisdictions in the Metropolis, where Magistrates exercise limited authority.—Of course, there are five inferior Courts of Justice, where lesser offences, committed in London and its vicinity, are tried by Justices of the Peace.

---

* The propriety of this suggestion is sanctioned by the recommendation of the Finance Committee of the House of Commons in their 27th and 28th Report; and forms part of that System of general controul and arrangement for the prevention of crimes, stated more at large in a subsequent Chapter.

1. The

1. The General and Quarter Sessions of the Peace; held eight times a year, by the Lord Mayor and Aldermen, at Guildhall—*for the trial of small Offences committed in London.*

2. The Quarter Sessions of the Peace; held four times a year, at Guildhall, Westminster, by the Justices acting for that City and Liberty—*for the trial of small Offences committed in Westminster only.*

3. The General and Quarter Sessions of the Peace; held eight times a year, at the New Sessions House on Clerkenwell-Green, (commonly called Hicks's Hall) by the Justices only of the County of Middlesex—*for the trial of small Offences committed in Middlesex and Westminster.*

4. The General Quarter Sessions of the Peace; held in the Sessions House in Well-Close-Square, by the Justices for the Liberty of the Tower of London—*for the trial of small Offences committed within the Royalty.*

5. The Quarter Sessions of the Peace; held by the Justices for the County of Surry, at the New Sessions House at Newington, Surry, in January;—At Reigate, in April;—At Guildford, in July;—and Kingston-upon-Thames, in October, each year;—*where small Offences committed in Southwark and the Neighbourhood are tried.*

These five inferior Courts of Justice take cognizance of *Petty Larcenies, Frauds, Assaults, Misdemeanors, and other offences punishable by fine, imprisonment, whipping, and the pillory:*—and in certain cases, the power of the Justices extends to transportation.

The higher and more atrocious offences committed in London and Middlesex, are tried at the Justice-Hall in the Old Bailey; by a special commission

mission of Oyer and Terminer to the Lord Mayor, and a certain number of the Judges, with the Recorder and Common Serjeant of the City of London.

Offences of this latter degree of atrocity, perpetrated in that part of the Metropolis which is situated in the Borough of Southwark and County of Surry, are tried at the assizes, held twice a year at *Kingston-upon-Thames, Croydon,* or *Guildford.**

Thus it appears, that five inferior and two superior Tribunals of Justice are established for trying the different crimes committed in the Metropolis.

As it may be useful, for the purpose of elucidating the suggestions already offered upon this branch of the subject, that a connected view of the result of these *Trials* should make a part of this Work;—the following Abstract, (including the discharges of Prisoners by Magistrates) has been made up for this immediate purpose: from authentic documents obtained from the keepers of the eight different prisons and houses of correction in the city of London, and in the counties of Middlesex and Surry.

---

* Considerable inconvenience arises (and, indeed, great hardship, where prisoners are innocent) from the length of time which must elapse, where offences have been committed in Southwark, before they can be brought to trial; either for inferior or more atrocious crimes. In the former case, prisoners must remain till the Quarter Sessions, (there being no intermediate General Sessions of the Peace) and in the latter case till the Assizes, held only twice a year; this occasions a confinement, previous to trial, lengthened out, in some instances, to three, four, five, and even nearly to six months.

It

It applies to the period, from September 1794, till September 1795, which is chosen as a sort of medium between Peace and War.

It is impossible to contemplate this collected aggregate of the prisoners annually discharged upon the Public, without feeling a strong anxiety to remedy an evil rendered extremely alarming, from the number which composes the dismal catalogue of Human Depravity.

Every inquiry in the progress of this Work proves a radical defect somewhere.

While the public tribunals are filled with Judges, the purity of whose conduct adds lustre to their own and the national character, why should not every subordinate part of the Criminal Jurisprudence of the Country be so organized, as to co-operate, in the greatest possible degree, with the efforts of those higher orders of the Magistracy in accomplishing the purposes of substantial justice?

Nothing could tend more to promote this object, than the appointment already proposed of a Public Prosecutor for the Crown.

An institution of this kind would terrify the hordes of miscreants now at open war with the peaceable and useful part of the Community, in a greater degree than any one measure that could possibly be adopted.

It would be the means of destroying those hopes and chances which encourage criminal people to persevere in their depredations upon the Public.

It

A Summary View of the Prisoners *committed, tried, punished, disposed of,* and *discharged* in the Metropolis, in *One Year*, ending in October, 1795.

SURRY		MIDDLESEX		LONDON				NAMES OF PRISONS
New Gaol, Southwark	Tothil Fields Bridewell	House of Correction, Cold Bath Fields	New Prison Clerkenwell	Bridewell Hospital	Giltspur Compter	Poultry Compter	Newgate	
22		2	4	5	4		7	Died
61	10						51	Capitally convicted
174	11	7		3			153	Sentenced to Transportation
85							85	Imprisoned in Newgate
563					249	334		Imprisoned in Bridewell Hospital
54							54	Imprisoned in the House of Correction of Middlesex
37		37						Imprisoned in Tothil Fields Bridewell
36	16						20	Imprisoned in Surry Goals
10						10		Sent to the Philanthropic and Marine Societies
216			58		75	44	39	Sent to serve his Majesty in the Navy and Army
1282	122	128		835	123	72		Passed to Parishes
115	1	26			44			Sent to Hospitals
2675	194	132	66	883	493	460	409	Total
1674	130	253	568	237	287	199		Discharged by Magistrates for want of Proof.
893	74	274	231	170	10		134	Discharged by Proclamation and Goal delivery
418	35	6	60	35	10		272	Discharged by Acquittal
24	2	1		9			12	Discharged after being whipt
56					45		11	Discharged after being fined
697	28	27	353	9	249	11	20	Discharged and suffering imprisonment
149			111		38			Apprentices discharged
422		154		127		114	27	Offenders bailed out of Prison
129							189	Discharged by Pardon
4462	269	715	1323	587	287	477	578	Totally discharged.

Left-margin notes: *16 executed* (against "Capitally convicted"); *106 transported* (against "Sentenced to Transportation").

Right-hand bracket headings: "Number of Prisoners, punished and disposed of." (upper section); "Number of Prisoners discharged by the Magistrates, and from the Eight Geols, in One Year." (lower section).

N. B. Although the Author has been at infinite pains to render this Summary as exact as possible yet, from the different modes adopted in keeping the accounts of Prisons, he is not thoroughly satisfied in his own mind that the View he has here given is accurate, to a point.—He is, however, convinced that it will be found sufficiently so for the purpose.

It would not only remove that aversion which Prosecutors manifest on many occasions, to come forward, for the purpose of promoting the ends of public justice; but it would prevent, in a great measure, the possibility of compounding felonies, or of suborning witnesses. *

It would also be the means of counteracting the various tricks and devices of old thieves; and occasion an equal measure of Justice to be dealt out to them, as to the novices in crimes:—It would do more,—It would protect real innocence,—for in such cases the Public Prosecutor would never fail to act as the friend of the prisoner.

The prevailing practice in criminal trials, in the

* Notwithstanding the severity of the Law, the composition of felonies and misdemeanors is carried to a much greater height than it is almost possible to believe; and various artifices are resorted to, to elude the penalties.—An instance occurred in August 1792; where a Jew was ordered to take his trial for a rape, committed on a married woman.—The offence appeared, on examination, to be extremely aggravated.—The Grand Jury, however, did not find a bill; which was thought a very singular circumstance, as the proof had been so clear before the Magistrate. The reasons were afterwards sufficiently explained; which shew, what corrupt practices, artifices, and frauds will be used to defeat the ends of justice:—In consequence of a previous undertaking between the Jew and the husband of the woman who had been so grossly abused, a sum of £.20 was left in the hands of a publican, which the prosecutor was to receive if the bill was not found. In this confidence the woman gave a different evidence from that which she had given before the Magistrate. The Jew, however, cheated both the husband and the wife; for he no sooner discovered that he was safe, than he demanded the money of the publican, and laughed at the prosecutor.

true

true spirit of mildness and humanity, induces the
Judge to act in some degree as counsel for the prisoner.—Without a Prosecutor for the Crown, therefore, every trifling inaccuracy in the indictment is
allowed to become a fatal obstacle to conviction;*
circumstances which would frequently throw great
light upon the charges, are not brought under the
review of the jury, and thus public justice is defeated.

Upon an average, the Magistrates of the Metropolis commit annually, (out of many times that number who are equally objects of punishment,) from
about 2500 to 3000 persons, male and female, for
trial, at the seven different Courts of Justice in and
near the Metropolis; charged with a variety of felonies, misdemeanors, and other petty offences. But
after fully convincing their own minds, from a careful, and in many instances, a most laborious investigation, that the parties are guilty, they are obliged,

---

* In criminal cases, a defective indictment is not aided by
the verdict of a Jury, as defective pleadings are in civil cases.
Indeed wherever life is concerned, great strictness has been at all
times observed. That able and humane Judge, SIR MATTHEW
HALE, complained above a century ago,† " *That this strictness*
" *has grown to be a blemish and inconvenience in the law and the*
" *administration thereof; for that more offenders escape by the*
" *over-easy ear given to exceptions in indictments, than by their*
" *own innocence: and many times gross murders, burglaries,*
" *robberies, and other heinous and crying offences remain un-*
" *punished, by those unseemly niceties; to the reproach of the Law,*
" *to the shame of the Government, to the encouragement of villainy,*
" *and to the dishonour of God.*"‡

† He died 1676.   ‡ Hale, P. C. 193.

from

from experience, to prepare themselves for the mortification of seeing their labour and exertions in a great
measure lost to the Community : the major part of
these criminals being returned upon Society, without
any effectual steps adopted for their reformation, or
any means used for the prevention of a repetition
of their crimes. A considerable proportion of this
wretched number may have suffered perhaps a slight
punishment for their demerits ; but which produces
no effect that is not ultimately mischievous to the
Community ; since it serves merely to initiate them,
in a greater degree, in the knowledge and means of
committing new acts of fraud and villainy.

To establish a System calculated to prevent criminals from returning to their evil practices after punishment is the very essence of good Police ; but notwithstanding its importance to the Community, no measures have ever yet been adopted, calculated to attain
so desirable an object. —It is, however, ardently to
be hoped, that the period is fast approaching, when
this great desideratum will be in a certain degree
obtained; and that the suggestions offered in the
subsequent Chapters, may tend to accelerate the
renovation of this forlorn and miserable class of
outcasts, by means of an appropriate *Penitentiary
System.*

CHAP.

C H A P. XVI.

On Punishments.—The mode authorized by the ancient laws.—The period when Transportation commenced. —The principal crimes enumerated which are punishable by Death.—Those punishable by Transportation and Imprisonment.—The courts appointed to try different degrees of crimes.—Capital punishments, extending to so many offences of an inferior nature, defeat the ends of justice.—The system of Pardons examined:—their evil tendency.—New regulations suggested with regard to Pardons and Executions.—An historical account of the rise and progress of Transportation.—The expedients resorted to, after the American War put a stop to that mode of punishment. —The System of the Hulks then adopted.—Salutary Laws also made for the erection of Provincial and National Penitentiary Houses.—The nature and principle of these Laws briefly explained.—An account of the Convicts confined in the Hulks for twenty-two years.—The enormous expence of maintenance and inadequate produce of their labour.— The impolicy of the system exposed by the Committee on Finance.—The system of Transportation to New South Wales examined.—Great expence of this mode of punishment.—Improvements suggested, calculated to reduce the expence in future.—Erection of one or more National Penitentiary Houses recommended.— A general view of the County Penitentiary Houses and

and Prisons:—their inefficacy in reforming Convicts. —The labour obtained uncertain, while the expence is enormous.—The National Penitentiary House (according to the proposal of Jeremy Bentham, Esq.) considered.—Its peculiar advantages over all others which have been suggested, with respect to health, productive labour, and reformation of Convicts.— General reflections on the means of rendering imprisonment useful in reforming Convicts.—Concluding observations.

IMPERFECT in many respects as the criminal Law appears, from what has been detailed and stated in the preceding Chapters, and much as the great increase of capital offences, created during the last and present Century, is to be lamented:—it cannot be denied that several changes have taken place in the progress of Society, favourable to the cause of humanity, and more consonant to reason and justice, in the appropriation and the mode of inflicting punishments.

The Benefit of Clergy, which for a long period exempted clerical people only, from the punishment of death in cases of felony, was by several statutes * extended to *peers, women,* and all persons *able to read;*

* 1 Edward VI. cap. 12 : 21 Jac. I. cap. 6 : 3 and 4 William and Mary, cap. 9 : 4 and 5 William and Mary, cap. 24.

who

who, pleading their Clergy, suffered only a corporal punishment, or a year's imprisonment; and those men who *could not read,* if under the degree of peerage, were hanged. *

This unaccountable distinction was actually not removed until the 5th of Queen Anne, cap. 6, which extended the benefit of clergy to all who were intitled to aſk it, *whether they could read or not.* †

In the course of the present century, several of the old sanguinary modes of punishment have been either, very properly, abolished by acts of parliament, or allowed, to the honour of humanity, to fall into disuse:—such as *burning alive (particularly women) cutting off hands or ears, slitting nostrils, or branding in the hand or face;* and among lesser punishments, fallen into disuse, may be mentioned *the ducking-stool.*

The punishment of death for felony (as has already been observed) has existed since the reign of Henry I. nearly 700 years.—Transportation is commonly understood to have been first introduced, anno 1718, by the act of the 4th George I. cap. 11; and afterwards enlarged by the Act 6th of George I. c. 23, which allowed the court a discretionary power to

* Blackstone.

† The benefit of Clergy originated in injustice and inhumanity, and can only be palliated by the rude state of society, when so disgraceful a privilege was legalized and interwoven in the criminal code.—It partakes of the nature of a compromise with villainy.—It perplexes the system of criminal jurisprudence; and since its sting is taken away it would be an improvement to discontinue it totally.

order

order felons who were by law entitled to their clergy, to be transported to the American plantations for seven or fourteen years, according to circumstances.*

Since that period the mode of punishment has undergone several other alterations ; and many Crimes which were formerly considered of an inferior rank, have been rendered capital ; which will be best elucidated by the following Catalogue of Offences divided into six classes according to the Laws now in force.

1. CRIMES *punishable by the* Deprivation of Life; *and where upon the Conviction of the Offenders, the sentence of Death must be pronounced by the Judge.—Of these, it has been stated, the whole, on the authority of Sir William Blackstone, including all the various shades of the same offence, is about* 160 *in number.*

The principal are the following :

Treason, and Petty Treason ; *See page* 38, &c. Under the former of these is included the Offence of Counterfeiting the Gold and Siver Coin, *See page* 191—211.

* It is said that exile was first introduced as a punishment by the Legislature in the 39th year of Queen Elizabeth, when a statute (39 *Eliz. c.* 4.) enacted that such rogues as were dangerous to the inferior people should be banished the realm, *Barr. Ant. Stat.* 269: and that the first statute in which the word Transportation is used is the 18th of *Charles* II. *c.* 3. which gives power to Judges at their discretion either to execute or transport to America *for life* the Moss-Troopers of *Cumberland* and *Northumberland;* a law which was made perpetual by the Act 31 *Geo.* II. *c.* 42. 2 WOOD. 498.

Murder,

Murder, *See page* 44, &c.

Arson, or wilfully and maliciously burning a House, Barns with Corn, &c. *See page* 56.

Rape, or the forcible violation of chastity, &c. *See page* 46.

Stealing an Heiress, *See page* 48.

Sodomy, a crime against nature, committed either with man or beast, *See page* 46.

Piracy, or robbing ships and vessels at sea; under which is included, the offences of Sailors forcibly hindering their captains from fighting, *See page* 55, 56.

Forgery of Deeds, Bonds, Bills, Notes, Public Securities, &c. &c. Clerks of the Bank embezzling Notes, altering Dividend Warrants; Paper Makers, unauthorised, using moulds for Notes, &c.

Destroying Ships, or setting them on Fire, *See page* 57.

Bankrupts not surrendering, or concealing their Effects

Burglary, or House Breaking in the night time, *See page* 57.

Highway Robbery

House Breaking in the day time, *See page* 54, 55.

Privately Stealing or Picking Pockets above one Shilling

Shop Lifting above Five Shillings, *See page* 55.

Stealing Bonds, Bills, or Bank Notes

Stealing Bank Notes, or Bills from Letters

Stealing above 40*s.* in any House, *See page* 55.

Stealing above 40*s.* on a River

Stealing Linen, &c. from Bleaching Grounds, &c. or destroying Linen therein

Maiming or Killing Cattle maliciously, *See* the Black Act, 9 Geo. I. cap. 22.

Stealing Horses, Cattle or Sheep

Shooting at a Revenue Officer: or at any other Person, *See* the Black Act

Pulling down Houses, Churches, &c.

Breaking

Breaking down the head of a Fish-Pond, whereby Fish may be lost, (*Black Act*)*

Cutting down Trees in an Avenue, Garden, &c,

Cutting down River or Sea Banks

Cutting hop Binds

Setting fire to coal mines

Taking a Reward for helping another to Stolen Goods, in certain cases, *See page* 295.

Returning from Transportation; or being at large in the Kingdom after Sentence

Stabbing a Person unarmed, or not having a weapon drawn, if he die in six months

Concealing the death of a Bastard Child

Maliciously maiming or disfiguring any person, &c. lying in wait for the purpose, *See page* 50.

Sending Threatening Letters (Black Act)

Riots by twelve or more, and not dispersing in an hour after proclamation

Being accessaries to Felonies deemed capital

Stealing Woollen Cloths from Tenter Grounds

Stealing from a Ship in Distress

Government Stores, embezzling, burning or destroying in Dock-Yards; in certain cases, *See pages* 261—263.

Challenging Jurors above 20 in capital felonies; or standing mute

Cottons, selling with forged Stamps

Deer-Stealing, second offence; or even first offence, under Black Act, not usually enforced

---

* The unwillingness which it must be expected a Jury would have to convict a man capitally for *this offence*, might be adduced among many other instances, to show to what extent public justice is defeated, merely from the severity of the laws, and the want of a Scale of punishments proportioned to the offences.

Uttering

I

Uttering counterfeit Money, third offence

Prisoners under Insolvent Acts guilty of perjury

Destroying Silk or Velvet in the loom; or the Tools for manufacturing thereof; or destroying Woollen Goods, Racks or Tools, or entering a House for that purpose

Servants purloining their Master's Goods, value 40s.

Personating Bail; or acknowledging fines or judgments in another's name

Escape by breaking Prison in certain cases

Attempting to kill Privy Counsellors, &c.

Sacrilege

Smuggling by persons armed; or assembling armed for that purpose

Robbery of the Mail

Destroying Turnpikes or Bridges, Gates, Weighing Engines, Locks, Sluices, Engines for Draining Marshes, &c.

Mutiny, Desertion, &c. by the Martial and Statute Law

Soldiers or Sailors enlisting into Foreign Service

2. CRIMES *denominated* Single Felonies ; *punishable by Transportation, Whipping, Imprisonment, the Pillory, and Hard Labour in Houses of Correction, according the Nature of the Offence.*

The principal of which are the following :

Grand Larceny, which comprehends every species of Theft above the value of One Shilling, not otherwise distinguished

Receiving or buying Stolen Goods, Jewels and Plate. *See page* 299.

Ripping and stealing Lead, Iron, Copper, &c. or buying or receiving, *See page* 295.

Stealing

Stealing (or receiving when stolen) Ore from Black Lead Mines

Stealing from Furnished Lodgings

Setting fire to Underwood

Stealing Letters, or destroying a Letter or Packet, advancing the Postage, and Secreting the Money

Embezzling Naval Stores, in certain cases, *See pages 261—263.*

Petty Larcenies, or Thefts under one Shilling

Assaulting with an intent to Rob

Aliens returning after being ordered out of the kingdom

Stealing Fish from a Pond or River—Fishing in inclosed Ponds, and buying stolen Fish

Stealing Roots, Trees, or Plants, of the value of 5s. or destroying them

Stealing Children with their apparel

Bigamy, or Marrying more Wives or Husbands than one (now punishable with transportation)

Assaulting and Cutting, or Burning Clothes

Counterfeiting the Copper Coin, &c.—*See page 191—211.*

Marriage, solemnizing clandestinely

Manslaughter, or killing another without Malice, &c. *See page 44.*

Cutting or Stealing Timber Trees, &c. &c. &c.

Stealing a Shroud out of a Grave

Watermen carrying too many passengers in the Thames, if any drowned

3. OFFENCES

5. OFFENCES *denominated* Misdemeanors, *punishable by Fine,*
Imprisonment, Whipping, and the Pillory.

The principal of which are the following:

Perjury, or taking a false Oath in a judicial proceeding, &c.

Frauds, by Cheating, Swindling contrary to the rules of common honesty, &c. &c.

Conspiracies, for the purpose of injuring or defrauding others

Assaults by striking or beating another person, &c.

Stealing Dead Bodies

Stealing Cabbages, Turnips, &c. growing

Cutting and Stealing Wood and Trees

Robbing Orchards and Gardens

Stealing Deer from Forests

Stealing Dogs

Setting Fire to a House to defraud the Insurance Office

Making and selling Fire-Works and Squibs

Throwing the same when on fire about the streets

Uttering Base Money

Selling Base Money under its denominated value

Embezzlement in the Woollen, Silk, and other Manufactures

Offences by Artificers and Servants in various Trades

Combinations and Conspiracies for raising the price of Wages, &c. (*See stat.* 39 *Geo.* III. *c.* 81.)

Smuggling Run Goods, and other Frauds relative to the Excise and Customs

Keeping Bawdy Houses and other Disorderly Houses

———

4. IDLE and Disorderly Persons, *described by the Act of the*
17*th Geo.* II. *cap.* 5. *and subsequent Acts:* punishable with
one Month's Imprisonment—*namely,*

1. Persons threatening to run away and leave their wives and
children on the Parish

2. Persons

2. Persons who tipple in Ale Houses, and neglect their Families, &c. as described in the 3d Geo. III. cap 45.

3. Persons who shall unlawfully return to the Parish or place from which they have been legally removed, without bringing a Certificate.

4. Persons, who not having wherewithal to maintain themselves, live idly without employment, and refuse to work for the usual Wages.

5. Persons begging in the streets, highways, &c.

5th. ROGUES and VAGABONDS *described by the said Act of the 17th Geo. II. cap. 5. and subsequent Acts;* punishable by Six Months' Imprisonment—namely,

1. Persons going about as Patent Gatherers, or Gatherers of Alms, under pretence of Loss by Fire or other casualty

2. Fencers, Bearwards, Strolling Players of Interludes, or other Entertainments

3. Minstrels, (except those licensed by the Lord Dutton in Cheshire)

4. Persons pretending to be, and wandering in the habit of, Gypsies

5. Fortune-Tellers, pretending skill in Physiognomy, Palmistry, &c. or using any subtle craft to deceive and impos. on others

6. Persons playing or betting at any unlawful Games or Plays

7. Persons who run away, and leave their Wives and Children upon the Parish

8. Petty Chapmen and Pedlars wandering abroad without a Licence

9. Persons wandering abroad, and lodging in Ale-Houses, Out-Houses, or the open Air, and not giving a good account of themselves

10. Persons

10. Persons wandering abroad, and pretending to be Soldiers or Sailors, without proper certificates from their Officers, or Testimonials from Magistrates.

11. Persons wandering abroad, pretending to go to work in Harvest, without a proper Certificate from the Parish.

12. Persons having Implements of House-breaking or Offensive Weapons, with a Felonious intent.

13. Persons concerned in illegal Lottery Transactions, as described in the Lottery Acts, 27th, 33d, 34th, and 35th Geo. III.

———

6th. INCORRIGIBLE ROGUES, *punishable with Two Years' Imprisonment and Whipping, or Transportation for Seven Years, if they break out of Prison—namely,*

1. Persons stiled End-Gatherers, buying, collecting, or receiving Ends of Yarn in the Woollen Branch, against the Stat. 18 Geo I. cap. 23.

2. Persons, who being Rogues and Vagabonds, have escaped after being apprehended, or who shall refuse to be examined by a Magistrate, or who shall give a false account of themselves after being warned of their punishment.

3. Persons who shall escape out of any House of Correction before the period of their imprisonment expires.

4. Persons, who being once punished as Rogues and Vagabonds, shall again commit the same offence.

☞ *There are a great many other trivial Offences denominated Misdemeanors, subject to pecuniary Fines, which it is not easy to enumerate. Since almost every statute, whether public or private, which passes in the course of a Session of Parliament, creates new offences—the shades vary as Society advances, and their number is scarcely within the reach of calculation.*

The

The crimes mentioned in the first and second classes of the foregoing Enumeration (except petty Larceny) are always tried by the Superior Courts :— The offences specified in the third class, as also Petty Larceny, and every species of misdemeanor and vagrancy, are generally tried, (with some few exceptions) by the Justices in their General and Quarter Sessions, where, in certain cases in Middlesex, they act under a commission of Oyer and Terminer. The Magistrates in Petty Sessions, and in several instances a *single Magistrate*, have also the power of convicting in a summary way, for a variety of small misdemeanors, and acts of vagrancy; and of punishing the delinquents with fine and imprisonment.

It generally happens in the Metropolis, that out of from 2000 to 2500 prisoners who were tried for different crimes, in the various Courts of Justice, above 5-6th parts are for larcenies, acts of vagrancy, and smaller offences; where the Benefit of Clergy either attaches, or does not apply at all. The major part are, of course, returned upon Society, after a short imprisonment, or some corporal punishment, too frequently to renew their depredations on the public.— But a vast proportion (as has already been shewn) are always acquitted*. In

* All endeavours towards the prevention of crimes will ever be attended with unconquerable difficulty, until some general House of Industry can be established in the Metropolis: where persons discharged for petty offences, as well as strangers and others out of work, may have an opportunity of finding, at least a temporary employment, sufficient to maintain them. An Institution of this sort would

In order to form a judgment of the proportion of the more atrocious offenders tried at the Old Bailey; the number acquitted; and the specific punishments inflicted on the different offences in case of conviction, one year has been selected; a year in which it was natural to expect from the immense, and indeed unparalleled bounties which were given for seamen and soldiers, that the number of thieves and criminals would be greatly reduced,—namely—*from the month of April* 1793, *to the month of April* 1794,—including eight Sessions at the Old Bailey.—

The following Table shews in what manner 1060 prisoners put on their trials during that period, were disposed of*.

would be a work of great charity and humanity; and it is earnestly to be hoped, that the view of the subject given in this Work may induce the Legislature to form a Police Establishment, calculated to promote such a multitude of good and useful objects; † more especially as with proper management it would very soon pay itself.

* In the year 1795, 1894 prisoners were tried at the Old Bailey, and the different Assizes in the country, exclusive of a much greater number at the General and Quarter Sessions of the Peace in the different Counties. These trials in the Superior Courts of Judicature, produced the following result:—

	London	Assizes in the Country	Total
Received Sentence of Death	44	174	218
- - - - - - Transportation	84	159	243
Imprisoned and Whipt - - -	129	411	540
Judgment respited to serve his } Majesty - - - -	23	25	48
Acquitted - - - - - - -	150	351	501
Discharged for want of Prosecutors	91	253	344
	521	1373	1894

† Vide *page* 99 *n.*   The

The Crimes for which the different Offenders were tried, were these following:

Murder	46	Felony	315	Manslaughter	29
Arson	5	Larceny	998	Bigamy	3
Burglary	101	Receiving } 61		Beastiality	2
Robbery	58	stolen Goods }		Rape	9
Horse & Cattle } 108		Frauds and } 101		Perjury	2
stealing }		Misdemeanors }		Sedition	2
Forgery	16	Rogues and } 21			
Coining	17	Vagabonds }			47
	351		1496		

A TABLE.

A TABLE, shewing the Prisoners tried at the Old Bailey, from April 1793, to March 1794, inclusive.

London, Middlesex, and Westminster.	Persons committed for trial.	Of whom acquitted and discharged.	Prisoners convicted, and their Punishments.								
			Death.	Transported for 14 years.	Transported for 7 years.	Whipt & imprisoned.	Imprisoned 6 months and upwards.	Imprisoned 3 months & otherwise disposed of.	Sent to serve the King.	Judgment respited.	Total punished.
London Sessions	199	70	6	1	50	10	29	20	8	5	129
Middlesex and Westminster }	861	497	62	1	117	38	51	49	30	16	364
	1060	*567	68	2	167	48	80	69	38	21	493

* The acquittals will generally be found to attach mostly to small offences which are punishable with death: where Juries do not consider the crime deserving so severe a punishment, the delinquent receives no punishment at all. If all were convicted who were really guilty of these small offences, the number of victims to the severity of the Law would be greatly increased.

Thus it appears, that in London only, of 1060 prisoners, tried in the course of a year, only 493 were punished; of whom 197, after a temporary confinement, would return upon the Public, with little prospect of being better disposed to be useful to Society, than before.—It may be estimated that in all England, including those offenders who are tried at the County Sessions, upwards of five thousand individuals, charged with criminal offences, are thrown back upon Society every year.—

But this is not all,—for according to the present System, out of about *two hundred* and upwards who are, upon an average every year, doomed to suffer the punishment of death, *four-fifths* or more are generally pardoned * either on condition of being transported, or of going into His Majesty's service, and not seldom without any condition at all.

Hence it is, that, calculating on all the different chances, encouragements to commit crimes actually arise out of the System intended for their prevention—*first, from the hope of avoiding detection and apprehension;—secondly, of escaping conviction, from*

---

* As punishments became more mild, clemency and pardons became less necessary.—Clemency is a virtue that ought to shine in the code, and not in the private judgment.—The Prince in pardoning gives up the Public Security in favour of an individual; and by the exercise of this species of benevolence proclaims a public act of impunity.—Let the Executors of the Laws be inexorable; but let the Legislature be tender, indulgent and humane.

BECCARIA, cap. 46.

the

the means used to vitiate and suborn the evidence;—thirdly, from the mercy of the Jury, in considering the punishment too severe;—and fourthly, from the interest of persons of rank or consideration, applying (under circumstances where humanity becomes the friend of every person doomed to die), for the interference of Royal Mercy, by Pardons.

God forbid that the Author of these pages should do so much violence to his own feelings, as to convey an idea hostile to the extension of that amiable Prerogative vested in the Sovereign ; and which His Majesty has exercised with a benevolent regard to the feelings of Humanity, and a merciful disposition truly characteristic of the mind of a great and good King.

These animadversions are by no means pointed against the exercise of a privilege so benign, and even so necessary, in the present state of the Criminal Law;—they regard only the impositions which have been practised upon so many well-intentioned, respectable, and amiable Characters, who have, from motives of humanity, interested themselves in obtaining *free pardons for Convicts,* or *pardons on condition of going into the Army or Navy.*

If these humane individuals, who exert themselves in applications of this sort, were to be made acquainted with one half of the gross impositions practised upon their credulity, or the evil consequences arising to Society from such pardons, (particularly unconditional pardons) they would shudder at the extent

of

of the cruelty exercised towards the Public, and even, in many instances, to the Convicts themselves, by this false humanity.

In a Country where, from the great caution which mingles in that part of the Criminal Jurisprudence which relates to the trial of Offenders,—it is scarcely possible that an honest or an innocent person can be convicted of a capital offence.*—It would seem to be a good criterion, that the Royal Mercy should only be extended on two indispensable conditions.

1. *That the Convict under sentence of death should, for the sake of Public Justice, (and to deter others from the commission of crimes) discover all his accomplices, and the robberies, or other crimes he has committed.*

2. *That he should be transported; or make retribution to the parties he has injured by being kept at hard labour for life; or until ample security shall be given for good behaviour after such retribution is made.*

The precaution not having been used of knowing *for certain*, before pardons were granted, whether the parties were fit for His Majesty's service or not; the Convicts themselves carefully concealing every kind of bodily infirmity;—and the pardons containing no eventual condition of ultimate Transportation, in case the persons should be found unfit for the

* It is not here meant to say there have not been some instances, and even one of a recent date, where an innocent man may be convicted; but they are certainly very rare, and when discovered, the Royal Mercy, of course, relieves the unfortunate person.

Army

Army or Navy;—the result has been, that many Convicts, who have been since actually Thieves upon the Town, were almost instantly thrown back upon the Public.—Some, even before they were attested by the Magistrate, in consequence of the discovery of bodily incapacity; and others, in a very short time after they had gone into His Majesty's Service, from the like unfitness being discovered; from some artful device practised to procure a discharge—or from desertion.—A professed Thief is never deficient in that species of artifice and resource which is necessary to rid him of any incumbrance.

This, however, is seldom taken into the calculation when Humanity urges philanthropic Characters to interest themselves in behalf of Criminals; nor could it perhaps otherwise have been known, or believed, that so many of these outcasts of Society have found means again to mingle with the mass of the people.

What impression must these facts make on the intelligent mind!—will they not warrant the following conclusion?

1. That every individual, restored to Society in this way, is the means of affording a species of encouragement, peculiarly calculated to bring others into the same dreadful situation, from which the unhappy convict is thus rescued.

2. That for this reason every pardon granted, without some lesser punishment, or removing the convicts from Society, is a link broken in the chain of justice, by annihilating that united strength which binds the whole together.

3. Tha

3. That by removing the terror of punishments by frequent pardons, the design of the Law is rendered in a great measure ineffectual; the lives of persons *executed* are thrown away, being sacrificed rather to the vengeance of the Law than to the good of the Public; and no other advantage is received than by getting rid of one thief, whose place, (under present circumstances,) will speedily be supplied by another.*

Nothing can sanction the punishment of death for crimes short of murder, *but the terror of the example operating as the means of prevention.*—It is upon this principle alone that one man is sacrificed to the preservation of thousands.—Executions, therefore, being exhibited as seldom as a regard to the public interest really required, ought to be rendered as *terrific* and *solemn* to the eyes of the people as possible.

The punishment now in use, considered in point

* That able and excellent Magistrate, the late Henry Fielding, Esq. (to whose zeal and exertions in the exercise of the duties of a Justice of the Peace, in the Metropolis, the Public were under infinite obligations)—manifested, half a century ago, how much he was impressed with the injuries arising from frequent pardons.—Those who will contemplate the character and conduct of this valuable man, as well as that of his brother, the late Sir John Fielding, will sincerely lament that their excellent ideas, and accurate and extensive knowledge upon every subject connected with the Police of the Metropolis, and of the means of preventing crimes, were not rendered more useful to the Public. It is to be hoped, however, that it is not yet too late, since the state of Society, and the progress and increase of crimes, call loudly for the establishment of a responsible preventive System.

of

of law to be next to that of deprivation of life, is *Transportation.*

It has been already mentioned that Parliament authorized this species of punishment in the year 1718 —when the general plan of sending Convicts to the American Plantations was first adopted. This System continued for 56 years; during which period, and until the commencement of the American War in 1775, great numbers of Felons were sent chiefly to the Province of Maryland. The rigid discipline which the colonial Laws authorized the masters * to exercise over servants, joined to the prospects which agricultural pursuits, after some experience was acquired, afforded to these *Outcasts,* tended to reform the chief part; and after the expiration of their servitude, they mingled in the Society of the Country, under circumstances highly beneficial to themselves and even to the colony. Possessed in general (as every adroit thief must be) of good natural abilities, they availed themselves of the habits of industry they acquired in the years of their servitude—became farmers and planters on their own account; and many of them, succeeding in these pursuits, not only acquired that degree of respectability which is attached to property and industry; but also in their turn

---

* By the Acts 4 George I. c. 11, and 6 George I. c. 23, the persons contracting for the transportation of convicts to the Colonies, or their assigns, had an interest in the service of each, for seven or fourteen years, according to the term of transportation.

became

became masters, and purchased the servitude of future Transports sent out for sale.*

The Convicts having accumulated greatly in the year 1776, and the intercourse with America being shut up, it became indispensably necessary to resort to some other expedient; and in the choice of difficulties the System of the *Hulks* was suggested, and first adopted under the authority of an Act of the 16th of his present Majesty.

The Legislature, uncertain with regard to the success of this new species of punishment, and wishing to make other experiments, by an Act of the same Session, † empowered the Justices of every county in England to prepare Houses of Correction for the reception of Convicts under sentence of death, to whom his Majesty should extend his Royal Mercy, to be kept at hard labour for a term not exceeding ten years.

The same Act, among many other excellent regulations, ordered the convicts to be kept separate, and not allowed to mix with any offenders convicted of crimes less than Larceny—and that they should

---

* For some years previous to the commencement of the American War, the adjudged services of Convicts became so valuable in Maryland, that contracts were made to convey them without any expence whatsoever to Government, who had formerly allowed 5l. a head; for the reasons already assigned, they generally were more adroit, and had better abilities than those who voluntarily engaged themselves to go to America.

† 16 George III, cap. 43, sect. 1st, 3d, and 11th.

be

be fed with coarse inferior food, water, and small beer, without permission to have any other food, drink, or cloathing, than that allowed by the Act, under certain penalties:—they were to be clothed at the public expence.

And as an encouragement to these delinquents, while such as refused to work were to receive corporal punishment, those who behaved well had not only the prospect held out of shortening the period of their confinement, but also were to receive decent clothes, and a sum of money not less than *forty shillings*, nor more than *five pounds*, when discharged.

This well-intentioned Act * (which certainly admits of many improvements,) was followed up, three years afterwards, by another Statute, (19 Geo. III.

* An enormous expence has been incurred in building Penitentiary-Houses in various Counties, and many philanthropic individuals have exerted their best endeavours to carry this Act into execution; but it is to be lamented, that crimes have been by no means diminished. The fact is, that the System is erroneous—Responsibility is no where established.—No uniformity of System prevails, and no general superintendance or center point exists.—Like the Poor Laws, the only part of the Act which is rigidly carried into execution is raising a fund, which, without imputing blame to Magistrates (for the error is in the System), has increased the expence of this branch of the Police of the Country very far beyond what could have been conceived—and it now becomes a heavy burden upon many of the Counties.—The reform began at the wrong end.—The same expence applied in establishing a System of Preventive Police, ought to render numerous penitentiary houses in a great measure unnecessary.

cap.

cap. 74,) which had two very important objects in view.

The first was to erect, in some convenient common or waste ground, in either of the counties of *Middlesex, Essex, Kent,* or *Surry, Two large Penitentiary Houses,* the one to hold 600 *male,* and the other 300 *female Convicts,* with proper *storehouses, workhouses,* and *lodging-rooms;* an *infirmary, chapel,* and *burying-ground;* a *prison, kitchen, garden,* and *air-grounds:* with proper *offices,* and other *necessary apartments.*

The expence of these grounds and erections was to be paid out of the treasury; and his Majesty was empowered to appoint three persons as a Committee of Management for regulating the Establishment; under the controul of the Justices of the Peace of the County, and Judges of Assize, with power to appoint a *clerk, governor, chaplain, surgeon,* or *apothecary, store-keepers,* and *task-masters;* and also a *matron* for the females;—and to allow salaries to each, which were to be paid out of the profits of the work, to be performed by the Convicts.

As soon as the buildings should be completed, the Court, before whom any person was convicted for a transportable offence, might, in lieu thereof, order the prisoner to be punished by confinement, in any of these Penitentiary Houses, there to be kept to hard labour in the proportion of 5 *years* instead of 7 *years' transportation,* and not exceeding 7 years in lieu of 14 *years' transportation;* limiting at the same time

time the number of Convicts to be sent annually from the Circuits in the Country, and from the different Sessions in the Metropolis.

This Act lays down various specific rules for the government of the Establishment, and for the employment of the Prisoners; and the following works, as being of the most servile kind and least liable to be spoiled by ignorance, neglect, or obstinacy, are selected, namely—

1. Treading in a wheel for moving machinery.
2. Drawing in a capstan, for turning a mill or engine.
3. Sawing stone
4. Polishing marble
5. Beating hemp
6. Rasping logwood
7. Chopping rags
8. Making cordage
9. Picking oakum
10. Weaving sacks
11. Knitting nets,
&c. &c.

The food of the different offenders, as in the former Act, was limited to bread and any coarse meal, with water and small beer; and the Prisoners were to be cloathed in uniform apparel, with badges affixed, agreeable to the Institution.

Certain other rules were established for the discipline of the house, under the direction of the Committee to be appointed by his Majesty; who were to attend every fortnight, and to have power to reward such offenders as should appear most diligent and meritorious, by giving them a part of their earnings, to be applied for the use of themselves and families.

And

And when an offender should be discharged, decent cloathing was to be delivered to him; with a sum of money for present subsistence, not less than *twenty shillings*, nor more than *three pounds*.

The second purpose of this Act (and which is the only part of it which was ever carried into effect,) regards *the continuation of the System of the Hulks.*

It declares that for the more effectual punishment of atrocious male offenders liable to be transported, the Court may order such Convicts as are of proper age, and free from bodily infirmity, to be punished by being kept on board ships or vessels; and employed in hard labour in raising sand, soil, and gravel, and cleansing the River Thames, or any other river, or port, approved by the Privy Council; or in any other works upon the banks or shores of the same, under the direction of superintendants approved of by the Justices, for a term not less than *one* year, nor more than *five;* except an offender be liable to transportation for 14 years, in which case his punishment may be commuted for 7 years on board the Hulks.

The mode of feeding is the same as already explained, and the cloathing is to be at the discretion of the superintendant. A similar discipline, varied only by local circumstances, is also established; and on the discharge of any of the convicts, they are to receive for present subsistence from 20s. to 3l. according to circumstances.

The

The concluding part of the Act obliges the governors and superintendants of the two Establishments to make annual returns to the Court of King's Bench: and also authorizes his Majesty *to appoint an Inspector of the two Penitentiary Houses, of the several vessels or hulks on the River Thames, and of all the other gaols and places of criminal confinement within the City of London and County of Middlesex;* these Inspectors are personally to visit every such place of confinement at least once a quarter, to examine into the particulars of each, and to make a return to the Court of King's Bench, of the *state of the buildings —the conduct of the officers—treatment of the prisoners—state of their earnings and expences,* and to follow up this by a report to both Houses of Parliament, at the beginning of each Session.

It is much to be lamented that neither of these two salutary Acts, so far as regarded *National Penitentiary Houses,* which seemed to hold out so fair a prospect of employing convicts, in pursuits connected with *productive labour, industry,* and ultimate *reformation,* without sending them out of the kingdom, have been carried into execution. In the year 1784, the System of Transportation was again revived, by the Act of 24th Geo. III. Stat. 2. cap. 56; " which empowers the Court, before whom a male Felon shall be convicted, to order the prisoner to be transported beyond seas, either within his Majesty's dominions or elsewhere; and his service to be assigned to the contractor who shall undertake such transportation."

The

The same Act continues the System of the Hulks for a further length of time; by directing the removal of Convicts, under sentence of death, and reprieved by his Majesty, and also such as are under sentence of Transportation (being free from infectious disorders) to other places of confinement, either inland, or on board of any ship or vessel in the River Thames, or any other navigable river; and to continue them so confined until transported according to law, or until the expiration of the term of the sentence should otherwise entitle them to their liberty.

This plan of transportation, through the medium of contractors, although some Felons were sent to Africa,* does not appear to have answered; from the great difficulty of finding any situation, since the Revolution in America, where the service of Convicts could be rendered productive or profitable to Merchants, who would undertake to transport them; and hence arose the idea of making an Establishment for these outcasts of Society in

---

* In 1785, George Moore, Esq. received for

transporting convicts	—	£.1,512	7	6
John Kirby for expences	—	540	19	4
1786, John Kirby; further expences		578	10	1
Anthony Calvert, for Transportation		286	14	0
Thomas Cotton, Esq. Cloathing, &c.	— — —	303	2	7
		†£.3,721	13	6

† See Appendix (L. 1.) to the 28th Report of Select Committee on Finance.

the

the infant colony of New South Wales, to which remote region it was at length determined to transport atrocious offenders.—Accordingly, in the year 1787, an Act passed, (27 Geo. III. cap. 2,) authorizing the establishment of a Court of Judicature for the trial of offenders who should be transported to New South Wales.

Another Act of the following year, (28 Geo. III. cap. 24,) empowered his Majesty, under his Royal Sign Manual, to authorize any person to make contracts for the Transportation of offenders, and to direct to whom security should be given for the due performance of the contract.

By the Act of 30 George III. cap. 47, the Governor of the Settlement may remit the punishment of offenders there : and on a certificate from him their names shall be inserted in the next General Pardon.

Under these various legislative regulations, the two Systems of Punishment, namely, the *Hulks* and *Transportation* to New South Wales, have been authorized and carried into execution.

The System of the Hulks commenced on the 12th day of July, in the year 1776; and from that time until the 12th of December 1795, comprehending a period of nineteen years, 7999 Convicts were ordered to be punished by hard labour on the river Thames, and Langston, and Portsmouth harbours, which are accounted for in the following manner :

1. Convicts

1. Convicts ordered to hard labour on the River Thames, from 12th July 1776, to the 12th January, 1778 — 2024.

2. Convicts, *under sentence of Transportation,* put on board the Hulks on the River Thames, from 11th January, 1783, to 12th December 1795 — — 4775

3. *Deduct,* under sentence of Transportation, put on board the Hulks in Langston and Portsmouth Harbours, received from the Hulks at Woolwich, on the 20th of June, 1791. — — 466
————— 4309

Additional Convicts sent from different prisons to Portsmouth and Langston, from 1791, to 1st December, 1795 — — 1200
To which, add those from Woolwich as above 466
————— 1666

Total 7999

Of the above convicts there have been

Discharged — —	1610	
Pardoned — —	790	
Escaped — —	130	
	— 2530	
Removed to other Gaols —	17	
Transported to New South Wales	2207	
* Died — —	1946	
	6700	

And there remain in the Hulks on the
Thames — — 523
And at Langston Harbour — 776
————— 1299

Total as above 7999

* A malignant fever, at one period, carried off a vast number, in spite of every effort to prevent it.

By

By a subsequent account laid before the Select Committee of the House of Commons on Finance, and stated in Appendix, M. of their 28th Report, dated the 26th of June, 1798, it appears that the number of Convicts stood thus:

In the Hulks on the Thames, at Woolwich	501
At Portsmouth — — —	948
Total	1449

Besides 415 under Sentence of Transportation in the different Goals, making in all 1864.

From the same authentic Documents, (pages 115, 116,) it appearss that of these Convicts, the following numbers will be discharged upon Society in the succeeding 13 years*:

	Portsmouth.		Woolwich.
In 1800 —	140	—	115
1801 —	106	—	43
1802 —	127	—	26
1803 —	107	—	46
1804 —	149	—	77
1805 —	33	—	3
1806 —	1	—	1
1807 —	1	—	1
1808 —	1	—	1
1809 —	1	—	0
1810 —	1	—	0
1811 —	10	—	4
1812 —	1	—	0
	—— 678		—— 317
For life	76	—	22

* See page 98 of this volume, for an Account of the Convicts enlarged the preceding eight years, in all 1383

To be discharged as above	—	995
Total		2378

RECAPITU-

RECAPITULATION.

Convicts discharged from the Hulks, from 1792 to
  1799 inclusive *(See page* 98 *of this Treatise)*   —   1388
To be discharged from the Hulks at Langston chiefly
  in 6 years   —   —   —   678
From Woolwich, chiefly within the same period   317

Total 2373

In the same authentic Documents, namely the
Appendix (L. 1 & 2) page 103 of the 28th Report of
the Select Committee on Finance, a Statement is
given of the Expence which has been incurred by
" Government, for or in respect of the Conviction,
" Confinement, and Maintenance of Convicts, from
" the 1st January, 1775, to the year ending the
" 31st December, 1797," of which the following
is an abstract:

			£	s.	d.
1 Jan. 1775 to 1 Jan. 1776 paid at the Exchequer		£.8,660	0	0
—— 1776	—	1777	—	7,950	16	10
—— 1777	—	1778	—	13,676	14	5
—— 1778	—	1779	—	17,939	18	0
—— 1779	—	1780	—	22,292	11	$1\frac{1}{2}$
—— 1780	—	1781	—	21,034	0	$1\frac{3}{4}$
—— 1781	—	1782	—	18,686	19	0
—— 1782	—	1783	—	22,320	10	9
—— 1783	—	1784	—	17,669	3	11
—— 1784	—	1785	—	31,555	18	11
—— 1785	—	1786	—	32,343	17	7
—— t 7 March	1786	—	9,353	17	0

Carried over £.223,484   7   8

To

Brought over £.223,484   7   8
To 31 December 1786 - - - -   22,282 18   4
——   1787 - - - - - 33,927   9   7
——   1788 - - - - - 34,059 14   8
——   1789 - - - - - 62,656 15   5
——   1790 - - - - - 46,865   4   6
——   1791 - - - - - 43,840   9   0
——   1792 - - - - - 22,300 12   7
——   1793 - - - - - 25,403 16   0
——   1794 - - - - - 25,751   3   7½
——   1795 - - - - - 14,195   7   4½
——   1796 - - - - - 36,174   7   9
1797 } - { 19,566 15 11
1797 }   { 12,574   0   0

Total Expence of Convicts in the
Hulks, from the Commencement } £.623,022 14   5
of the System to 1 January, 1798

The Contractors for the Convicts at Woolwich and Langston Harbour, (as appears from documents laid before the House of Commons) entered into an agreement with the Lords of the Treasury obliging themselves for *the consideration of* 1s. 3d. *per day*, (being 22l. 16s. 3d. a year *for each Convict*,) to provide at their own cost or charge, *one* or more *Hulks*, to keep the same in proper repair, to provide proper Ship's Companies for the safe Custody of such Convicts; and sufficient *meat, drink, clothing* and *medical assistance*, for the Convicts; as also to sustain all other charges (excepting the expence of the *Chaplain, Coroner*, and bounties to discharged Convicts;*) obeying,

* This expence, by an account laid before the House of Commons, for one Year, ending the 15th Feb. 1792, appears to be—
Expence of Chaplain, Coroner, and Bounties for
Convicts at Woolwich — — £.221 17 4
At Langston and Portsmouth Harbours — 153 19 8

Total £.375 17 0
at

at the same time, all the orders of his Majesty's Principal Secretary of State for the Home Department, respecting the Convicts. A subsequent contract was made at 14½d. which reduced the expence to 22l. 1s. 0½d. per man : and which is the allowance made to the present Contractors.

The terms of these contracts appear to be as favourable for Government as could reasonably be expected, under all circumstances; and it would appear, that some advantages are reaped by the Public, as the documents laid before the House of Commons, in 1792 and 1798, shew that the labour performed by the Convicts is productive in a certain degree.— The following Statements explain how their labour is valued :—

From the 1st of January 1789 to the 1st of January 1792, it appears that 653,432 days' work had been performed at Langston Harbour, Portsmouth, and Woolwich Warren; which being estimated at 9d. a day, is   £.24,503 14 0

and

From the 1st of January 1789 to the 1st of January 1792, it also appears that 260,440 days' work had been performed at the Dock yard at Woolwich; which being partly performed by artificers in a more productive species of labour, is estimated at 1s. a day 13,022 0 0

Total value of Convicts' labour in 3 years £.37,525 14 0

It

It appears from the 28th Report of the Select Committee on Finance, Appendix, No. 7 and 8—

That the work done by Convicts confined on board the Hulks in Langston Harbour, during the year 1797, was performed by about 421 convicts upon a daily average, and computing the labour of each artificer at 19l. 8s. 9d. per annum, and each labourer at 11l. 13s. 3d. it will amount to £.5,997 18 3

The work performed in the same year by about 250 convicts, confined on board the Hulks at Portsmouth, computed as above will amount to 3,226 15 0

9,224 13 3

From which is to be deducted, to make the amount correspond with the valuation made by the Ordnance Board 1,440 5 3

£.7,784 8 0

The work done by Convicts, confined on board the *Prudentia* and *Stanislaus* Hulks at Woolwich Dock-yards and Warren, performed by 359 convicts, rated at 1s. and 1s. 2d. for labourers, and 1s. 5d. per day for artificers, is calculated to amount to 6,578 4 7

£.14,362 12 7

Deduct allowances made, and articles supplied, by the Board of Ordnance 1,498 14 10½

Total Estimate of the value of the labour of Convicts in 1797 . . . . £.12,863 17 8½

Upon

Upon this last statement the Select Committee on Finance (whose various elaborate Reports on the State of the Nation, do them immortal honour as Patriots and Legislators) very justly observe, that it is extremely difficult to calculate the value of labour, performed under such circumstances, with any degree of accuracy; and after several views of the subject a conclusion is drawn, that the net expence to the Public, for the maintenance of 1402 Convicts in 1797, after deducting the estimated value of labour, amounted to 20,878*l*. 14*s*. 10¼*d*. being at the rate of 14*l*. 17*s*. 9½*d*. per man.

It appears, however, that out of the whole number of 1402 maintained in 1797, only 1030 were actually employed. The labour of the remaining 370 was, therefore, in a great measure, lost to the Community.

At any rate, the value of this species of labour must be precarious, and the advantages resulting from it problematical.

Since the mere " possession of so many idle hands " will sometimes be a temptation to engage in works, " which but for this inducement, would not recom- " mend themselves by their intrinsic utility."*

While it is admitted, that considerable improvements have been made with regard to the reduction of the expence; that provision has also been made for religious and moral instruction, by established sa-

* See 28th Report of Finance Committee, page 17.

laries

laries to chaplains;—and that the contractors have honourably performed their part of the undertaking; it is much to be lamented, that this experiment has not been attended with more beneficial consequences to the Public; not only in rendering the labour of the Convicts productive in a greater degree, so as at least to be equal to the expence; but also in amending the morals of these miserable out-casts; so that on their return to Society, they might, in some respect, atone for the errors of their former lives, by a course of honest industry, useful to themselves and to their country. On the contrary, experience has shewn, that although an expence exceeding 623,000*l.* has been incurred by Government in the course of 22 years, most of them, instead of profitting by the punishment they have suffered (forgetting they were under sentence of death, and undismayed by the dangers they have escaped) immediately rush into the same course of depredation and warfare upon the public: nay, so hardened and determined in this respect have some of them been, as even to make proposals to their old friends, the Receivers, previous to the period of their discharge, to purchase their newly acquired plunder. It has already been shewn, that those few also, who are less depraved, and perhaps disposed to amend their conduct, can find no resource for labour; and are thus, too frequently, compelled, by dire necessity, to herd with their former associates in iniquity, and it is

much

much to be feared, that the chief part of the multitudes, who have been periodically discharged, have either suffered for new offences, or are actually at present afflicting Society by reiterated depredations.*

After maturely considering the enormous expence, and the total inefficacy of the System of the Hulks, aided by the new lights which have been thrown upon the subject by the important documents called for by the Select Committee on Finance, it appears clear to demonstration, that it would be for the interest of the Country to abandon the present System; and the Author heartily joins in the opinion expressed by those respectable members of the Legislature,—
" *That our principal places of Confinement, and modes*
" *of punishment, so far from the Conversion and Re-*
" *formation of the Criminal, tend to send him forth at*
" *the expiration of the period of his imprisonment more*
" *confirmed in vice; and that the general tendency of*
" *our œconomical arrangements upon this subject, is*
" *ill calculated to meet the accumulating burdens,*
" *which are the infallible result of so much error in*
" *the System of Police.*"

Having thus explained the nature and effect of the punishment inflicted on convicts, through the medium of the Hulks, and also the expence attending these establishments; it will be necessary in the next place, to examine the authentic documents, as they

---

* See the Examination of the Author before the Select Committee of the House of Commons.

relate,

relate to the transportation of Felons to New South Wales.

From the Appendix, page 122, of the 28th Report of the Select Committee on Finance, printed the 26th of June 1798, it appears that the number of Convicts sent to New South Wales and Norfolk Island* from the year 1787 to the year 1797 inclusive, stood thus :—

	Men and Women.	Children.	TOTAL,
1787	778	17	795
1789	1251	22	1273
1790	2029	9	2038
1791	408	11	419
1792	412	6	418
1794	82	2	84
1795	133	3	136
1796	279	13	292
1797	393	10	403
	5765	93	5858

It appears also from another document in the same Report (being the last return of Convicts in the two Settlements) that their numbers stood as stated in the following Table,—

	Convicts		Convicts Victualled		Convicts Emancipated		Total		Total Men and Women
	Men	Women	Men	Women	Men	Women	Men	Women	
In New South Wales on the 31 Aug. 1796.	1638	755	78	5	20		1731	769	2500
In Norfolk Island on the 22 Oct. 1796.	379	167	53	0	12	3	444	170	614
	2012	922	131	5	32	12	2175	930	3114

To which add the Convicts sent in 1796 and 1797, including Children 695

Total 3809

The diminution of Convicts from 5858 to 3809 is to be accounted for, by a certain proportion leaving the Settlement after the expiration of their time, and also by deaths,* which in the natural course of things must be expected.

In resorting to this mode of disposing of Convicts, which at the time must be considered as a choice of difficulties, a very large sum of money has been expended.—Certainly much more than could have been foreseen at the commencement: Since it appears from the 28th Report of the Select Committee on Finance, who certainly have bestowed infinite pains in the investigation, that the total amount exceeds *One Million Sterling*, as will be seen from the following Statement, extracted from page 120 of that 28th Report, viz;

Disbursed for 5858 Convicts including 93 Children, transported to New South Wales

	£.	s.	d.		£	s.	d.
				Brought over	337,449	7	1½
In 1786	28,346	3	6	In 1792	104,588	2	3¼
— 1787	29,242	11	10½	— 1793	69,961	16	6½
— 1788	18,008	9	2	— 1794	79381	13	11½
— 1789	88,057	18	2	— 1795	75,280	19	0¼
— 1790	44,774	4	6¼	— 1796	83,854	18	0
— 1791	129,019	19	10¾	— 1797	120,372	4	8¾
Carried over	337,449	7	1½	Carried over £.	870,889	1	8¾

* Norfolk Island is a small fertile spot, containing about 14,000 acres of land, situated about 1200 miles distant from Sydney Cove, in New South Wales, where the seat of Government is fixed.

† In 21 months after the arrival of the first Convicts in May 1788, there were 77 deaths and 87 births in the whole Settlement.

To

Brought over £.870,880   1   8¼
To which add the total Naval Expences   166,341   4   11

Total Expences in 12 Years   £.1,037,230   6   7½

Specification of the heads of Expences above stated—

Expences of the first Establishment of the
Settlement and Transportation of Convicts 264,433 11   0
Expences of Victualling Convicts and the
Settlement from hence - - - - -   186,270   1   3¼
Expences of Cloathing, Tools, and Sundry
Articles   - - - - - - - - -   116,658 15   3
Bills drawn for the purchase of Provisions,
&c. for the use of the Colony - - -   138,225   9   8¾
Expence of the Civil Establishment - -   48,134   0   2¼
Expence of the Military Establishment -   94,993 11   3
Expence of the Marine Establishment -   22,173 13   0½
Naval Expences as above - - - -   166,341   4   11

Total   £.1,037,230   6   7¾

Thus it appears, that in executing the sentence of the Law on 5765 Convicts more than one Million Sterling has been expended, nearly equal to 180l. for each Convict, exclusive of the expence incurred by the Counties, and by Government in the maintenance at home; and without taking into the account the very considerable charge, which must have been borne by the private Prosecutors in bringing these Offenders to Justice.

The

The Select Committee in their laborious investigation of the effects of this System, very justly observe, " that the numbers of the Convicts do not
" appear to have kept pace with the increase of the
" expence."—They proceed to state (page 27 of the
Report) "that after a trial of twelve years, it seems
" not too early to inquire whether the peculiar ad-
" vantages likely to arise from this plan are such as
" may be considered as compensating for its proba-
" ble expence. The security held out by the dif-
" ficulty of return on the part of the convicts is
" the only advantage that strikes the eye: but the
" nature of this advantage, the amount of it, and
" the certainty of it, seem not altogether undeserv-
" ing of inquiry; nor whether a security of the same
" sort more at command, and more to be depended
" on, might not be purchased on less exceptionable
" terms. It may be also worthy of inquiry (add the
" Committee) whether the advantages looked for
" from this establishment may not be dependent on
" its weakness; and whether as it grows less disad-
" vantageous in point of finance, it will not be apt to
" grow less advantageous in the character of an in-
" strument of Police? The more thriving the Settle-
" ment the more frequented: The more frequented
" the less difficulty of return.—The more thriving
" too the less terrible. To persons in some circum-
" stances;—to persons who otherwise would have
" been disposed to emigrate, it may lose its terrors
                                        " altogether,

" altogether, especially if by money or other means
" the servitude be avoidable. This inconvenience
" had already become sensible in the instance of
" the comparatively old planted Colonies. Many,
" though innocent, went thither voluntarily even at
" the price of servitude, while others under the no-
" tion of punishment, were sent thither for their
" crimes; so that while to some the emigration re-
" mains a punishment, to others it may become an
" adventure; but a punishment should be the same
" thing to all persons, and at all times."

Contingencies, the Committee remark, may diminish the utility of the Establishment, or may increase
the expence.   " Bad seasons, and the destruction
" of the vegetable part of the stock of food : Mor-
" tality among the as yet scanty stock of cattle.*

* An account of the Live Stock in the possession of, and Land
in cultivation by Government, and the Officers civil and military,
1st September 1796, extracted from page 123, of the above
Report of the Select Committee on Finance.

	Government.	Civil and Military Officers.	Settlers.	Total.
Mares and Horses -	14	43	0	57
Cows and Cow Calves -	67	34	0	101
Bulls and Bull Calves -	37	37	0	74
Oxen - -	46	6	0	52
Sheep - -	191	1310	30	1531
Goats - -	111	1176	140	1427
Hogs - -	59	889	621	1869
	525	3495	1091	†5111

Land

" Mischief from the natives—from insurrection
" among the convicts, or from the enemy.

" Here, as at Sierra Leone, malice may produce an
" expedition of devastation. The illusions to which
" the spirit of rapine is so much exposed may give
" birth to an enterprize of depredation ; apprehen-
" sions of any such event entertained here would
" necessarily give birth to preparations of defence.
" The apprehensions may be well or ill grounded—
" The measures taken for defence successful or un-
" successful ; but the expence in the mean time
" is incurred. The distance is unexampled, and all
" danger, as well as all expence swells in proportion
" to the distance : these topics appear to merit con-
" sideration.

" Another circumstance is, that the labour of the
" whole number of persons sent to these colonies,

Land in cultivation, viz :—	Acres.
Government - - - - - - - - -	1700
Civil and Military Officers - - - - -	1172
Settlers - - - - - - - - - -	2547
	5419

The above 1700 acres were unemployed in 1796, on account of
the want of public labourers, and the many buildings required—
about 4-5th parts of 1172 acres were sown with wheat—much
timber cut, but not burnt off, on the 2547 acres belonging to the
settlers.

† In addition to the above Stock 61 head of Cattle were discovered in the year
1795, about 50 miles S.W. of the town of Sydney, which must have been produced from three Cows which strayed from the Settlement in 1788. This
proves that at least one of the Cows at the time must have been big with a
Bull Calf, and also gives the date for calculating the rate of the increase.

" whether

" whether as Convicts or Settlers, *is entirely lost to*
" *the Country*, nor can any return, to compensate
" such a loss, be expected till that very distant day,
" when the improved state of the Colony may, by
" possibility, begin to repay a part of the advance,
" by the benefits of its trade.

" Supposing abundance established, and remain-
" ing for ever without disturbance, it may be de-
" serving of consideration, in what shape and in
" what degree, and with what degree of assurance,
" Government, in point of Finance, is likely to
" profit by the abundance ; for the stock of the in-
" dividuals, which each individual will consume, lay
" up or sell, is on his own account ; is not the
" Stock of Government. The saving to Govern-
" ment depends upon the probity and zeal, and in-
" telligence of the Bailiffs in Husbandry, acting
" without personal interest in the concern at that
" immense instance."

After opinions so decided, the result of an inquiry, aided by extensive information, and conducted
by men of talents and judgment, it would ill become
the author of this Work to offer (if he could suggest,) additional arguments to prove the disadvantages which have attended, and which are likely to
attend the transportation of Convicts to New South
Wales. Although with regard to mere *subsistence*
there may be a prospect (and it is yet a distant
one), of the Colony becoming independent of supplies from this Country ; yet with respect to most
ether

other articles, its wants will experience no diminution, and having once engaged in the project, humanity requires that the Settlement should be supplied at the expence of the Nation.

When the measure of establishing this Colony was adopted, a hope was probably entertained that while the great difficulty and expence of the passage home, joined to the fertility of the soil and the salubrity of the climate, might induce convicts to remain after the expiration of the period specified in their sentence, so as not to become offensive again to their native Country; the removal to an unknown region, inhabited by Savages, and situated at such a remote distance from Great Britain, would exhibit this species of punishment in so terrific a light as to operate powerfully in preventing crimes.

Experience however, has shewn that this salutary effect has not been produced, and that crimes are not to be diminished by the dread of punishment in any shape. This great desideratum is only to be attained by a well-regulated Police, calculated to destroy the sources from whence evil propensities spring, and to remove the facilities by which criminality is nourished and assisted.

Under the present circumstances, where the mind continues depraved, and where the harvest is so prolific, it ceases to be a matter of wonder that a considerable proportion of the convicts transported to New South Wales, have found their way back to their native Country;—and that not a few of them have

have again afflicted Society by renewing their depredations on the Public.—It is, indeed, lamentable to
reflect, that after the extreme labour which has been
bestowed, and the unparalleled expence which has
been incurred, no effect whatsoever favourable to
the interest of the Community, or to the security of
innocence, has been produced.   Looking back to the
period when Government was relieved of the expence
of Convicts, almost of every description under sentence of Transportation, and reflecting on the enormous expence which has been incurred since the
channel of disposal, through the medium of the late
American Colonies, has been shut up ; considering
that within the short period of twenty-five years no
less a sum than 1,663,974l.* has been expended in
transporting and maintaining about 15,000 Convicts,
which would have cost nothing under the old System ;—it cannot be sufficiently lamented, that so
liberal a provision had not been employed in establishing systems of Prevention.   One fourth part of
this enormous sum expended in a proper establishment of preventive Police, would probably have
rendered transportation and punishment in a con-

* Expence of maintaining about 9000 Convicts in
   the Hulks from January 1, 1795, to January 1,
   1798 - - - - - - - - - - - - - £. 623,022
Expence of Transporting Convicts in 1785 and 1786   3,
Expence of Transporting and Maintaining Convicts
   from 1786 to 1797, New South Wales   -   1,037,230
                                    Total   £.1,663,974

siderable

siderable degree unnecessary, while the Country would have benefited by the industry of a large proportion of these outcasts, who would then have been compelled to earn an honest livelihood by their labour.

Deploring the mass of turpitude which has drawn from the resources of the Country so enormous a portion of wealth, it is no little consolation to be able to look forward to a measure recommended by the Select Committee, and in the train of being adopted by Government, which holds out so fair a prospect not only of gradually diminishing this expence in future, but also of rendering the labour of Convicts productive, and of securing the Public against the repetition of those depredations which have been rather increased than prevented, by the System of punishments which have been heretofore adopted.

The advantages in contemplation are to be attained by carrying into effect a *proposal for a new and less expensive mode of employing and reforming Convicts,* which has been offered to the consideration of Government by Jeremy Bentham, Esq. and which appears to have been fully investigated by the Finance Committee, who state it (p. 20, of Report 28) " to " be no small recommendation to the plan, that the " Contractor proposes to employ the prisoners on his " own account, receiving a proportionally smaller " sum from the Public for their maintenance. — " That the great and important advantages which " distinguish that plan from any other which has " been

" been hitherto suggested, consist in the certain
" employment and industrious livelihood which it
" insures to those whose terms of confinement are
" expired. In the responsibility which the Con-
" tractor proposes to take upon himself, for the fu-
" ture good behaviour of Criminals entrusted to his
" care, even when they shall be no longer under his
" control : in the publicity which is meant to be
" given to the whole conduct and effect of the Es-
" tablishment, *moral, medical,* and *œconomical,* as well
" by an annual report of the state and proceedings,
" as by the constant facility of inspection, which
" will in an unusual manner be afforded by the
" very form and construction of the building, upon
" which the prompt and easy exercise of the superin-
" tending power of the Governor himself principally
" depends."

These advantages appear to the Committee of more
importance, when the periods of the enlargement of
the several Convicts now on board the Hulks are
taken into consideration. The pernicious effects
produced upon the unfortunate persons confined in
these seminaries of vice; and the circumstance of
1411 destined to be enlarged in the course of 7 years,
to afflict the Society from which they have been
separated—the Committee consider as deserving of
very serious consideration : and they conclude their
view of the subject, by expressing an uncommon degree of solicitude, that no delay should take place in
the execution of the contract with Mr. Bentham,
" because

" because it would deprive the Public for a longer
" time of the benefits of a plan, which they cannot
" but look to as likely to be productive of the most
" essential advantage both in point of œconomy and
" Police."

The object in view is, by the aid of ingenious
machinery, to render the labour of every class of
Convicts so productive to the Contractor, as to admit of their being maintained at 25 per cent. less
than the expence incurred on board the Hulks;
while a rational prospect is held out of reforming
these Convicts and returning them upon Society,
not only with purer morals, but with the knowledge
of some trade or occupation by which they may afterwards earn their bread;—but this is not all.—The
proposer of this important design insures to the Convicts, after the expiration of their time, the means of
obtaining a *livelihood;* by setting up a *Subsidiary Establishment,* into which all who found themselves otherwise destitute of employment would be admitted,
and where they would be continued in the exercise of
the trades in which they were employed during their
confinement.

It is, however, impossible to do justice to the merit of this *Proposal,* without laying it wholly before
the Public. It seems to embrace every object, calculated to remove the errors and difficulties of the
present System, while it promises in a short time to
relieve the Finances of the Country from the enormous and unparalleled expence which is incurred by
the

the Establishment of the Hulks, and by Transportation to New South Wales.

PROPOSAL

FOR A NEW AND LESS EXPENSIVE MODE OF
EMPLOYING AND *REFORMING CONVICTS.*

THE AUTHOR, having turned his thoughts to the Penitentiary System from its first origin, and having lately contrived a Building in which any number of persons may be kept within the reach of being inspected during every moment of their lives, and having made out, as he flatters himself, to demonstration, that the only eligible mode of managing an Establishment of such a nature, in a Building of such a construction, would be by *Contract*, has been induced to make public the following Proposal for Maintaining and Employing Convicts in general, or such of them as would otherwise be confined on board the Hulks, for 25 per cent. less than it costs Government to maintain them there at present; deducting also the average value of the work at present performed by them for the Public : upon the terms of his receiving the produce of their labour, *taking on himself the whole expence of the* BUILDING, *fitting up and stocking,** without any advance to be made by Government for that purpose, requiring only that the abatement and deduction above-mentioned shall be suspended for the first year.

Upon the above mentioned Terms, he would engage as follows :

I. To furnish the Prisoners with a constant supply of wholesome *Food*, not limited in quantity, but adequate to each man's desires.

* All these articles taken into the account, the originally-intended Penitentiary Houses on the late Mr. Blackburne's plan, would not have cost so little as 200l. per man:—for 1000 Prisoners, 200,000l. exclusive of the whole annual expence of maintenance, &c. to an unliquidated amount.

II. To

II, To keep them *clad* in a state of tightness and neatness, superior to what is usual even in the Improved Prisons.

III. To keep them supplied with *separate Beds* and Bedding, competent to their situations, and in a state of cleanliness scarcely any where conjoined with liberty.

IV. To insure them a sufficient supply of artificial *warmth* and *light*, whenever the season renders it necessary : and thereby save the necessity of taking them prematurely from their work, at such seasons (as in other places,) as well as preserve them from suffering by the inclemency of the weather.

V. To keep constantly from them, in conformity to the practice so happily received, every kind of *strong* and spirituous liquor; unless where ordered in the way of medicine.

VI. To maintain them in a state of inviolable, though mitigated seclusion, in *assorted* companies, without any of those opportunities of promiscuous association, which in other places disturb, if not destroy, whatever good effect can have been expected from occasional solitude.

VII, To give them an interest in their work, by allowing them a share in the produce.

VIII. To convert the prison into a *school*, and, by an extended application of the principal of *the Sunday Schools*, to return its inhabitants into the world instructed, at least as well as in ordinary schools, in the most useful branches of vulgar learning, as well as in some trade or occupation, whereby they may afterwards earn their livelihood. Extraordinary culture of extraordinary talents is not, in this point of view, worth mentioning: it would be for his own advantage to give them every instruction by which the value of their labour may be increased.

IX. To pay a penal sum for every *escape*, with or without any default of his, irresistible violence from without excepted ; and this without employing *irons* on any occasion, or in any shape.

                                                    X. To

X. To provide them with *spiritual* and *medical* Assistants, constantly living in the midst of them, and incessantly keeping them in view.

XI. To pay a sum of money for every one who *dies* under his care, taking thereby upon him the insurance of their lives for an ordinary premium: and that at a rate grounded on an average of the number of deaths, not among imprisoned Felons, but among persons of the same ages in a state of liberty within the Bills of Mortality.

XII. To lay for them the foundation-stone of a *provision for old age*, upon the plan of the *Annuity Societies.*

XIII. To insure to them a *livelihood*, at the expiration of their terms, by setting up a *Subsidiary Establishment*, into which all such as thought proper, should be admitted, and in which they would be continued in the exercise of the trades in which they were employed during their confinement, without any further expence to Government.

XIV. To make himself personally responsible for the reformatory efficacy of his management, and even make amends, in most instances, for any accident of its failure, by paying a sum of money for every Prisoner convicted of a Felony after his discharge, at a rate, increasing according to the number of years he had been under the Proposer's care, viz. a sum not exceeding 10*l*. if the Prisoner had been in the Penitentiary Panopticon *one* year: not exceeding 15*l*. if *two* years; not exceeding 20*l*. if *three* years; not exceeding 25*l*. if *four* years; not exceeding 30*l*. if *five* years or upwards : such sum to be paid immediately on conviction, and to be applied to the indemnification of the persons injured by such subsequent offence, and to be equal in amount to the value of the injury, so long as it did not exceed the sums respectively above specified.

XV. To present to the Court of King's Bench, on a certain day of every Term, and afterwards print and publish, at his own expence, a Report, exhibiting, in detail, the state, not

only

only moral and medical, but economical, of the Establishment ; showing the whole profits, if any, and in what manner they arise ; and then and there, as well as on any other
day, upon summons from the Court, to make answer to all
such questions as shall be put to him in relation thereto,
not only on the part of the Court or Officer of the Crown,
but, by leave of the Court, on the part of any person whatsoever : questions, the answers to which might tend to subject him to conviction, though it were for a capital crime,
not excepted : treading under foot a maxim, invented by
the guilty for the benefit of the guilty, and from which
none but the guilty ever derived any advantage.

XVI. By neatness and cleanliness, by diversity of employment,
by variety of contrivance, and above all, by that peculiarity
of construction, which, without any unpleasant or hazardous
vicinity, enables the whole Establishment to be inspected at
a view from a commodious and insulated room in the centre,
the Prisoners remaining unconscious of their being thus
observed, it should be his study to render it a spectacle such
as persons of all classes would, in the way of amusement, be
curious to partake of ; and that not only on Sundays, at the
time of Divine Service, but on ordinary days, at meal-times,
or times of work ; providing thereby a *system of superintendance, universal, unchargeable and uninterrupted*, the most
effectual and *indestructible* of all securities against abuse.

Such are the methods that have occurred to him for accomplishing that identification of " *interest with duty*," the effectuating of which, in the person of the Governor, is declared
to be one of the leading objects of the Penitentiary Act.—
[19 GEO. III. ch. 74.]

The station of Gaoler is not in common account a very
elevated one : the addition of Contractor has not much tendency to raise it.   He little dreamt, when he first launched
into the subject, that he was to become a suitor, and perhaps

in

in vain, for such an office.   But inventions unpractised might
be in want of the inventor ; and a situation, thus clipped of
emoluments, while it was loaded with obligations, might be
in want of candidates.   Penetrated, therefore, with the importance of the end, he would not suffer himself to see any
thing unpleasant or discreditable in the means.

Outline of the Plan of Construction alluded to in the above Proposal.

The Building *circular*—about the size of *Ranelagh*—The
Prisoners in their Cells, occupying the Circumference—The
Officers, (Governor, Chaplain, Surgeon, &c.) the Centre.

By *Blinds*, and other contrivances, the Inspectors concealed
(except in as far as they think fit to show themselves) from
the observation of the Prisoners : hence the sentiment of a
sort of invisible omnipresence.—The whole circuit reviewable
with little, or, if necessary, without any change of place.

One Station in the Inspection-Part affording the most perfect view of every Cell, and every part of every Cell, unless
where a screen is thought fit occasionally and purposely to
be interposed.

Against *Fire* (if, under a system of constant and universal inspection any such
accident could be to be apprehended) a pipe, terminating in a flexible hose, for
bringing the water down into the central Inspection-Room, from a cistern, of a
height sufficient to force it up again by its own pressure, on the mere turning of
a cock, and spread it thus over any part within the Building.

For *Visitors*, at the time of Divine service, an *Annular Gal-
lery*, rising from a floor laid immediately on the ceiling of the
Central Inspection-Room, and disclosed to view, by the descent of a central *Dome*, the superior surface of which serves,
after descent, for the reception of Ministers, Clerk, and a
select part of the Auditory : the Prisoners all round, brought
forwards within perfect view and hearing of the Ministers,
to the front of their respective Cells.

Solitude,

Solitude, or *limited Seclusion*, *ad libitum.*—But unless for punishment, limited seclusion in assorted companies is pre- ferred : an arrangement, upon this plan alone, exempt from danger. The degree of *Seclusion* fixed upon may be pre- served, in all places, and at all times, *inviolate*. Hitherto, where solitude has been aimed at, some of its chief purposes have been frustrated by occasional associations.

The *Approach*, *one* only—*Gates* opening into a walled *avenue* cut through the area. Hence, no strangers near the building without *leave*, nor without being *surveyed* from it as they pass, nor without being known to come *on purpose*. The gates, or *open* work, to *expose hostile* mobs : On the other side of the road, a wall with a branch of the road behind, to *shelter peaceable* passengers from the fire of the building. A mode of fortification like this, if practicable in a city, would have saved the *London Prisons*, and prevented the unpopular accidents in *St. George's Fields*.

The *surrounding Wall*, itself surrounded by an open palisade, which serves as a fence to the grounds on the other side.—Except on the side of the Approach *no public path* by that fence.—A *Centinel's Walk* between ; on which no one else can set foot, without forcing the fence, and declaring himself a trespasser at least, if not an enemy. To the four walls, four such walks *flanking* and *crossing* each other at the ends.—Thus each Centinel has two to check him.

In contemplating the whole of this important de- sign, it is impossible to avoid congratulating the Public on the prospect which now opens by a recent vote of Parliament,* for the purpose of carrying it speedily into effect.

It comprizes in its structure every thing humanity can dictate, or which a mind full of resource, and a judgment matured by great depth of thought could

---

* At the close of the Session in June 1798, the House of Com- mons voted 36000*l.* to Mr. Bentham, towards the expence of carrying his plan into execution. See the Appropriation Act, 39 Geo. III. c. 114.

suggest,

suggest, for the purpose of relieving Society from a dreadful and oppressive evil.

It is even to extend comforts to offenders in the course of punishment; and they are to be returned to Society after the period expires, not as at present, polluted and depraved beyond what the human mind can conceive; but impressed with the force of religious and moral instructions, with an abhorrence of their former course of life, and with a resource for obtaining an honest livelihood by the trade or occupation which they were taught during their confinement.—And if employment should fail, when at liberty to make their own election, an asylum is provided, into which they will be admitted, and where they may continue to exercise the trades in which they were employed during their confinement, with certain advantages to themselves.

These Convicts are, moreover, while in confinement, to have an interest in the work they perform, by being allowed a share of the produce, which may be either partly or wholly applied in laying the foundation-stone of a provision for old age, upon the plan of the Annuity Societies, which is to form one of the œconomical arrangements of this excellent Establishment.

Among many other advantages calculated to improve the morals of delinquents, and to render them useful to Society, it will possess, after a certain period, the singular faculty of extending to the Public these

these incalculable benefits, *perhaps without any ex-pence whatsoever;* since it may be reasonably expect-ed, that by training both Sexes to productive labour, extended and rendered valuable by the proposed in-troduction of ingenious machinery, it will hereafter become an object of advantage to new Contractors, (after the System is fully matured, and the profits arising from it clearly ascertained), to take upon them the conduct of the design, without stipulating for any annuity or assistance whatsoever from Govern-ment. Nay, the certainty of this profit, and its magnitude arising from labour alone, may, perhaps, ultimately even create a competition of Contractors, who, instead of *receiving,* will be induced to *offer* a premium to Government for the appointment to the situation; the value of which will be evidenced by the increasing annual profits.

It is, indeed, highly probable, that as the Insti-tution advances to maturity, under a plan so admi-rably adapted to render labour productive in the greatest possible degree; in the same manner will the profits gradually increase year after year until they shall be rendered obvious and certain, and not as at present depending on speculative opinions.

The proposed annual report to the Court of King's Bench, through which medium the progressive pro-fits will be generally promulgated, will create noto-riety, and excite attention; and it is by no means improbable, that when the contract becomes open,

by

by the decease of the two Gentlemen to whom the Public are to be indebted for this invention, that it will acquire *a precise value*, like any other saleable commodity.

This was exemplified in the instance of Convicts sent to America, which for a great length of time cost Government a large sum annually, until a discovery of the profits, arising from the disposal of the services of Felons, created a competition, which eased the Public of every expence whatsoever on account of their Transportation.

But these are not the only advantages which the Country will derive from this New Penitentiary System. Its success will rapidly change the œconomy of the many unproductive Houses of Correction, which have been erected at an enormous expence to the different Counties, under the Act of the 16th of Geo. III. cap. 43. Those in the management of these respective Establishments will gladly follow an example which mingles in so great a degree—*humanity with reform and profit*, thereby holding out a prospect both of diminishing crimes, and reducing the County Rates, now estimated by the Finance Committee at *fifty thousand pounds a year* for prisons, and criminal Police alone.

Such are some of the benefits which may be reasonably expected to arise from the proposed Penitentiary System. If they shall be realized to the extent which is contemplated, so as to render transportation,

as

as well as the Hulks, unnecessary, the pecuniary saving to Government in twenty years will be immense. This may be ascertained by referring to a preceding page, where the disbursements in the criminal department are inserted, which have taken place since the commencement of the American war, which rendered a new System necessary. If to this sum is added the expences incurred by the Counties, it will probably be found to have exceeded *Two millions sterling in all.*

But still further advantages may be contemplated in addition to those of a pecuniary nature.—By retaining delinquents in the Country, and rendering their labour profitable to the State, a new source of wealth is opened which never existed at any former period, since the labour of Convicts transported, whether to America or New South Wales, has been totally unproductive to the Country.

The success of such a design, once clearly manifested, would give a new and favourable turn to the System of Punishments. Labour would be exacted in almost every case, not more for the benefit of the State than the advantage of the Prisoner, since labour and reform generally go hand in hand.—Without the aid of labour, it is in vain to expect an improvement in the morals or habits of delinquents— without an asylum to which discharged prisoners can resort for employment, their punishment produces no advantage. On the contrary, the vices of a Gaol

send

send them forth more hardened in iniquity, and greater adepts in the trade of thieving than before.

Nothing, therefore, can be more hostile to the diminution of crimes than the present mode of punishment for small offences, by a short imprisonment, without being employed in useful and productive labour.

Under this defective System the different Gaóls in the Metropolis and the Kingdom, are periodically vomiting forth hordes of Minor Delinquents, who serve as recruits to the more desperate gangs, and remain in a course of turpitude until cut off by the commission of higher offences. Some exceptions, doubtless, there are; but while the resource for honest labour is so effectually shut out, many who have totally lost character, and are without friends, seem to have no other resource.

To all who may be confined in the proposed Penitentiary Establishment, this difficulty will be removed. —A difficulty in the present state of things, the magnitude of which cannot be estimated, since it generates most of those evils to which are to be attributed the extensive corruption of morals, and the increase and multiplication of crimes.

Upon the whole, it would be expedient to give full effect to the new Penitentiary System as soon as possible; which, to use the language of the Select Committee, (p. 30) " seems to bid fairer than any
" other

" other that was ever yet offered to the Public, to
" diminish the Public expenditure in this branch,
" and to produce a salutary reform in the objects
" of the proposed institution."

At the same time for the purpose of rendering
the System of Punishments useful in the greatest
possible degree to the Community, and that they
may operate, in the fullest extent, as an example,
tending to the prevention of crimes, it would seem
that the following general principles should be
adopted.

1st. That examples of punishment by death (except, perhaps, in cases of Murder), should only
take place twice a year: and that the impression
upon the Public mind may be stronger from the
less frequency of such painful exhibitions, they
ought on all occasions to be conducted with a
degree of solemnity suited to the object in the
view of the Legislature, when the life of a fellow-
creature is sacrificed, that it may really prove
useful in deterring others; and not be contemplated with indifference, as is too often the case
at present, without making the least impression,
or being in any degree beneficial to the great ends
of Public justice.

2d. That the System of the Hulks should be at once
wholly abandoned, as a source of great expence,
producing in the result infinitely more evil than
good,

good, and thereby exhausting the Finances of the Country without any one beneficial consequence.

3d. That Transportation to New South Wales and Norfolk Island, should be limited to a few of the most depraved, incorrigible, and irreclaimable Convicts, whose vicious and ungovernable conduct, while under the discipline of a Penitentiary House, rendered their reform hopeless.—That shipments should only take place once in three years, and that the Civil and Military Establishment of the Colony should be gradually reduced, so as to bring the National Expenditure on this branch of Police within moderate bounds.

4th. That every thing should be done to accelerate the erection of National Penitentiary Houses. —That their capacity, including appendages, should be equal to the accommodation of 3,500 Convicts of all descriptions, so as to admit of different degrees of treatment and labour, according to the *age, sex, and state of health of the Convicts.*

5th. That the local Penitentiary Houses in the different Counties, destined for the Punishment of persons convicted of Larcenies, and other minor offences, should be conducted, as nearly as possible, upon the plan of the National Establishments; and also by contract, under circumstances where the labour of the Convicts may, by the resources

of

of the Contractor, be rendered (without hardship) equal, or nearly equal, to the expence; a measure conceived to be almost, in every instance, practicable, where knowledge of business, stimulated by interest, shall form an ingredient in the executive management.

6th. That there should be attached to each County Penitentiary House, a Subsidiary Establishment, into which all discharged prisoners should be admitted who choose it, and where they might be continued in the exercise of the trades in which they were employed during their confinement, and for which they should receive wages in proportion to their earnings, until they could otherwise find a settled employment through an honest medium : thus giving those who are desirous of reforming an opportunity of sheltering themselves from the dangers of relapse, which arise from being afloat upon the Public—idle, and without the means of subsistence.

In carrying the Penitentiary System into effect, it ought not to escape notice, that the hardship imposed on Convicts, with respect to manual labour, would be no more than every honest artisan who works industriously for his family, must, during the whole course of his life, impose upon himself. The condition of a Convict would, even in some respects, be superior, inasmuch as he would enjoy medical assistance, and other advantages tending to the preservation

servation of health, which do not attach to the lower classes of the people, whose irregularities not being restrained, while their pursuits and labours are seldom directed by good judgment and intelligence, often produce bad health, and extreme indigence and distress.

The difficulty which has heretofore been experienced with respect to productive labour in the Provincial Houses of Correction will vanish, when the System shall be exemplified in the National Penitentiary Establishment. To conduct a Plan of this nature with advantage to the Public and to the individual, an assemblage of *qualities, dispositions,* and *endowments,* which rarely meet in one man, will be necessary—namely, *education, habits of business, a knowledge of the common affairs of life—an active and discriminating mind—indefatigable industry—the purest morals, and a philanthropic disposition, totally divested of those hurtful propensities which lead to idle amusements.*

Such men are to be found, and would come forward, as Contractors, with ample security as often as opportunities offered, after the System became matured. It is only by the uncontrolled energy of talents, where duty and interest go hand in hand, that labour is to be obtained from Convicts.—No fluctuating management, nor any superihtendance whatsoever, where a spring is not given to exertion by motives of interest, can perfect any Penitentiary design; or, indeed, any design where profit is to be derived from labour. Hence the ill success of almost
all

all the well meant establishments with respect to the Poor, and to most of the local Penitentiary Houses. In some instances a few establishments at first hold out prospects of success; but at length they dwindle and decay, and in the result they have mostly all been unprofitable. The death or removal of an active or philanthropic Magistrate produces a languor, which terminates often in the ruin or the abandonment of the design.

The National Penitentiary System is guarded against this contingency; and until the local Establishments can enjoy equal advantages, success in any degree is scarcely to be expected, and *permanent success* is altogether hopeless.

The object to be attained is of great magnitude.— Let an appeal be, therefore, made to the good sense of the country, and to the feelings of humanity in behalf of an unfortunate and noxious class of individuals. Let the effects of the present System be candidly examined, in opposition to the benefits which may result from that which is proposed, and let the decision be speedy, that Society may no longer be tormented by the evils which arise from this branch of the Police of the country.

The suggestions which are thus hazarded on the subject of punishments, are by no means the refinements of speculation doubtful and uncertain in their issue.

The System accords either with what has been already enacted by the Legislature or recommended by

the

the Finance Committee. And the whole has been admitted to be practicable under an able and permanent superintendance. A hope may, therefore, be indulged, that where the interest of Society and the cause of Humanity is so deeply concerned, a design which holds out so many advantages, will experience that general support which it unquestionably merits; since its object is not only to reclaim the Out-casts of the present generation, but also to rescue thousands yet unborn from misery and destruction.

CHAP.

C H A P. XVII.

*The Police of the Metropolis examined—Its organiza-
tion explained, with regard to that branch which relates to the prevention and suppression of Crimes.—
The utility of the new System, established in 1792,
examined and explained.—Reasons assigned why this
System has not tended, in a greater degree, to the
suppression and prevention of atrocious Crimes—
Its great deficiency from the want of funds, by
which Magistrates are crippled in their exertions,
with regard to the detection and punishment of
Offenders.—Reasons in favour of a New System.—
The Police of the City of London (as now constituted) explained and examined.—Suggestions relative to established Justices, and the benefits likely
to result from their exertions in assisting the City
Magistrates: from whose other engagements and
pursuits, that close and laborious attention cannot
be expected which the Public interest requires.—
The Magistrates of London the most respectable,
perhaps, in the world.—The vast labour and weight
of duty attached to the chief Magistrate.—The
Aldermen have certain duties assigned them, which
ought not, in justice, to be augmented, as they act
gratuitously.—The benefits which result to the
Community from established Police Magistrates,
considered in different points of view; and exemplified*

plified in the advantages which have arisen from the System under the Act of 1792.—General Reflections on the advantages which would arise from the various remedies which have been proposed in the course of this Work.—These benefits, however, only of a partial nature, inadequate to the object of complete protection, for want of a centre-point and superintending Establishment, under the controul of the first Minister of Police.—Reasons assigned in favour of such a System.—The advantages that would result from its adoption.—The ideas of enlightened Foreigners on the Police of the Metropolis explained.—Reflections suggested by those ideas.—Observations on the Police of Paris previous to the Revolution in France: elucidated by Anecdotes of the Emperor Joseph the Second and Mons. de Sartine.—The danger of an inundation of Foreign Sharpers and Villains on the return of Peace.—The situation of Europe requires, and the necessity of a well-regulated Police points out the utility of, a Central Board of Commissioners for Managing the Police.—This measure recommended by the Select Committee of Finance, since the publication of the last Edition of this Work.

HAVING in the preceding Chapters endeavoured to bring under the review of the Reader, not only those prominent causes which have occasioned that great increase of Public Wrongs, which every good man

man must deplore, but also the *various classes of delinquents* which compose the melancholy catalogue of human depravity; having also stated such observations and facts, relative to *detection, trials, and punishments*, as seemed to be necessary for the purpose of elucidating a subject of great importance to be understood; it remains now to explain and develope the *System* hitherto established for the purpose of protecting the Public against those enormities; and from which is to be expected that energy, and those exertions which have been shewn to be so indispensably necessary, for the suppression and prevention of crimes.

The POLICE *of this great Metropolis* is undoubtedly a System highly interesting to be understood, although heretofore (as far as the author has had access to know) it has never been, at any period, fully explained through the medium of the press ;—and hence it is, that a vast proportion of those who reside in the Capital, as well as the multitude of strangers who resort to it, have no accurate idea of the principles of organization, which move so complicated a machine.

It has been already stated in a preceding Chapter, that twenty-six Magistrates, forming that respectable body, comprehending the Lord-Mayor and Aldermen,* sit in rotation every forenoon, at the Mansion-house,

* The following are the names of the Aldermen at present in the Magistracy of the City, arranged according to their Seniority.
1772 Sir

house, and at Guildhall, and take cognizance of all matters of Police within the ancient jurisdiction of the City of London; while twenty-six established Magistrates appointed for every other part of the Metropolis,* including the River Police, having particular offices

1772	Sir Watkin Lewes, Knt.	Bridge Ward Without
74	Nathaniel Newman, Esq.	Vintry
84	Sir Brook Watson, Bart.	Cordwainers
85	Sir William Curtis, Bart.	Tower
89	Sir J. W. Anderson, Bart.	Aldersgate
90	Sir Richard Carr Glynn, Bart.	Bishopsgate
90	Harvey C. Combe, Esq.	Aldgate
93	Sir William Staines, Knt.	Cripplegate
95	Sir John Eamer, Knt.	Langborne
98	Sir Charles Price, Bart.	Farringdon Without
98	John Perring, Esq.	Broad-street
98	James Shaw, Esq.	Portsoken
99	Sir William Leighton, Knt.	Billingsgate
1800	John Ansley, Esq.	Bread-street
01	Charles Flower, Esq.	Cornhill
02	Thomas Smith, Esq.	Farringdon Within
03	Thomas Rowcroft, Esq.	Walbrook
03	Joshua Jonathan Smith, Esq.	Castle-Baynard
03	Richard Lea, Esq.	Coleman-street
03	Sir Matthew Bloxam, Knt.	Bridge Within
04	Claudius Stephen Hunter, Esq.	Bassishaw
04	John Prinsep, Esq.	Lime-street
04	Josiah Boydell, Esq.	Cheap
05	George Scholey, Esq.	Dowgate
06	John Peter Hankey, Esq.	Candlewick
06	William Domville, Esq.	Queenhithe

John Sivester, Esq. Recorder of London, a Magistrate holding rank above the Aldermen who have not served the office of Lord Mayor.—He assists at the General and Quarter Sessions of the Peace, and in the principal affairs of the City; but does not sit in rotation.

Richard Clark, Esq. Chamberlain, acting judicially with respect to Apprentices.

Mr. Hobler, Clerk to the Lord Mayor, or sitting Alderman at the Mansion-house.

Mr. Fitzpatrick, Clerk to the sitting Alderman at Guildhall.

* The following are the Public Offices in the Metropolis; (exclusive of the City of London;) and the respective Magistrates who *preside*, and the Clerks who *officiate* at each.

Westminster

offices or courts of justice assigned them at convenient distances in Westminster, Middlesex, and Surry, sit

Westminster.

Bow-street, CoventGarden
- Sir Richard Ford, Knt.
- Nicholas Bond, Esq.
- Aaron Graham, Esq. } *Magistrates.*
- Mess. Stafford, Thomas & Keen *Clerks.*

The following seven Public Offices were established by the Act 32 Geo. III. cap. 53. and continued for 5 years by 36 Geo. III. cap. 75.

Queen'sSquare St. Margaret's Westminster.
- Henry James Pye, Esq.
- Patrick Colquhoun, Esq.
- William Phillips, Esq. } *Magistrates.*
- Mess. G. Skeen, & W. Jones. *Clerks.*

Great Marlbo-rough-street, Oxford-Road.
- Nathaniel Conant, Esq.
- Philip Neave, Esq.
- William Brodie, Esq. } *Magistrates.*
- Mess. H. P. Butler & J. Thornton, *Clerks.*

Middlesex.

HattonGarden Holborn.
- Robert Baker, Esq.
- John Turton, Esq.
- Thomas Leach, Esq. } *Magistrates.*
- Mess. A. Todd and W. Upton, *Clerks.*

Worship street Finsbury Squ.
- John Nares, Esq.
- John Gifford, Esq.
- Joseph Moser, Esq. } *Magistrates.*
- Mess. Chas. Lush & J. Chalmers, *Clerks.*

Lambeth str. Whitechapel
- Rice Davies, Esq.
- Henry Reynott, D. D.
- Sir Daniel Williams, Knt. } *Magistrates.*
- Mess. John Smith and J. Thompson, *Clerks.*

High Street, Shadwell
- George Storie, Esq.
- Rupert Clarke, Esq.
- ——— Reed, Esq. } *Magistrates.*
- Mess. W. Telcampff & *Clerks.*

Surrey.

Union-street, Southwark
- Gideon Fournier, Esq.
- Rich. Carpenter Smith, Esq.
- Thomas Evance, Esq. } *Magistrates.*
- Mess. E. Lavender & G. Graves *Clerks.*

Marine Police, Wappping New Stairs
- P. Colquhoun, Esq. superintending Magistrate, gratis
- John Harriot, Esq. Resident Magistrate
- Henry Lang, Esq. Chief Clerk
- William Brook, Cashier
- Three Junior Clerks, & Ten Surveyors, &c.

N. B. The whole Fees and Penalties taken and received at the seven Offices, established by 32 Geo. III. cap. 53. are paid in to the

sit every day (Sunday excepted) both in the morning
and evening, for the purpose of executing all the
multifarious duties, connected with the office of a
Justice of the Peace, which unavoidably occur in
large societies*.

This Institution of established Justices (except
with regard to the three Magistrates at Bow-street,
and the Justices at the Marine Police Office,) was
suggested to the Legislature, in consequence of the
pressure felt by the Public, from the want of some
regular and properly-constituted Tribunals for the
distribution of Justice; where the System should be
uniform; and where the purity of the Magistrates,
and their regular attendance, might insure to the
People, the adjustment of their differences, at the least
possible expence; and the assistance of gratuitous
advice in every difficulty; as well as official aid, in
all cases within the sphere of the Magistrates in their
respective districts.

The duty of these established Magistrates, (in conjunction with other Justices of the Peace, who find
it convenient to give their assistance,) extends also to
several important judicial proceedings; where, in a
great variety of instances, they are empowered and

the *Receiver* on account of the Public, and the whole expences
of the Establishments are defrayed from the funds placed in his
hands for that purpose.

* The Marine Police Magistrates, on account of the extent of
the Establishment, and the number of River Officers under their
Control, never leave the Office from the time that business commences in the morning, until a late hour in the evening.

required

required to *hear* and *determine*, in a summary way ; particularly in cases relative to the *customs, excise, and stamps—the game laws—hawkers and pedlars— pawn-brokers—friendly societies—highways—hackney coaches, carts and other carriages—Quakers and others refusing to pay tythes—appeals of defaulters in parochial rates—misdemeanors committed by persons unlawfully pawning property not their own—bakers for short weight, &c.—journeymen leaving their services in different trades—labourers not complying with their agreements—disorderly apprentices—alehouse keepers keeping disorderly houses—nuisances by different Acts of Parliament—acts of vagrancy by fraudulent lottery insurers—fortune tellers; or persons of evil fame found in avenues to public places, with an intent to rob—As well as a multitude of other offences, in which Justices have power to proceed to conviction and punishment, either by fine or imprisonment.*

The duty of the Magistrates also extends to a vast number of other objects, such as *licensing Public Houses*, and establishing Rules and Orders for Publicans,* *watching over the conduct of Publicans—swearing in, charging and instructing parochial constables and headboroughs from year to year, with regard to their duty—issuing warrants for privy searches ; and in considering the cases of persons charged with being disorderly persons, or rogues and vagabonds, liable to be*

* See Tract on Public Houses, by the Author of this Treatise.

punished

*punished under the Act of the 17th George II. cap. 5,
and subsequent acts of Parliament—in making orders
to Parish Officers, Beadles, and Constables, in a variety of cases—in Parish Removals— in billetting soldiers—in considering the cases of poor persons applying
for assistance, or admission to workhouses—in granting
certificates and orders to the wives of persons serving
in the Militia,* and also *in attesting recruits, for the
Army—in attending the General and Quarter Sessions
of the Peace, and in visiting the Workhouses, Bride-
wells, and Prisons*.*

In addition to these various duties, many criminal
cases occur in the course of a year, which are examined for the purpose, if necessary, of being sent
to superior tribunals for trials :—such as charges of
*Treason, Murder, Coining, and uttering Base Money,
Arson, Manslaughter, Forgery, Burglary, Larceny,
Sedition, Felonies of various descriptions, Conspiracies,
Frauds, Riots, Assaults, and Misdemeanors of different
kinds :*—all which unavoidably impose upon every
official Magistrate, a weight of business requiring
great exertion, and an unremitting attention to the
Public Interest in the due execution of this very important Trust.

When the Police System was first established in

* The Magistrates at the Marine Police confine their attention
almost wholly to the cognizance of offences, either committed on
the River, or connected with Maritime Affairs, and his Majesty's
Stores in the Public Arsenals.

                                                    the

the year 1792, the public mind became impressed with an idea that the chief, if not the only object of the institution was to prevent *Robberies, Burglaries,* and other *atrocious Offences;* and that the suppression of those crimes, which bore hardest upon Society, and were most dreaded by the Public at large, was to be the result. These expectations shewed, that neither the powers nor authorities granted by the Act of Parliament, nor the other duties imposed upon the Magistracy of the Police, were understood. For this Statute, useful as it certainly is in a very high degree in many other respects, does not contain even a single regulation applicable to the prevention of crimes; except that which relates to the apprehension of suspected characters, found in the avenues to public places, with intent to commit felony, who are liable to be punished as rogues and vagabonds,—and even this provision does not extend to the city of London.

But this is not all—an establishment has been created, without the most necessary of all engines to give vigour and effect to the exertions of the Magistrates; namely, a pecuniary Fund to defray the expences of detecting criminals, and of rewarding those who bring informations useful to Public Justice. The expence of each Public Office being restricted to *two thousand pounds* a year, and the establishment in *salaries, rents, taxes,* and other *contingencies* exhausting that sum, nothing remains for one

of

of the most necessary purposes of the Institution—the *Prevention* and the *Suppression of Crimes.**

It is in vain to expect that either vigour or energy can enter into that part of the System, where a great deal of *both* is necessary, *without Funds*.

If criminals, at war with the Community, are to be detected—if risks are to be run to effect this purpose—if it is to be done, (as it must frequently be) at the hazard of the loss of health, and *even of life*, by watching desperadoes in the night time—if accurate informations are necessary, either to discover where stolen property is deposited, or where the delinquents are to be found; a Fund must be provided, or the Public cannot be protected. Those, whose province it is to watch over the Police must not expect that men, capable of giving them useful information, will return a second time, if they have not some adequate reward bestowed upon them for their labour, risk, and trouble. Without such power of granting small rewards, (so far as that part of his duty which relates to the discovery of property plundered, and the de-

---

* It is by no means to be understood, that this deficiency arose from any want of real attention or public spirit on the part of the respectable individuals who framed and promoted this act. It was perhaps as much as could reasonably be expected at the time, until the Public mind could be more fully informed. It was by the operation of this act that a correct view of the improvements necessary to complete the System, were to be obtained. This first step was, therefore, of great importance; and it is but justice to state, that to the Authors of this Act the Public will be indebted for every subsequent arrangement, which may be adopted for perfecting the Police of the Metropolis.

tection

tection of the offenders is of importance to the Public,) a Magistrate is placed in the situation of a person pledged to work, *without tools or implements of labour*, by which he can in any respect accomplish his purpose. And hence it is, that among the numerous causes assigned in the course of this Work, for the increase of Crimes,—this is none of the least.

Not that it is meant that any additional burthen on the Public, by an extensive expenditure of money, would be necessary—A very moderate sum judiciously and œconomically laid out, would bring to Commissioners of the Police, or to the *disbursing Magistrates*, through some medium or other, an early account of most of the depredations committed upon the Public, as well as every circumstance relative to coiners and sellers of base money.—This would lead to the detection and apprehension of most of the offenders : and thereby strike such an universal terror, as (assisted by the other salutary regulations proposed in this Work) would soon reduce the number of Thieves, Coiners, and other delinquents; and thus, of course, diminish the ultimate and great additional expence which follows conviction, in all cases where felons are in the course of punishment.

In this view of the subject, it would prove a Regulation calculated greatly to reduce the aggregate expence; for surely, if *a few guineas* judiciously laid

out,

out, in the first instance, would save *fifty* afterwards to the State, it must be a wise and a good arrangement: and in this way it would probably operate. But this would not be the only saving to the Nation: by preventing crimes, all those concerned in projects of mischief must, instead of preying upon the industry of others, assist the State by contributing their share to the national stock of labour.

Next to the want of a sufficient pecuniary Fund, the most obvious deficiency in the present System of executive Police in the Metropolis, is that which regards the Magistracy of the City of London; *where the case is precisely reversed;* for *there* the funds for the detection and discovery of offenders, may be made as ample as the Corporation shall think fit; but the want of a *Stipendiary Establishment* must prevent the operation of that System of vigour and energy, which the increase of criminals and the present state of Society demand.

The Magistrates of the City of London form a body, perhaps the most *respectable,* and *independent* of any in the world; but besides the unavoidable, important, and multiplied affairs of the Corporation, in attending the various Courts of the Lord-Mayor—Aldermen—Common Council—Common Hall—Wardmotes—Conservancy—Courts of Requests—Court of Orphans—and General and Quarter Sessions of the Peace, and Justice Hall at the Old Bailey, they have avocations and engagements in business,

business, which must necessarily occupy their minds. It cannot, therefore, reasonably be expected, that they should forego their own important private interests, and bestow upon the business of the Public that attention which their situation as Magistrates seems to require.*

The Chief Magistrate cannot, in the nature of things, while the immense load of municipal affairs, joined to his own private concerns, presses constantly upon his mind, bestow either time or attention in considering the cases of delinquents brought before him; or in following up informations, and devising plans necessary to detect offenders; and yet this detail of duty, even from the pass-vagrant to the most atrocious villain, is imposed on him, by ancient immemorial custom and usage; at the very moment when he is overpowered with other official business, of great magnitude and importance, which can be transacted by no other person. Hurried with constant engagements, inseparable from the functions and dignity attached to his high office, and the general government of the City, a Lord-Mayor is just beginning to understand the duties attached to the

* The Author having had occasion to represent to a late Chief Magistrate, of great talents and respectability, the enormous evil arising from *base coin* :—He very judiciously observed, that to do any good in protecting the Public against this species of offence, *it would require the mind of a Magistrate to be given up to that object alone.* This pointed and accurate remark is sufficient to elucidate, in an eminent degree, the necessity of Magistrates with salaries, in all large Communities.

Chief

Chief Magistracy, at the period when he must lay it down.

The other Magistrates of the City, having had a precise line of duty anciently chalked out, when Commerce and Society had made less progress, the same System continues ; nor would it be proper to expect an augmentation of labour, or a greater proportion of time, from Magistrates who serve the Public gratuitously.—The unremitting attendance and indefatigable industry, which the Public interest requires, it would be vain and unjust to expect, from any but Magistrates selected for that purpose, and that only*.

With

* The select Committee of the House of Commons on Finance, in their 28th Report (already repeatedly quoted), appear to be very strongly impressed with the necessity of Police Magistrates, and a Concurrent Jurisdiction for the City of London.—They express themselves in the following words : " It is further to be " stated, that a considerable defect is felt in the Police of the Me- " tropolis, from the limited jurisdiction of the present Magistrates " in every part of it, and from the want of an Institution similar " to that of the Police Offices to be established in the City of " London, as was originally intended and proposed : that the " delay which necessarily takes place in obtaining the sanction of " the local Magistracy in either case, to the warrants of those " presiding in other districts, operates in all cases to the advan- " tage of offenders against the Laws, and to the obstruction of " Public Justice : add to which, that the numerous and import- " ant avocations, both public and private, of the truly respec- " table Magistracy of the City, is too often inconsistent with " that constant and unremitting attention which the due preser- " vation of the Police of the Metropolis requires. That it would " be unfortunate indeed if any local jealousy founded upon no " just grounds, though entertained by honourable minds, should

" continue

With the increase of those blessings which are supposed to arise from a course of prosperity and wealth, there is generally an increase also of *evils* and *inconveniences;* and hence it is that while an influx of riches preponderates in *one scale,* an augmentation of crimes acts as a counterbalance in the *other :*—thus requiring the constant and progressive application of such antidotes and remedies as will preserve the *good,* while the *evil* is diminished or kept within bounds.

It seems that the Metropolis is now in that situation where the active and unceasing attention of Magistrates with salaries, has become necessary to promote a vigorous and energetic execution of the Law, for the general protection of property, and the safety of individuals*.

" continue to deprive even the inhabitants of the City itself, as
" well as those of the rest of the Metropolis, of that security
" which a more permanent attendance, and a perfect intercom-
" munity of Jurisdiction in Criminal matters between the Magis-
" trates of every part of the Metropolis, and of the five adjoin
" ing Counties, could not fail to produce."—See p. 13, 28th Report, 26th of June 1798.

* If this were the case, neither the Bank, nor the avenues to every part of Cheapside, &c.† would be beset with gangs of rogues and sharpers, both men and women, who support themselves principally by the resource which the vast amount of moving property, in money and portable goods, affords them, in this part of the Metropolis; where it appears, capital offenders are rarely detected ; since, at the Old Bailey, those convicted in the course of a year, from the City and County, run in the proportion of about 1-7th part for London, and 6-7th parts for Middlesex‡.

† See p. 106.   ‡ Vide Table, p. 429.

Contem-

Contemplating the various existing evils detailed in this Work, and which form so many prominent features of Police, requiring the constant and watchful eye of the Magistrate, it seems clear to demonstration, that unless official duties become the sole business and pursuit of the parties engaged in them, the Public interest must suffer; and (although imperceptible in their progress), Crimes will increase and multiply: at a time when the comfort, happiness, and security of Society, require that they should be diminished.

In consequence also of the great accumulation of the Statute Laws, requiring the attention of Justices in a vast number of instances, which did not occur a century ago, their duty has so multiplied as to require the *whole time* of Magistrates acting in all great Societies; an observation which applies not merely to the Metropolis, but to many large Provincial Towns. It follows, therefore, almost as a matter of course, that Stipendiary Justices have become indispensably necessary*.

---

* In the measures finally proposed by the Finance Committee, in the 9th Article (page 30), they recommend it to Parliament, "That
" two additional Offices of Police should be established in the
" City, consisting each of three Magistrates, to sit at the Mansion-
" house, and at Guildhall, for the purpose of assisting the Lord-
" Mayor and the Court of Aldermen: such Magistrates to be
" named by the Lord-Mayor and Court of Aldermen; and paid
" out of the General Funds arising from the proposed regulations,
" to sit permanently, as at the other Offices, with Commissions
" from the Crown, extending over the whole Metropolis, and the
" counties of Middlesex, Kent, Essex, and Surry.

If

If men of business, integrity, and talents, could once be prevailed on to accept of such employments, and execute the trust reposed in them with zeal and attention to the public interest, and with firm and independent minds, attached to no Party, infinite advantages must result to the Community from their services*.

Where men of this description pledge themselves, as they must necessarily do, to give up every other pursuit, assiduously and constantly to execute the laborious duties of a Police Magistrate; Justice also requires that the reward should be commensurate to the sacrifices which are made. It is the interest of the Community that it should be so; for in the present extended state of Commerce and Society, no gratuitous System can ever be expected to answer any purpose of real utility.

While the higher order of Magistrates receive the just reward of their useful labour, bestowed in the exercise of their functions in promoting the Public good—where can be the impropriety of extending the same species of remuneration to inferior Magistrates; who must devote even a greater portion of time and attention to the multifarious duties assigned them?

* A Police Magistrate has nothing to do with the politics of the Country; and he is incapable, and unworthy of the trust reposed in him, if he permits any bias, or influence, but that which is immediately connected with a correct and chaste execution of the Laws, to take hold of his mind.—It is only by this line of conduct, that he can either render himself useful or respectable.

The

The office of *Assistant Magistrates* in the City might be assigned to six active and honourable men, who would give *their whole attention* to the criminal department of the Police. The proceedings of these Magistrates should be sanctioned by the presence of the Aldermen, as often as one or more could conveniently attend; on which occasions they could necessarily preside, as holding within their own district the highest rank in the Magistracy.

The difference in point of benefit to the Community between a *Mind* constantly occupied in objects of public utility, and that which is only occasionally employed, is great beyond all possible calculation.—Nor is the measure without precedent, even in the City of London, since the Recorder may, in his high office, be fairly considered in the light of a Magistrate with a salary.

Ready on every occasion at their Sittings in the morning and evening, to offer their advice or assistance to the labouring people, as well as all ranks of the Community, who apply for it—to adjust their differences, and to protect them against wrongs and oppressions: prepared also, as a matter of business, to receive and follow up informations where crimes have been committed, and never to lose sight of the object while it is practicable to attain it; these Assistant Magistrates would afford incalculable advantages to the City: which would be still farther increased, if a System of co-operation of the other Police Magistrates were established, upon a plan

which

which would unite their energy, and render their jurisdiction co-extensive. (See *ante*, pages 419 420.)

It is a well-known fact, that since the establishment of Police Magistrates for Westminster, and the parts of Middlesex and Surry, contiguous to the City of London, great benefits have been experienced from the assistance and advice which have been afforded to the indigent, and the ignorant.

Many quarrels and little law-suits have been prevented, and innumerable differences immediately reconciled without any expence.

It is in this manner that Magistrates, acting up to the spirit of their Public Duty, and bestowing their *whole* attention upon whatever relates to that duty, confer those obligations upon the Community which no moderate remuneration can pay.

The office of a Police Magistrate is not like other public situations:—for the business is multifarious, seldom admits of any recess or a vacation.—it is, or ought to be, *constant, laborious,* and without *intermission**.

But

---

* In the month of October, 1793, a respectable Committee, representing the great body of the Manufacturers in Spitalfields, waited on His Majesty's Principal Secretary of State for the Home Department, with an Address of Thanks for the Establishment of the Police System ; the substance of which is as follows:

" That it is the opinion of this Society, that great benefits have arisen, with regard to the fecurity of property, from the correct and regular manner in which the judicial business has been conducted by the Magistrates of Police; in consequence of whose vigilance and attention, an effectual check has been given to a System of depredation

But with all these advantages, even improved by competent funds appropriated to the different Public Offices, still a *Centre-point* is wanted to connect the whole together. so as to invigorate and strengthen every part, by a superintending establishment, under the immediate controul of the Secretary of State for the Home Department: There, indeed, the constitutional superintendence of the Police of the Metropolis, as well as of the whole country, rests at present; but from the vast weight and increase of other Public Business, connected with the general affairs of the State, foreign, colonial, and domestic, it has been found impracticable to pursue that particular System which has now become, more than ever, necessary for the detection of criminals. It seems then, that in executing a task so complicated and multifarious, a delegation of subordinate *Responsible Management* to a *Central Board of Police* should be resorted to: as the only means of giving strength, vigour, and energy to a System, heretofore only partially useful; and which, in it spresent disjointed state, is incapable of extending that Protection and

dation which heretofore occasioned a loss of many thousands per annum to the silk Manufacturers :—And it wasResolved,—" That the thanks of this Society are due to the Right Honourable Henry Dundas, one of his Majesty's Principal Secretaries of State ; and also to Mr. Burton, and the other Members of Parliament, who proposed and supported the Police System, for the share they had in the establishment of a judicial Tribunal, which has been found to extend, to the Silk Manufacturers, many advantages in a just and proper execution of the Laws which were not heretofore experienced."

Security,

Security, which has been shewn in the course of this Work, to be so much wanted, and so indispensably necessary.

To understand the Police of the Metropolis to that extent which is necessary to direct and super-intend its general operations, it must be acted upon *practically ;* and those who undertake the *superintend-ence* and *management* alluded to, must be men *able, intelligent, prudent,* and *indefatigable:* devoting their whole attention to this object alone. Clerks might be continually employed with great advantage in en-tering and posting up under the proper heads, such new information as should be obtained from day to day ; and hours should be appointed for receiving such intelligence from all proper and well-informed persons, who might choose to offer the same ; so far as such information related to Public wrongs, and offences against the peace, safety, and well-being of Society.

Under such a System, with a proper power of re-munerating Officers and others, scarcely a *Robbery, Burglary, Larceny,* or *fraudulent Transaction* could be committed, where the perpetrators would not be very speedily detected and brought to justice ; for then the Magistrates, in their respective districts, would be enabled to act with confidence, vigour, and energy, in the discovery and apprehension of offenders ;—and the effect would be to excite a general terror in the minds of every class of delin-quents ; which could not fail to operate strongly as

a means

a means of preventing crimes, and improving the morals and the happiness of the lower orders of the People.

In addition to this these responsible Commissioners of Police might with great propriety, and with no little public utility, have committed to them the superintendence of *all Receipts and Disbursements of the accounts*, and of *all monies applicable to objects of Police :* these they should lay annually before Parliament, if required, accompanied by a General Report; that the Legislature, as well as the Public at large, might see in what manner the funds had been applied; and what progress had been made in the prevention of crimes, and in restoring among the Labouring People that sense of morality, which never, perhaps, was at a lower ebb than at present.

The most enlightened Foreigners who have visited this Metropolis, and contemplated the nature and organization of our Police System, join in one general remark upon it ; viz.—" *That we have some sha-* " *dow of Police, for apprehending Delinquents, after* " *crimes are actually committed ; but none for the pur-* " *pose of preventing them.*"—This certainly is, in one sense, literally true ;—and from this source, combined with the imperfection of the Criminal Code, have arisen all those enormities and inconveniencies already so amply detailed.

Attached to the Laws and Government of his country, even to a degree of enthusiasm, the Author of this Work will not be too prone to seek for greater
perfection

perfection in other nations : or to quote them as examples to be imitated in the Metropolis of the British Empire ; and still less if such examples should tend, in the slightest degree, to abridge that freedom which is the birth-right of every Briton. But as all true liberty depends on those fences which are established in every Country, for the protection of the Persons and Property of the People, against every attack whatsoever : and as prejudices ought to be banished from the mind in all discussions tending to promote the General Weal, we ought not to be ashamed of borrowing good Systems from other Nations ; wherever such can be adopted, consistent with the Constitution of the Country, and the Liberty of the Subject.

In France, under the Old Government, how much soever many parts of the System of that Country were justly reprobated, by all who were acquainted with the blessings of Freedom, yet, in the management and regulation of what was denominated *The Police*, there existed that kind of Establishment, with regard to personal security, and protection against the depredations of the most depraved part of the community, which Englishmen have certainly never enjoyed ; who, on the contrary, have suffered manifold inconveniences from an idea, (surely a very erroneous one,) " that we must endure these public wrongs, and expose our property and lives to the attack of murderers, robbers, and highwaymen, as the price of *Liberty*."

When

When difficulties are felt, it is our duty to look at them dispassionately; to face them with fortitude, and to discuss them with intelligence—divested of all prejudices generated merely by habit and education. By pursuing this mode of investigation, it will be discovered that in other Governments there may be some Establishments worthy of imitation; and which, perhaps, might in part be adopted, not only in perfect consistency with the Freedom of the Subject; but with the advantage of extending to the mass of the People, who are not in a course of delinquency, more real liberty than they at present enjoy.—

At the commencement of the troubles in France, it is a curious fact, that the Lieutenant-General of the National Police, as well as that of the Metropolis, had upon his Registers the names of not less than twenty thousand suspected and depraved characters, whose pursuits were known to be of a criminal nature: yet by making this part of Police the immediate object of the close and uniform attention of one branch of the Executive Government, Crimes were much less frequent than in England; and the security extended to the Public, with regard to the protection of Life and Property against lawless depredation, was infinitely greater.—To elucidate this assertion, and to shew to what a wonderful height the System had advanced, the Reader is referred to the following Anecdotes; which were mentioned to the Author by a Foreign Minister of great intelligence

gence and information, who resided some years at the Court of France.

" A Merchant of high respectability in Bourdeaux had occasion to visit the Metropolis upon commercial business, carrying with him bills and money to a very large amount.

" On his arrival at the gates of Paris, a genteel looking man opened the door of his carriage, and addressed him to this effect :—" *Sir, I have been waiting for you some time ; according to my notes you were to arrive at this hour ; and your person, your carriage, and your portmanteau, exactly answering the description I hold in my hand, you will permit me to have the honour of conducting you to Monsieur De Sartine.*

" The Gentleman, astonished and alarmed at this interruption, and still more so at hearing the name of the Lieutenant of the Police mentioned, demanded to know what *Monsieur De Sartine* wanted with him ; adding, at the same time, that he never had committed any offence against the Laws, and that he could have no right to interrupt or detain him.

" The Messenger declared himself perfectly ignorant of the cause of the detention, stating, at the same time, that when he had conducted him to *Monsieur De Sartine*, he should have executed his orders, which were merely ministerial.

" After some further explanations, the Gentleman permitted the Officer to conduct him accordingly. *Monsieur De Sartine* received him with great
politeness ;

politeness ; and after requesting him to be seated, to his great astonishment, he described his portmanteau ; and told him the exact sum in bills and specie which he had brought with him to Paris, and where he was to lodge, his usual time of going to bed, and a number of other circumstances, which the Gentleman had conceived could only be known to himself. —*Monsieur de Sartine* having thus excited attention, put this extraordinary question to him,— *Sir, are you a man of courage ?*—The Gentleman, still more astonished at the singularity of such an interrogatory, demanded the reason why he put such a strange question, adding, at the same time, that no man ever doubted his courage. *Monsieur De Sartine* replied,—*Sir, you are to be robbed and murdered this night !—If you are a man of courage, you must go to your hotel, and retire to rest at the usual hour : but be careful that you do not fall asleep ; neither will it be proper for you to look under the bed, or into any of the closets which are in your bed-chamber ;* (which he accurately described);—*you must place your portmanteau in its usual situation, near your bed, and discover no suspicion :—Leave what remains to me.—If, however, you do not feel your courage sufficient to bear you out, I will procure a person who shall personate you, and go to bed in your stead.*

" The Gentleman being convinced, in the course of the conversation, that *Monsieur De Sartine's* intelligence was accurate in every particular, he refused to be personated, and formed an immediate resolution,

tion, literally, to follow the directions he had received; he accordingly went to bed at his usual hour, which was eleven o'clock.—At half past twelve (the time mentioned by *Monsieur De Sartine*), the door of the bed-chamber burst open, and three men entered with a *dark lantern, daggers* and *pistols*.—The Gentleman, who of course was awake, perceived one of them to be his own servant.—They rifled his portmanteau, undisturbed, and settled the plan of putting him to death.—The Gentleman, hearing all this, and not knowing by what means he was to be rescued, it may naturally be supposed, was under great perturbation of mind during such an awful interval of suspense; when, at the moment the villains were prepared to commit the horrid deed, four Police Officers, acting under *Mons. De Sartine's* orders, who were concealed under the bed, and in the closet, rushed out and seized the offenders with the property in their possession, and in the act of preparing to commit the murder.

" The consequence was, that the perpetration of the atrocious deed was prevented, and sufficient evidence obtained to convict the offenders.—*Monsieur De Sartine's* intelligence enabled him to *prevent* this horrid offence of robbery and murder; which, but for the accuracy of the System, would probably have been carried into execution."

Another Anecdote was mentioned to the Author by the same Minister, relative to the Emperor Joseph the Second : " That Monarch, having in the year

1787,

1787, formed and promulgated a new Code of Laws relative to criminal and civil offences;* and having also established what he conceived to be the best System of Police in Europe, he could scarcely ever forgive the French Nation, in consequence of the accuracy and intelligence of *Mons. De Sartine* having been found so much superior to his own; notwithstanding the immense pains he had bestowed upon that department of his Government.

" A very notorious offender, who was a subject of the Emperor, and who committed many atrocious acts of violence and depredation at Vienna, was traced to Paris by the Police established by His Majesty, who ordered his Ambassador at the Court of France to demand that this delinquent should be delivered up to Public Justice.

" *Mons. De Sartine* acknowledged to the Imperial Ambassador, that the person he inquired after had been in Paris;—that, if it would be any satisfaction, he could inform him where he had lodged, and the different gaming-tables, and other places of infamous resort, which he frequented while there—but that he was now gone:—

" The Ambassador, after stating the accuracy and correct mode by which the Police of Vienna was conducted, insisted that this offender must still be in Paris; otherwise the Emperor would not have commanded him to make such an application.

---

* Vide page 63 & *seq.* of this Volume.

" *Monsieur*

" *Monsieur De Sartine* smiled at the incredulity of the Imperial Minister, and made a reply to the following effect :—

" *Do me the honour, Sir, to inform the Emperor, your Master, that the person he looks for left Paris on the* 10*th day of the last month ; and is now lodged in a back room looking into a garden in the third story of a house, number* 93, *in* —— *street, in his own Capital of Vienna ; where his Majesty will, by sending to the spot, be sure to find him.*—

" It was literally as the French Minister of Police had stated.—The Emperor, to his astonishment, found the delinquent in the house and apartment described ; but he was greatly mortified at this proof of the accuracy of the French Police ; which, in this instance, in point of intelligence, *even in Vienna*, was discovered to be so much superior to his own."—

The fact is, that the French System had arrived at the greatest degree of perfection ; and though not necessary, nor even proper, to be copied as *a pattern*, might, nevertheless, furnish many useful hints, calculated to improve the Police of this Metropolis, consistent with the existing Laws ;' and even to extend and increase the Liberty of the Subject without taking one privilege away ; or interfering in the pursuits of any one class of individuals ; except those employed in purposes of *mischief, fraud,* and *criminality.*

The situation of this Country, (indeed of every country

country in Europe,) has changed materially since the dissolution of the ancient Government of France.— The horde of sharpers and villains, who heretofore resorted to Paris from every part of Europe, will now consider London as their general and most productive theatre of action ; for two obvious reasons :— 1st. Paris being exhausted of riches, its Nobility banished, and the principal part of the active property there annihilated, the former resources for the support of criminal and depraved characters no longer exist; while that Metropolis holds out no allurements similar to what were formerly experienced. 2dly. The ignorance of the English language (a circumstance which formerly afforded us some protection), will no longer be a bar to the resort of the continental sharpers to the Metropolis of this kingdom. At no period was it ever so generally understood by Foreigners ; or the French language so universally spoken, by at least the younger part of the People of this Country.—

The spirit of gaming and dissipation which prevails in London, promoted already in no inconsiderable degree by profligate characters from the Continent, the opulence of the People, and the great mass of active property in circulation, will afford a wide field for the exercise of the invention and wits of that description of men, both foreigners and natives, who infested Paris under the old Government, and which rendered a more than ordinary attention to its Police indispensably necessary.—

The

The termination of the present war will probably throw into this country a vast number of idle, profligate, and depraved characters, natives of this, as well as of other nations, who will require to be narrowly watched by a vigilant and well-regulated Police. The probability of such an accession to the numbers already engaged in acts of delinquency, serves to establish new and incontrovertible arguments in favour of the proposed *Board of Responsible Commissioners,* for managing the affairs of the Police of the Metropolis : to form a *Centre-point,* and to bind the System together.

To be well prepared against every possible evil, is one great step towards prevention ; and among the many advantages already detailed, as likely to result from a *Board of Police Revenue,* this would be none of the least.

In every view in which the subject can be considered, such a System, strengthened by good and apposite Laws, could not fail to be productive of vast benefits to the Community. *Petty Thefts,* affecting all ranks who have any property to lose, and destroying the moral principle, would be greatly abridged :—as would also the plunder from vessels in the River Thames, as well as from the public Arsenals, Dock-yards, and Ships of War. The more atrocious Crimes of Burglary and Highway Robbery, would suffer a severe check, in the embarrassments which would arise from the System of Detections and Rewards—from the restrictions pro-

posed

posed to be laid upon Receivers of Stolen Goods; upon Night Coaches,—and from other regulations applicable to those particular offences.   A large proportion of the *Coiners, Dealers,* and *Utterers of Base Money,* feeling the risk of detection, as well as of punishment, greatly extended and increased, would probably abandon the business as hazardous and destructive.   The completion of the General System would also, either collaterally or immediately, reach the tribe of Cheats, Swindlers, and Lottery Offenders, in such a manner as to occasion a considerable reduction of their number, by narrowing the ground, and destroying the resources by which they at present flourish.

The establishment of such a System would be an immediate benefit to every man of property, as an individual, independent of the Public at large ; but even in another point of view, it is doubly necessary at this juncture, when new events are daily occurring, of a nature truly interesting to the peace and well-being of Society, and to the tranquillity of the State ; rendering it more than ever necessary to establish a System of unremitting vigilance.   It is a fact well established, that it was principally through the medium, and by the assistance, of many of the twenty thousand miscreants who were registered, previous to the anarchy of France, on the books of the Lieutenant of Police, that the contending Factions in that distracted country, were enabled to perpetrate those horrid massacres and acts of atrocity,

which

which have been beheld with detestation, abhor-rence and astonishment, by every civilized nation in the world.

Let it be recollected, at the same time, that Man-kind, in a state of depravity, arising from a long course of criminal turpitude, are nearly alike in every country ; and that it becomes us to look with a jea-lous eye on the several thousand miscreants of the same description which now infest London ; for they too, upon any fatal emergency, (which GOD forbid !) would be equally ready as their brethren in iniquity were, in Paris, to repeat the same atrocities, if any opportunity offered.

As the effectuating such an object has become so great a desideratum ;—and as it is to confer those blessings which spring from a well-regulated Police,. calculated to extend a species of protection * to the inhabitants

---

* In mentioning what regards the protection of the Metropolis, with the inefficiency of the existing Civil Force in Constables, it is impossible to overlook those eminent advantages which have arisen from the excellent institutions of the Honourable Artillery Company, the Light Horse Volunteers, and the other associated Corps, who have so nobly stood forth in the hour of danger to support the deficient Police of the Country.

To these Patriotic individuals, the inhabitants of the Metro-polis are under infinite obligations.

Regardless of their own *ease, convenience, interest,* or *personal safety,* the members of these public-spirited associations have ever stood forward in the hour of tumult and disorder, gratui-tously, and at their own expence, for the protection of their Fellow citizens and for the preservation of the Public peace.

The

inhabitants of this great Metropolis, which has never been heretofore experienced;—it can scarcely fail to be a matter of general satisfaction to know that the Select Committee of the House of Commons on Finance, have strongly recommended to Parliament a System of Police, similar to that which had been submitted to the consideration of the Public in the former editions of this Work.

In order that improvements, sanctioned by such high authority, and the adoption of which are so important to the best interests of Society, may be fully explained and elucidated; a detail of the measures, which have been recommended, with general observations on the proposed System, are reserved for the ensuing Chapter.

The assistance they have, on every occasion, afforded the civil power, and the sacrifices of valuable time which they have made, at the risk of health, and under circumstances where they were compelled to forego that ease and comfort, which in many instances, from their opulence and rank in life, are attached to their particular situations—it is to be hoped, will never be forgotten by a grateful Public.

CHAP

CHAP. XVIII.

*The System of Police recommended by the Select Com-
mittee on Finance explained.—A proposition to consolidate the two Boards of Hawkers and Pedlars,
and Hackney Coaches, into a Board of Police Revenue.—The whole Revenues of Police from Fees,
Penalties and Licence Duties, to make a common
Fund.—Accounts to be audited.—Magistrates to
distribute small rewards.—A Power to the Board to
make Bye-Laws.—A concurrent jurisdiction recommended—also the Penitentiary House for reforming
Convicts.—Other measures proposed after the Board
is established—namely, a Public Prosecutor for the
Crown.—A Register of Lodging Houses.—The
establishment of a Police Gazette.—Two leading objects to be attained.—The prevention of Crimes:
and raising a Revenue for Police purposes.—The
enumeration of the Dealers who are proposed to be
Licenced.—A General View of the annual expence
of the present Police System.   Observations on the
effect of the System recommended by the Finance
Committee, with respect to the Morals and Finances
of the Country.—Suggestions respecting a chain of
connection with Magistrates in the Country, and the
mode of effecting it.—Licences to be granted by select
Magistrates in the Country, and by the Central Board
in London and the neighbourhood.—The Functions*

of

of the proposed Board explained.—Specifications of the Trades to be regulated and Licenced.—General Reflections on the advantages likely to result from the adoption of the plan recommended by the Finance Committee.—Concluding Observations.

———

IMPRESSED with a deep sense of the utility of investigating the nature of the Police System, the Select Committee of the House of Commons on Finance turned their attention to this, among many other important objects in the Session of the year 1798: and, after a laborious investigation which occupied several months, (during which period the Author of this Treatise underwent several examinations) * they made their *final Report*—in which after stating it as their opinion, " that the general tendency of our " œconomical arrangements upon this subject is ill " calculated to meet the accumulating burdens, " which are the infallible result of so much error in " our System of Police"—they recommended it to Parliament to reduce or consolidate " the two offices " of Hawkers and Pedlars, and Hackney Coaches, " into a Board of Police Revenue, under the direc- " tion of a competent number of Commissioners, " with such Salaries as should bid fair to engage

* See Appendix to the 28th Report of the Committee.

" talents

" talents adequate to the situation, and as should
" be sufficient to command the whole exertion of
" those talents.—That the Receiver of the Police
" offices, should be the Receiver-General of the
" funds proposed to be collected by this Board.—
" That the superintendants of aliens should form a
" part of its business.—That the fees and penalties
" received at the several offices of Police, together
" with the Licence-duties and penalties, if any,
" which shall be in the collection of this consoli-
" dated Board, shall make one common fund, out
" of which all salaries and expences of the several
" offices of Police should be defrayed, as well as all
" those of the Consolidated Board, and that all pay-
" ments whatever should be made by the Receiver,
" under the sanction of this Board, subject to the
" approbation of the Lords Commissioners of his
" Majesty's Treasury.—That the accounts of the
" Receiver should be audited and signed by the
" Board before being delivered to the Treasury, or
" the office for auditing accounts.—That the ba-
" lances in the hands of the Receiver, after retain-
" ing what may be sufficient for current expences,
" should be paid into the Exchequer at frequent
" and fixed periods.—That Magistrates of Police
" should be empowered to distribute small rewards
" to Constables or others, for meritorious services,
" to be paid by the Revenue, after receiving the
" sanction of the Board: And further, that the
" Board should have power to make Bye-laws, for
" the

" the regulation of such Minor Objects of Police
" as relate to the objects of their superintendence,
" and to the control of all Coaches, Chairs, Carts,
" Barrows, and the conduct of all Coachmen, Chair-
" men, Carters, &c. and the removal and preven-
" tion of annoyances, and the correction of all of-
" fences against the cleanliness, the quiet, and the
" free passage of the Streets of the Metropolis, si-
" milar to the powers now possessed by the Com-
" missioners of Hackney Coaches, and subject in
" like manner to the approbation of the Superior
" Judges in the Courts in Westminster Hall."—
The Committee further recommend that two additional Police Offices should be established in the
City of London, consisting each of three Magistrates,
to be named by the Lord Mayor and Aldermen, and
paid out of the General funds, and to have Commissions from the Crown, extending over the whole
Metropolis, and the Counties of Middlesex, Kent,
Essex, and Surry; and that the Commissions of
the Magistrates of the other eight Offices should
extend in like manner over the whole Metropolis,
and the four above-mentioned Counties*.   And
finally, the Committee recommend that no time
should be lost in carrying into effect the Plan and
Proposal of Jeremiah Bentham, Esq. for employing

---

* It is not proposed in the Bill, now in preparation, hereafter
stated, to introduce any thing respecting the City of London,
unless the consent of the Lord Mayor, Aldermen, and Common-
Council, shall be previously obtained.

and

and reforming Convicts as a measure which bids fairer than any other that was offered to the Public, to diminish the Public expenditure in this branch, and to produce a salutary Reform in the object of the proposed Institution.

Other measures are stated by this Committee as well calculated to facilitate the means of detection and conviction of Offenders, and to reduce the expence which is now borne by the Public, or sustained by private Individuals, in the maintenance of a very inefficient Police; while they seem calculated to lessen the growing Calenders of Delinquency, but which may be better matured after the consolidation of the Offices here proposed shall have taken place. —" Such as the appointment of Counsel for the " Crown, with moderate Salaries, to conduct all " Criminal Prosecutions, and rendering the Solicitor " to the Board useful, either in such Prosecutions as " any of the Public Offices might find it necessary " to institute; or in such Criminal Prosecutions at " the suit of Individuals, as the Public Justice of the " Country should render expedient.—Such as a Re- " gister of Lodging-houses in the Metropolis.—Such " as the establishment of a Police Gazette, to be " circulated at a low price, and furnished gratis to " all persons under the superintendence of the Board; " who shall pay a licence duty to a certain amount: " And such also as an Annual Report of the State of " the Police of the Country."

In

In considering this Report in general, it is no slight gratification to the Author of this Treatise, to discover that all the great features of his original design for giving to Police its genuine character, unmixed with those judicial Powers which lead to Punishment, and properly belong to Magistracy alone, have been sanctioned by such high authority.

In taking a general view not only of what is specifically recommended by the Select Committee of the House of Commons, but also of the Report itself, two leading objects appear to be in contemplation, namely—

1st. The prevention of crimes and misdemeanors, by bringing under regulations a variety of dangerous and suspicious trades;* the uncontrolled exercise

of

---

* The Trades alluded to are these following,—vide Appendix (C) 28th Report of Select Committee of the House of Commons on Finance, page 45, 46, and 47.

New Revenues.

1. Wholesale and Retail Dealers in old Naval Stores, Hand-stuff, and Rags.
2. Dealers in second-hand wearing Apparel, Stationary, and Itinerant.
3. Dealers in old Iron and other Metals, &c.
4. Founders and others using Crucibles.
5. Persons using Draught and Truck Carts for conveying Stores, Rags, and Metals.
6. Persons Licenced to slaughter horses.

7. Persons

of which by persons of loose conduct, is known to contribute in a very high degree to the concealment, and by that means to the encouragement and multiplication of crimes.

2d. To raise a moderate Revenue for Police purposes from the persons who shall be thus controlled, by means of Licence Duties, and otherwise so modified as not to operate as a material burden ; while a confident hope is entertained, that the amount of this revenue will go a considerable length in relieving the finances of the country, of the expences at present incurred for objects of Police, and that, in the effect of the general System, a considerable, saving will arise, in consequence of the expected diminution of crimes, particularly as the chief part of the expence appears to arise after delinquents are convicted*.

By

7. Persons keeping Livery Stables, and letting Horses for hire.
8. Auctioneers, who hold periodical or diurnal Sales.

Existing Revenues proposed to be transferred with a view to a more effectual control, and to an improved Finance.

9. Hackney Coaches and Chairs.
10. Hawkers and Pedlars.
11. Pawn Brokers.
12. Dealers in Horses.

N. B. The new Revenues are estimated to yield   £.64,000
The increase of the existing Revenues is stated at   19,467
_____
83,467
_____

* The amount of the general expence of the Criminal Police of
the

By the consolidation of the two Boards of Hackney Coaches, and Hawkers, and Pedlars, the functions

the Kingdom as stated by the Committee on Finance in their
28th Report is as follows :

1st. The annual average of the total expence
   of the Seven Public Offices in the Metropolis, from the institution in August
   1792 to the end of the year 1797, being
   a period of 5½ years   -   -   £.18,281 18   6

2d. The total expence of the Office at Bow-
   street, in the year 1797, including remunerations to the Magistrates in lieu
   of fees, perquisites, and special services, and the expence of the patrole
   of 68 persons   .   -   -   7,901   7   7
                                          _____

            Total expence for the Metropolis 26,183   6   1

3d. The money paid to the several Sheriffs
   for the conviction of Felons in 1797   9,650   0   0

4th. The expence of maintaining Convicts on board
   the Hulks, (exclusive
   of 415 under Sentence
   of Transportation in
   the different gaols), a-
   mounted in 1797 to £.32,080 0 0

5th, The expences incurred in
   the employment of
   Convicts by the Navy
   and Ordnance Boards,
   probably amounting to
   not less than from 10l.
   to 20l. per Man per
   annum, were by com-
   putation   -   1,493 14 10¼
                        _____   _____

         Carried over   33,578 14 10¼   35,833   6   1
                                             6th. The

tions of the Commissioners will become very extensive and laborious, since in addition to the inspection
and control of the different suspicious trades proposed
to be licenced, it will be useful to the Public, and,
indeed, the System will be incomplete, unless they
not only keep constantly in their view the general
Calendar of delinquency, but also carry into effect
such plans as, on mature deliberation, and (many
will unquestionably be found practicable), shall, in
a great measure, prevent the terror—dangers—losses
and inconveniences which arise from foot-pad and
highway robberies, burglaries, and other atrocious

Brought over £.33,578 14 10¼ £.35,833 6 1

6th. The annual average of
cloathing, victualling,
and transporting Con-
victs, and of the Civil,
Military, and Marine
Departments of New
South Wales, and Nor-
folk Island, from 1786
to 1797   86,457 19 11½

                                 120,036 7 9¼

                                 155,869 13 10¼

To which add the farther sums
annually charged on the
County Rates, or incurred
in places having peculiar
Jurisdiction in England - 50,000 0 0
Borne by the Sheriffs in Eng-
land   -   -   - 10,000 0 0 - 60,000 0 0

Total for all England   -   215,869 13 10¼

1

offences, which are so prevalent in and near the Metropolis at present.—This duty will naturally attach to the Central Board, and which the Commissioners, (from the accurate. information their situation will enable them to procure, and the Civil Force they may have at their disposal,) will be well qualified to execute with advantage to the Community; and while competent pecuniary resources will arise from the Licence Duties imposed, aided by legislative regulations, applicable to this, and other objects tending to the general prevention of Crimes, blame may fairly be imputed wherever a considerable degree of success is not manifest, by the gradual diminution of the more atrocious, as well as the minor offences.

The Select Committee of the House of Commons having stated it as their opinion, that the principle upon which the plan which has been brought under their review is founded, " *is liable to no error; and that supposing it faithfully executed it gives the fairest prospect of success*;" the Public will naturally become anxious for an enjoyment of the benefits which may be expected to result from its adoption.

As its leading feaure is the security of the *rights of the innocent*, with respect to their Life, Property, and Convenience, the measures of this Board must, in a peculiar degree, be directed with prudence and discretion to this particular object. This will be effected not only by increasing the difficulty of perpetrating

perpetrating offences, through a control over those Trades by which they are facilitated and promoted, but also by adding to the risk of detection, by more prompt and certain mode of discovery wherever crimes are committed. Thus must the idle and profligate be compelled to assist the State, by resorting to habits of industry, while the more incorrigible delinquents will be intimidated and deterred from pursuing a course of turpitude and criminality, which the energy of the Police will render too hazardous and unprofitable to be followed up as a trade; and the regular accession of numbers to recruit and strengthen the hordes of criminal delinquents, who at present afflict Society, will be in a great measure prevented.

These objects (in the opinion of the Select Committee) are to be attained by the establishment of a *Central Board of Police Revenue;* the views of the Members of which should be directed to the means of adding " Security to the Person and Property " of the peaceful Subject; the Morals of the " People, and the general Finances of the Coun- " try ; by those powers of action which are likely " to operate most beneficially towards the prevention " of Crimes."

To accomplish these purposes it would seem, (after mature deliberation), to be necessary not only to extend the Licensing System over the whole Kingdom; but also to form *a chain of connection*
between

between the Central Board, and every district of the Country, with a view as well to a more effectual Control over those suspicious Traders, who are to become immediate objects of attention on the part of the Police, as to establish a more correct and certain mode of collecting the proposed Revenue.

This chain of connection would appear to be only attainable through the medium of Select local Magistrates,* to whom a certain degree of responsibility would attach, and who by means of Stationary Surveyors, (being Constables), appointed by themselves, and under their immediate Control, would be enabled to superintend the collection of the Licence Duties, and in a particular manner to inspect into, and regulate the general Police of the District, while in conjunction with other Justices in the division, they granted the Annual Licences to the different Dealers, upon the same plan which is at present pursued with respect to Alehouses.

From this general rule, however, on account of

* It is presumed, that the distinction of *Select Magistrates,* joined to the patronage arising from the appointment of inferior Officers of Police in their respective Districts of the Country, (as Surveyors and Collectors of Licence Duties), would be considered as a sufficient inducement to men of property, talents, and respectability, to undertake this very honourable Trust: to which it may reasonably be hoped, that many would be stimulated, in a particular degree, by the impulses of patriotism, and a desire to introduce a correct and improved System of Police in their respective Districts.

the

the peculiar situation of the Metropolis, a deviation might be necessary and useful to the Public. It would, therefore, seem that the Dealers resident within a certain distance round the Metropolis, should receive their Licences from the Central Board, and be immediately under its control.—The advantages resulting from this arrangement are obvious.— The chief part of the Receivers, and Criminal Dealers, who contribute in so great a degree to the increase and concealment of the numerous offences, which are committed in and near the Metropolis, require that the superintendance should not be divided, but that it should be confined entirely to the Board, where all intelligence is supposed to center; and whose peculiar duty it will be to watch the progress of Crimes in all their ramifications, and to adopt measures for preventing the growing corruption of Morals, by which every species of delinquency is generated.

For the purpose therefore of compassing this and every other object in the view of the Select Committee, it is suggested that the proposed Board should be authorized to exercise the following

FUNCTIONS:

I. To manage that branch of the Police which relates to Hackney Coaches and Chairs.—To enforce strictly the laws now in being for the better ordering this system so necessary to the comfort and convenience of the Metropolis.—To obtain new

powers

powers (where wanting) to compel a greater degree of cleanliness and security, with respect to these vehicles.—To banish, if possible, from the fraternity those criminal characters denominated *Flash Coachmen*, and to secure civility, and prevent imposition.—For this last purpose a department should be continued, as at present, (a part of the Institution,) having a concurrent jurisdiction with other Magistrates, for the purpose of hearing and determining disputes between Coachmen and the Public.

II. To execute the laws relative to Hawkers and Pedlars.—To regulate and improve the System respecting this suspicious class of Dealers, and more effectually to extend the control over them by means of the Select Magistrates in each District of the country where they travel, for the purpose of more narrowly watching their conduct.

III. To grant Licences in the Town District (*i. e.* within the limits of the Penny-Post,) while the Select and other Justices grant similar Licences in the Country; under the authority of the proposed general Police Bill, to the following Traders, and others,* viz.

1st. Pur-

* Nothing can exceed the pains and labour which have been bestowed in settling the description of the persons, proposed to be licenced, with a view to an accurate system of Legislation. A regard to this accuracy made it necessary to abandon those classes recommended by the proposer to the Select Committee; because on

attempting

1st. Purchasers of second-hand, and other Household goods, for Sale.

2d. Wholesale purchasers of Rags, and unserviceable
Cordage, for Sale to Paper-makers.

3d. Retail Purchasers of Rags, and unserviceable
Cordage, for Sale to Paper-makers.

4th. Purchasers of second-hand Apparel, made-up
Piece Goods, and Remnants for Sale.

5th. Walking or Itinerant Purchasers of second-hand
Apparel, made up Piece-goods, and Remnants for
Sale.

6th. Purchasers of second-hand Naval Stores, for
Sale.

7th. Wholesale Purchasers of second-hand Metals,
for ale.

8th. Retail Purchasers of second-hand Metals, of
persons in general, for working up.

9th. Every Worker of second-hand Metals purchasing the same, from persons in general, and
not from Licensed Dealers.

10th. Purchasers of second-hand Building Materials
for Sale.

11th. Persons keeping Draught-Carts for second-
hand-goods, purchased for Sale.

12th. Persons keeping Hand or Truck Carts for second-hand goods, purchased for Sale.

attempting to frame a Bill, it was found impracticable in one case,
and impolitic in another, to apply Legislative rules that would
not either be defeated or invade the privileges of innocence*.

* Persons keeping Crucibles, and Auctioneers.

13th. Sel-

13th. Sellers of Unredeemed Pledges, otherwise than by Auction : and also to control and inspect the conduct of these dealers, so as if possible to confine them to the innocent part of their trades ; and to collect and receive the respective Licence Duties.*

IV. To grant Licences also in like manner to other Traders, which are already under some degree of Legislative regulations ; (but which require a more efficient Control), provided it shall be thought expedient by the Legislature to transfer these branches to the proposed Board, as requiring in a particular degree the superintendance of the Police System, viz.

1st. Pawnbrokers in Town and Country

2d. Persons keeping Slaughtering-houses for Horses, and other Animals, not for the food of Man.

3d. Dealers in Horses, and persons hiring, keeping at Livery, and transferring Horses from hand to hand, with a view to establish a check against

---

* If Twine Spinners and Rope Spinners of a certain class could be brought under similar regulations, it would prove extremely beneficial, inasmuch as the small Manufacturers in this line are known to give considerable facilities to the Stealers of Hemp on the River Thames.—A number of small Rope and Twine Manufacturers have undersold the fair trader, by working up Stolen Hemp, purchased at half price ; and it is but too evident from discoveries which have recently been made, that this evil has gone to a very great extent, and that considerable benefits would be derived to the Public, by placing *Twine and White Rope Spinners* under the control of the Police, at least within the proposed District of the Metropolis.

Highway

Highway Robberies, and to defeat those subtle tricks which prevail in the Sale of Horses.

And also to collect the Licence and other Duties, (which might, in respect to the transfer of Horses, be rendered extremely productive without being felt as a burden), and to inspect the conduct of these classes with a view to the prevention of Frauds, and other offences.

V. To grant Licences in like manner to all persons (except those employed in his Majesty's Mints), who shall erect or set up any cutting Engine for cutting round Blanks by the force of a Screw ; or any stamping Press, Fly, Rolling Mill, or other instrument for stamping, flatting, or marking Metals, or Bank Notes ; or which, with the assistance of any Matrix, Stamp, Die, or Plate, will stamp Coins or Notes—so as to prevent the enormous evils constantly experienced by the Coinage of Base Money, and the counterfeiting of Bank Notes :—A System whereby the criminal part of ingenious Artists could be kept under the immediate view of the Police, is so obvious in a Commercial Country, as to require no elucidation. And the measure is the more desirable, as the reputable part of the Artists and Manufacturers who have occasion to keep Presses for innocent and useful purposes, have no objection to such regulations.*

VI. These

---

* See the Chapter on the subject of Base Coin, in this *Treatise;* and the remdies ultimately proposed for suppressing this
enormous.

VI. These Commissioners, after deducting the necessary expences, should pay into the Exchequer weekly, through the medium of a Receiver, the whole Revenues collected by them for Police purposes; and it is to be hoped, notwithstanding the very low Rates of the Licence Duties proposed, that, *including the Horse Police*, the aggregate Collection would go very far towards easing the resources of the Country of the expence of what the Select Committee of the House of Commons denominate, *a very inefficient System of Police.* *

VII. It would be the duty of the Commissioners to superintend, with great strictness, the conduct of their

enormous evil.—The Author has great satisfaction in stating that a Bill is now nearly prepared, grounded chiefly on his suggestions, for improving the Coinage Laws; and that sanguine hopes are entertained of its passing during the present Session of Parliament.—The proposition now made of bringing this feature of Police, so far as relates to *Presses*, and other *Machinery*, under the inspection of the proposed *Central Board*, will certainly have a powerful effect in deterring evil-minded persons from following the Trade of Coiners of Base Money, or Engravers and Stampers of forged Bank Notes.—In this kind of Control, the Police Revenue Board would have an advantage arising from the nature of the System, which may be considered as *invaluable in a national point of view*, since no part of the Country, however remote, could be said to be out of their reach, as Officers, under their immediate direction, would be found every where.

* From an estimate which has been made, the three Classes mentioned in division IV. might be made to produce above 100,000l, for Police purposes, in addition to what is received at present from Pawnbrokers, and Horse Dealers.—The chief part would arise from the transfer of Horses.

Subordinate

Subordinate Officers, both in the Town and Country Districts, and to be careful that those who were entrufted with the collection of the Licence Duties gave proper Security;† and that in their conduct, in Surveying and Watching the Movements of the different Dealers, they manifested the greatest degree of vigilance, prudence, and discretion—Above all, that they were regular in their Payments, and remittances, so as not to incur the penalties inflicted by the proposed Act on defaulters.

VIII. To correspond with the Select Magistrates in every District in the Kingdom, and not only to receive from them useful information, relative to offences which have been committed, and all other matters within the scope of the Functions of these Select Magistrates; but also to give them their advise and assistance in every case where it is found necessary, for the purpose of the preservation of peace and good order, and the due administration of the Laws, and particularly as it may apply to

† The most œconomical mode would, apparently, be to consolidate in one person the office of *Constable* and *Collector of Licence Duties* in the respective Districts: having it understood that the poundage received on the money paid to the Board, should not only be considered as a remuneration for the Collection, but also as a reward for occasional Services in the general Police Department. By such an arrangement, a chain of Select and reputable Officers may be established all over the Country, without being felt as a burden of any kind on the Community; while those Services under the general arrangements of the Board, could not fail to be productive of infinite benefits in the well-ordering of Society.

those

those Select Magistrates who reside near the Sea-Coasts of the Kingdom, that in all cases of Ship-wreck, measures may be pursued, and the laws enforced, to prevent those horrid barbarities, pillage and spoliation, which have, to the disgrace of civilized Society, prevailed on such melancholy occasions.*

IX. To make arrangements with the Select Magistrates in the Country, relative to the due execution of the proposed General Police Act, with respect to the Control over the persons Licenced, and all other Duties which may be required under such a Legislative System.

X. To obtain accurate Information, by means of regular returns from Clerks of Assize, Clerks of the Peace, Keepers of Prisons, Houses of Correction, Penitentiary Houses, and other places of Confinement; and to have constantly in view the state of delinquency in the Metropolis, and in every part of the country; preserving such accounts in registers for the purpose of reference, as occasions might arise to render them useful to public Justice.—To assist the acting Magistrates in Town and Country by conveying all useful information applicable to their local situa-

* The Registers of our Courts of Record, and other well-attested accounts have developed scenes of unfeeling Cruelty and Rapacity, in cases of Shipwrecks, which would have disgraced the rudest and most ferocious Savages, and would lead a Stranger to suppose that we have no Laws for the prevention of such outrages.

tions,

tions, respecting the commission of crimes, and the detection of offenders, and which might tend to the prevention of disorders, or offences meditated against the Laws.

XI. To watch the proceedings of the herds of criminal delinquents who generally leave Town every year in the month of March, after the drawing of the English Lottery, for the purpose of attending *fairs, races,* and other places of amusement and dissipation in the country, carrying with them quantities of *base Money and EO Tables,* with a view to commit frauds on the unwary—And to give notice to the Select local Magistrates, that they and their officers may be upon their guard in defeating the nefarious designs of these miscreants, who are often disguised as farmers and labourers, the better to enable them to effect their purposes, by cheating and stealing, particularly *horses,* to the great loss and injury of the country.

XII. It is recommended by the Select Committee of the House of Commons, that the Commissioners of this Central Board should have it in their power to distribute rewards to Constables or others for meritorious services, through the medium of the Magistrates of Police, and to use such other means as should best promote the ends of Justice, and the general utility of the Institution to the community.

XIII. Under the direction of the principal Secretary of State for the Home Department, these Commissioners

missioners should avail themselves of the knowledge their situation would afford them of the degree of depravity and danger attached to the character of the different convicts; to select such as they thought proper objects for transportation to New South Wales; and to follow any other instructions they may receive for œconomizing this branch of the criminal Police of the nation, so as, if possible, to reduce the annual expence.

XIV. These Commissioners being authorized by the Lords of the Treasury, might take under their management all matters relative to the Lottery; not only with a view to a more œconomical mode of drawing the same, but also for the purpose of rendering the Revenue productive to the State, without the evil consequences which at present arise from it to the morals of the lower orders of the people, and the distresses and miseries to which its fascinating delusions subject them.

XV. It would be the duty of the Board, availing itself of the practical knowledge which may be obtained by means of a System of general superintendance in the Police Department, to attend closely to the operation of the whole of the present code of penal Laws, with respect to its efficacy and utility; and where imperfections are discovered, to suggest from time to time such improvements as may appear useful and beneficial to the Police, and to the Revenue.

XVI. The Select Committee in their Report recommend, that the proposed Board should have power
" to

" to make Bye-Laws for the regulation of such
" minor objects of Police as relate to the objects
" of their superintendence, and to the control of
" all Coaches, Chairs, Carts, Barrows, and the
" conduct of all Coachmen and Chairmen, Cart-
" ers, &c. and the removal and prevention of all
" annoyances, and the correction of all of-
" fences against the cleanliness and quiet, and the
" free passages of the streets of the Metropolis, in
" like manner as is now possessed by the Com-
" missioners of Hackney Coaches, and subject to
" the approbation of the Superior Judges."

XVII. To superintend the general receipts and disbursements of the Establishment, and to report the
same quarterly to the Treasury, and to the principal Secretary of State for the Home Depart-
·ment.

XVIII. To receive and execute the instructions of
the Treasury in all matters respecting Finance and
Revenue; and the instructions and directions of
His Majesty's Secretary of State for the Home
Department in all matters of Police.

XIX. To establish a more correct System through
the medium of the Select Magistrates, whereby
the Laws for the prevention and punishment of
offences may be more effectually and universally
carried into execution, and not in many instances
remain a dead letter, as at present, to the great
injury of the community; or be partially carried
into effect in particular parts of the country,
against

against a few individuals, or for mere temporary purposes.

XX. Finally, it will be the duty of the Board to report to his Majesty in Council, and to Parliament (if required) the state of the Metropolis and the Country, with respect to criminal *Police* in all its branches, so as to bring under the review of the Executive Government *the whole criminality of the Country*, at a given period each year, where it will be accurately discovered whether it increases or diminishes.

Such are the functions apparently necessary to be assigned to the proposed Board of Commissioners, for the purpose of accomplihing the objects of improvement in the Police System, which have been recommended to Parliament by the Select Committee.

These objects are of too much importance to the Public, to the Security of the State, and to the peace and good order of Society, to be lost sight of, even for one moment.

While the morals and habits of the lower ranks in Society are growing progressively worse and worse— while the innocent and useful part of the Community are daily suffering evils and inconveniences originating from this source—while crimes multiply in all instances under the existing systems, (the Thames Police only excepted*) it becomes of importance to

apply

* Nothing can be offered as a more irrefragable proof of the utility of a Police Institution, such as has been recommended by the

Select

apply a remedy. In legislating with this view, the same disadvantages and difficulties do not present themselves as in many other cases, since much previous labour and investigation has been bestowed in forming a ground-work for the proposed General Police System.

Under the Sanction of his Majesty's Principal Secretary of State for the Home Department, a Bill has been prepared, in which, while every attention has been paid to the means of accomplishing the views of the Select Committee, nothing can exceed the pains which have been bestowed *in preserving the rights of innocence, and in divesting power of the faculty of abuse.*

A line has been carefully drawn between the *noxious* and the *blameless* and useful part of the community; and while the injuries arising from the pursuits of the former are checked and restrained, the privileges of the latter are extended and enlarged.

Select Committee on Finance, than the effect of the Marine Police Establishment upon the River Thames; where, inspite of a crippled System, and deficient Laws, the energy of the superintendance and the strength of the Civil force, has, at a very trifling expence, applied with strict œconomy, worked such a change in the Port of London, both with respect to the security of commercial property, and the Revenue, as would scarcely have been conceived possible. For an Account of this System, see the 8th Chapter of this Work: but for a more enlarged and comprehensive view of the nature and effect of the design, recourse must be had to the Author's *Treatise on the Commerce and Police of the River Thames, &c.* in which the whole plan is developed, together with the Legislative System necessary to give permanent effect to the design.

This

This, when properly contemplated, will be found to be the *true essence of good Police*—and this explains in the shortest compass that is possible, the *ultimate object of the design.*

The Bill comprehends five divisions:—The *first* authorizes *the imposition of Licence Duties on certain classes of Dealers already enumerated :*—The *second* establishes a *Board of Police Revenue, and explains its powers and functions :*—The *third* explains *the powers and regulations which apply to the Licensing System :*—The *fourth* relates to *penalties* and *procedure :* and the *fifth* transfers the functions of *the Commissioners of Hackney Coaches and Chairs, and Hawkers and Pedlars, to the new Establishment, and makes provision for such Officers as may cease to be employed.*— While the proposed duties, although light upon the individuals, promise to be productive to a certain extent; the Licensing System is likely " to purge " the occupations placed under control from the im- " putations which are now but too deservedly cast " upon them ; and to make them by gradual steps " the instruments of detection, instead of the means " of concealment, of every species of fraud and vio- " lence."*

The functions of the Board, by comprehending whatever relates to the delinquency of the country, will establish a general responsibility which does not now exist, and which never has existed, with respect to the evils arising from the multiplication of crimes,

* See the 28th Report of the Select Committee, page 4.

while

while their diminution will depend on the zeal, ability, and discretion to be manifested by those to whom this important duty may be assigned.

By this establishment of a general Police System, it will become the duty of one class of men to watch over the general delinquency of the Metropolis, and the country ;—to check its progress by lessening the resources of the evil-disposed to do injuries, and to commit acts of violence on the peaceful subject ; and gradually to lead the *criminal,* the *idle,* and the *dissolute* members of the community into the paths of innocence and industry.

The collateral aids to be derived from this System of Control over Dealers and others of loose conduct, in pursuit of evil courses, will give considerable strength to the Legislative measures which are in contemplation, with respect to the *Police of the River Thames ; The frauds and plunder in the Naval and other public departments :—The Coinage of base Money,* and the *fabrication of counterfeit Bank Notes*—Whatever has been contemplated for the purpose of checking and preventing these evils cannot be complete or effectual, until the proposed Board is established, and the Licensing System in full action. The control of this Board is absolutely necessary to contribute to the success of the measures proposed, and to the security of public and private property against the present extensive depredations. In fact the whole System is linked together, and its energy and success will depend on the passing of the respective Laws applicable

cable to each object of which the Police Board may
not improperly be denominated *the key-stone.*

It is this responsible superintendance which is to
give *life, vigour,* and *effect,* not only to the Laws
which are in contemplation, but to many other excellent Statutes which remain at present as *a dead
letter.*—Let it once become the duty of one body of
men to charge themselves with the execution of the
Laws for the prevention of crimes, and the detection of offences—let them be armed with proper and
apposite powers for that purpose, and the state of
Society will speedily become ameliorated and improved ; a greater degree of security will be extended
to the peaceful subject, and the blessings of civil liberty will be enlarged.

A new æra in the world seems to have commenced, which imperiously calls for the adoption of
such measures ; not only in this country, but all
over Europe. The evil propensities incident to human nature appear no longer restrained by the force
of religion, or the influence of the moral principle.

On these barriers powerful attacks have been made
which have hitherto operated as curbs to the unruly
passions peculiar to vulgar life : they must therefore be strengthened by supports more immediately
applicable to the object of preserving peace and good
order.

The period is approaching when to the phalanx of
delinquents who at present prey upon Society, will
be added multitudes of idle and depraved characters
                                         discharged

discharged from the Army and Navy on the return of Peace.——Policy and humanity require that an adequate remedy should be provided for such a con-tingency.——*Qui non velat peccare cum possit, jubet.* Where the powers of a State are not employed to avert apparent and threatened evils, a tacit assent is given to the commission of crimes. On the con-trary, where means are used to check the progress of turpitude and vice, and to compel obedience to the Laws, the comfort of Society is promoted, and the privileges of innocence are secured.

If in the accomplishment of the design which has been recommended by the highest authority, these objects shall be gradually attained——If it shall ope-rate in preventing acts of violence and fraud from being committed upon the peaceful subject ; while means are discovered through the medium of a well-regulated Police, whereby the unfortunate, and even the idle and the dissolute, may possess a resource for subsistence by honest industry, without having any pretended plea of necessity for resorting to Crimes ; great, indeed, would be the benefits which would result to the Public. This would be at once the triumph of both reason and humanity.

The first step is, to attend to the Morals and the Habits of the rising Generation; to adapt the Laws more particularly to the manners of the People, by minutely examining the state of Society, so as to lead the inferior orders, as it were, insensibly into better Habits, by gentle restraints upon those propensities
which

which terminate in Idleness and Debauchery ;—to remove temptations, in their nature productive of evil, and to establish incitements to good and useful pursuits.

Among a variety of other functions which would devolve on the proposed Commissioners, perhaps one might be to offer suggestions to the Executive Government, with respect to such useful Regulations as might arise from the extensive knowledge which they must necessarily acquire as to the condition and pursuits of the labouring People ; and hence would result one of the greatest means of preventing Crimes, and improving the Condition of human Life.

But while it is acknowledged to be a vain hope to reduce the tumultuous passions of Men to absolute regularity, so as to render the Commission of offences impracticable ; it is equally clear (and it is even proved by the State of Society, where Public Morals have been more effectually guarded), that it is possible to diminish the Evil very considerably.

By the establishment of a well-conducted Board of Police, a confident hope is entertained that this purpose is attainable ; and in this view (although it is to take nothing from the present Resources of the State), it is a blessing to the Nation, which could scarce be too dearly purchased at any price.

CHAP.

C H A P. XIX.

*The unparalleled Extent and Opulence of the Me-
tropolis manifested in the number of streets, lanes,
alleys, courts, and squares, estimated at above
8000; containing above 4000 Churches and Places
for religious Worship,—more than 400 Seminaries
of Education;—several Institutions for promoting
Religion and Morality;—11 Societies for promoting
Learning, and the useful and the fine Arts;—a
great number of charitable Asylums for the indigent
and forlorn;—Hospitals and Dispensaries for the
lame, sick, and diseased;—and above 1700 Institutions of various other kinds for Charitable and Humane Purposes.—A detail of the Courts of Law,
and other Establishments connected with the distribution of Justice.—The public Prisons in the metropolis.—A view of the number of Persons employed
in the different departments of the Law, estimated
in all at about 7000.—Suggestions for improving the civil Jurisprudence in the Metropolis, so far
as relates to the recovery of small Debts.—The
Evils arising from the present System, exemplified in
the multiplicity of actions for trivial sums in the
course of a year; the enormous expence, and the ill
effects of the severity of the punishment in such
cases; debasing the mind, and proving the destruction
of many families, in their morals; and injuring the
State.—The necessity of an Alteration of the System,*

*tem, farther enforced by the propriety of relieving
the supreme Judges from a weight of labour unreasonable in the vast increase of business, which the
extensive and growing intercourse of Commerce occasions.—The same Observations extended to the great
Officers of State; and the necessity and utility of a
division of labour, in proportion to the increase of
public duty, explained; as a means of preventing
inconveniences.—A view of the Municipal Regulations which have been established in the Metropolis
for the accommodation and convenience of the inhabitants; grounded on various acts of the Legislature,
passed at different periods, during the last and the
present century.—Each district of the Metropolis, a
separate Municipality; where the power of assessing
the inhabitants, for the purposes of paving, watching, lighting, cleansing, and removing nuisances, is
placed in the hands of Trustees, under a great number of local acts of Parliament.—These regulations
mostly founded on Laws made in the last and in the
present Reign.—The principal public acts detailed,
viz:—The General Act of the 2d William and
Mary, cap. 8, for paving the Metropolis;—the 10th
Geo. II. cap. 22, for watching the City of London;
11th Geo. III. cap. 29, for removing signs, and
establishing a complete System of Municipal Police.—
The Acts relative to Westminster and Southwark
for similar purposes.—The Statutes relative to Common Sewers detailed; their origin, and the great advantages resulting from them.—The Laws relative*

to

to Hackney Coaches and Chairs—also to Carts and other Carriages.—The Acts relative to Watermen on the Thames,—The Law for restraining bullock-hunting. And finally, the Regulations by the 14th Geo. III. cap. 78, relative to the Mode of building Houses, and the Rules laid down for extinguishing Fires. Concluding Observations, on the advantages which would result to the Metropolis at large from these numerous Acts of Parliament being rendered uniform, and conformable to the excellent Regulations established for the City of London.—The advantages of simplifying the System.—The burden upon the Inhabitants equal to one million a year for the expence of Municipal Police.—Suggestions for improving the System and reducing this expence,—Concluding Reflections.—The present epoch, more than any other, presses for arrangements calculated to amend the Morals of the People, by improving the Laws of the Country.

IT cannot fail to prove an interesting inquiry, not only to the inhabitants of the Metropolis, but also to Strangers, by what means that department of its œconomy and government, which may be denominated *Municipal Police,* is regulated; so as to convey the comforts, and procure the various accommodations and conveniences which, with some few exceptions, are felt to exist in every part of the Capital and its environs.

When

When it is known that this great City, (unparalleled, as will be hereafter shewn, in extent and opulence, through the whole habitable Globe,) comprehends, besides *London, Westminster,* and *Southwark,* no less than forty-five Villages, now exceedingly inlarged, independent of a vast accession of buildings upon the open fields in the vicinity; it becomes less a matter of surprize, to learn, that it extends to nearly eight miles in length,—is three miles at least in breadth, and not less than twenty-six in circumference; containing above eight thousand streets, lanes, alleys, and courts, and sixty-five different Squares; in which are more than one hundred and sixty thousand houses, warehouses, and other buildings; besides *Churches* and *Chapels* for religious worship, of which the following enumeration is imagined not to be very distant from truth :—

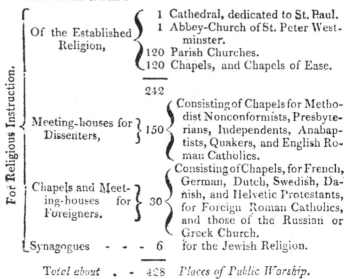

For Religious Instruction.

Of the Established Religion,
- 1 Cathedral, dedicated to St. Paul.
- 1 Abbey-Church of St. Peter Westminster.
- 120 Parish Churches.
- 120 Chapels, and Chapels of Ease.

242

Meeting-houses for Dissenters, 150
Consisting of Chapels for Methodist Nonconformists, Presbyterians, Independents, Anabaptists, Quakers, and English Roman Catholics.

Chapels and Meeting-houses for Foreigners. 30
Consisting of Chapels, for French, German, Dutch, Swedish, Danish, and Helvetic Protestants, for Foreign Roman Catholics, and those of the Russian or Greek Church.

Synagogues - - - 6   for the Jewish Religion.

Total about . - 428 *Places of Public Worship.*

The

The number of Inhabitants of this great Metropolis, occupying these various houses and buildings, may, under all circumstances, be rationally estimated at one million at least; for whose accommodation, convenience, and security, the following Institutions have been formed, *namely,*—1st. *For Education ;*—2d. *For promoting good Morals ;*—3d. *For useful and fine Arts;*—4th. *For objects of Charity and Humanity ;*—5th. *For distributing Justice ;—and* 6th. *For punishing Offenders.*

EDUCATION.

1st. For Education.

16 Inns of Court and Chancery, for educating Students to the profession of the Law, &c. &c.

5 Colleges— viz. One for the improvement of the Clergy, London Wall; one for Divinity and Astronomy, called Gresham College; one for Physicians, Warwick Lane; one for the study of Civil Law, Doctors Commons; and the Heralds College.

62 Schools or public Seminaries; the principal of which are Westminster School, Blue-coat School or Christ's Hospital, St. Paul's, Merchant Taylors, Charterhouse, St. Martin's School, &c. &c. &c. where about 5000 young persons are educated.

237 Schools belonging to the different Parishes; where about 9000 male and female Children are educated in Reading, Writing, and Accompts.

3730 Private Schools, for all the various branches of male and female Education; including some for Deaf and Dumb.

——

4050 Seminaries of Education.

The following Schools seem to deserve particular Enumeration; though probably there are many others which might equally deserve notice :—

1. Asylum

For Education.

1 Asylum for poor friendless, deserted girls, under twelve years of age, Vauxhall Road   1758

2 Orphan Working School, for Children of Dissenters, City Road

3 Philanthropic Society, St. George's Fields, for children of criminal parents, and young delinquents

4 Freemasons' School, for Female Orphans, St. George's Fields   1788

5 Marine Society for educating poor destitute boys to the Sea, in Bishopsgate-street   1756

6 British or Welsh Charity School, Gray's Inn Lane   1718

7 French Charity School, Windmill-street, Tottenham Court Road   1747

8 School for Soldiers Girls, at Chelsea, supported by Ladies   1709

9 Neal's Mathematical School, for teaching Navigation, &c. to poor Children, King's Head Court, Gough Square, Fleet-street   1715

10 School for Children of the Clergy; the Boys at *Acton*, Middlesex; the Girls at *Lisson Green*, Paddington.—Treasurer, H. Stebbing, Esq. No. 2, Bloomsbury Place   1749

11 Day School of Industry, for Boys and Girls, Paradise-street, Mary-le-bone   1791

12 Another, No. 68, Edgware Road, for Girls   1784

13 Ladies' Charity School, King-street, Snow Hill   1702

14 Walworth Female Charity School

15 Saint Anne's Society, hitherto at Lavenham, Suffolk, now removed to Peckham, for Boys and Girls, (extended in 1783 and 1791)   1709

16 Grey Coat Hospital, Artillery Ground, Westminster

17 Green Coat Hospital, Ditto

RELIGION AND MORALS.

Religion and good Morals.

1 The Society for giving effect to his Majesty's proclamation against Vice and Immorality   1787

2 The Society for promoting Christian Knowledge, Bartlett's Buildings, Holborn   1699

3 The Society for propagation of the Gospel in Foreign Parts, Dean's Yard, Westminster   1701

4 The Society for promoting Religious Knowledge, by distributing books among the poor,—Secretary, Mr. T. D. Harriot   1715

5 The

2. For promoting Religion and good Morals.

5, The Society for promoting Charity Schools in Ireland, Merchants Seamen's Office.

6 The Society for Religious Instruction to the Negroes in the West Indies — 1793

7 The Society for preventing Crimes, by prosecuting Swindlers, Sharpers, and Cheats; Gough-Square, Fleet-street — 1767

8 British Society for the encouragement of Servants, No. 27, Hay-market — 1792

9 Society for giving Bibles to Soldiers and Sailors, No. 427, Oxford-street — 1780

10 Dr. Bray's Charity for providing parochial Libraries, No. 5, Ave Maria Lane.

11 Society for Relief of poor pious Clergymen — 1788

12 Queen Anne's Bounty for the augmentation of Small Livings of Clergymen.—Secretary, R. Burn, Esq. Duke-street. Westminster — 1703

13 Sunday Schools, in various parishes

14 Sunday School Society, for giving Bibles, &c. and otherwise furthering the purposes of Sunday Schools.—Secretary, Mr. Prestill, No. 47, Cornhill — 1785

THE ARTS.

3. For learning, and the useful and fine Arts.

1 Royal Society, incorporated for promoting useful Knowledge ;—*Instituted* — 1663

2 Antiquarian Society, Somerset Place — 1751

3 Society or Trustees of the British Museum — 1753

4 Society of Artists of Great Britain, Strand — 1765

5 Royal Academy of Arts, Somerset Place — 1773

6 Society for the encouragement of Learning, Crane Court, Fleet-street

7 Society for encouragement of Arts, Manufactures, and Commerce, Adelphi Buildings

8 Medical Society of London, Bolt-court, Fleet-street — 1773

9 Society for the improvement of Naval Architecture

10 Veterinary College, near St. Pancras Church

11 Royal Institution for applying the Arts to the common purposes of Life — 1799

107 Alms-

107 Alms-houses endowed at different periods, where 1352
old men and women are supported; the principal of
these houses are—*The Trinity Alms-houses*, for 28 decayed Ship Masters, in Mile End; *Bancroft's Alms-
houses*, Mile End, for 24 Poor Men; *Fishmonger's
Alms-houses*, Newington Butts; *Haberdasher's Alms-
Houses* in Hoxton; *Jeffries' Alms-houses*, Kingsland
Road; *Sir John Morden's College*, for decayed Merchants, at Blackheath; *Emanuel*, or *Lady Dacre's Hospital*, Tothilfields, Westminster.

1 London Workhouse, Bishopsgate-street, for decayed
old Men*.

1 Bridewell Hospital, an asylum for apprentices to different trades, Bridge-street, Blackfriars.

1 Charter-house Hospital, an asylum for 80 indigent persons, in Charter-house Square, *founded* 1611

1 Scottish Hospital for decayed natives of Scotland, in Crane-court, Fleet-street.

1 Welsh Hospital, for decayed Natives of Wales,
in Gray's Inn Lane.

1 French Hospital, for decayed Frenchmen, in St.
Luke's, Middlesex　　　　　　　　　　　　　1719

1 Foundling Hospital, for deserted Infants, Lamb's
Conduit street　　　　　　　　　　　　　　1739

1 Magdalen Hospital, for the admission of seduced Females, St. George's Fields　　　　　1769

1 Lock Asylum, for penitent Female Patients,
cured in the Lock Hospital　　　　　　　　　1787

1 Chelsea Hospital, for worn out and disabled
Soldiers　　　　　　　　　　　　　　　　　1670

1 Greenwich Hospital, for worn out and disabled
Seamen　　　　　　　　　　　　　　　　　1694

118

4. Asylums for the Indigent and Helpless.

* London Workhouse is a large building, which might, with great advantage, be turned into a house of Industry, or Penitentiary House for petty
offenders, for which purpose it was used in ancient times. Although it is said
to be sufficient to lodge about 500 people, it is now used only as an asylum
for a few old persons; and is a sinecure for the Keepers and Officers, who
live comfortably as the servants of the Community without doing any good.
This house is amply endowed by a power of levying contributions on all the
parishes for its support.

ASYLUMS

ASYLUMS FOR SICK, LAME, DISEASED, AND FOR
POOR PREGNANT WOMEN.

<table>
<tr><td>1. St. Bartholomew's Hospital, in West Smithfield, for the reception of afflicted and diseased persons</td><td>1539</td></tr>
<tr><td>2. St. Thomas's Hospital, Southwark, for the reception of sick and lame, especially sailors</td><td>1553</td></tr>
<tr><td>3. Guy's Hospital, Southwark, for sick and impotent persons, and lunatics</td><td>1721</td></tr>
<tr><td>4. London Hospital, Whitechapel Road, for the reception of all persons meeting with accidents</td><td>1740</td></tr>
<tr><td>5. St. George's Hospital, Hyde Park Corner, for the reception of Sick and Lame</td><td>1733</td></tr>
<tr><td>6 Westminster General Infirmary, James-street, Westminster, for sick and diseased persons</td><td>1719</td></tr>
<tr><td>7. Middlesex Hospital, Charles-street, near Oxford-street, for sick and lame, and pregnant women</td><td>1745</td></tr>
<tr><td>8. Lock Hospital, Hyde Park Turnpike, for persons afflicted with the venereal disorder</td><td>1746</td></tr>
<tr><td>9. Hospital Misericordia, Goodman's-fields, for the same purpose</td><td>1774</td></tr>
<tr><td>10. Small-pox Hospital, St. Pancras, for inoculation of poor persons</td><td>176</td></tr>
<tr><td>11. London Lying-in Hospital, Aldersgate-street, for poor married women</td><td>1750</td></tr>
<tr><td>12. City of London Lying-in Hospital, Old-street, City Road, idem</td><td>1751</td></tr>
<tr><td>13. British Lying-in Hospital, Brownlow-street, Long-Acre, id.</td><td>1749</td></tr>
<tr><td>14. Westminster Lying-in Hospital, Surry Road, Westminster Bridge, for poor pregnant women generally</td><td></td></tr>
<tr><td>15. Queen's Lying-in Hospital, Bayswater-hall, Oxford Road, id.</td><td></td></tr>
<tr><td>16. Lying-in Hospital, Store-street Tottenham Court Road, id.</td><td>1767</td></tr>
<tr><td>17. Lying-in Charity, for delivering pregnant women at their own houses: W. Manning, Esq. Governor; Physician, Dr. Sims, Blackfriars</td><td>1757</td></tr>
<tr><td>18. Society for delivering married women in their own habitations, by whom 32 Midwives are employed, No. 18 Strand</td><td>1757</td></tr>
<tr><td>19. Bethlem Hospital, for Lunatics, Moorfields</td><td>1553</td></tr>
<tr><td>20. St. Luke's Hospital for Lunatics, Old-street Road</td><td>1751</td></tr>
<tr><td>21. Samaritan Society for relieving Persons discharged from Hospitals</td><td>1791</td></tr>
<tr><td>22. Society for visiting and relieving the Sick in their own Houses</td><td></td></tr>
</table>

Hospitals for Sick, Lame and Diseased, and Pregnant Women.

1. Eastern

Dispensaries for Sick, Lame, and Diseased.

1 Eastern Dispensary, Whitechapel
2 Western Dispensary, Charles-street, Westminster
3 Middlesex Dispensary, Great Ailiff-street
4 London Dispensary, Primrose-street, Bishopsgate-street
5 City Dispensary, Bevis Marks
6 New Finsbury Dispensary, West Smithfield
7 Finsbury Dispensary, St. John's Square, Clerkenwell
8 General Dispensary, Aldersgate-street
9 Public Dispensary, Cary-street, Lincoln's Inn Fields
10 Infant Poor Dispensary, Soho-square
11 St. James's Dispensary, Berwick-street, Soho
12 Westminster Dispensary, Gerard-street, Soho
13 Mary-le-bone Dispensary, Well-street, Oxford-street
14 Ossulton Dispensary, Bow-street, Bloomsbury
15 Surry Dispensary, Union-street, Borough
16 Royal Universal Dispensary, Featherstone Buildings, Holborn

Institutions for Charitable and Humane Purposes.

Humane Society, for the recovery of drowned and suffocated Persons, Spital square, and London Coffee-house 1773
Society for the Relief of Clergymens' Widows, Paper Buildings, Temple
Society for the Relief of Widows and Orphans of Medical Men, founded by Dr. Squires, and Mr. Chamberlaine 1788
Laudable Society for the benefit of Widows, Crane-Court, Fleet-street
Society for the support of Widows, Surry-street, Strand
Society for the support of poor Artists, and their Widows, Strand
Three Societies for the Support of decayed Musicians, their Widows and Children
Society for Relief of decayed Actors
Abc-darian Society, for the relief of decayed School-masters
Society for the Relief of Authors in distress
Society for the Relief of Officers, their Widows, Children, Mothers, and Sisters
Society for Annuities to Widows, Old Fish-street, St. Paul's, No. 25
Society for the Relief of sick and maimed Seamen in the Merchants' Service 1747
Society for the Relief of poor Widows and Children of Clergymen, instituted by Charter 1768
Rayne's Hospital for 40 girls, who receive 100l. portion on their marriage 1736
Society called the Feast of the Sons of the Clergy, for apprenticing their indigent Children, No. 2, Bloomsbury Place

Free-

Institutions, &c.

Freemason's Charity

Society for the relief of Persons confined for Small Debts, Craven-street, Strand

Society for bettering the condition, and increasing the comforts of the Poor

Society for improving the condition of Chimney-Sweepers

Five Soup Societies

Workhouses

Private Asylums for Lunatics

91 Public Companies in the City of London, who give in charity above £75,000 a year

Stock's Blind Charity, distributed by the Painter-Stainers' Company

Hetherington's Blind Charity, payable at Christ's Hospital - - 1787

Asylum for Deaf and Dumb Poor, Grange Road, Bermondsey - - 1792

Charitable Society for Industrious Poor, School House, Hatton Garden

Society for Charitable Purposes, Wardour-street, Soho - - - 1773

1600 Friendly Societies in the Metropolis and its vicinity, of which about 800 have enrolled themselves under the act of Parliament, 33 Geo. III. cap. 54. They are composed of mechanics and labouring people, who distribute to sick members, and for funerals, sums raised by monthly payments, amounting on an average to 1s. 8d. a month, or 20s. a year, and consisting of about 80,000 members, who thus raise annually about 80,000l.

Reflecting on the foregoing list of various laudable Institutions, which it cannot be expected should be altogether perfect, but which may be said to be unparalleled in point of extent, as well as munificence, and conferring the highest honour on the National Character for Charity and Humanity, the mind is lost in astonishment, that greater and more extensive benefits have not arisen to the inhabitants

of

of the Metropolis : not only in improving their morals, but in preventing the lowest orders of the
People from suffering that extreme misery and
wretchedness, which has been already stated to exist
in so great a degree in London.

When it is also recollected, that large sums are
annually expended by Societies instituted for promoting religion, virtue, and good morals, it must
be evident, as human misery does not appear to be
alleviated, and the morals of the People grow worse
—that there must be some cause to produce effects
so opposite to what might have been expected from
such unparalleled philanthropy; the cause, indeed,
may easily be traced to that evident deficiency in the
general System of Police, which has so often been
mentioned in the course of this Work.*

In the next place, it may be useful, and certainly
cannot be improper, in a Treatise on the Police, to
insert a brief detail of the different Courts of Law,
and public Prisons, established in the Metropolis ;
for the distribution of Justice, and the punishment
of delinquents, for civil as well as criminal offences ;

* But particularly that branch of it, which relates to the
management of the Poor, than which nothing in a greater
degree requires immediate improvement; since it is unquestionably true, and has, indeed, been already shewn, that from this
source incalculable evils have arisen, which must propor-
tionately increase, until some effectual remedy is applied.—
See Chapter 13th, where a remedy is proposed.

together

together with the number of professional men attached to these various Law establishments.

COURTS OF JUSTICE

IN THE

METROPOLIS.

Supreme Courts.

The High Court of Parliament.

The House of Lords ; being the Appeal in the last resort in all causes criminal and civil.

The Court of Exchequer Chamber, before which Writs of Error are brought on judgments in the Court of King's Bench and other Courts ; it is composed, in certain cases, of all the Twelve Judges, and the Lord Chancellor; but sometimes of a smaller number.

The High Court of Chancery—at Westminster Hall—and Lincoln's Inn Hall.

The Court of King's Bench, held in Westminster Hall.

The Court of Common Pleas, held in Westminster Hall.

The Court of Exchequer—a Court of Law, Equity and Revenue ; held at Westminster Hall and Serjeant's Inn.

The Court of Appeals in Colonial and Prize Causes; before the Lords of his Majesty's Privy Council at Whitehall.

The High Court of Admiralty, for Prizes, &c. at Doctors' Commons ; and in Criminal Cases, twice a year, at the Old Bailey.

Four Ecclesiastical Courts.

Prerogative Court, for Wills and Administrations

Court of Arches, for Appeals from inferior Ecclesiastical Courts in the Province of Canterbury ; the Court of Peculiars is a branch of this Court.

Faculty Court, to grant Dispensations to marry, &c.

Court of Delegates for Ecclesiastical Affairs.

Doctors' Commons.

COURTS

COURTS of JUSTICE in the METROPOLIS.

The Court of Oyer and Terminer and Goal-Delivery for trying Criminals at the Justice Hall, Old Bailey. } Held by His Majesty's Commission to the Lord-Mayor, Judges, Recorder, and Common Serjeant, &c.

Seventeen Courts in the City of London.

Court of Hustings { The Supreme Court of the City for Pleas of Land and Common Pleas.

The Lord-Mayor's Court { For Actions of Debts and Trespass, and for Appeals from inferior Courts and for foreign attachments; giving decisions in all cases whatever, in 14 days, at an expence not exceeding 30s. held in the King's Bench, Guildhall, by the Lord Mayor, Recorder, and Aldermen.

Court of Requests { Held by two Aldermen and four Members of the Common Council, appointed by the Lord-Mayor and Aldermen; three of whom form a Court for the recovery of small debts under 40s. at the expence of 10d.

Chamberlain's Court { Held every day to determine differences between masters and apprentices; and to admit those qualified to the freedom of the City.

Sheriff's Court { Held every Wednesday, Thursday, Friday, and Saturday, at Guildhall; where Actions of Debt and Trespass, &c. are tried by the Sheriff, and his Deputy, who are Judges of the Court.

Court of Orphans. { Held before the Lord-Mayor and Aldermen, as Guardians of the Children of deceased Freemen under twenty-one years of age, &c.

Pie Poudre Court { Held by the Lord-Mayor and Stewards, for the administering instantaneous justice between Buyers and Sellers at Bartholomew Fair, to redress all such disorders as may arise there.

COURTS

COURTS of JUSTICE in the METROPOLIS.

Seventeen Courts in the City of London.

Court of Conservancy — Held by the Lord Mayor and Aldermen four times a year, in Middlesex, Essex, Kent, and Surry; who inquire by a Jury into Abuses relative to the Fishing on the River Thames, and redress the same; from Staines *West*, to Yenfleet *East*.

Court of Lord-Mayor and Aldermen. — Court of Common-Council. — Court of Common Hall. — Court of Wardmotes — These relate to setting the Assize on Bread and Salt—to the municipal Officers of the City—to the Elections of Lord Mayor, Sheriffs, and Officers of the City—and to the management of the public property of the City, and removing Nuisances. The Wardmotes are held chiefly for the Election of Aldermen and Common Councilmen.

General and Quarter Sessions of the Peace, held by the Lord-Mayor and Aldermen, eight times a year.

Petty Sessions for small Offences, &c. held at the Mansion House by the Lord Mayor and one Alderman; and at Guildhall by two Aldermen in rotation — Daily, in the forenoon

Coroners' Court — To inquire into the causes of sudden deaths, when they arise.

Court of the Tower of London — Held within the verge of the City by a Steward, appointed by the Constable of the Tower, before whom are tried actions of Debt, Trespasses, and Covenants.

Courts of Justice within the City and Liberty of Westminster.

Court of the Duchy of Lancaster — A supreme Court of Record, held in Somerset Place, for deciding by the Chancellor of said Duchy, all matters of Law or Equity belonging to the County Palatine of Lancaster.

Quarter Sessions of the Peace — A Court of Record, held by the Justices of the City and Liberty of Westminster, four times a year, at the Guildhall, Westminster, for all Trespasses, Petty Larcenies, and other small Offences, committed within the City and Liberty.

Westminster Court — Or Court Leet, held by the Dean of Westminster, or his Steward, for choosing parochial Officers, preventing and removing Nuisances, &c.

COURTS

COURTS of JUSTICE in the METROPOLIS.

Courts of Justice within the City and Liberty of Westminster.

Court of Requests, Castle-street, Leicester-square — Held by Commissioners, being respectable Housekeepers, for deciding without appeal, all Pleas for Debts under 40s. for the parishes of St. Margaret, St. John, St. Martin, St. Paul Covent Garden, St. Clement Danes, St. Mary le Strand, and that part of the Dutchy of Lancaster which joins Westminster

Court of Requests, Vine-street, Piccadilly. — Held in the same manner, and for the same purposes; for the parishes of St. Anne, St. George Hanover-square, and St. James, Westminster

Petty Sessions or Police Court, held at Bow-street. — A Court of petty Sessions, held by two Magistrates every day, (Sunday excepted) morning and evening, for matters of Police, and various Offences, and Misdemeanors, &c.

Police Court or Petty Sess. Queen-sq. Westminster — A Court of petty Sessions established by Act of Parliament, held every morning and evening, (Sunday excepted) by two Magistrates, for matters of Police and various Offences, Misdemeanors, &c.

Courts of Justice in that part of the Metropolis, which lies within the County of Middleesx.

Police Court or petty Sess. Great Marlborough-st. — The same.

St. Martins-le-Grand Court. — A Court of Record, subject to the Dean and Chapter of Westminster, held every Wednesday for the trial of all personal Actions. The process by Capias against the body, or an Attachment against the goods, in this particular Liberty

East Smithfield Court. — A Court Leet and Court Baron, held for this Liberty, to inquire into Nuisances, &c.—In the Court Baron Pleas are held to the amount of forty shillings

Finsbury Court. — A Court Leet held once a year by a Steward of the Lord-Mayor as Lord of the Manor of Finsbury, for inquiring into nuisances competent for Leet Juries, and swearing in Constables for the Manor

St. Catherine's Court. — Two Courts are competent to be held within this small Precinct, for actions of Debt and Trespass, at St. Catharine's

Whitechapel Court. — A Court held by the Steward of the Manor of Stepney, by whom, and a Jury, are tried Actions of Debt for 5l. and under, &c.

COURTS of JUSTICE in the METROPOLIS.

Courts of Justice in that part of the Metropolis, lying within the County of Middlesex.

Sheriff's Court	For the County of Middlesex, for Actions of Debt, Trespasses, Assaults, &c.
Quarter and Gen. Sess. of Peace & Sess. of Oyer and Terminer	Held by the Justices of the County of Middlesex, eight times a year, at the New Sessions House, Clerkenwell Green, for all Trespasses, Petty Larcenies, Misdemeanors, &c. and for Roads, Bridges, and other County Affairs
Petty Sessions or Police Court, established by Act of Parliament	A Court of Petty Sessions, held every morning and evening. (Sunday excepted) by two Magistrates, at the Public Office, in Hatton Garden, for matters of Police and various Offences, Misdemeanors, &c.
Petty Session, or Police Court	At the Public Office, Worship Street, near Finsbury-square, by two Justices, for objects of Police, &c.
Idem	At the Public Office, Lambeth-street, Whitechapel
Idem	At the Public Office, High-street, Shadwell
Two Coroners' Courts	For inquiring into causes of sudden death
Court of Requests	For small debts under 40s. without appeal, held in Fulwood's Rents, Holborn, for the Division of Finsbury
Court of Requests	For small debts under 40s. without appeal, held in Osborn-street, Whitechapel, by Commissioners under the Act of Parliament, chosen annually by the several Parishes in the Tower Hamlets
General and Quarter Sessions of the Peace for the Liberty of the Tower of London	Held by the Justices of that Liberty, 8 times a year, for petty Larcenies, Trespasses, Felonies, and Misdemeanors, &c. within that particular District

Courts of Justice in the Borough of Southwark, Surry.

Court of Record	Held at St. Margaret's Hill, Southwark, by the Lord Mayor's Steward, for Actions of small Debts, Damages, Trespass, &c.
Court of Record	For the Clink Liberty, held near Bankside, Southwark, by the Bp. of Winchester's Steward, for Actions of Debt, Trespass, &c. within that Liberty.
Marshalsea Court	A Court of Record (or the Court of the Royal Palace) having jurisdiction 12 miles round Whitehall (exclusive of the City of London) for actions of Debts, Damages, Trespasses, &c. and subject to be removed to a higher Court of Law, when above 5l.

COURTS of JUSTICE in the METROPOLIS.

Courts of Justice in the Borough of Southwark, Surry.

Court of Requests	For the recovery of small Debts under 40s. without appeal, held at St. Margaret's Hill by Commissioners chosen under the Act of Parliament, by the different Parishes
Coroners' Court	To inquire into causes of sudden Death— in Southwark, &c.
Quarter Sessions of the Peace	Held by the Lord Mayor and Aldermen, at St. Margaret's Hill, for the Borough of Southwark
Quarter Sessions of the Peace for the County of Surry	Held at the New Sessions House in Southwark, by the Magistrates of the County of Surry.
Petty Sessions, or Police Court, established by Act of Parliament	A Court held every morning and evening, by two Justices, at the Public Office, Union Hall, Union-street, Southwark, for Objects of Police, &c.

PRISONS *in the* METROPOLIS.

1. King's Bench Prison, for Debtors on Process of Execution in the King's Bench, &c. St. George's-fields
2. Fleet Prison, for Debtors on Process, &c. in the Common Pleas, &c. Fleet Market
3. Ludgate Prison, Bishopsgate-street ⎱ For the City of
4. Poultry Compter, in the Poultry ⎰ London
5. Giltspur-street Compter, Giltspur-street
6. Newgate, or City and County Gaol, Old Bailey
7. New Prison, Clerkenwell—Gaol for the County of Middlesex
8. Prison for the Liberty of the Tower of London, Well-close-square
9. Whitechapel Prison for Debtors in the five pound court
10. Savoy Prison for Deserters and Military Delinquents

Houses of Correction

11. City Bridewell—Bridewell, Bridge-street, Blackfriars
12. Tothill Fields Bridewell—Tothill Fields
13. Spa Fields Penitentiary House
14. New Bridewell in the Borough of Southwark

15. County Gaol for Surry in the Borough of Southwark
16. Clink Gaol, in   ditto
17. Marshalsea Gaol, in the Borough, for Pirates, &c.
18. New Gaol, in the Borough.

Nothing

Nothing, perhaps, can manifest, in a greater degree, the increased commerce and population of the Metropolis of the Empire, than the following summary detail of the different classes of professional men connected with the various departments of the Law.

It appears from the preceding Statements, that there are in the Metropolis

   9 Supreme Courts; to which are attached **270** officers*
   4 Ecclesiastical Courts   -   -   54 do.
 18 Inferior Courts for small Debts   146 do.
   1 Court of Oyer and Terminer, and Gaol } 27 do.
     Delivery   -   -
   4 Courts of General and Quarter Sessions } 46 do.
     of the Peace   -   -
 10 Courts and Petty Sessions for purposes } 190 do.
     of Police   -   -
   5 Coroners' Courts   -   -   20 do

                           753

King's Serjeants, Attorney and Solicitor General, and King's Advocate   -   8
Serjeants at Law   -   -   14
Doctors at Law   -   -   14
King's Counsel   -   -   25
Masters in Chancery   -   -   10
Barristers at Law   -   -   400
Special Pleaders   -   -   50
Proctors in Doctors' Commons   -   50
Conveyancers   -   -   40
Attorneys at Law in the different Courts   1,900
Clerks, Assistants, and others, estimated at 3,700
Notaries Public   -   -   36

            Total about   7,000

* See for some further particulars the 27th Report of the Finance Committee.

It

It is impossible to contemplate this view of a very interesting subject, without being forcibly struck with the vast extent of the wealth and commercial intercourse of the Country, which furnish advantageous employment for such a multitude of individuals, in one particular profession. Every good man, and every lover of his country, must anxiously wish that the advantages may be reciprocal; and that men of talents, integrity, and ability, in the profession of the Law, while they extend their aid to the removal of those evils which are a reproach to the criminal jurisprudence of the Country, would also assist in procuring the removal of the inconveniences at present felt in the recovery of small debts. This is peculiarly irksome to every well-disposed person, who in the course of business, having transactions with the mass of mankind, cannot avoid frequently meeting with bad or litigious characters by whom disputes are unavoidably generated.

According to the prevailing System, if the debt exceeds 40s. the action may be brought in a superior Court, where, if contested or defended, the expence, at the lowest computation, must be upwards of fifty pounds. Prudent men, under such circumstances, will forego a just claim upon another, or make up a false one upon themselves, as by far the least of two evils, in all cases where they come in contact with designing and bad people; and hence it is, that the worthless part of mankind, availing themselves in *Civil,* as others do in *Criminal Cases,* of the imperfections

fections of the Law, forge these defects into a rod of oppression, either to defraud the honest part of the Community, of a just right, or to create fraudulent demands, where no right attaches; merely because those miscreants know that an action at Law, even for 20*l.* cannot either be prosecuted or defended, without sinking three times the amount in Law expences; besides the loss of time, which is still more valuable to men in business.

To convince the Reader that this observation is not hazarded on weak grounds, and that the evil is so great as to cry aloud for a remedy, it is only necessary to state, that in the County of Middlesex alone in the year 1793, the number of bailable writs and executions, for debts from *Ten* to *Twenty* pounds, amounted to no less than 5,719, and the aggregate amount of the debts sued for was the sum of 81,791*l.*

It will scarcely be credited, *although it is most unquestionably true*, that the mere costs of these actions, although made up, and not defended at all, would amount to 68,728*l.*—And if defended, the aggregate expence to recover 81,791*l.* must be— *(strange and incredible as it may appear)*, no less than 285,905*l.*! being considerably more than three times the amount of the debts sued for.

The mind is lost in astonishment at the contemplation of a circumstance, marking, in so strong a degree, the deficiency of this important branch of the jurisprudence of the Country.

Through

Through this new medium we discover one of the many causes of the increase of crimes.—And hence that caution which men in business are compelled to exercise (especially in the Metropolis), to avoid transactions with those who are supposed to be devoid of principle.

Whenever the Laws cannot be promptly executed, at an expence, that will not restrain the worthy and useful part of the Community from the following up their just rights, bad men will multiply, the morals of the People will become more and more corrupted, and the best interests of the State will be endangered.

In a political as well as in a moral point of view, it is an evil that should not be suffered to exist; especially when it can be demonstrated, that a remedy may be applied, without affecting the pecuniary interest of the more reputable part of the Profession of the Law, while it would unquestionably produce a more general diffusion of Emolument.

If, instead of the various inferior Courts for the recovery of debts, (exclusive of the Courts of Conscience) which have been mentioned in this Chapter, and which are of very limited use on account of appeals lying in all actions above 5*l.*—the Justices, in General Sessions of the Peace, *specially commissioned,* were to be empowered to hear and determine *finally by a Jury*, all actions of debt under 50*l.* and to tax the Costs *in proportion to the amount of the Verdict,*

great

great benefits would result to the Public. *At present, the rule is to allow the same cost for forty shillings as for ten thousand pounds !*—It depends only on the length of the pleadings, and not on the value of the action.

Humanity, Justice, and Policy, plead for an improvement of the System; more particularly when it is recollected that, between *Six* and *Seven Thousand* unfortunate persons are arrested annually on *mesne process* in Middlesex alone, one half of whom are for debts *under twenty pounds.* In the kingdom at large, the number is not less than *Forty Thousand* for trifling debts in the course of a year !—The unavoidable expence, therefore, at the lowest computation, is a most grievous burden, which on many occasions, sends both the plaintiff and defendant to a

* The following authentic table, divided into four Classes, will shew in forcible colours, the evils which arise from there being no distinction between the amount of the sum to be recovered in one action and another, in settling the costs. In the county of Middlesex, in the year 1793, the actions for recovering debts stood thus :

Classes		Number of Writs.	of which	Bailable	Executions	Costs of Actions undefended at 12l. each	Costs of Actions defended at 50l. each.	Net Amount of Debts sued for
						£	£	£
1	from 10 to 20l.	5,719		4,966	753	68,728	285,950	81,791
2	20 to 30	2,267		1,878	389	21,096	113,350	85,675
3	30 to 100	4,367		2,492	1,875	52,404	238,350	257,358
4	£.100 & upw.	2,324		1,769	555	27,160	116,200	1,010,379
		14,677		11,105	3,572	169,388	753,850	1,385,203

Thus it appears, that upwards of one million of money, in the 4th class, is recovered at considerably less than half the expence of 81,791l. in the 1st class.

gaol,

gaol, for the Attorney's bills, to the total ruin of themselves, and often to the destruction of their families.

The Evil, in this view, is exceedingly prominent.—— It involves in it consequences which trench upon the best interests of the Country. The Mischief increases, unperceived by the people at large, and Remedies are not applied; because few men will subject themselves to investigations of great labour, without which facts are not to be obtained; and without facts it is impossible to reason with accuracy, or to draw just conclusions upon any subject.

It will be found upon inquiry, that the miseries of a gaol, by which the inferior orders of the people are often punished, do not so frequently attach to the worthless and profligate part of the Community, as to those who have been useful members of the State— Like the adroit thief, encouraged to proceed by many escapes, Knaves are seldom victims to the severity of the Law.—The Innocent, and often the Industrious, unfkilled in the tricks and artifices which bad men pursue to rid themselves of incumbrances, (for which there is abundant resource in the chicane of the Law), are generally the sufferers.

To incarcerate one member of the body politic, whose misfortunes and losses may have arisen from giving credit to another, who is relieved by a Commission of Bankrupt,* because his debts amounted to
more

* It is to be observed, that the Debtors comprised in the first three classes mentioned in the foregoing note, page 587, are generally

more than 100*l.* seems not well to accord with Justice, Humanity, or State Policy. It debases the minds of thousands whose conduct never deserved such a fate—who were from the nature of their dealings, *although small,* entitled upon the principle adopted by the Legislature, to the same relief which is extended to the higher classes by whom they often suffer—and sometimes too by the most worthless and depraved.—While no good can arise from their confinement, it is thus rendered infinitely more severe than that, which is, in many instances, inflicted on criminal offenders.—Their labour is lost to the Community.—Their families are neglected—and perhaps reared up in vice and idleness to become Nuisances in that Society, of which they might have been virtuous and useful Members.

rally the objects of imprisonment; while the bankrupt-laws relieve the fourth, the insolvency of which class generally produces the distress of the other; who must languish in a gaol and suffer a severe punishment, although it is clear to demonstration, that the Debtor for *ninety-nine* pounds is equally an object of commiseration as another whose debt amounts to *one hundred;* and almost in the same degree subject to accident and misfortune.

Under a System so contrary to reason, and so shocking to humanity, too much praise cannot be bestowed on the founders and supporters of the excellent Institution for the relief of honest, industrious persons imprisoned for small debts. The immense number relieved by this benevolent Society, who have appeared upon inquiry not to have brought misfortunes upon themselves by imprudence, is one of the strongest proofs that can be adduced of the imperfection of the laws; which are tacitly acknowledged to be erroneous, in the case of every person who is discharged by the bounty of the Public.

This,

This, therefore, is a most important branch of what may be called *Civil Police*, highly deserving the attention of the Legislature; because it is not only contrary to Reason, but pregnant with evils which tend to the increase of crimes in a greater degree than is generally supposed.

The extensive and growing intercourse in commercial dealings, and the diffused state of property, must, of course, progressively increase the number of Appeals to Courts of Justice, even under the present System; till at length the duty of the Judges (infinitely more extensive than their predecessors experienced, and increasing every day,) will so multiply, as to render it an act of great cruelty and injustice, not to ease them of the unreasonable labour arising from small Law-suits.

The same reasoning applies to the Members of the Executive Government. As we advance in riches, population, and crimes, the management of the Country becomes more complicated. The labour attached to the higher departments of the State of all descriptions is infinitely greater than a century ago; and yet there is no increase in the number of the first executive responsible officers.—This, (although it has not heretofore attracted notice), when duly considered, will be found to be a. very serious misfortune.

The mind, however active or enlightened, can only compass certain objects. It requires relaxation; it cannot always be upon the stretch.—There

is

is a point beyond which human exertion cannot go—
and hence the necessity of the division of labour, in
proportion to the increase of responsible public duty.
Wherever this does not take place, the Country suffers; an unreasonable burden attaches, by which
means matters of great consequence to the Community must be overlooked, because it is impossible to
compass every thing.

Having thus briefly explained that branch of the
Police of the Capital which is connected with the
department of the Law, together with some of the
most prominent features of abuse, which have grown
out of the present System; as well as the Remedies
which have occurred, as apparently best calculated to
remove these accumulating evils; it remains now
to bring under the review of the Reader, the various
Municipal Regulations, which have been established
for the comfort, accommodation, and convenience of
the inhabitants: and the means used in carrying
them into execution.

The Metropolis of the Empire having been extended so far beyond its ancient limits;—every
parish, hamlet, liberty, or precinct, now contiguous
to the Cities of *London* and *Westminster,* may be considered as a separate Municipality, where the inhabitants regulate the Police of their respective districts,
under the authority of a great variety of different Acts
of Parliament; enabling them to raise money for
paving the streets, and to assess the householders for
the interest thereof, as well as for the annual expence

of

of *watching, cleansing, and removing nuisances and an-noyances.* These funds, as well as the execution of the powers of the different Acts, (excepting where the interference of Magistrates is necessary) are placed in the hands of Trustees, of whom in many instances, the Church Wardens, or Parish Officers for the time being, are Members *ex officio;* and by these different Bodies, all matters relative to the immediate safety, comfort and convenience of the inhabitants are ma-naged and regulated.

These Regulations, however, are mostly founded upon Statutes made in the last and present Reign.

The Act of the 2d of William and Mary, cap. 8, for paving, cleansing, &c. within the City and Liberties of *Westminster*, and the Bills of Mortality, not having been found applicable to modern im-provements, new regulations became necessary; and an incredible number of private Statutes applicable to the different Parishes, Hamlets, and Liberties, composing the Metropolis, have been passed within the last 50 years.

The Act of the 10th George II. cap. 22, esta-blished a system for paving and lighting, cleansing, and watching the City of London: but the Statute which removed *signs, and sign-posts, balconies, spouts, gutters,* and those other *encroachments* and *annoy-ances,* which were felt as grievances, by the inhabi-tants, did not pass till the year 1771.—The 11th of Geo. III. cap. 29, contains a complete and masterly System of that branch of the Police which is con-nected

nected with municipal regulations, and may be considered as a model for every large City in the Empire. This excellent Act extends to every obstruction by carts and carriages, and provides a remedy for all nuisances, which can prove, in any respect, offensive to the inhabitants; and special Commissioners, called *Commissioners of Sewers*, are appointed to ensure a regular execution.   It is further improved by the 33d of his present Majesty, cap. 75, by which the power of the Commissioners is increased, and some nuisances arising from Butchers, Dustmen, &c. further provided against.

In the City and Liberty of Westminster also, many useful Municipal Regulations have been made within the present Century.   The Acts of the 27th of Elizabeth, and the 16th of Charles I. (private Acts) divided the City and Liberties into 12 Wards, and appointed 12 Burgesses to regulate the Police of each Ward; who, with the Dean, or High Steward of Westminster, were authorised to govern this District of the Metropolis.

The Act of the 29th of George II. cap. 25, enabled the Dean, or his High Steward, to choose 80 Constables in a Court Leet; and the same act authorised the appointment of an Annoyance-Jury of 48 inhabitants, to examine weights and measures; and to make presentments of every public nuisance, either in the City or Liberty.—The Acts of the 31st of George II. cap. 17 and 25, improved the former Statute, and allowed a free market to be held in
West-

Westminster.—The Act of the 2d of George III. cap. 21, extended and improved the System for *paving, cleansing, lighting, and watching* the City and Liberty, by including six other adjoining Parishes and Liberties in Middlesex : This Act was afterwards amended by the 3d of his present Majesty, cap. 23.—The Acts 5th Geo. III. caps. 13, 50 ; 11th Geo. III. cap. 22 ; and particularly 14th Geo. III. cap. 90, for regulating the nightly Watch and Constables, made further improvements in the General System by which those branches of Police in Westminster are at present regulated.

In the Borough of Southwark also the same System has been pursued; the Acts 28th Geo. II. cap. 9 ; and 6th Geo. III. cap. 24, having established a System of Municipal Regulations, applicable to this District of the Metropolis ; relative to *markets, hackney-coach stands, paving, cleansing, lighting, watching, marking streets*, and *numbering houses*, and placing the whole under the management of Commissioners.

In contemplating the great leading features of Municipal Regulation, nothing places England in a situation so superior to most other countries, with regard to cleanliness, as the *System of the Sewers*, under the management of special Commissioners, in different parts of the Kingdom ; introduced so early as by the Act 6th Henry VI. cap. 5, and regulated by the Acts 6th Henry VIII. cap. 10 ; 23d Henry VIII. cap. 5 ; and 25th Henry VIII. cap. 10:

—after-

—afterwards improved by the 3d and 4th Edward VI. cap. 8; 1st Mary, Stat. 3, cap. 11; 13th Elizabeth, cap. 9; 3d James I. cap. 14; and 7th Anne, cap. 10.

Sewers being so early introduced into the Metropolis, as well as into other Cities and Towns, in consequence of the general System, every offensive nuisance was removed through this medium, and the inhabitants early accustomed to the advantages and comforts of cleanliness.

Another feature strongly marking the wisdom and attention of our ancestors, was the introduction of *Water*, for the supply of the Metropolis, in the reign of James I. in 1604. The improvements which have been since made for the convenience of the inhabitants, in extending the supplies by means of the New River, and also by the accession of the Thames water, through the medium of the London Bridge, Chelsea, York Buildings, Shadwell, and other water works, it is not necessary to detail.

The Act 9th Anne, cap. 23, first established the regulations with regard to *Hackney Coaches* and *Chairs*, which have been improved and extended by several subsequent Statutes, *viz.* 10 Anne, cap. 19; 12 Anne, stat. 9, cap. 14; 1 Geo, I. cap. 57; 12 Geo. I. cap. 12; 30 Geo. II. cap. 22; 4 Geo. III. cap. 36; 7 Geo. III. cap. 44; 10 Geo. III. cap. 44; 11 Geo. III. caps. 24, 28; 12 Geo. III. cap. 49; 24 Geo. III. stat. 2. cap. 27; 26 Geo. III. cap. 72; 32 Geo. III. cap. 47; 33 Geo. III. cap. 75.

These

These Acts authorize *one thousand coaches, and four hundred hackney chairs,* to be licensed for the accommodation of the inhabitants of the Metropolis ; and Magistrates, as well as the Commissioners, are empowered to decide, in a summary way, upon all complaints arising between Coachmen or Chairmen, and the inhabitants who may have occasion to employ them.

Carts and other carriages have also been regulated by several different Acts, *viz.* 1 Geo. I. stat. 2. cap. 57; 18 Geo. II. cap. 33; 24 Geo. II. cap. 43; 30 Geo. II. cap. 22; 7 Geo. III. cap. 44; and 24 Geo. III. cap. 27. The Statutes contain a very complete System, relative to this branch of Police ; by virtue of which all complaints arising from offences under these Acts, are also cognizable by the Magistrates, in a summary way.

The Act of the 34th of George III. cap. 65, established an improved system, with regard to *Watermen plying on the River Thames.*—The Lord Mayor and Aldermen are empowered to make Rules and Orders for their Government* ; and, with the Recorder and the Justices of the Peace of the respective Counties, and places next adjoining to the Thames, have equal jurisdiction in all situations between Gravesend and Windsor, to put in execution not

---

* No Rules or Orders have yet been published, although nearly six years have elapsed since the passing of this Act. The Public are, therefore, without the means of punishing or controlling Watermen, which is felt as a serious misfortune.

only

only the *Laws,* but also the Rules and Orders relative to such Watermen, which shall be sent to the several Public Offices in the Metropolis, and to the Clerks of the Peace of the Counties joining the Thames, within 30 days after such Rules are made or altered. The Magistrates have power given them to fine Watermen for extortion and misbehaviour: and persons refusing to pay the fares authorised by Law, may be compelled to do so, with all charges, or be imprisoned for one month; and whoever shall give a Waterman a fictitious name or place of abode, forfeits 5l.

Offences relative to the Driving of Cattle improperly, usually termed *Bullock Hunting,* are also determined by the Magistrates, in the same summary way, under the authority of an Act 21st Geo. III, cap. 67; by which every person is authorised to seize delinquents guilty of this very dangerous offence.

The last great feature of useful Municipal Police which the Author will mention, consists in the excellent regulations relative to *Buildings, Projections,* and *Fires;* first adopted after the Fire of London in 1666, and extended and improved by several Acts of Parliament passed, from that time, down to the 14th of his present Majesty.

The Act of the 14th of George III. cap. 78, which repeals the former Acts, besides regulating the mode of building houses in future, so as to render them *ornamental, commodious,* and *secure* against the accidents of fire, established other useful rules for the prevention

tion of this dreadful calamity; by rendering it incumbent on Churchwardens to provide one or more engines in every parish, to be in readiness, on the shortest notice, to extinguish fires, and also ladders to favour escapes: And that every facility might be afforded with regard to water, it is also incumbent on the Churchwardens to fix stop-blocks and fire-plugs at convenient distances, upon all the main pipes within the parish; and to place a mark in the street where they are to be found, and to have an instrument or key ready to open such fire-plugs, so that the water may be accessible on the shortest possible notice. That every thing also might be done to ensure dispatch, the person bringing the first parish engine to any fire is entitled to 30s. the second to 20s. and the third to 10s. paid by the parish; excepting in cases where chimnies are on fire, and then the expence ultimately falls upon the person inhabiting the house or place where it originated.

This excellent Statute, so salutary in its effects with regard to many important Regulations of Police, also obliges all Beadles and Constables, on the breaking out of any fire, to repair immediately to the spot, with their long staves, and to protect the sufferers from the depredation of thieves; and to assist in removing effects, and in extinguishing the flames.

These outlines will explain, in some measure, by what means the System of the Police, in most of its great features, is conducted in the Metropolis—to which it may be necessary to add, that the Beadles of
each

each Parish, are the proper persons to whom application may be made, in the first instance, in case of any inconvenience or nuisance. The City and Police Magistrates, in their respective Courts, if not immediately authorized to remedy the wrong that is suffered, will point out how it may be effected.

It is, however, earnestly to be wished, that (like the Building Act just mentioned), one general Law, comprehending the whole of the excellent regulations made for the City of London, so far as they will apply, could be extended to every part of the Metropolis, and its suburbs ; that a perfect uniformity might prevail, in the penalties and punishments to be inflicted for the several Offences against the comfort or convenience of the Inhabitants.—At present it often happens, that an Offence in one Parish, is no act of Delinquency in another.

The great object is to simplify every System as much as possible ;—complicated Establishments are always more expensive than is necessary, and constantly liable to abuses.

The annual expence to the Inhabitants, in consequence of all those Municipal Regulations just detailed, is, perhaps, higher than in any other City in the world.—Including the Poor's-rate, it amounts, on an average, to full 25 per cent. on the gross rental of the Metropolis: and is supposed to exceed one million sterling a year !

A superintending Police would, in many instances, correct the want of intelligence, which is apparent,

and

and enlighten the local Managers in such a manner, as not only to promote objects of œconomy, calculated to abridge and keep within bounds an enormous and growing expence, but also to suggest improvements by which it might be reduced, and many solid advantages be acquired by the Community.

It is impossible to examine, with the mind of a man of business, the various Establishments which have become necessary for promoting the comfort and convenience of great Societies, without lamenting, in many instances, the unnecessary waste that prevails, and the confusion and irregularity which often ensue, merely for want of system, judgment, and knowledge of the subject.

Various, indeed, are the evils and disorders which Time engenders, in every thing connected with the affairs of civil Society, requiring a constant and uniform attention, *increasing, as the pressures increase,* for the purpose of keeping them within bounds ; that as much happiness and comfort may be extended to the People as can possibly arise from a well-regulated and energetic Police, conducted with purity, zeal, and intelligence.

We are arrived at an epoch full of difficulties and dangers, producing wonderful events, and still pregnant with consequences, in their nature, stretching beyond the usual course of human conjecture, where it is impossible to judge of the ultimate issue.

Under

Under such circumstances, it becomes, more than ever, necessary to make prudent arrangements for the general safety, for amending the morals, and promoting the happiness of the People; by improved Laws, extending protection to all, and correcting those evils, which are felt as a burden upon the Community.

CHAP.

C H A P. XX.

A summary View of the Evils detailed in the preceding Chapters.—The great opulence and extensive Trade of the Metropolis assigned as a Cause of the increase and multiplication of Crimes, and of the great extent of the Depredations which are committed.—Arguments in favour of a more energetic Police as the only means of remedying those Evils.—A wide Field opened to Men of Virtue and Talents to do good.— A general View of the estimated Depredations annually in the Metropolis and its Vicinity, amounting in all to Two Millions Sterling.—General Observations and Reflections on the strong Features of degraded Humanity, which this Summary of Turpitude exhibits.—Observations on the further Evils arising from the deficiency of the System with respect to Officers of Justice.—The want of a Prosecutor for the Crown, and the inadequacy of Punishments. A View of the Remedies proposed—1st. With respect to the Corruption of Morals.—2d. The means of preventing Crimes in general.—3d. Offences committed on the River Thames.—4th.—Offences in the Public Arsenals and Ships of War.—5th. Counterfeiting Money and fabricating Bank Notes; 6th. Punishments.—7th. Further advantages of an improved System of Police.—Concluding Reflections.

IN

In taking a summary view of the various evils and remedies, which have been detailed in this Work, it may be right, previously to apprize the Reader, that in contemplating the extent and magnitude of the aggregate depredations, which are presumed to be committed in the course of a year, it is necessary to measure them *by a scale proportioned to the unparal-leled amount of moving property exposed in transit in this great Metropolis*, as well as the vast and unexampled increase of this property, within the last half century; during which period there has certainly been an accumulation of not less than two-thirds, in commerce as well as in manufactures.

It has not, perhaps, generally attracted notice, that, besides being the Seat of the *Government—of the Law—Learning*, and the *Fine Arts*,—the resort of the Nobility and the Opulent from every part of the British Empire, however distant; LONDON, from being a great *depôt* for all the manufactures of the country, and also the goods of foreign nations as well as East India and colonial produce, is not only the first Commercial City at present existing, but is also one of the greatest and most extensive Manufacturing Towns, perhaps in the World; combining in one spot every attribute that can occasion an assemblage of moving property, unparalleled in point of extent, magnitude, and value in the whole Globe. —From the abstract of Imports and Exports in
page

page 215 of this Work, it appears that above 13,000 vessels,* including their repeated voyages, arrive at, and depart from, the Port of London, with merchandize, in the course of a year; besides a vast number of river craft, employed in the trade of the interior country, bringing and carrying away property, estimated at above *Seventy Millions Sterling.*†

In addition to this, it is calculated, that above 40,000 waggons and other carriages, including their repeated journies, arrive and depart laden, in both instances, with articles of domestic, colonial, East India and foreign merchandize; occasioning a transit of perhaps (when cattle, grain, and provisions sent for the consumption of the inhabitants, are included) *Fifty Millions more.* If we take into the account the vast quantity of merchandize and moveable property of every species deposited in the various *maritime magazines, timber-yards, piece-goods' warehouses, shops, manufactories, store-houses, public markets, dwelling-houses, inns, new buildings,* and *other repositories,* and which pass from one place to another, it will establish a foundation for supposing that, in this way, property to the amount of *Fifty Millions* more at least, is annually exposed to depredation; making a Sum of *One Hundred and Seventy Millions;* independent of the moving articles in ships of war and transports, and

* See Table in page 215. † See page 216.

in

in the different Arsenals, Dock-yards, and Repositories in the Tower of London, and at Deptford,
Woolwich, Sheerness, and various smaller magazines, in the daily course of being received and sent
away, supposed to amount to *Thirty Millions* more;
making in the whole an aggregate sum of *Two Hundred Millions.* Thus an immense property becomes
exceedingly exposed, in all the various ways already explained in the course of this Work; and
the *estimated* amount of the *annual depredations* hereafter enumerated under these respective heads will
cease to be a matter of surprise, if measured by the
enormous scale of property above particularized.
Although it is supposed to amount to about *Two
Millions* sterling, it sinks to a trifle, in contemplating
the magnitude of the capital, *scarcely reaching one
per cent. on the value of property passing in transit
in the course of a year.*

It is not, therefore, so much the actual loss that
is sustained (great as it certainly is) which is to
be deplored *as the mischief which arises from the destruction of the morals of so numerous a body of people; who must be directly or collaterally engaged in
perpetrating smaller offences, and in fraudulent and
criminal pursuits.*

This, in a political point of view, is a consideration of a very serious and alarming nature, infinitely
worse in its consequences than even those depredations which arise from acts of violence committed
by more atrocious offenders; the numbers of which
latter

latter have been shewn to be small, in comparison with other delinquents, and not to have increased in any material degree for the last 50 years; while *inferior thefts, river-plunder, pillage, embezzlement, and frauds, in respect to public property, coining base money, forgeries under various ramifications, cheating by means of swindling and other criminal practices, and purchasing and dealing in stolen goods*, have advanced in a degree, commensurate to the great and rapid influx of wealth, which has arisen from the vast increase of the commerce and manufactures of the Country, and the general accumulation of property by British subjects in the East and West Indies, and in foreign Countries.

The evils, therefore, are the more prominent, as they have become so exceedingly diffused; and implicate in criminality numerous individuals, of whom a very large proportion were formerly untainted with any of that species of Delinquency, which now renders them, (for their own sakes—for the benefit of their families—and for the interest of public morals,) objects of peculiar attention on the part of the Legislature, as well as the Police of the Country.

The habits they have acquired are, doubtless, very alarming, as in the destruction of their own morals, they also destroy those of the rising generation; and still more so, as the existing Laws, and the present System of Police, have been found so totally inadequate to the Object of Prevention.

Indeed

Indeed it is but too evident, that nothing useful can be effected without a variety of Regulations, such as have been suggested in different parts of this Work. It is not, however, by the adoption of any one *remedy* singly applied, or applied by piece-meal, but by a combination of the whole Legislative *Powers, Regulations, Establishments,* and *superintending Agencies* already suggested, (and particularly by those recommended by the Select Committee of the House of Commons, *which may be considered as the Ground Work*) that Crimes are, in any degree, to be prevented, or kept in check. And it is not to be expected, that such Remedies can be either complete or effectual, unless there be a sufficient Fund appropriated for the purpose of giving vigour and energy to the General System.

The object is of such astonishing magnitude, and the abuses which are meant to be corrected, are of so much consequence to the *State,* as well as to the *Individual,* and the danger of a progressive increase is so evidently well established by experience, that it is impossible to look at that subject with indifference, when once it is developed and understood.

It opens a wide field for doing good, to men of virtue, talents, and abilities, who love their country, and glory in its prosperity. Such men will speedily perceive, that this prosperity can only be of short duration,—if public morals are neglected,—if no check is given to the growing depravity which prevails, and if measures are not adopted to guard the
rising

rising generation against the evil examples to which they are exposed.

Philanthropists will also, in this volume, find abundant scope for the exercise of that benevolence, and those efforts in the cause of humanity, which occupy their attention, and constitute their chief pleasure.—It is earnestly to be hoped, that it may produce an universal desire to attain those objects, which are shewn to be so immediately connected with the Public good.

For the purpose of elucidating, in some degree, the dreadful effect of the profligacy and wickedness, which have been opened to the view of the Reader, and occasioned the perpetration of Crimes and offences of every species and denomination, the following Estimate has been made up from information derived through a variety of different channels.—It exhibits at one view, the supposed aggregate amount of the various depredations committed in the Metropolis and its environs, in the course of a year.

The intelligent reader will perceive at once, that in the nature of things, such a calculation cannot be perfectly accurate; because there are no precise data upon which it may be formed; but if it approaches in any degree near the truth, (and the Author has discovered nothing in the course of four years to alter the opinion he originally formed in any material degree,) it will fully answer the purpose intended; by affording many useful and important hints favourable to those improvements which are felt to be necessary by all; though till of late, understood by very few.

It

It is introduced also (merely as a calculation) for the purpose of arresting the attention of the Public, in a greater degree, and of directing it not only to inquiries similar to those upon which the Author has formed his conjectures; but also to the means of procuring those improvements in the Laws, and in the System of the Police, which have become so indispensably necessary for the security of every individual possessing property in this great Metropolis.

———

AN ESTIMATE *of the annual Amount and Value of the Depredations committed on Public and Private Property in the Metropolis and its Vicinity,* IN ONE YEAR. *Specifying the Nature of such Depredations under Six different Heads, viz :—*

1. *Small Thefts,* committed in a little way by *menial Servants, Chimney Sweepers, Dustmen, Porters, Apprentices, Journeymen, Stable Boys, Itinerant Jews, and others,* from *Dwelling-Houses, Stables, Out-Houses, Warehouses, Shops, Founderies, Workshops, New Buildings, Public Houses,* and in short every other place where property is deposited, which may be specifically estimated and subdivided as follows:

	Tons.	£.
Articles new and old, of iron and steel - -	5000	100,000
——————— brass	1500	150,000
——————— copper	1000	120,000
——————— lead	2500	50,000
——————— pewter; solder, and tin - -	300	35,000

Carried over   £.455,000

Pewter

Brought over   £.455,000

Pewter pots, stolen from 5204 Pub- *Tons.*

licans   -   -   500   *55,000

Small articles of plate, china, glass -
    ware, sadlery, harness, and other
    portable articles of house and table
    furniture, books, tea, sugar, soap,
    candles, liquors, &c. &c. &c.   -   100,000

Piece-Goods from shops and ware-
    houses, by servants, porters, &c.   50,000

Wearing apparel, bed and table
    linen, &c.   -   -   -   40,000

Silk, cotton, and worsted yarn, em-
    bezzled by Winders and others in
    Spitalfields, &c. formerly 20,000*l.* a
    year, now supposed to be   -   10,000

—————£.710,000

2. *Thefts upon the River and Quays,*
    committed in a little way on board
    ships in the River Thames, whilst
    discharging their cargoes ; and af-
    terwards upon the Wharfs, Quays,
    and Warehouses, when the same
    are landing, weighing, and storing ;
    by glutmen, lumpers, jobbers, la-
    bourers, porters, lightermen, boys
    called mudlarks, and others em-
    ployed, or lurking about for
    plunder, *viz.*

Carried over   £.710,000

---

* The Publicans in their petition to the House of Commons
(1796) estimated their loss at 100,000*l.* But there is some reason
to suppose this was exaggerated.

Raw

Brought over   £.710,000

Raw sugars, rum, coffee, chocolate, pimento, ginger, cotton, dying, woods, and every other article of West-India produce, estimated at the commencement of the Marine Police Establishment at 232,000*l.* a year; but now reduced to   -   50,000

East-India goods, and merchandize from Africa, the Mediterranean, America, the Baltic, the Continent of Europe, coasting trade, &c. &c. 274,000*l.* now reduced by the Marine Police Institution to   -   155,000

Ship stores and tackling, including cordage, sails, tar, pitch, tallow, provisions, &c. taken from above 10,000 different vessels, estimated at 100,000*l.* but now reduced since the Establishment of the Marine Police, according to Estimate, to   45,000

————£.250,000

3. *Thefts and Frauds* committed in his Majesty's Dock-yards and other public Repositories, situated on the River Thames; including the plunder, pillage, and frauds, by which public property (exclusive of metals) is embezzled in the said stores, and from ships of war. (Besides the frauds, plunder and pillage, in the Dock-yards, and from ships of war at Chatham, Portsmouth, Ply-

Carried over   £960,000

mouth,

Brought over　　　£.960,000

mouth, &c. at all times enormous, but especially in time of war; when public property is unavoidably most exposed, equal at least to 700,000*l.* a year more:) making in all, one million sterling, at least; but reduced by the Marine Police from 300,000*l.* to　-　-　-　200,000

4. *Depredations* committed by means of burglaries, highway robberies, and other more atrocious thefts, viz.

　1. Burglaries by Housebreakers, in plate, and other articles　-　100,000

　2. Highway Robberies, in money, watches, bank-notes, &c.　55,000

　3. Private stealing, and picking of pockets, &c.　-　-　25,000

　4. Stealing horses, cattle, sheep, poultry, corn, provender, potatoes, turnips, vegetables, fruits, &c. in London and the Vicinity　100,000
　　　　　　　　　　　　———£.280,000

5. *Frauds* by the coinage and recolouring of base money, counterfeited of the similitude of the current gold, silver and copper coin of the Realm　　310,000

6. *Frauds* by counterfeiting bank notes, public securities, powers of attorney, bonds, bills, and notes; by swindling, cheating and obtaining money and goods by false pretences, &c. &c.　-　-　-　250,000
　　　　　　　　　　　———————
　　　　　　　　　　　£.2,000,000

RECAPITU-

RECAPITULATION

1. Small Thefts - - -	£.710,000
2. Thefts upon the Rivers and Quays -	250,000
3. Thefts in the Dock-yards, &c. in the Thames	200,000
4. Burglaries, Highway-Robberies, &c. &c.	280,000
5. Coining base Money - - -	310,000
6. Forging Bills, Swindling, &c. -	250,000
Total	* £2,000,000

The foregoing Estimate, grounded on the best information that can be procured, exhibits a melancholy picture of the general depravity which prevails; and

* This sum will, no doubt, astonish the Reader at first view; and may even go very far to stagger his belief: but when the vast extent of the trade and commerce of London is considered, the great quantity of money, Bank notes, and stationary or fixed property of a portable nature, as well as moving effects, all which has been estimated, exclusive of horses, cattle, corn, provender, fruit, vegetables, &c. at two hundred million sterling, (*See p.*605.) it will cease to be a matter of surprize, that under an incorrect System of Police and deficient Laws, the depredations are estimated so high. It would have equally attracted attention with a view to an improvement in the Police, and of course have answered the Author's purpose full as well to have reduced the estimate to *one half the present sum ;* but being solicitous to approach as nearly to the truth as possible, he considered himself bound to offer it in its present form, which after being four years under the view of the Public, not only stands unimpeached; but although the Author himself, after the additional experience he has acquired, has attempted a new modification; and although the River Plunder is greatly reduced, the aggregate remains nearly as before.

which

which is heightened in a considerable degree by the reflection, that among the perpetrators of the crimes there particularized, are to be numbered persons, who from their rank and situation in life would scarcely be suspected of either committing or conniving at frauds, for the purpose of enriching themselves at the expence of the Nation.

Avarice is ever an eager, though not always a clear-sighted passion; and when gratified at the price of violating the soundest principles of honesty and justice, a sting must remain behind, which no affluence can banish,—no pecuniary gratification alleviate.

In contemplating these strong features of degraded Humanity, it cannot escape the observant Reader, how small a part of the annual depredations upon public and private property is to be placed to the account of those Criminals who alone attract notice, from the force and violence they use; and to whose charge the whole of the inconveniences felt by the Public, is generally laid, namely, *common thieves and pick-pockets; highway-men and foot-pad robbers.*—But for this Estimate, it could not have been believed how large a share of the property annually plundered, stolen, embezzled, or acquired in a thousand different ways, by means *unlawful, unjust* and *immoral,* in this great Metropolis, is acquired by Criminals of other descriptions; whose extensive ravages on property are the more dangerous, in proportion to the secrecy with which they are conducted.

Next to the evils which are experienced by the
general

general corruption of morals, and by the actual depredations upon public and private property as now brought under the review of the Reader, by means of a summary detail, it has been shewn, in the course of this Work, that many pressures arise from the defects in the Laws relative to the detection, trial, and conviction of Offenders, from the want of an improved System respecting Constables, and particularly from the deficiency of Jurisdiction in the City and Police Magistrates,—the want of Funds to remunerate Officers of Justice, and to reward Watchmen, Patroles, and Beadles, who may act meritoriously in apprehending Delinquents; and lastly, in the trial of Criminals, for want of a general *Prosecutor for the Crown*, to attend to the Public interest, and to prevent those Frauds (in suborning evidence, and in compounding Felonies,) whereby many of the most abandoned are let loose upon Society, while those who are novices in crimes are often punished.

The next stated in the class of evils is, that which arises from the laws as they now stand, relative to *Punishments.*—Their extreme severity, in rendering such a multitude of crimes capital, which Juries can never be made to believe are of that nature, in point of actual atrocity, has proved a very serious misfortune to the Country, in the administration of criminal Justice.—Because the punishment is too severe, it frequently happens that the Delinquent is sent back upon Society, encouraged to renew his depredations upon the Public by his having escaped (although guilty) without any chastisement at all.

It

It is unquestionably true, and little doubt will be entertained by any who attentively examine this Work, that the dread of severe punishment, in the manner the Law is executed at present, has not the least effect in deterring hardened Offenders from the commission of Crimes.

An opinion seems to have been formed, that Crimes were to be prevented by the severity of the punishment. That this opinion has been erroneous seems to be proved by incontestible evidence adduced in various parts of this Work ; and elucidated by a variety of reasoning, which it is hoped cannot fail to bring conviction to the mind of every Reader, who will bestow time in the investigation of a subject of so much importance to Society.

Last, in the enumeration of the evils detailed, are those deficiencies and imperfections which arise from the *Police System;* as explained in the 16th and 17th Chapters.—A variety of inconveniences, it appears, originate from this source ; and reasons are adduced to demonstrate that the National Security, and Prosperity, are more dependent on a well-regulated and correct System of Police, than has been generally supposed ; and that the adoption of the Plan of Police, explained in the 18th Chapter, and recommended by the Select Committee on Finance, would prove an inestimable blessing to the Country.

Having thus briefly glanced at the Evils detailed in this Work, it now becomes necessary to lay before the Reader a similar collected view of THE REMEDIES.

In

In accomplishing this object, while the Author ventures to indulge a hope that these which have been suggested, or at least a part of them, may be brought in due time, under the consideration of the Legislature, for the purpose of being enacted into Laws, or otherwise carried into effect; they are now presented to the Reader under the following heads, *viz.*

I. THE PREVENTION OF THE PRESENT CORRUPTION OF MORALS, as originating from ill-regulated Public Houses, Tea-Gardens, Theatres, and other places of Public Amusement; indecent Publications; Ballad-Singers—Female Prostitution—Servants out of Place—The Lotterry ; Gaming—Indigence, and various other causes.

II. THE PREVENTION OF OFFENCES ; and first of those denominated *Misdemeanors* ; such as Cheating and Swindling ; Robbing Orchards; Petty Assaults, and Perjury.—Next of Counterfeit Coinage ; River Plunder ; Plunder in Dock-yards, &c. Lastly of the Prevention of Crimes in General, under *twelve* different heads, specifying the Remedies proposed on this subject in the course of the Work.

III. AMENDMENT OF THE EXISTING LAWS ; respecting the obtaining *Goods* and *Chattels* under false pretences — Pawnbrokers — Forgeries — Receiving Stolen Goods—Arson—Lodgers—Registering Lodging Houses—Plunder on Houses—Gypsies—Milk—Speedy Trial of Offences committed within five Miles of the Metropolis—Imprisonment for Debt, and Recovery of Debts under 50*l.*

CONCLUDING OBSERVATIONS.

SUMMARY

SUMMARY VIEW

OF THE

REMEDIES PROPOSED.

THE First Step to all improvements in Civil Society is that which relates to the *Morals of the People.*—While in the higher and middle ranks of life a vast portion of Virtue and Philanthropy is manifested, perhaps in a greater degree than is to be found in any Country or Nation in the World, it is much to be lamented, that among the lower Class a species of profligacy and improvidence prevails, which as it applies to the Metropolis of the Empire, is certainly not exceeded in any other Capital in Europe.—To this source may be traced the great extent and increasing multiplication of Crimes, insensibly generating evils calculated, ultimately, to sap the foundation of the State.

The grand object, therefore, must be to devise means for the purpose of checking, and gradually preventing the evils arising from the

Corruption of Morals.

To effect so valuable a purpose to the Community at large—to render the labour of the lower orders of the people more productive to themselves, and more beneficial to the Nation, recourse must be had to that superintending System of *preventive Police* which has been recommended generally by the Select Committee of the House of Commons, and which

which has been particularly detailed in the 18th Chapter of this Treatise.

It is thus by giving Police its true and genuine character, and divesting it of those judicial functions which are the province of Magistrates alone, that a proper line will be drawn between *Prevention,* and those proceedings which lead to *Punishment* after an offence is actually committed. It is through this medium also that a change is to be effected in the Morals of the People, calculated to abridge the number of acts of delinquency, and to lead the perpetrators gradually into the walks of innocence, sobriety, and industry.—One of the first steps towards the attainment of these objects will be a Systematic attention to

PUBLIC-HOUSES.

In the Eleventh Chapter of this Work, the progress of the corruption of Morals through this medium, from the Infant to the Adult, is brought under the review of the Reader; and it is considered as of the highest importance that general and apposite rules for the proper conduct of those houses, now the haunts of vice and profligacy, should be formed and recommended by a Board of Police to the Magistrates acting in all the Licensing Divisions of the Country. The benefits arising from an uniform and well-digested System might thus be extended throughout the Country: and an accurate and permanent administration of this branch of Police secured thro' the medium of a general *Centre,* where responsibility

should

should rest, and from which the Licensing Magistrates should receive *information, assistance,* and *support,* in whatever related to the proper regulation of Alehouses, particularly in the Metropolis and the surrounding Counties.

Regular reports of the number of these Alehouses in each Licensing District in proportion to the extent of population; and details of the effects produced by an adherence to the general Rules which may be prescribed, would lead to new and useful suggestions which must ultimately give a favourable turn to the manners of the lower classes of the people, not only with respect to the diminution of Crimes, but also with regard to their domestic Comforts.—They would be rendered more independent of Parochial aid; and, above all, the education and habits of the rising generation would be easily improved—*Apprentices* thus secured against the evil examples of which young minds are but too susceptible, would enter upon life with dispositions differently formed, and with that sort of bias which stimulates to industry and virtue, instead of idleness, profligacy, and vice.—In this, as in many other instances, the happiness and virtue of the individual are intimately combined with the best interests of the state.

Such prudent and discreet regulations would have a general tendency to make Public-houses what they were originally intended to be by the Legislature— *Places of mere refreshment,* and not haunts of idleness as at present.—The resource now afforded

by

by them to actual *Thieves*, *Burglars*, *Pickpockets*, *Highwaymen*, *Swindlers*, *Cheats*, *Gamblers*, and *Dealers* in *Counterfeit Money*, would not only be cut off, but those who have been accustomed to resort to these houses from the temporary want of employment:—such as persons broke down by misfortune and indiscretion—servants out of place, and strangers resorting to the Metropolis, would no longer be assailed by those temptations which contribute in so great a degree to recruit the gangs of Criminal Depredators. Nothing but a well-regulated Police, under a proper System of Controul, can remedy those evils arising from Public-houses, and it is earnestly to be hoped, that the Functions proposed to be exercised by the Central Board of Police would effect this valuable purpose.

Public Gardens.

The corruption of Morals has been in a considerable degree promoted, not only by the assemblage of lewd and debauched company who have of late years crowded to Public Gardens; but also by the unrestrained Licence which has been permitted in these places of amusement.—This circumstance has not only called upon the Magistrates to refuse the renewal of the Licences to several of the Occupiers, Lessees, and Proprietors, but it has precluded the more decent and respectable part of the Public in the middle walks of life, from what might, under proper regulations, be considered as an innocent and
a desirable

a desirable recreation for the Inhabitants of an overgrown Metropolis.—Most of the remaining Public Gardens have of late years fallen into disrepute, to the injury of the Proprietors, who, under the present deficient System of Police, have no means of protecting themselves against the consequences of those irregularities which operate powerfully in diminishing the number of visitors, upon which their emolument depends.

While profligate and debauched characters of both Sexes find not only an easy access to these places of amusement, but also have permission to insult Public Morals, by doing violence to the rules of decency and decorum; it is evident that they must gradually cease to be desirable as a recreation to the virtuous part of the Community; and there appears to be no remedy but by means of *Police regulations,* prescribing proper rules, with officers appointed by the Central Board, for the purpose of carrying them into effect*. Indeed, if such places of resort were licensed only by the proposed Central Board, it might be productive of the greatest advantages; and they might be a fair source of Revenue for Police purposes, to a certain moderate extent.

* See pages 345, 346, and 347.

PLACES

PLACES OF PUBLIC AMUSEMENT LICENSED BY MAGISTRATES.

The general concourse of loose and immoral cha- racters of both Sexes who frequent the Summer Exhibitions, and the irregularities which are un- avoidable under such circumstances, tend in no small degree to the corruption of Morals; and while it is admitted that such amusements are necessary in great Communities, it is of the utmost importance that they should not only be regulated by the Police, with respect to the nature of the *Spectacle* or *Exhi- bition*, so as clearly to ascertain that it has no im- moral tendency,† but also that the utmost decorum should be preserved by means of proper Officers acting under the proposed Central Board.—This be- comes the more important, as a large proportion of the frequenters of these places of amusement are of the middle and inferior ranks of life, and many of them very young and susceptible of loose impressions, which renders it highly necessary that authority should be vested only in the responsible Board of Police, to grant or to refuse Licences: to which a moderate Revenue might be attached to defray the expence of a regulating System.

THE THEATRES.

Without entering upon a discussion how far many of the Theatrical exhibitions which are brought for-

† See page 348.

ward

ward tend to improve, or to injure the Morals of the People—it is, at least, evident that the unrestrained Licence which is permitted to Males and Females in the walks of Prostitution in the Lobbies, and even in the Boxes of the Playhouses, and the indecent behaviour and unbecoming language which is frequently uttered in the view and hearing of the respectable part of the Community who frequent these places of resort, with the younger branches of their families, must tend in no inconsiderable degree to the corruption of Morals *. It is, therefore, suggested that a Police, applicable to this object, should be formed by the proposed Central Board; and also for the purpose of effectually securing the Public against the attacks and depredations of the hordes of Pickpockets who infest the avenues of the Theatres, and have long been a reproach to the Police of the Metropolis.

IMMORAL AND INDECENT PUBLICATIONS, AND PRINTS.

Nothing can exhibit in a stronger point of view the deficiency of the Police System than the number of immoral Books which are published and circulated, and the indecent Prints which are exhibited and sold in the various streets of the Metropolis, all tending in no inconsiderable degree to the corruption of Morals.—Let it once become a part of the Functions of the proposed Board of Police to take cognizance of these abuses, and they will

* See page 338.

soon

soon ceases to convey that poison to young minds, which ultimately leads to dissolute manners and loose conduct in the general intercourse of life.

Ballad-Singers.

Since it has never been possible, under the existing Laws, to suppress the herd of Ballad-Singers which are to be found in such multitudes in every part of the Metropolis, and, indeed, in all the large Towns in the Kingdom : and which at present are under the controul of a very feeble Police, which does not, and indeed cannot, restrain effectually the immoral, and often seditious tendency of the Songs sung to the listening multitude—Why might not this lowest cast of amusement be turned to good purposes, tending to counteract and prevent the corruption of Morals, which are at present generated through this medium ? Under a responsible Board of Police such an object is certainly attainable *, and the present state of things points out the policy and necessity of carrying it into effect.

Female Seduction.

In contemplating the excessive evils, and the dreadful consequences which result from Female Seduction, whether it applies to married or single women †, it would seem to be a matter of astonishment that no punishment has been inflicted by the

* See page 349.   † See pages 33, and 34.

criminal

criminal Law, by which the destroyers of innocence, and of the peace of families, could be held up as public examples of infamy.—A corporal punishment accompanied with circumstances of obloquy and disgrace, is certainly not too severe where a delinquent plunges a Female (whether married or single) into a situation, in most instances, worse than death itself; since when abandoned by her Seducer, she is not only exposed to the reproach and contumely of the World, but subjected to herd with the phalanx of Prostitutes who contribute so much to the corruption of Morals, and where the miserable victim may be said to die, perhaps, *a thousand deaths* before her actual dissolution.—Surely an offence producing such dreadful consequences should, as a mean of prevention, be marked not only as an object of *Criminal Punishment*, but of *pecuniary retribution to the injured party.*— Were such a law in force, the numerous instances of Female Seduction would be greatly diminished: while the injured woman, under such unhappy circumstances, might, after the Conviction of a Jury, have a fair prospect of being again restored to her friends, and, perhaps, to Society.

FEMALE PROSTITUTION.

In the 12th Chapter of this Treatise,* a general view is given of the shocking corruption of Morals, which is generated by the vast increase of common

* See pages 333 to 34.

Prostitutes

Prostitutes in the Metropolis.—It now becomes necessary to explain the specific remedies which the Author had in view for the purpose of lessening this enormous and afflicting evil.

Its magnitude, and the wrongs that result from it, are too vast and extensive to admit of any common remedy.—The excellent Institution of the Magdalen Hospital in the course of 40 years, has only been able to reform or reconcile to their friends, 2,217, out of 3,250 who have been actually admitted within that period—and even some of these have relapsed into their former errors : though others, who have been discharged at their own request, have behaved well.

But when a survey is taken of the aggregate number of unhappy women who have entered the walks of Prostitution within the last 40 years in the Metropolis, succeeding one another perhaps every 13 years upon an average, it is probable that from 80 to 100,000 have passed through a miserable life, the irreclaimable victims to this debasing turpitude, without the means of rescuing themselves from a situation so pitiable and calamitous.

The fact is, that the evil is of too great a magnitude to admit of a cure through the medium of private benevolence.—Relief without *reform*, and *reputable employment*, or reconciliation to relations, will do nothing towards a diminution of the evil.—It will require an extensive System and a corresponding expence, which can only be compassed by a

Police

Police applicable to this particular object, aided by appropriate regulations.

After the maturest consideration of the subject, the Author ventures to offer the following Propositions as the most likely, in the first instance, to excite a desire in many of those unhappy women to alter their degrading course of life, and to facilitate their introduction into situations, where, through the medium of a reconciliation with their friends, or otherwise, at least a considerable part might be restored to Society who are lost at present; while, under the regulations hereafter proposed, the streets of the Metropolis will no longer hold out allurements to vice and debauchery, ruinous to the Morals of youth, and disgraceful to the Police of the Metropolis.

1st. It is proposed, with a view to prevent common Prostitutes from walking the streets to assail passengers, and promote the Seduction of Youth, that a Select Body of discreet Officers should be appointed, under the direction of the Central Board, who fhould apprehend all who can be clearly ascertained to be in pursuit of objects of Prostitution.—That each should be conveyed to their respective homes, and when the Landlord's name, or the person to whom they pay rent or lodging, is by that means ascertained, that such person's name and place of abode, and the names of his or her lodgers be registered, and a penalty of 10s. for the first, and an advance of 5s. more

for

for every additional offence, be inflicted on each hirer of Board or Lodgings for every Female apprehended in the streets, upon proper proof of an overt act leading to Prostitution.

In all cases where Prostitutes refuse to discover their real place of abode, they shall be detained in a house to be provided for their reception until such discovery be made.

2d. That every male person who shall be proved to have made, or to have accepted, overtures from any Female walking the streets, shall in like manner be apprehended, and shall give security for his appearance before a Magistrate next day, or be detained in the Watch-house, and shall, on conviction, forfeit and pay a penalty of *Twenty Shillings.*

3d. That for the purpose of holding out encouragement to that class of unfortunate Females who have been abandoned by their Seducers, and whose minds are not yet debased by an indisriminate intercourse of Prostitution ; and also such others as may have friends likely to assist them, *Twelve* or more *sensible and discreet Matrons* shall be appointed, under the Board of Police, with a moderate Salary, and residing (with proper accommodation) in different parts of the Town, on whom it shall be incumbent to receive into their houses and to provide a temporary residence for every unfortunate Female who may apply, for the purpose of stating her case, with a view to a reconciliation

ciliation with her friends, and to the exposure of her Seducer, as a check upon such acts of villainly hereafter.—That it shall be the duty of the Matron, after being mistress of the whole case, to open a negociation with the nearest relations or friends of the unfortunate Female, and to use every means to effect a reconciliation; or where that is found impracticable, to endeavour to procure her some reputable employment.

And as an encouragement to such Matrons, to use all diligence in promoting the object in view, they shall be entitled to a certain premium from the Police funds, (independent of what private Societies of benevolent Individuals may be induced to bestow,) for every unfortunate Female who shall be thus rescued from the walks of Prostitution: to be paid at the end of 12 months, in case such Female shall then be in society with her relation, or in some reputable employment, and shall not have relapsed into her former course of life.—That these Matrons shall be distinguished for talents and humanity, and shall be capable of exercising such powers as could, in other instances, be employed to promote reconciliation with relations and friends; and also to devise employments by which the unfortunate persons, *ad interim*, under their care should be able to subsist, by taking in *Military Shirts*, *Slop-work*, and other branches of Female labour; to procure which, it is not doubted, but Societies of benevolent Individuals

dividuals would contribute their aid, so as to secure, at all times, the means of full employment for all the various applicants in succession.

In so noble a work of humanity, especially when it is understood that the labour of the Matrons would be remunerated by such a moderate Salary, as might be an object to many deserving well-educated women, little doubt can be entertained of there being many Candidates for such Situations, who, from having no family, would be perfectly competent to the execution of so benevolent a design.

4th. That with a view to the reformation of Prostitutes who have no relations or friends, or in cases where a reconciliation is hopeless, and who may be disposed to abandon their evil courses, *Houses of Industry* shall be provided in different parts of the Town, with large Kitchens for the purpose of preparing wholesome and nourishing food at a cheap rate, into which all who apply for an asylum will be received; on condition that a true and faithful account of the various circumstances of their lives shall be given, and that they agree not only to submit to the discipline of the Establishment, but also to perform such labour as shall be assigned them for their subsistence, lodging and apparel. That these *Houses of Industry* shall also be superintended by *discreet Matrons*, who shall receive a moderate Salary, and a certain portion of the profit arising from the work done, and a premium for

for every Female restored to Society, or to their
friends by their means; and in honest employment or living with relations, for the space of 12
months, in addition to such other premiums as
benevolent Societies of Individuals may choose to
bestow, in consequence of the impression made
on their minds of the utility of such Establishments, and the success which may appear to attend
them.

5th. That all the laws now in being against Prostitution, and against the Keepers of Brothels, shall
remain in full force; with this alteration only, that
instead of proceeding against Offenders in the
latter case, by the difficult, expensive, and circuitous mode of Presentment and Indictment,
which has heretofore proved so ineffectual, the
proceedings shall be *summary* before two Magistrates, as in Lottery and other offences, and the
Delinquents if convicted shall be subject to immediate punishment.

These are the regulations which the Author would
humbly propose, as a mean of preventing the dis-
asters and miseries which arise from Seduction, and
of diminishing the number of Prostitutes in this great
Metropolis.—Perhaps, after the experiment is tried
of the House of Industry, it might be expedient to
convert the whole into a large Penitentiary House,
where only unfortunate women should be admitted.
—The suggestions which are now offered, appear
to

to be not only easy with respect to their execution, but likely to be compassed at a moderate expence.— They are, however, to be considered as mere outlines of a practicable design, which should certainly precede the removal of the unfortunate Females from the Streets, as humanity points out the necessity of offering them asylums; since by suddenly abridging their present resources, however iniquitous and reprehensible they may be, without such asylums, it would certainly be the means of many of them perishing for want.

The object to be attained is of vast importance; but it is too unwieldy for the efforts of private benevolence, and certainly cannot be accomplished through any other medium than that of *Public Institutions*, under the protection of a Superintending Police.

MENIAL SERVANTS.

Among the various evils, which, in the present state of Society, tend to the corruption of Morals, the state and condition of Menial Servants, Male and Female, are none of the least: particularly those who are out of place, and who swarm in multitudes, idle and unemployed, at all times in this great Metropolis—This is chiefly to be attributed to the want of those legal restraints and punishments for improper behaviour, which apply to other classes of labourers.

Such regulations, independent of infinite advantages

tages which must, in other respects, arise to the Community, would be *an act of great humanity to the Individuals* who compose this class; since they would check, or in most instances prevent, those indiscretions which are the result of being under no controul, and by restraining the influence of ungovernable and ill-regulated passions, would produce that degree of steadiness which is the characteristic of a good Servant; and of course the constant disposition to shift about would not be felt, while they would be rescued from the vices which are generated at those intervals of idleness, when Servants, Male and Female, out of place, are exposed to every species of Seduction, till at length, by loss of character, they too frequently become Thieves and Prostitutes.*

It would certainly promote in an eminent degree the cause of Morality, if the whole Laws respecting Servants of every description were revised, and accommodated in a greater degree to the present state of Society. Some of them might perhaps be stript of their severity; while the penalties or breaches of moral duty, and refusal to fulfil a civil contract, or Conspiracies and Associations for mischievous purposes, ought certainly to apply to menial Servants, in the same manner as to Servants in Husbandry, Handicrafts and Labourers. A general exclusive Re-

---

* It is calculated that there are seldom less than Ten Thousand Servants of both Sexes, at all times out of place in the Metropolis. This shews, in strong colours, the importance of the regulations which are proposed.

gister of Servants out of place, under the inspection of an appropriate branch of the general Police System, would also have an excellent effect in bringing to light the evil pursuits of bad Servants; while it operated favourably to those who were deserving of confidence. Much might be done through this medium, favourable both to the interest of the Master and Servants; and this with many other benefits are to be attained, by means of a Superintending System of Police. In no other way can it be effected.*

The Lottery.

In spite of the persevering efforts of Government, who incur a great annual expence† for the purpose of restraining the baneful effects of illegal Insurances among the lower classes of the people, the evil still continues; *its consequences are lamentable,* for the delusion of this infatuation tends, in a very eminent degree, to the corruption of morals, producing scenes of distress, by which thousands suddenly descend from a state of comfort to extreme indigence.—In the 6th Chapter of this Treatise, a general view is given of the effects of this contagion, and various remedies are proposed, which, under the conduct of a Board of Police, would certainly be effectual; while the Revenue drawn from the sale of Tickets

* See page 150.
† Said to be above Two Thousand pounds a year.

might

might certainly be preserved. In the mean time, the following are suggested as useful expedients:

1st. That in every Parish and District in the Metropolis, Masters, and heads of Families, should sign and publish an engagement to discharge all Servants who shall be concerned in Insurances in the Lottery; to be printed and hung up in every Servant's Hall and Kitchen, that none might pretend ignorance.

2d. That all Members of Friendly Societies, should, by a regulation of their own, and enforced by Parliament, be excluded from the benefits of such Societies, on being convicted of any concern whatever in such Insurances.*

GAMING.

The magnitude and extent of the pernicious propensity to Gaming have at all times proved a prolific source from whence has sprung an extensive corruption of morals. The reader is referred to the 6th Chapter of this work for details, which will fully elucidate the baneful effects of this evil, in generating *Cheats, Swindlers, and Sharpers of every description.* For the purpose of more effectually checking this mania, and the consequences which flow from it, it might be expedient to extend the Laws now in being respecting Lottery vagrants, *to the Proprietors or Keepers of Gaming-Houses, and also to the Waiters, Servants and Assistants, who, on being apprehended, should, on proper proof, be punished as*

* See page 151 to 170.

rogues

rogues and vagabonds.—It is, however, by the operation of the General Police System, that this and other
evils are to be checked or remedied.

THE LOWER CLASSES OF THE JEWS.

Nothing would be more desirable than the adoption of some effectual plan, through the medium of
the opulent and respectable individuals of the Jewish
persuasion, whether of the Dutch or Portuguese
Synagogues, by which the lower classes, particularly
of the German Jews, might be regularly trained to
some useful employment, since their present pursuits
not only tend, in an eminent degree, to the corruption
of Morals, but also to the commission of Crimes:
and under circumstances, where the necessity of the
case imperiously calls for a remedy, Legislative
regulations might be resorted to; which might not
only better the condition of this miserable class of
the community, by compelling parents to bind their
children to some employment, but also render them
useful, instead of being too generally noxious members of the Body Politic,* from the idle and useless
pursuits in which they are engaged.

INDIGENCE AND BEGGARY.

The various causes which produce Indigence in
the Metropolis, discoverable through the medium of
Beggary or Idleness, tend, in an eminent degree, to

* See pages 319 to 323, Chap. 11th.

the

the corruption of Morals, and the consequent increase of Crimes.—In the 13th Chapter of this
Treatise this subject is examined, and *a remedy pro-*
posed, through the medium of a *Pauper Police,* for
the purpose of examining into the circumstances of
the numerous class of individuals who have no parochial settlements in the Metropolis, or perhaps in
any part of England, and are, from that circumstance,
denominated *Casual Poor.*—There could not be a
greater act of humanity to these often afflicted, and
sometimes oppressed individuals, or of greater utility
to the Public at large, than the establishment of a
System whereby the most deserving could be propt
up, rescued from despondency, and enabled to help
themselves; while by discriminating between the
virtuous and *vicious* poor, a proper line might be
drawn, and the streets of the Metropolis freed from
the multitude of Beggars, without doing violence to
humanity.*

Various other causes might be assigned for the
general corruption of Morals, which has in so great
a degree increased the calendars of delinquency.—
Among these might be mentioned *Smuggling,* or
illicit Trade; the evil examples arising from an indiscriminate *mixture in Workhouses* and Prisons; the
profligate examples of parents, and the want of religious and moral education, so universal among the
children of the labouring people.—And the too

* See pages 351 to 380.

frequent

frequent cohabitation without marriage among the lowest classes of the Community. These, like other evils, which have been more particularly detailed, are objects to which the proposed Police System would gradually attach, and through which preventive medium the Public are to expect those ameliorating designs, which are to secure the privileges of innocence, and better the condition of Society.

Prevention of Offences.

MISDEMEANORS.

CHEATING AND SWINDLING.

The 5th Chapter of this Treatise developes the extensive mischiefs and evils which arise from the phalanx of Cheats and Swindlers who infest the Metropolis.—There appear to be two remedies, namely—

1st. To look accurately at the evil in all its branches, and then to improve the two Statutes now in being* by framing an act of Parliament that would include all the various cases which have been shown to have occurred, where the barrier of common honesty is broken down.—These cases are detailed from page 115 to 132.

2d. The Establishment of a Board of Police on the plan detailed in the 18th Chapter of this Work, with functions calculated to check and prevent this evil, by giving to Police the full energy of the Law.

* 33 Henry VIII. cap. 1. and 30 Geo. II. cap. 24.

STEALING

Stealing Fruit from Orchards, &c.

This offence is only punishable by the act of 43 Eliz. c. 7. by compelling the party to refund the value of the fruit stolen, or in default suffer the punishment of whipping, which never takes place, as the small value of the fruit detected is always paid. It is probable at that early period Fruit was not a species of property of much consequence.—The case is, however, different at the present time, and surely it would not be thought too severe to place this offence on the same footing as stealing Cabbages, Turnips, &c.

Assault and Battery.

It would seem to be a great improvement in the Police, if Magistrates in Petty Sessions had a power finally to determine on offences denominated Assaults—subject, however, to an appeal to the Quarter Sessions.—It would even be an act of humanity to the labouring people, who are often imprisoned from the time of the charge till the Sessions, when a confinement of a shorter duration might atone for the offence.—It would likewise save much trouble and expences to the parties, and the time and attention of Courts and Juries would not be wasted by matters extremely frivolous; but by which a certain expence is incurred, and a loss of valuable time to the parties, who are not seldom both in the wrong.

Perjury.

Perjury.

This shocking offence, particularly prevalent among the inferior ranks in Society, is to be attributed in no small degree to the want of proper *solemnity* and previous explanation on the administration of oaths.—Nothing can exceed the unimpressive and careless manner which is in practice in calling upon witnesses to make *this solemn appeal to the Supreme Being.*—It would seem highly necessary that all oaths should be administered in the most impressive manner by the Judge, and that a form should be devised, calculated in the greatest possible degree, to impress upon the mind of the party a high sense of the obligation he or she has come under to speak the truth.

On the whole, it may be asserted that nothing could tend to improve the Police of the Country and the Metropolis more than a general revision of the Laws respecting Misdemeanors, and particularly the Act of the 17th Geo. II. cap. 5. and subsequent Acts respecting vagrants, and rogues and vagabonds; so as to assimilate them in a greater degree to the present state of Society, and to render their execution more certain and beneficial to the Community.

Prevention of the Coinage of Base Money.

In the 7th Chapter of this Work, the various modes in practice, by which the Public is defrauded by the coining,

coining, fabricating, and colouring of Base Money are fully developed, and specific Remedies proposed from page 195 to 210, to which the Reader is referred.

A confident hope is entertained, that those Remedies will speedily be brought under the consideration of Parliament, in the form of a Bill.—If this should be passed into a Law, and accompanied by a new Coinage of Silver, and aided by the energy of an appropriate Police, little doubt can be entertained of the measure being effectual in securing the Public against the enormous evil of Counterfeit Coin.

PREVENTION OF PILLAGE AND PLUNDER ON THE RIVER THAMES.

The 8th Chapter of this Treatise displays not only the immense importance of controlling the evil habits of aquatic labourers and others on the River Thames and in the Warehouses adjacent; but also the advantages to be expected *from a general Police System;* reasoning on the extensive success which has attended the partial experiment on the same principle *of vigilance* applied to this object.

The extensive benefits which are known and acknowledged to have been derived from the *Marine Police* (even under all the disadvantages of a *Crippled System* and *Deficient Powers*) joined to a review of the state of the River *before* and *since* this important measure was adopted, afford the best proof that can be adduced of its utility; and also of the indispensable

necessity,

necessity, not only of immediately perfecting a System, by which the Commerce and Revenue of the Port of London have been in so great a degree secured; but also of extending the same beneficial designs, wherever the state of things require a similar antidote.

It remains only for the Legislature to pass a Bill which has been prepared, grounded on more than a year's experience of the powers and regulations requisite for the purpose of giving full effect and permanency to this important Establishment, in order to secure to the Commerce and Revenue of the River Thames, those advantages which will arise from the Preservation of Property against the numerous and unexampled Depredations to which it was exposed; and the Revenue of the Crown from many frauds which arose not only from the loss of the Duties of Customs and Excise on goods plundered, but also from an extensive illicit trade, which has been controlled and prevented by the known vigilance of the River Guards, particularly during the night.

If to those advantages shall be added an increase of Salaries to the inferior Officers of the Customs and Excise employed on the River, the renovated morals and improved habits of multitudes heretofore deeply implicated in a species of turpitude, hurtful in the extreme to the Public interest, will become no less a matter of triumph than advantage to the Government of the Country. Every individual concerned

in

in the Commerce of the Port, will rejoice to see so useful an Institution supported and rendered permanent by that Legislative Aid, upon which its ultimate success must in a great measure depend.

An evil of unexampled magnitude existed, for which an effectual remedy has been found:—not in *Speculation*, but proved in *Practice* to answer the purposes of *future security*.

Let the Legislature, therefore, avail itself of the measures which are proposed, by which incalculable benefits will be extended both to the *Commerce, Revenue*, and *Police* of the Port of London, especially when strengthened and invigorated by a Central Board.

PREVENTION OF PLUNDER OF PUBLIC STORES: IN SHIPS OF WAR, DOCK-YARDS, &c.

The collateral Influence of the Marine Police System, in checking in an eminent degree, the Embezzlements and Pillage of his Majesty's Stores in Ship's and Public Arsenals, within the limits of its Jurisdiction, is the strongest proof which can be adduced of what may be expected by applying a similar System to all the Dock-yards in the kingdom. In the 9th Chapter of this Treatise, the *Evils*, and the *Remedies* are so minutely detailed as to render a reference only necessary to pages 264 to 287—If the measures there suggested shall be adopted by the Legislature and the Lords of the Admiralty, little
                                                              doubt

doubt can be entertained of complete success in securing the Public Property (*unparalleled in point of extent in any nation in the world*)* against those Frauds and Depredations to which it has heretofore been exposed to a very large amount annually.

PREVENTION OF CRIMES IN GENERAL.

It has been demonstrated in the course of this Work, that the more atrocious offences of Highway and Footpad Robberies, Burglaries, and other acts of Felony† may be greatly diminished, if not nearly annihilated by improved Laws and a responsible Agency, through the medium of a well-regulated Board of Police to carry those Laws into effect.

It must, however, be obvious to the Reader, from what has been repeatedly stated, that it is not by any *single regulation*, nor by any portion of civil strength, however well it may be systematized, that this desirable object is to be effected.

Success in any material degree is only to be expected from a *combination of the various controlling regulations which have been proposed, with a vigorous and energetic civil force*, and a correct and pointed execution of the Laws and Regulations, upon which the Preventive System is founded.—These *Regulations* may be summed up under the following heads:

* The floating Public Property is estimated, including Ships of War, Naval, Victualling, Ordnance and Military Stores, in time of War, at upwards of Forty Millions sterling.

† See Chapters III. and IV.

1st. The

1st. The adoption of eight propositions contained in the 10th Chapter, pages 503 to 307, relative to *the Receivers of Stolen Goods, &c.*

2d. An improved mode of granting rewards to officers of Justice and others, for meritorious services, in the detection and conviction of offenders—as elucidated and explained in Chapter XIV. pages 390 to 396.

3d. An improved and modernized System, with respect to Parochial Constables, so as to restore to the Community the original efficacy of this useful institution—as explained in Chapter XIV. pages 401 to 410.

4th. An improved System also, with respect to Watchmen and Patroles—with a view to render this branch of the Police *efficient*, and to ensure to the Public, that vigilance and protection to which the expence they incur justly intitles them.

5th. An extension of the Jurisdiction of the City Magistrates, over the whole of the Metropolis and the four adjoining Counties, and a power to Police Magistrates to issue Search Warrants, and to follow and apprehend persons charged with offences, who take shelter within the limits of the City of London—as explained in chapter XIV. pages 418 to 420.

6th. The appointment of a Prosecutor for the Crown to obviate the difficulties which occur at present in bringing Offenders to Justice; and which is elucidated and explained in the 15th Chapter, particularly in pages 426 to 432.

7th. The Establishment of certain general Rules and Conditions, according to which the Royal Mercy might be extended to Offenders, on terms beneficial to themselves and to the Community—as explained in the 16th Chapter, pages 450 to 452.

8th. An improved System with respect to the Punishment of Convicts, by means of Penitentiary Establishments, calculated to ensure the reformation of Felons, and to render this

class

class useful afterwards to the Community—as explained in the 16th Chapter, pages 481 to 494, and 497 to 500.

9th. General Rules laid down with respect to different modes of Punishment, under six heads, pages 495 to 497, with an immediate view to render them more useful in the Prevention of Crimes.

10th. An improved System of Police, aided by competent Funds, and an extension of the Police Establishments, under the 32 Geo. III. (1792) to the City of London— as explained in Chap. XVII. pages 509 and 514 to 523.

11th. By the adoption of the General System of Police, recommended by the Select Committee of the House of Commons, and explained in Chapter XVIII.—By licensing and regulating certain dangerous and suspicious Trades therein specified; and by raising a Revenue for Police purposes, from persons who shall be thus controlled.—See pages 536 to 546.

12th. By the Establishment of a Board of Police Revenue, who shall exercise the specific Functions detailed and explained in Chap. XVIII. pages 546 to 559 : and finally, by an Act of Parliament, authorising such a system, the heads of which and the elucidating observations are also specified in pages 560 to 564.

Let these measures only be adopted by the Legislature, not by *piece-meal*, but *in the gross*; and little doubt need be entertained of the most beneficial effects being experienced by the innocent part of the Community, whose privileges will be extended, in proportion as the Licence which an imperfect Police afforded to Robberies, Burglaries, and other acts of violence on the person and property of the peaceful subject is abridged.

The

The General Police, and the powers of making it effectual, will then be a charge committed to responsible Agents; whose duty it will be to penetrate into all its mazes, and to accomplish its purposes by a variety of Regulations, all tending to embarrass, and to render difficult and hazardous, the pursuits and operations of Criminals.—Experience will suggest modifications, which, aided by competent funds, must in a short time attain that point which shall establish *Security*.—But this is not all.—Without taking large sums (as at present) from the Revenue of the Country, the effect of the System will unquestionably be, to add to its resource in the diminution of the enormous expence now incurred in the punishment of convicts*; and which still must continue a burden on the Finances of the Country, until the General Police System is fully (not partially) in activity.

It will collaterally extend to every thing that can improve the Morals of the People, and better the condition of Human Life —Its influence will be felt by giving vigour to the Systems proposed for checking all Misdemeanors, for securing Commercial Property, and also the Public Stores, from embezzlement and depredation; while the offences against the mint Laws, under the new Regulations which are suggested, will tend much to the prevention of that enormous evil.

---

* See Chapter VI. page 430, where it is stated, that in 25 years about 15,000 Convicts have cost the Nation no less than 1,663,974l.

Amend-

Amendment of the Existing Laws.

When in addition to the adoption of the foregoing measures, further improvements shall be made in the Laws now in force, or perhaps a general consolidation of the whole Criminal Code be effeted, so as to render the System more simple, and in a greater degree applicable to the attainment of the ends of Public Justice, great indeed will be the blessings conferred on the Metropolis, and on the Nation at large.

The celebrated Lord Bacon denominated them almost two centuries ago, when they were much less voluminous, and infinitely more simple than at the presed ay —

"An heterogeneous mass, concocted too often
"on the spur of the occasion, and frequently
"without that degree of accuracy, which is the
"result of able and minnte discussion, or a due
"attention to the revision of the existing Laws."

But voluminous as they certainly are, many omissions are apparent, partly arising from the causes assigned by the able Lawyer whose strictures have been just quoted, and more particularly from the rapid changes, which Commerce and Property have made in the state of Society.

Among

Among these, the following have occurred to the Author as highly deserving attention.—

1st. The Act of the 30 Geo. II. Cap. 24. makes it transport-able Misdemeanor, to obtain *Goods* or *Chattels* by false pre-tences.—But as *Horses, Cattle, Poultry, Bank Notes, Bills of Exchange,* or *Notes of Hand,* although equally objects of Fraud, are not deemed in Law to be *Goods* or *Chattels,* offences of equal, if not of greater magnitude, or not with-in the meaning of the Statute, and hence appears the neces-sity of an Amendment.

2d, The present Act relative to Pawnbrokers is extremely de-ficient, and not only in several important points ambiguous; but also inapplicable in a variety of instances to the general views of the Legislature, as they regard the security and in-terests of the Poor, while in others, perhaps unnecessary and useless restrictions are imposed on the Pawnbrokers them-selves.

3d. As the Laws respecting Forgeries now stand—the act of forging the Firm of a Commercial House, and obtaining goods on the Credit of such Firm, is only punishable as a Misdemeanor; although in this case this offence is of a ten-dency *the most dangerous that can be conceived,* in a Com-mercial country, where (from the unbounded confidence which prevails) it is so easy to obtain credit.

A case occurred and came under the cognizance of the Au-thor in 1796, where a Swindler assuming the Firm of a respect-able House in Bristol, ordered goods from Manchester to be sent to Portsmouth, where the person (committing the Forgery) stated, that one of the Partners meant to go to meet them.— Two parcels of goods were obtained by this device, and imme-diately sold at half the value by the sharpers, which led to a
discovery,

discovery, and enabled the Author to guard the unsuspecting Manufacturers in York and Lancashire, against the injuries they were likely to sustain, by the operation of a very complicated and artful conspiracy to rob them of their property to a great amount.

4th. The Receiving of *Cash or Specie, Bank Notes, Bills of Exchange, or Notes of Hand, knowing the same to be stolen,* is not at present a Criminal Offence: In a Commercial Country where such offences may be productive of much evil to Society, Why should not the Law extend to every species of Property in the same manner as to Goods and Chattels?

5th. Although Arson is considered (and justly so) as a high Criminal Offence, yet the offence of a person setting fire to his own house, with a view to defraud the Insurers, is considered only *a simple Misdemeanor,* and punished as such; and where a house at a distance from others is set on fire so as to occasion no danger to the neighbourhood, *it is not an Offence known in the Criminal Code,* even although it may appear to have been done for the purpose of defrauding the Insurers.

With a view to the prevention of this very atrocious crime (of which there have been but too many instances of late years) it would seem right that it should be *clearly defined;* and that it would not be too severe to punish offenders by Transportation; since in all cases, where the fire extends to a neighbouring house the offence of Arson is committed, and the punishment is Death.

6th. Much inconvenience is at present experienced from the circuitous and expensive process of Law, which must be resorted to for the purpose of removing bad and profligate *Lodgers.*—In cases of small concern, where the rent does not exceed a few shillings a week, it would be an act of great humanity to empower Magistrates to decide in a summary

way.

way,—It would check that spirit of litigation which is the destruction of the Labouring People.

7th. As a means of controlling many offences, which are generated by an assemblage of loose and immoral characters, who are constantly afloat in the Metropolis, *a General Register of Lodging Houses*, would certainly be attended with very beneficial effects: and to use the language of the Select Committee of the House of Commons in their 28th Report, page 31,— would also "be a Regulation, which, if discreetly used, "might probably afford the means of materially assisting "both the Police and the Revenue*."

8th. The extensive Plunder committed on the Farmers round the Metropolis, under the pretence of *Gleaning in Harvest*, is a very serious evil, and calls aloud for a remedy.—The practice is pernicious and ruinous to the Morals of the Families of the Labouring People in every part of the Country, since through this medium children learn pilfering habits, before they know that it is a crime.

A slight punishment on all who gleaned in any case previous to a complete removal of the corn or vegetables, and on every occasion without first obtaining leave of the Proprietor, would prove a very salutary Regulation—for it appears that every Thief charged with stealing corn pretends it was obtained by *Gleaning*.

9th. The existing Laws being found ineffectual in controlling the habits, and in turning into a course of useful industry the labour of the herds of Gypsies, who surround the Metropolis, and commit depredations in every part of the Country, it would be exceedingly desirable†, both with respect to policy and humanity, to provide some effectual Legislative Remedy, since the idle, vagrant, and miserable life of this profligate community can be as little desirable to themselves

---

* See pages 105 and 539 in this Work.   † See pages, 84, 5.

as it is hurtful to the Public.—Compelling a residence which shall be *stationary*, and obliging them to bind out their children apprentices at a certain age, so as to incorporate them with the mass of the people, would certainly prove a very salutary Regulation.

10th. The frauds and adulterations in the article of *Milk* sold in the Metropolis, as detailed in the 3d Chapter of this Work, pages 89 to 92, seem to justify the inteference of Parliament for the purpose of placing *Milk Dealers* under the inspection and controul of the Police : Here the injury is not merely confined to the frauds thus practised on the Public, but the healths of the Consumers are in some measure endangered from the infamous devices which are practised.

11th. For the purpose of saving much unnecessary expence, and also to remove the inconvenience arising from the length of time, which frequently elapses before persons charged with offences, in Southwark, Greenwich, and the villages surrounding the Metropolis, make it lawful to try offences committed in Surry, Kent and Essex, within five miles of the three Bridges, at the Justice Hall of the Old Bailey, which may be done before a Jury of the Vicinage, with great advantages to Public Justice, and without touching on the rights of the Accused*.

12th. To establish certain Legislative Regulations, for the purpose of preserving the Morals of unfortunate unoffending families, by restoring to them such parents whose misfortunes and not their crimes, have doomed them to the horrors of perpetual Imprisonment.—And to establish arrangements for the improvement of what may be denominated *Civil Police*, by adopting inferior Tribunals for distributing Justice in all actions of Debt under 50l. for the purpose of reducing the present enormous expence, and extending relief to traders in general †.

* See pages 428 and 429.　　　† See pages 584 to 590.

THUS

THUS has the Author of this work endeavoured develope that infinite variety of crimes and misfortunes, which have been long felt and deplored as a pressure upon the innocent part of the community.

In travelling over so extensive a field, where almost every step is stained with turpitude and depravity, no little consolation is derived from being able thus to place upon record *practicable Remedies*, applicable to the chief part of the evils, which have been brought under the review of the Reader.

Nor is it less a matter of gratification to the Writer of the preceeding pages, than it must be satisfactory to the Public at large, to discover that the leading features of the whole improvements which he suggested in the preceding editions of this Work, *have attracted the notice, and received the sanction of the Select Committee of the House of Commons.*

The conclusion which may naturally be drawn is, that the laborious efforts of the Author in bringing a new and interesting subject under the review of the Public have not been in vain; and that a confident hope may now be entertained that his humble endeavours, for the good of his Country, will ultimately produce arrangements *in the New Science of Police,* calculated to secure and protect the peaceful subject against injury, and to ameliorate the state and condition of Civil Society, particularly in this great Metropolis, by the adoption of such measurs *as shall*

be

be conducive to the more effectual Prevention of Crimes ;—by lessening the demand for Punishments :—by diminishing the expence and alleviating the burden of Prosecutions :—by turning the hearts and arresting the hands of evil doers : by forewarning the unwary, and preserving the untainted in purity; thus attaching to Police its genuine preventive character, unmixed with those judicial powers which lead to Punishment, and properly belong to Magistracy alone.

FINIS.

INDEX.

A

	Page
Abstract of the annual Imports into, and Exports from the Port of London - - *(table)*	215,16
———of Persons committed, and discharged from Prisons in one year, and extraordinary document - - - *(table)*	430
Account of Pawnbrokers in the Metropolis, and the vast property in their houses belonging to the poor - - - -	110
—— of various descriptions of Cheats	123,4,5,6,7
—— of the number of Streets, Lanes, Houses and Families in the Metropolis - -	562
—— of the previous Plans and Arrangements of Thieves when a Robbery or Burglary is contemplated - - -	291
—— of the usual Mode of proceeding to recover stolen property - - -	383
—— of the Number of Persons engaged in fraudulent Lotteries. - - - -	156
—— of the Trials at the Old Bailey in 1790 and 1791	394,5
—— of ditto in 1793 and 1795 - - -	446—448
—— of the Officers of Justice in the Metropolis	397
—— of the Watchmen and Patroles there -	414
—— of the Magistrates there - - -	398,9
—— of the Criminal Courts there - - -	428
—— of the specific Criminals punishable by Law	437—444
—— of the Convicts in the Hulks - -	455
—— of the Names of the City and Police Magistrates	504,5
—— of the Churches and other places of Worship in the Metropolis - - -	568
—— of the Seminaries of Education in the Metropolis	569,70
—— of the Societies for promoting Religion and Morality - - -	570,1
—— of the Societies for promoting the Arts	571
—— of the Asylums for the Indigent and Helpless	572
—— of the Hospitals for the Sick and for Pregnant Women in the Metropolis - -	573
—— of the Institutions for Charitable and Humane Purposes - - -	574,5

Account

INDEX.

Page

Account of the Charity annually distributed in the Metropolis, estimated at 850,000*l.* a year   -   357,8

———— of the Courts for Civil and Criminal Justice in the Metropolis   -   -   -   577——582

———— of the Prisons in the Metropolis   -   *ibid.*

———— of the different Classes of Professional Men connected with the departments of the Law about 7000 in all   -   -   -   583

———— of the Number of Writs issued in Middlesex in 1793, with an extraordinary statement of the Expences on small Law-suits   585,6,7

Acquittals, See Prisoners.

Actions at Law for small Debts   -   -   584.7

        Expence enormous beyond all credibility   -   *ibid.*

ACTS OF PARLIAMENT referred to in this Work.

2 Geo. 3. *c.* 28. for preventing Frauds by Persons navigating Bum-boats on the River Thames   237, *n.* 269

31 Elizabeth, *c.* 4 ⎫
22 Charles 2d. *c.* 5 ⎪
 9 & 10 William 3d. *c.* 11 ⎪
 1 George 1st. *stat.* 2. *c.* 25 ⎬ Relative to the Protection of his Majesty's Stores   -   261——263
 9 George 1st. *c.* 8 ⎪
17 Geo. 2d. *c.* 40 ⎪
 9 Geo. 3d. *c.* 35 ⎪
12 Geo. 3d. *c.* 24 ⎭

14 Geo. 3d. *c.* 90, for regulating the Westminster Watch, &c.   -   -   -   107

25 Edward 3d. *stat.* 5. *c.* 2 ⎫
 1 Mary *stat.* 2. *c.* 6 ⎪
 1 & 2 P. & M. *c.* 11 ⎪
 5 Eliz. *c.* 11 ⎪
14 Eliz. *c.* 3 ⎪
18 Eliz. *c.* 1 ⎪
 7 William 3d. *c.* 3 ⎪ Relative to the Coinage and disposal of Base Money   192,3,4
 8 & 9 William 3d. *c.* 26 ⎬
 9 & 10 William 3d. *c.* 21 ⎪
 7 Anne, *c.* 24, 25 ⎪
15 & 16 Geo. 2d. *c.* 28 ⎪
11 Geo. 3d. *c.* 40 ⎪
37 Geo. 3d. *c.* 126 ⎪
38 Geo. 3d. *c.* 59——67 ⎪
39 Geo. 3d. *c.* 75 ⎭

33 Henry 8th. *c.* 1 ⎫ Relative to Cheats and Swindlers   113,14
30 Geo. 2d. *c.* 24 ⎬

 9 Anne, *c.* 14 ⎫
 8 Geo. 1st. *c.* 2 ⎬ Relating to Gaming   134,5
12 Geo. 2d. *c.* 28 ⎭

 9 Geo. 2d. *c.* 5 relative to Fortune-tellers being punished by standing four time in the Pillory   -   130

        3 & 4 Wil-

INDEX.

Page

3 & 4 William 3d. *c.* 9
1 Anne, *c.* 9
5 Anne, *c.* 31
4 Geo. 1st. *c.* 11
29 Geo. 2d. *c.* 30
30 Geo. 2d. *c.* 24 — Relative to Receivers of Stolen Goods 298—300
2 Geo. 3d. *c.* 28
10 Geo. 3d. *c.* 48
21 Geo. 3d. *c.* 69
22 Geo. 3d. *c.* 58

5 Edw. 3d. *c.* 14 — Relative to the Office & power of Constables 387
34 Edw. 3d. *c.* 1
8 Geo. 2d. *c.* 16 relative to Hue and Cry 389

4 William & Mary, *c.* 8
6 & 7 William & Mary *c.* 17
10 & 11 William 3d. *c.* 23
5 Anne, *c.* 31
6 Geo. 1st. *c.* 23 — Relative to Rewards for apprehending different Classes of Offenders 390—392
3 Geo. 2d *c.* 16.
14 Geo. 2d. *c.* 6
15 Geo. 2d. *c.* 34
15 & 16 Geo. 2d. *c.* 28
16 Geo. 2d. *c.* 15
3 Geo. 3d. *c.* 15

25 Edward 3d. *stat.* 5 *c.* 2; 36 Geo. 3d. *c.* 7, relative to *High Treason* - - - 38,9
25 Henry 8th. *c.* 6. Sodomy made capital - 46
18 Eliz. *c.* 7, Rape made capital - - 46,7
3 Henry 7th. *c.* 2 — Forcible Marriage and Defilement made capital 48
39 Eliz. *c.* 9
5 Henry 4th. *c.* 5 — Mayhem or Maiming made capital 49
22 & 23 Charles 2d. *c.* 2
35 George 3d. *c.* 67, Polygamy punished by Transportation - - - *ibid.*
King Athelstan's Law (anno 936) punished theft with Death, if above the value of One Shilling 51
9 Henry 1st. punished Theft with Death (anno 1108) 52
23 Henry 8th. *c.* 1
1 Edw. 6th. *c.* 12
5 & 6 Edw. 6th. *c.* 9
39 Eliz. *c.* 15 — As to Felonies in Dwelling Houses 54,5
3 & 4 William & Mary *c.* 9
10 & 11 William 3d. *c.* 23
12 Anne, *stat.* 1. *c.* 7
23 Henry 8th. *c.* 1 — Relative to Arson and Burning Houses, Barns, Corn, Underwood, Ships, &c. 56,7
43 Eliz. *c.* 13
22 & 23 Charles 2d. *c.* 7. 11
1 Geo. 1st. *c.* 48

4 Geo.

INDEX.

4 George 1st. *c.* 12

9 ――― 1st. *c.* 22

10 ――― 2d. *c.* 32 — Relative to Arson and Burning Houses, Barns, Corn, Under-wood, Ships, &c.   56,7

27 ――― 2d. *c.* 15

9 ――― 3d. *c.* 21

12 ――― 3d. *c.* 24

18 Eliz. *c.* 7

3 & 4 William and Mary, *c.* 9 — Relative to Burglary   57

12 Anne, *Stat.* 1. *c.* 7

1 Edw. 6th. *c.* 12

21 Jac. 1st. *c.* 6

3 & 4 William & Mary, *c.* 9 — Relative to the Benefit of Clergy -   435

4 & 5 William & Mary, *c.* 24

5 Anne, *c.* 6

4 Geo. 1st. *c.* 11 ; 6 Geo. 1st. *c.* 23, legalizing Trans-portation to the Colonies - -   436,7

The same Statute appropriated to the Services of Convicts   454

16 Geo. 3d. first legalized the system of the Hulks   455

16 Geo. 3d. *c.* 23, legalized Penitentiary Houses in Coun-ties - - - - -   *ibid.*

19 Geo. 3d. *c.* 74, legalized two National Penitentiary Houses - - - - -   456

24 Geo. 3d. *stat.* 2. *c.* 56, relative to Transportation and the Hulks - - - -   460

27 Geo. 3d. *c.* 2 ; 30 Geo. 3d. *c.* 47, relative to New South Wales - - -   462

28 Geo. 3d. *c.* 24, contracts for Convicts -   *ibid.*

2 Will. & Mary, *c.* 8, relative to paving the Metropolis   592

10 Geo. 2d, *c.* 22

11 Geo. 3d. *c.* 29

14 Geo. 3d. *c.* 78 — Relative to the Police of the City of Lon-don -   592—597

33 Geo. 3d. *c.* 75

34 Geo. 3d. *c.* 65—(*Watermen*)

27 Elizabeth — divided the City

16 Chars. 1st. — into Wards

29 George 2d. *c.* 25

31 ――― 2d. *c.* 17

2 ――― 3d. *c.* 21 — Relative to the Police of London and West-minster -   593,4

3 ――― 3d. *c.* 23

5 ――― 3d. *c.* 13 & 50

11 ――― 3d. *c.* 22

14 ――― 3d. *c.* 90

28 ――― 2d. *c.* 9 — Relative to the Police of Southwark   594

6 ――― 3d. *c.* 24

6 Henry 6th. *c.* 5

6 ――― 8th. *c.* 10

23 ――― 8th. *c.* 5 — Relative to the System of the Sewers   594,5

25 ――― 8th. *c.* 10

3 & 4 Edw. 6th. *c.* 8

1 Mary,

INDEX.

Page

1 Mary, *stat.* 3 c. 11
13 Eliz. c. 9 } Relative to the Sestem
8 James, c. 14 of the Sowers   594,5
7 Anne, c. 10

9 Anne, c. 23
10 ———— c. 19
12 ———— *stat.* 1. c. 14
1 Geo. 1st. c. 57
12 ——— Geo. 1st. c. 2
30 ——— 2d. c. 22
4 ——— 3d. c. 36   Relative to Hackney
7 ————— c. 44   Coaches and Chairs 595
10 ————— c. 44
11 ————— c. 24, 28
12 ————— c. 49
24 ————— *stat.* 2. c. 27
26 ————— c. 72
32 ————— c. 47
33 ————— c. 75

1 Geo. 1st. c. 57
18 ——— 2d. c. 38
24 ——— 2d. c. 43   Relative to Carts and
30 ——— 2d. c. 22   other Carriages in
7 ——— 3d. c. 24   the Metropolis 596
24 ——— 3d. c. 27

21 Geo. 3d. c. 57, relative to Bullock-hunting 597
26 Geo. 3d. c. 71, as to Slaughtering Horses 104 *n.*
Adultery, not in the Criminal Code - - 35
Advertising Bill-discounters and Money-lenders to be regulated - - - - 118,19
Alehouses, a great source of Crimes and Nuisances when ill-regulated - - 85, 311, &c. 324, &c.
   In 500 Alehouses within the Bills of Mortality upwards of 3,300,000*l.* a year spent in Beer, Spirits, &c. - - 327
   Profligate Characters entrusted with Licences a source of much mischief - 325,6
Alfred, His Laws relative to Murder - - 44
Alston's Liquid Test to detect counterfeit Gold and Silver Coin - - - 180
Ancestors, Their Laws had an immediate reference to the prevention of Crimes - - 3
Anecdotes—Of an American Vessel plundered in the Thames in an extraordinary manner 219
———— of a Guinea Vessel plundered - *ibid.*
———— of the plunder and imposition on a Canada Merchant - - 229
———— of an Officer of Justice, who discovered an instance of pillage in one of the dock-yards 283

Anecdotes

INDEX.

Page

Anecdotes respecting the Lottery, the astonishing number
of persons supported by fraudulent insurances   156, *n.*

———— of the Jews in London, the extraordinary depravity of the lowest orders   148—150

———— of the different Classes of Cheats   -   130

———— of a Robbery in the Drawing-room at St. James's   -   -   127

———— of a Female Money-lender to Barrow Women   *ibid.*

———— of a Fortune-teller   -   -   129

———— of a Police Officer watching the house of a Receiver of Stolen Goods   -   306, *n.*

———— of a Jew who had committed a Rape   431, *n.*

———— of Sir Matthew Hale   -   -   432, *n.*

———— of the Justices of Chester, a singular circumstance   -   -   52,3

———— of a respectable Magistrate of the City   513, *n.*

———— of Monsieur De Sartine, Minister of the Police of Paris, an extraordinary circumstance   525—530

———— of the Emperor Joseph the Second   527, 8, 9

Apprentices corrupted by Receivers of Stolen Goods, &c.   12

———— harboured in Public-houses, in Clubs for purposes of lewdness and debauchery   315, *u.*

———— their immoral education, one cause of the origin of Crimes   314—317

———— Neglect of superior Tradesmen in boarding Apprentices out of their houses   -   316, 17, *n.*

Arrests for Felony, four modes practised   -   388

———— deficiency in the Law protecting Lottery vagrants and others from being arrested on Sundays   390

Arson, punished capitally   -   -   -   56

Asylums, an establishment recommended for discharged convicts   -   -   -   99, 100

———— for the Indigent in the Metropolis   572

———— for Sick, Lame, and Diseased   573

Athelstan's Laws relating to Death   -   -   51

Athenian Laws relative to Murder   -   43

Auctioneers called *diurnal,* with Puffers   -   117

B

Bacon, Lord—suggested a revision of the Criminal Code   7

Ballad Singers—might, from an Evil, be made an advantage to Society   348

Bank Notes and Bills received, knowing the same to be stolen—not an offence by any existing Law   8, 114, *n.*

Barkers at auctions   -   -   -   117

Beadles ought to be rewarded for useful public services   415

———— The proper persons to apply to when nuisances are to be removed   -   -   598

Beccaria, Marquis, his opinion of Punishments   53, *n.*

Beccaria,

INDEX.

	Page
Beccaria, Marquis, his maxim relative to Pardons	449, *n.*
Beggars. See Poor.	
Benefit of Clergy extended to all ranks -	436
Bentham (Jeremy, Esq.) his proposal for a Penitentiary	
House for Convicts, and remarks thereon	481—495
Bill Discounters, or Advertising Money-lenders	118—19
Board of Police. See Police.	
Bolton, Matthew, Esq. of Birmingham, number of Penny	
Pieces supplied by him. - -	186, *n.*
Botany Bay. See Convicts, New South Wales.	
Brokers, in pawns, to be registered - -	108, 304
Building Materials, dealers in, to be licensed -	549
Bullock-hunting, the Laws relative to it -	597
Burglary, not so frequent on the Continent as in England	94
———— by what classes of men committed	95, 6
———— systematically planned and executed	101, 3
———— remedies proposed - -	104
———— definition of Burglary and how punished -	57
———— called Hamsockne in the North of England	58

C.

Carts and other Carriages, the Laws relative to them	595, 6
Casual Poor. See Poor.	
Chance Medley, how punished - -	45
Charities in the Metropolis :	
Parish Schools for Education -	569
Societies for promoting Religion and Mo-	
rality - - -	570
Asylums for the Helpless and Indigent	572
Hospitals for the Sick and Pregnant Women	573
Dispensaries for the Poor -	574
Institutions for Charitable Purposes *(See Poor)*	*ibid.*
Cheapside, a general rendezvous for Thieves, and the	
reason - - -	106, 7
Cheats, the offence of cheating defined by Law -	113
The different classes of Cheats explained; who	
are more or less engaged in acts of Fraud, in	
the Metropolis - - 109,10, &c.	131
China, its Laws, and Punishment for High-Treason	40
Parricide 41—Murder 44 ;—Theft -	52
Chips. See Dock-yards.	
Churches and Places of Worship in the Metropolis	568
Coaches and Chairs in the Metropolis *(and See Hackney*	
Coaches; Night Coaches) -	595, 6
Coasting Vessels, &c. purchase embezzled Stores -	255
Coin counterfeited, and Coiners :	
Extensive circulation of base Coin -	15, 16
The Evils attending it - -	117, 18
Foreign Coin fabricated in England -	*ibid.*

INDEX.

Page

Coiners, 120 discovered - - 18
 Vast amount of Coin counterfeited - 181
 Different Coins fabricated - 173
 The process used in making the different kinds of
  base Money - - 174, 184
 The period when the trade dealing in base
  Money acquires its greatest v gour 188
 Deficiences of the present Laws - 208
 Remedies proposed - - 191—208
Colleges, five in London - - 569
Commons and waste Lands, the source of evil by encou-
 raging the idle Poor - 83
Constables, in the Metropolis, 1040, in London, West-
 minster, Middlesex, the Tower Liberty and
 Southwark - - 397,8,9
 Their power by the Common Law extensive,
  explained - - - 390
 Rewards necessary to excite attention - 392
 Rewards to Constables, and persons appre-
  hending various classes of Criminals 390
 Propositions for rendering them more useful
  and respectable - - 405—410
Convicts discharged from the Hulks from 1792 to 1799 98
 Number sent to the Hulks from the commence-
  ment of the Establishment, to December
  12, 1795, 7999 - - 463
 Expence of the support of Convicts transported
  in the Hulks - - 465,6—480,n.
 General Statements shewing the periods of
  their discharge, and the number par-
  doned, escaped, and discharged 463—465
 A statement of their Earnings at Woolwich and
  Langston Harbour - 467,8
 The inefficacy of this mode of Punishment 469,70
 Transported to New South Wales—Accounts of
  the Number and Expence - 472—474
 Opinion of the Finance Committee on the in-
  efficacy of the whole System - 475,&c.
 Proposals for employment of Convicts in Peni-
  tentiary Houses, by Jeremy Bentham, Esq. 481—495
 Further Regulations in the Penitentiary System
  suggested - - 495,500
Copper Money. *See* Coiners.
Corn and Provender stolen in the Country, how disposed
 of in the Metropolis - - 88
Courts of Justice in the Metropolis:
 Courts for the trials of Crimes, Misdemeanors,
  Trespasses, &c. *Two* superior and *Five* in-
  ferior - - 528

9 Supreme

INDEX.

Pag

9 Supreme Courts in the Metropolis - 577
4 Ecclesiastical Courts, Doctors Commons *ib.*
17 Courts of Justice in the City of London 478,9
8 Courts of Justice in Westminster 579,80
15 Courts of Justice in that part of Middlesex
    which joins the Metropolis - 580,1
8 Courts of Justice in Southwark - 581,2
Crimes, Specification of some not punishable by Law 8,356,6
    The cause of their increases, &c. - 24,5
    should be prevented rather than punished 32,3
    punishable with Death—a List of them 437,8,9
    punishable with Transportation - 440,1
    punishable with Fine and Imprisonment 442
    punishments on Rogues and Vagabonds 443
    the encouragements to Crimes held out by the
      present System - - 449
    increased by the imperfections of the Law, rela-
      tive to small Debts - - 585,6
    See Offenders : Thieves.
Criminal Code, a Revision of proposed - 7,8
———— its imperfections - 24,5
———— its great severity - 33,53
    See Emperor Joseph's Criminal Code
Criminal People, their boldness and many chances of
      escaping - - 20,1
———— many thousands in the Metropolis who subsist
      illegally - - 21
———— likely to be increased - - 24
———— although unfit for the Navy and Army from
      diseases, ruptures, &c. are yet capable of
      crimes - - 99,100
———— the measures used to effect their purposes 100,4
———— they make contracts with Receivers 104
———— increase by means of base Money 211
Custom-House Officers, called Glut-men, connive at
    pillage and plunder - - 232

D

Dead Horses, and other Animals, Dealers in, to be regulated 109
Dealers in old Metals and Stores, their great increase 12
———— their mischievous tendency - - 292,3
———— Regulations proposed - 292,3. 303, 548,9
Death. The number of Crimes punishable with Death
    by the English Law - - 5, 437
———— Abrogated in the Roman Empire, by the Portian
    Law - - 6
———— Inadequate to the ends of Justice - 6
———— Impropriety of inflicting death, except for the
    highest offences - 30,53,8

Death,

INDEX.

Page

Death, Jewish Law relative to death - 43
———— Athenian Law - - *ib.*
———— Roman ditto - - *ib.*
———— Chinese ditto - - 44
———— Persian ditto - - 43
———— Saxon ditto - - - 44
———— Alfred's ditto - - *ib.*
———— Athelstan's ditto - - - 51
———— Abolished in the Imperial Dominions of Jo-
        seph II. anno 1767 - - 60
———— Theft first punished by death by Henry I.
        nearly 700 years ago - - 437
———— A specification of the several offences punish-
        able with death by the Laws of England 437,8,9
Debts, The difficulty and expence of recovering small sums 584,5,6,7
———— An astonishing Document, proving the vast extent
        of the injury - - 587, *n.*
———— A Remedy proposed - - 586,8
Depredations on the Public, in the River and Dock-
        yard   Chap. viii. 214, &c. ix. 250, &c.
———————— on Sugar and West India Produce 240,1
———————— from Sugar Samples, upwards of 60,000*l.* a
        year - - 235, *n*
———————— does not much exceed 15*s.* per cent. on
        the Moving Property - - 215
Detection of Offenders;
———————— The deficiency of the Law in this respect
                12, 13, 14, 15—20
———————— further elucidated and explained 381,421,2
Die Sinkers for base Money, the number employed 184
Directions and Cautions to avoid being cheated 124 ,,6,7, &c.
———————— As to the mode of proceeding in case of
        Fraud or Robbery - - 383, *n.*
Dispensaries, in London - - 574
Distresses of the Poor arising from the delusion of the
        Lottery (See *Lottery*) - 154,5
Docks in the River will not supersede the necessity of a
        River Police - - 217, *n.*
Dock-yards, on the plunder and peculation therein 249—287
———————— Fees to Officers one source of the Evil 251
———————— Frauds in receiving, detaining, and selling
        Stores - - - 253—259
———————— The perquisite of Chips - - 256,7, *n.*
———————— The amount of Public Property in Navy,
        Victualing, and Ordnance Stores, estimated
        at 7,000,000*l.* - - 260
———————— Laws now existing for protecting of this Pro-
        perty - - 361—3
        Their Deficiency, and Remedies proposed
                through

Page

through the means of the Legislature, by
a General Police System - 264
———— A Local Police for the Dock-yards 265
———— Legislative Regulations in aid of these Systems 269
———— Through the Admiralty, by regulating the
sale of old Stores - - 274—280
———— Abolishing the Perquisite of Chips - 281
———————————— of Fees; and increasing Salaries 282
———— Improving the mode of keeping Accounts 284
———— Making an annual inventory of Stores 286
Dollars, counterfeited - - - 173
———— (stamped) the iniquities practised in counter-
feiting and exporting, detected by the Author
of this Work - - 172,3, *n.*
Draco, his sanguinary boast - - 53

E.

Education, The great inattention to in the lower ranks
one cause of Crimes - 34,311
———— Seminaries for, in the Metropolis, estimated
at 4050 - - - 569
Egyptians. Their Laws for the punishment of certain
offences - - 41
Embezzlement of Public Stores. See *River Plunder—
Dock-yards.*
Emperor Joseph the Second abolished the punishment
of Death - - - 60
———— His edict on promulgating his New Criminal
Code - - - 61
———— Abstract of his New Code - 63
———— A singular Anecdote concerning this Prince 528,9
Estimates, That Receivers of stolen Goods have increased
from 300 to 3000 in the Metropolis 9, 12
———— of moving Property on the River Thames *(table)* 215
———————————————————— arriving, departing, and
circulating in the Port of London 216,17
———————————————————— belonging to the Public,
Naval and Warlike Stores, &c. 260
———— of Chips in Dock-yards - - 256,7. *n.*
———— of Streets, Houses, and Families in London 411, *n.*
———— of Public Houses - 110
———— of Persons employed in fraudulent Lotteries 156, *n.*
———— of the number of Members of Friendly Societies 157
———— of the number of Jews - - 147,8
———— of the Officers of Justice, Beadles, Watchmen,
and Patroles 2044 ; - 413,14
———— of Magistrates, acting in the Metropolis 416,17,18
———— of Convicts and others discharged from Prisons 95,*n*.97
———— of Prisoners tried in 1793 and 1794 448

Estimates

INDEX.

	Page
Estimates, of the Produce of Labour of Convicts in the Hulks. (See *Convicts : Police*)	467
Exports from the River Thames in one year 29,640,000*l.* (*table*) -	215,16

F

Farmers, petty Depredations on them -	86,9
Faro Tables and Games of Chance, their evil Tendency	135,6
———— particularly in private Houses of Persons of Rank - - -	148
Felo de se, how punished by different Laws -	43,4
Felonies public and private defined - -	43
———— A specific Detail of the different Felonies, distinguishing the Punishments	437,8,9, 440,1
Female Prostitution. See Prostitutes.	
Fielding, Henry }Excellent Magistrates, &c. *Fielding*, Sir John }	453, *n.*
Finance Committee of the House of Commons, their useful Labours and Opinions on various Subjects (See *Police).* 251, *n.* 264, 419, 427, 469, 514, 16, 558, *n.*	
Fires in London, the Laws relative to them -	597,8
Forcible Marriage, how punished by different Laws	48
Foreign Coin counterfeited in England	17, 18, 184, 190
Foreigners, their opinion of the English System of Police	522
———— the insecurity likely to arise from so many of them acquiring a knowledge of the English Language - -	530
Fortune-tellers, their evil tendency, &c. -	128,30
Founders of Metals, an object of regulation as a means of preventing Crimes -	108, 540, *n.*
France, its Laws relative to Receivers of stolen Goods	302, *n.*
———————— to Sodomy -	46
———— its former Police, curious Anecdotes of	525
Frauds on the Public in the Metropolis:	
———— in the Naval Department of two sorts	256,7
———— and Forgeries specifically detailed	111, 12, &c.
French language, the inconvenience and insecurity from its being so generally spoken	530
Friendly Societies, an Estimate of the number of Members	575
———————— a proposition to guard them against the Evils of the Lottery -	157

G.

Gaming, among the lower Ranks in Public Houses, a vast source of Crimes -	324
———— the Law relative to, and Penalties -	134,5
———— The systematic confederacy of certain Gaming Establishments fully developed	136—147
———— Estimated amount of the Money annually lost and won by Gaming -	143

Gaming,

INDEX.

Page

Gaming, the evil consequences of Gaming, and dreadful
    effects to many respectable Families -   143
———— the bad example to menial Servants of Persons
    of Fashion -   -   -   150,1
Gin, the astonishing quantity drank in London -   327 .n.
———— the advantages arising from a High Price -   328,n.
Grecian Law relative to Sodomy -   •   -   46
———————— to Polygamy -   -   49

H.

Hackney Coaches, to be regulated by the Police, (and see
            Night Coaches)   105,6, 305, 547,56
———————————— Laws relating to them -   -   402
Hale, Sir Matthew, his opinion of criminal Indictments   432, *n.*
Hawkers and Pedlars, to be licensed by Magistrates   116,17
———————————— their fraudulent practices -   116, &c.
High Treason. See *Treason.*
Highway Robberies, by what classes committed -   95
———————————— systematically planned and executed   102,3
———————————— suggestions for preventing them by
            means of a travelling Police -   109, *n.*
Homicide -   -   -   -   45,6
Horse Patroles proposed -   -   -   109, *n.*
Horses Stolen, receiving them as such no Crime -   9, *n.*
———————— how to be remedied -   -   303,550
———— Frauds and Felonies respecting, immense   103, *n.* 115, *n.*
Hospitals in the Metropolis -   -   -   577
Houses in the Metropolis, 160,000, and upwards -   568
Houses of Correction, authorized in different Counties -   455
———————————— Regulations -   -   459, 60
Hue and Cry, a particular means of arresting Criminals   388,9
Hulks, the depravity of the Convicts confined in them -   24
———— First instituted in 1776 -   -   -   455
———— Regulations by Parliament   (See *Convicts*) 461

I & J.

Idle Poor, the Funds appropriated for their support a Pub-
    lic Evil -   -   -   -   80,2, &c.
Jews, (Dutch) their mode of Education a National In-
    jury, as it promotes Idleness and Profligacy
    among the lower ranks -   -   119, 319
———— Objects of regulation as Dealers in old Metals and
    Apparel -   -   -   -   120
———— the principal Utterers of base Coin -   -   182, 190
———— the deplorable state of the lower orders belonging
    to the Dutch Synagogues, and the difficulties in
    making them useful -   -   120, 319, &c.
———— they are generally the medium by which stolen
    Goods are concealed and sold -   -   292

Jewish

INDEX.

Page

Jewish Synagogues in London - - - 568
Jewish Laws relative to Murder - - - 43
——————— —— Sodomy - - 46
——————— —— Rape - - 47
——————— —— Theft - - - 52
Immorality of worse consequence than Political Crimes 34
——————— striking proofs adduced - - 35,6
Imports and Exports to and from the Port of London, ab-
   stract of - - (*table*) 215,16
——————— of Sugar and Rum for a year to March 25, 1799 234, *n.*
Imprisonment for Debt, its impolicy and evil consequences
   in producing moral Crimes - 390,94, &c.
Indigence, one cause of Crimes (*See Poor*) 352
Inhabitants of London, number estimated at one Million
   at least - - - - 569
Inns of Court and Chancery in London - - *ib.*
Institutions for useful, charitable, and humane purposes in
   the Metropolis - - - 376,81
Irish, the lower Ranks great utterers of base Money 189
Iron Shops, great Receptacles of stolen Goods - 293
Judges of England, their great purity adds lustre to their
   own and the National Character - - 430
——————————— the extreme labour attached to their
   Situations; a Proposition for the re-
   ducing it - - - 590

K.

KING, his Majesty's goodness and love of Mercy exem-
   plified in pardon to Convicts - - - 22
King's Stores, Men employed to remove the *broad arrow*
   from Public Stores - - 258
——————— Abuses and Evils from the Sale of Old Stores 256
——————— Stolen, embezzled, &c. in the Thames, 257

L.

Landed Interest Depredations on by petty Thefts calcu-
   lated at 4s. per Acre per annum - 89
Larceny, the Definition of this Offence, and the punishment 50
——————— Grand Larceny defined - - - 50,5
Law, the different classes of Professional Men in the Me-
   tropolis - - - - 583
Laws of England, (*Criminal*) Deficient with regard to
   the prevention of Crimes, abridging Liberty,
   and rendering Property insecure, and in some
   instances even Life itself - - 94,5, 100
—— Punishments, from their severity, defeat the ends of
   Justice - - - 43, 53
—— Above 160 Offences punishable with Death 5, 437
—— When incompatible with Justice Law should be
   repealed - - - - 8, 301

Laws

INDEX.

Page

Laws, Some Offences, injurious to Society, not punished
 at all - - - - 8, 9, 34,5,6
—— Criminal Law explained, with respect to various
 Offences :
    High Treason - - - 38
    Public Felonies against the State - 42
  Private Felonies specifically considered, viz :
       Murder - - 43,4
       Manslaughter - 44,5
       Homicide by Misadventure 45
       Chance Medley - ib.
       Self-Defence - - ib.
       Rape - - 46,8
       Forcible Marriage - 48
       Polygamy - - 49
       Mayhem - - ib.
       Grand Larceny - 50
       Petty Larceny - 50,1
       Mixed Larceny - 54,5
 Offences punishable by the Laws of England ; a
  List of - - - - 437, &c.
Lawsuits, See *Writs, Debts.*
Lewdness and Debauchery prevail in all ill-regulated Pub-
 lic Houses   (See *Alehouses*) 311
Liberty of the Subject abridged by Thieves and Robbers 2,93
—— not by salutary Regulations to prevent Robbery
         13, 14, 508, 9, 545
Licences proposed on Milk Dealers - - 92
—— on various trades connected with the Receivers
 of stolen Goods (See *Police*) 540; *n.* 549, 50
Lightermen on the Thames assist in Pillage and Plunder 228
Lighting, &c. in the Metropolis - - - 592
Little Goes, a private Lottery, a contrivance of a recent
 date, brought forward by the Lottery Cheats
 to keep alive the delusion and fever on the
 minds of the Poor all the year round - 152
Livery Stable Keepers, proposed to be regulated (See *Horses*) 109,541
Lodgers, and Lodging Houses, proposed to be registered 105,539
London, comprehending the Metropolis. Its Commerce
      (See *River Plunder*)
—— The Magistrates, a list of ; also Public Offices 504,5
—— Houses, Streets, Families, and Inhabitants - 411
—— Its prodigious Extent and Opulence - 561
—— Places of Religious Worship - 482
—— Seminaries for Education - - 569
—— Institutions for promoting Morality - 570
—— For the Arts - - - - 571
—— Asylums for the Indigent and Helpless - 572
—— For the Sick, Lame, &c. - - 573
—— Dispensaries - - - - 574

London,

INDEX.

		Page
London, Charitable Institutions	- - -	574
——— Courts of Justice	- - 577,8,9,	580,1,2
——— Prisons	- - - -	582
——— Municipal Regulations of the Metropolis, relative to Watching, Lighting, Fires, &c. &c.		591
London, so called, (the City):		
——— The utility of a closer Connection between the Aldermen and Police Justices	-	420
——— The great respectability of the Magistrates of London	- - - -	512
——— The vast Labour of their official Situation	-	513
——— Magistrates with Salaries proposed, to ease them of that part of the Labour which relates to Criminal Offences	- - - - -	518
——— The great Labour attached to the Office of Lord Mayor	- - - - -	513
——— Reasons assigned in favour of an Improvement of the Police of the City, by means of assisting Justices	- - - -	*ib.*
——— The advantages which would result from such a System	- - - - -	517
Lottery, A great means of corrupting the Morals of the Lower Orders of the People	- -	11
——— Lottery Insurers cheats of the worst class		151—9
——— Their evil Practices explained, and their devices to carry them on in despite of the Law	-	152,3
——— Menial Servants contribute considerably to their support	- - - -	153,4
——— The astonishing extent of their Transactions		154,5
——— The misery attendant on the Lottery delusion to the poor, who fill the Pawnbrokers' Shops during the drawing of it	- - - -	155
——— The amazing amount of the premiums for Insurances yearly	- - -	154, 6, *n.*
——— Estimated amount of fraudulent Insurances per annum 10,460,000*l.*	- - -	143
——— The astonishing number of Lottery Insurers, with their Appendages, consisting of *Clerks, Morocco-men, Bludgeon-men,* and *Ruffians,* employed during the Drawing of the Two Lotteries each year	- - - -	156, *n.*
——— The Lottery might be rendered useful to the State if the poorer classes could be shielded from its mischief	- - - -	157, 556
——— The evils attending on its present Plan, and the audacious conduct of the miscreants engaged in fraudulent Insurances in resisting the Civil Power, explained	- -	156, *n.* 158,9
——— Their Profits said to be immense during the English Lottery, 1796	- - -	159

Page

Lottery, The exertions of the Magistrates rendered more
  peculiarly necessary to check this evil during
  the time of drawing the Lotteries - 159
—— Expedients proposed for guarding the Poor
  against the mischiefs of future Lotteries,
  digested under eight different Heads 160,1,2
—— Three plans for drawing the Lottery in such a
  manner as to prevent Insurance - 163, 170
Louis d'Ors, coined in England - - 17, 190
Loyal Military Associations, the Country much indebted
  to them - - - - 533, *n.*
Lumpers or Labourers on the River (See *River Plunder*) 226

M.

Magistrates, their Duty with regard to Public Houses
  (See *Alehouses*.)
—— Their great utility when their Power and
  Influence are prudently and judiciously
  employed - - 383, 422, 3
—— The number of Magistrates in the Metro-
  polis - - - - 270
—— The number who sit daily in rotation 417,18
—— The number of persons committed annually ⎫
  for Trial 2500 to 3000 ⎪
—— The mortification experienced by the Ma- ⎪
  gistrates in seeing their labour lost in ⎬ 432,3
  consequence of the chief of these Prisoners ⎪
  thrown back on Society without pu- ⎪
  nishment ⎭
—— A List of the City Magistrates - 504
—— the Police Magistrates - 505
—— Their Duty explained - - 506
—— Their Labours cramped for want of pecuniary Funds - - - 509,10
—— Magistrates with salaries necessary in every
  part of the Metropolis, and benefits arising
  from them - - - 517
—— Avocations of the City Magistrates explained - - - - 522
Manslaughter defined, how punished - - 44
Marine Police Institution, Origin and Progress of 239,248
—— Annual Advantages resulting
  therefrom to the West India
  Planters, and the Revenue
  estimated at 160,000*l.* and
  upwards 240, 1,*n.*242,*n.*
—— The effect in restraining River
  Plunderers - - 242,3
—— Necessity of its being sanc-
  tioned

INDEX.

Page

tioned by Legislative Regulations - - 245, &c.

Marine Police Institution, Testimonies to the utility of the System, and the benefits it has already produced

242, n. 247,8, n. 558, n.

——————————— The number employed in this Establishment - 399, n. 418

Marriage, The evil consequence of the prevailing practice of Cohabitation without it - 340

Martin, Matthew, Esq. his benevolent exertions for relieving the Poor - - 360,1,n.

Mayhem, Laws relative to it - - 49

Menial Servants, Their Morals corrupted, how - 154,5

Metals, Dealers in proposed to be regulated 108, 540, 9

Metropolis, vide *London*.

Milk, curious particulars as to the Adulteration of 89, 90, &c.

Misadventure, Homicide by, defined - 45

—————— how punished - - 45,6

Misdemeanors, A list of them punishable by Law - 442

Money, counterfeit, vide *Coin*.

Montesquieu, Baron, his opinion relative to Thefts, &c. 30, 53

Morals, The moral Principles destroyed among the Lower Ranks - - - 11, 310, &c.

—————— Can only be preserved by preventing Crimes 14

—————— Bad education and bad habits destroy Morals, and are the chief causes of atrocious Crimes

34,5, 94,5, 310, &c.

—————— The deficiency of the System for guarding the Morals of the Lower Orders one great cause of the Corruption of Manners - 36

Other Causes, The temptations of a great Capital - 35

——————————— The habit of living improvidently and luxuriously - - - 312

——————————— The temptation of fraudulent Lotteries 151,2, 9

——————————— The facilities held out by Pawnbrokers, Old Iron Shops, and other Receivers of Stolen Goods, enabling persons to raise Money on pilfered articles in an easy way 288,323

——————————— The bad examples in ill-regulated Public Houses one great cause of the Corruption of Morals - - - 310—324

——————————— The habit recently practised of Men, Women and Children spending their time in the Tap-rooms of Alehouses, where all sorts of Profligacy prevails, exhibited in language and conduct - 310,14,24

——————————— The profligate Characters intrusted with Licences to keep Alehouses (See *Alehouses*) 325,6

Morals.

INDEX.

Page

Morals, The immoral or careless Education of Appren-
tices - - - - 314
———— The failure in Business by Mismanagement, Idle-
ness, &c. - - - - 317
———— Servants out of Place - - - 318
———— The mode of Education and Superstition of the
Jews, which prevent them from being appren-
ticed to Mechanical Employments - 319
———— The vast temptations to plunder, which are held
out to Lumpers, Scuffle-hunters, Mudlarks,
Scullers, Lightermen, &c. on the Thames,
from the want of proper Guards, and a proper
System for protecting Property. (See *River
Plunder: Dock-yards*) - 322
———— The temptations held out to fraud from the shock-
ing state of the Silver and Copper Coinage, and
the imperfection of the Mint Laws - 171,2
———— The temptations held out in a great Metropolis
from the resource which the influx of Wealth
affords to commit acts of Criminality, giving
so many opportunities to live in Idleness 111, 12
———— The deficiency of the Laws in not taking cog-
nizance of Moral Crimes - - 35,6
———— Morals of Public Depredators - - 251
Morality—Men of pure Morals make the best Subjects 36
———— Against its principle to punish small offences
with Death - - - - 59
———— Societies for promoting it - - 570
Mudlarks, See River Plunder - - - 230
Murder, Laws relative to it, in this and other Countries 43,5

N.

Naval Embezzlements and Plunder, &c.
Reasons why not heretofore corrected - 252
Gratuities given, a great evil - - 251
The Depredations enormous (*See River
Plunder—Dock-yards*) - - 253
New South Wales. Transportation there when first lega-
lized (*See Convicts*) 460,2
Night Coaches, a great means of promoting Burglaries 105
———————— Propositions for regulating them 106,305,547,556,7

O.

Offences, 160 punishable with Death - - 58
Some not punishable by the Laws 8,30,5
A general List of the various classes of Of-
fences - - - 437, &c.
See further *Punishments.*

x x 2 *Officers*

INDEX.

Page

Officers of Justice—Their Zeal always proportioned to that shewn by the Magistrates under whom they act   -   -   384

The importance of choosing men of Respectability   -   -   ibid.

The absurd prejudices against Officers of Justice   -   -   385

The Antiquity and Power of the Officers of Justice   -   -   386

Number of them in the Metropolis 397,411,*n.*

Officers subjected to considerable risks   400

Ought to be rewarded—vide *Rewards.*

Old Bailey—Its registers shew the necessity of a Prosecutor for the Crown   -   -   21

Trials anno 1790 and 1791, eight Sessions 394,5,6

Idem and Convicts 1793 and 1794   -   448

Old Iron Shops, Owners, for the most part, generally Receivers   (See *Receivers*)   10

Origin of Crimes, Traced to Alehouses—Bad education of Apprentices—Servants out of Place—Jews — Receivers — Pawnbrokers—Low Gaming Houses—Smuggling—Prisons   Chap. XI. 310—332

————— Female Prostitution (See *Prostitutes*) Ch. XII. 333—345

————— Tea Gardens   -   -   -   346,7

————— Ballad Singers   -   -   -   348,9

————— State of the Poor   (See *Poor*) Chap. XIII.   351—380

P.

Pagoda, of Arcot, counterfeited in London   17, 184, 190

Pardons—The devices used to obtain them   -   22

Granted to four-fifths of those found guilty of death   -   -   -   449

Marquis Beccaria's Opinion of Pardons   450,*n.*

Impositions practised to obtain them   -   ibid.

Conditions under which they ought to be granted   -   -   -   451

The evil consequences of free Pardons   451,2

A tacit disapprobation of the Law, *(Beccaria)*   59

Parents, their Profligacy and inattention to the Education of their Children   -   311, &c.

Parochial Officers in the Metropolis   -   -   397,8, 416

————————— of little use to the Police in the Metropolis, why   -   -   -   400

Parricides, their punishment by the Roman Law   41

By the Chinese and Egyptian Laws   ibid,

Patroles and Watchmen, their number   -   -   399

————————— frequently conspire with Thieves   106,8

Pawnbrokers hold out many temptations to the Poor   115

Pawnbrokers,

INDEX.

Page

Pawnbrokers, A proposition for regulating them   116,550

———— To give security for good behaviour   -   116

———— The number in London and the Country   115,*n.*

———— The immense amount of the Goods of the Poor at all times in their hands   -   116, *n.*

Peace, an epoch when much danger is to be apprehended from the return of Criminals   -   100, 529,30

Peace-Officers—Safeguards of the Community   -   384,5

———— The ill effects of the absurd prejudice against them   -   385

———— The number in the Metropolis   408, 413,14

Penitentiary Houses. Two national ones authorised, but never erected   -   456,7,9

An Inspector of Penitentiary Houses should be appointed. (See *Convicts*)   460

Penny-Pieces, 40 Millions of them coined by Mr. Bolton of Birmingham   -   186, *n.*

———— why not likely to be much counterfeited   183, *n.*

Petty Larceny, how punished   -   -   50,1

Pewter Pots and Pewter, purchased by Dealers in Old Iron—Protected by Act 21 Geo. 3d c. 69   299

Piracy a capital offence   -   -   -   55

Pirates on the River, their audacious conduct, (See *River Plunder*).

Plunder on the River, and Dock-yards (See those titles).

Police—The advantages resulting from it when well regulated   -   -   -   1,2

The insecurity from a deficient Police no where so great as in England   -   3,4

One cause for the increase of Criminals is the insufficiency of the Police   -   4, 310

The specific causes of the deficiency explained, and the means of improvement   -   24,5,6

The disjointed State of the Police one of the causes of the increase of Stolen Goods   289

The Establishment of an active Principle strongly enforced   -   -   307

The expences of the Police might be defrayed by itself, under an improved System   -   410

No place of Industry provided by the Police for discharged Prisoners, (See *Convicts*)   99

Police of the Metropolis explained   -   503

City and Police Magistrates now acting, their Names   -   -   -   504,5

Their Duty explained   -   -   506,7

Inconveniences arising from want of Funds; Robberies and Burglaries not prevented, from this among other Causes   -   509,10

Police Magistrates should have power to give small Rewards for useful Services   _   510,11

INDEX.

POLICE—Police Magistrates necessary in all large Societies - - - -   514

Police Magistrates have nothing to do with Politics - - - -   517, *n.*

Police System approved by the Manufacturers of Spital Fields - -   519,20, *n.*

The great deficiency of the System for want of a Centre Point - - -   520

Constitutional superintendance of Police rests with the Secretary of State for the Home Department - - -   521,22

The increase of State Business, and the increase of Crimes, renders a delegation of subordinate management necessary -   520

The utility and absolute necessity of such a System explained - -   521,2

The opinion of Foreigners of the Police of London - - - -   *ibid.*

The Police of France under the old Government, observations upon it illustrated by two Anecdotes of M. de Sartine -   524,5, &c.

The situation of this as well as every Country in Europe makes a correct System of Police necessary, on account of the profligate Characters who will infest the Metropolis on the return of Peace - - -   529,30

A Board of Police proposed as the only means of binding together a disjointed System, and of giving it that energy which the interest of the Country requires - -   531

The new System of Central Police recommended by the Finance-Committee fully detailed and explained, Chap. XVIII. - -   535

Reasons suggested by the Committee   535—539

The leading object the prevention of Crimes and the raising a Revenue by Licence Duties   540,1

Trades proposed to be Licensed   540, *n.* 549,50

Expence of the Police of the Kingdom near £216,000 - - - -   542,3

A Central Board of Police Revenue to be formed by the Consolidation of the two Boards of Hackney Coaches, & Hawkers, &c. 542—545

The Licensing System to be extended over the Kingdom under the Controul of this Board 545—547

Functions of the Commissioners of this Central Board of Police amply detailed under 20 heads - - -   547—558

Outline of the Bill proposed to be brought into Parliament for establishing this Central Board of Police - -   559, &c.

Polygamy,

I N D E X.

Page

Polygamy, an improved mode of punishment for - 49

Poor, their Distresses - - - 312, 13, *n*.

—— Particularly from the Lottery delusion - 151,2

—— State of, Cap. XIII. - - 352—380

—— Casual, the erroneous System respecting them one
great cause of the increase of Crimes - 351

—— Estimate of Voluntary Contributions for their Relief, £850,000 *per Ann.* - - 358

Present expence of the Casual Poor not less than
£10,000 *per Ann.* - - - 362,3

This Relief ill applied - - - ibid.

Propriety of consolidating and superintending this
Relief - - - - - 364

Poverty not an Evil if it does not degenerate into
Indigence - - - - 365,6

The Poor divided into five Classes:

    The useful and industrious - - 366

    Vagrant - - - - 367

    Indigent - - - 368

    Aged and Infirm - - - 369

    Infants - - - - ibid.

The Statute 43 Elizabeth unexceptionable in its
principle, but its execution deficient 370,3,575

Proposals for a *Pauper Police*, to regulate Street
Beggars and Casual Poor - - 373—376

Expence thereof £5,230 to be defrayed by contributions from the Parishes proportioned to the
sums now paid by them for Casual Relief - ibid.

Benefit of consolidating the Funds of all the Parishes
in the Metropolis - - 377,8

The System should be perfected by the joint efforts
of well-informed individuals - - ibid.

Prisoners. An Asylum proposed for those that are discharged, to prevent their returning to evil
practices for want of Work, (See *Convicts*)

                            97,8, *n.* 486

—————— Abstracts of the number committed and discharged in the Metropolis in the course of a
year, ending Oct. 1795. (*Table*) 430

—————— Number discharged from the eight Gaols in
the Metropolis in a period of four years:

————————— 1st. by Proclamation 5,592

————————— 2d. Acquittals 2,962

————————— 3d. After Punishment 2,484
                                 —————

                            11,038 96,7

INDEX.

Page

Prisoners. Discharged from 1792 to 1799:

———————— 1. - 8,650 ⎫
———————— 2. - 4,935 ⎬ 20,510   97
———————— 3. - 6,925 ⎭

———————— from the Hulks, ditto - 11,283

                                   21,893   98

———————— Tried at the Old Bailey from Sept. 1790 to 1791 - - - - 394
———————— Tried at the Old Bailey from April 1793 to 1794 - - - - 448
———————— Tried in the year 1795, their Crimes and Sentences - - - 446,7
———————— Committed annually for trial in the Metropolis from 2,500, to 3000 - - 96

Prisons in the Metropolis - - - 331,582

Prosecutor for the Crown—The Utility of such an Establishment - - 21,6
           The injury occasioned by the want of it in defeating Justice 426,7
           A severe Burden on the subject to prosecute - - 426
           Further Reasons in favour of the Proposition - - 430,2,539

Prostitutes—Their unhappy Situation, and the dreadful consequences of it, Cap. XII. - 333
           The evil cannot be prevented, but may be alleviated - - - 337
           Number of Prostitutes of various classes estimated at 50,000 - - - 340
           Proposals for regulating them not inconsistent either with Religion or Morality - 343
           The example of Holland and India quoted 345

Public Houses, vide *Alehouses*

Punishments—defeat their ends by too much Severity 6
           Death should be inflicted as seldom as possible - - - - *ibid.*
           Disproportionate to the Offences 6, *n.* 8
           A Definition of Punishments - 29
           Should be proportioned to the Offence, &c. 29,30
           The objects of inflicting Punishments *ibid.*
           General Rules relative to Punishments 32,3
           The Severity of Punishments exposed 34,5,6,94
           Punishments examined as they apply to the various Offences known in the English Law - - - 38,9, &c.
           Punishments by the New Code of the Emperor Joseph - - - 60,3
           Marquis Beccaria's Opinion and Maxims 53, *n.*

Punishments

INDEX.

Page

Punishments—The System of Punishments fully considered, Cap. XVI. - - 434—500
 Punishments inflicted on various offences
 by the English Law - 437,8,9, &c. &c.
 Punishments as now regulated tend to in
 crease Crimes, (See *Convicts*) - 449—452

Q.

Quarter Sessions of the Peace :
———— and General Sessions of Middlesex, in certain
 Cases act under a Commission of Oyer and
 Terminer. - - - - 445
———— Held in London, eight times a year - 428
———— in Westminster, four times a year - *ibid.*
———— in Middlesex, eight times a year - - *ibid.*
———— in Tower Liberty, eight times a year - *ibid.*
———— in Surry, four times a year - - *ibid.*
Quays—Plunder committed upon—See *River Plunder.*

R.

Rape, Laws relative to it in England, Death by 18 Eliz.
 c. 7. - - - - - - 47
 The Egyptian Law relative to this Crime - *ib.*
 The Athenian ditto - - - *ib.*
 The Roman ditto - - - - *ib.*
 The Jewish ditto - - - - *ib.*
Receivers of Stolen Property :
 Receivers of Cash, or Bank Notes, not punish-
 able - - - - - 8
 nor of Horses and Cattle - - 9, *n.*
 3000 estimated to be in the Metropolis - 10
 The greatest encouragers of Thieves - 9
 Their wonderful increase in the last 20 years 12
 Restraints upon them a public benefit - 13, 14, 104
 Make previous contracts with Thieves - 103, 291
 Hostlers at Watering Houses often Receivers
 of Corn, &c. - - - 88
 Journeymen Butchers receive Cattle - 104
 Receivers considered separately, Cap. VIII.
  288, 308, &c.
 The chief cause of Public Depredation - 289
 The different Classes detailed - - 292,3
 By 3 and 4 William and Mary, *c.* 9. made Ac-
 cessaries after the fact - - 294
 By 4 Geo. I. *c.* 11. punishable by Transporta-
 tion for fourteen years - - 295,301
 The laws enumerated relative to Receivers,
 and their defects pointed out - 293,301
 A proposition to make the Receiving Stolen
 Goods an original Offence - - 302
       Receivers

INDEX.

Page

Receivers—Remedies proposed under eight different heads
by regulating certain Classes of Dealers   303,7
A system of inspection recommended   -   308
Applied to for their assistance in recovering va-
luable Property which is stolen   -   384
Religion, Places of Public Worship in the Metropolis   568
Register of delinquency proposed to be kept by the Cen-
tral Board of Police   -   -   554
Remedies for Evils mentioned in this Work:
To remove the Imperfections in the Criminal
Code   -   -   -   -   24
To improve the System of the Hulks   -   27
To improve also the Mode of Transportation,
and the Employment of Convicts   -   481, &c.
To establish National Penitentiary Houses   457, 460
To improve the System in granting Licences to
Public Houses—See *Alehouses.*
To regulate Dealers in Old Iron, Metals,
Stores, Old Wearing Apparel, Founders of
Metals, &c. by Licence   -   -   304
To improve the Laws relative to the preven-
tion of Pillage and Plunder in the River
Thames—See *River Plunder.*
To improve the Laws relative to the preven-
tion of Frauds, Embezzlements, Pillage and
Plunder in Ships of War, and Transports,
and in the Naval and other public Arsenals
(See *Dock-yards*)   -   26,253,4,5,6,7,8
To prevent Highway Robberies and Burglaries   103
To prevent the Coinage of base Money, and
the Sale and Circulation of the same   190,211
To prevent the evil effects of the Devices of
Cheats, Swindlers, Gamblers and Fraudulent
Persons, viz.
Swindlers in general   -   -   113, 150
Fraudulent Pawnbrokers   -   -   109
Hawkers and Pedlars   -   -   116
Puffing diurnal Auctioneers   -   -   117
Puffing Money Lenders   -   -   118
Illegal Lottery Insurers   -   151, 162
Itinerant Jews   -   -   -   147,8
Various Classes of Cheats and Swindlers, &c.
with Cautions to Tradesmen and others
to beware of them   -   -   131
A general Remedy proposed   -   131,2
To prevent the evil of receiving Stolen Goods,
and through this medium the Commission
of Robberies, Burglaries, Thefts, Larcenies,
Embezzlements, Frauds and Swindling, &c.
under eight different heads   -   302,3,4,&c.

Remedies.

INDEX.

Page

Remedies. To prevent Justice from being defeated in the apprehension of Offenders, by Rewards to Officers and others apprehending them (See *Rewards*) - - 392,3

To prevent Frauds in the trial of Offenders by appointing a Prosecutor for the Crown 21,6

To proportion all punishments to the nature of the Offence, and to abolish sanguinary and severe Punishments - 28,9,59,60

To improve the System with regard to Pardons—(See *Pardons*) - - 27

To improve the System of Police for the Metropolis, by establishing a Fund for Rewards 509,12

To establish a concurrent Jurisdiction over the whole of the Metropolis - 419,20

To establish Police Magistrates in London 513,*n.*

To establish a Board of Police as a centre point, where a responsible superintending agency, under the Secretary of State for the Home Department, should be pledged to attend to the great outlines of the Police of the Metropolis—(See POLICE) 25,6

A System for the more easy recovery of small Debts - - 584,5,6,7

To improve the Municipal Police, by extending the same Laws, Penalties and Punishments to every part of the Metropolis 599, &c.

General View of all the remedies proposed in this Work, against the existing Evils which at present infest the Metropolis, Ch. XX. p. 602, &c.

Restraints imposed on Criminal People cannot affect the Liberty of the Subject

Those already established to obtain Revenue, severer - - 14

Revenue of the Customs greatly injured by River Plunder - - - 241,*n.*

Rewards—To be given by Magistrates in order to enable them to detect Offenders— The utility explained 509—511

Rewards necessary to all classes of Public Officers of Justice, for the purpose of exciting vigilance 409,10

Rewards granted at present for ten specific Offences, detailed - 390,1

Amount paid by Sheriffs from 1786 to 1797, £.94,430 - 393,*n,*

Rewards paid on Prosecutions at the Old Bailey from Sept. 1790 to 1791 394,5

Small Rewards recommended for detecting inferior Offences - 393,4

Rewards

INDEX.

Page

Rewards——The quantum of the Reward to be left to the discretion of the Judge, and allowed according to the merit of the parties, whether there is a conviction or not - - 393,6

Rewards proposed for the detection of Coiners and utterers of Base Money 207

For the detection of Plunderers in the Dock-yards - - 272

River Plunder, its amazing extent, probably not less than *Half a Million per annum*, Cap. VIII. 215,237,8,9

Yet not exceeding 15s. per Cent. on the value of the Property exposed 215,16,& *table*

13,000 Vessels and more discharge and receive three millions of Packages annually in the River - 217

Various classes of River Plunderers:

River Pirates, (particular instances of their audacious depredations) 218,20

Night Plunderers - 220,3

Light Horsemen, or nightly Plunderers of West India Ships - 223,6

Heavy Horsemen, or Lumpers - 226,7

Game Watermen - - *ibid.*

Game Lightermen - - 228,31

Mud-Larks - - 230

Revenue Officers - - 231,2

Scuffle-hunters - - 233,4

Copemen, or Receivers - 233,6

See further *Marine Police*.

Robberies and Burglaries—not prevented by the Police System of 1792, and the reason why 509

Chiefly for want of giving small Rewards 510

Robbery, defined - - - 54

Roman Laws relative to Murder, Theft - 41,51

S.

Salaries, proposed to be increased to the Servants of the Crown, on the abolition of Perquisites 282

Sartine, M. de, Minister of Police in Paris, two singular Anecdotes of - - 525,6,&c.

Saxon Laws relative to Murder - - 44

Schools in the Metropolis - - 569

Scuffle-hunters, A class of Labourers who hunt after Work when Ships are discharging, chiefly with a view to plunder - 233,4

Sequin of Turkey, counterfeited in London 18,184,190

Servants—Corrupted by the temptations of the Metropolis - - - 12

Particularly by the Lottery - - 153,5

Sewers,

INDEX.

	Page
Sewers, their origin and great utility, the Acts relative to them - - -	594
Sharpers, an account of noted Females concerned in different kinds of Frauds -	127,30
Sharpers and Swindlers, their various devices to defraud the Public -	114,15
——————Ought to find security for their Good Behaviour -	135
Ships, in the River Thames, the Loss and Inconvenience arising from the present mode of discharging, (See *River Plunder*)	
Silk Manufacturers of Spital-Fields, their Address of Thanks for the Establishment of the Police System in 1792 -	519,20,*n.*
Societies in London for Morals, Arts, &c. -	570,1
Society for the Relief of Persons imprisoned for small Debts, an excellent Institution -	589
Sodomy, the Laws relative to it, and the Punishment	46
—————— Introduced into England by the Lombards	*ibid.*
Soup Charities, their peculiar excellence in relieving the Poor - -	81,2,*n.* 356
Southwark, the Acts relative to its Police -	594
Spirituous Liquors, the astonishing Consumption of, &c.	327,*n.*
Statutes. See *Acts of Parliament*.	
Statute Law—Necessity of its Revisal, and the steps taken for that purpose -	7, *n.* 32
Stolen Goods. See *Receivers*.	
Stores, Government. See *Embezzlement; Naval Embezzlements; Acts* -	257
Streets in the Metropolis estimated at 8000 -	411
Sugars, the Plunder of, estimated at £.97,000 a year lost by the Planters and Merchants, and £. 25,000 by the Revenue -	241,*n.*
—————— Annual losses by Samples, £.50,000 and upwards	235,*n.*
Suicide, the effect of Gambling in the Lottery -	144,*n.*
Summary View of the Causes of the Insufficiency of the Police, under nine different heads	24,5,6,7
—————————Of Prisoners committed in one year	429
Superstition of the Jews. See *Jews*.	
Swindlers. See *Sharpers*.	

T.

Tea Gardens, Public Evils - -	345
—————— Proposals for regulating them -	347
Thames (River). See *River Plunder—Marine Police*	
Thefts (petty) Causes and Progress of, Cap. III.	74 & seq.
—————————By Persons not belonging to the Fraternity of Thieves, estimated at £700.000	10
—————————From Ships in the River and upon the Wharfs. See *River Plunder*.	
—————————From Dock-yards, Ships of War, &c. See *Dock-yards*.	

Thefts

INDEX.

Page

Thefts (petty) Burglaries, Highway Robberies, &c.   93,4,1(3
Theft. First punished with Death by Henry I. 1108   52
   The Laws relative to Theft in this and other
   Nations - - -   51
Thieves. Professed Thieves not intimidated when put
   on their Trial; reasons assigned   424,5,6,449,50
   The different classes of persons who resort to
   thieving and robbing -   95,6
   Many Thieves taken off by the War, but many
   remain behind on account of ruptures and
   other disabilities, which, however, do not
   prevent their committing Crimes -   99,100
   The means used by them to accomplish their
   purposes - -   101,132
Tokens, Provincial Coins, respecting which Regulations
  are proposed - -   198
Transportation, when first introduced as a Punishment   454
   Offences punishable in this way detailed   440
   Expence of the Transportation of Con-
   victs to New South Wales, and their
   Confinement in the Hulks -   460,9
Travelling Police, A plan of hinted at -   109,*n.*
Treason, The Laws relative to it explained, viz.
   Of High Treason - -   38,9,40
   The great inaccuracy of the Act of Edward III.
   in blending together Crimes dispropor-
   tionate in their nature -   39
   The Laws of China relative to High Treason   40
   Petty Treason, how punished -   41
Twenty Thousand rise every morning in the Metropolis,
   without knowing how they are to be
   subsisted through the day -   313, *n.*
Tyburn Ticket, A premium given for apprehending and
   prosecuting Burglars, House-Breakers
   and Horse-stealers, explained   391, *n.*

U.

Useful Cautions, to Tradesmen and others against the
   devices of Cheats and Swindlers, and
   to prevent Frauds and Impositions   124,31

V.

Vagrants and Vagrancy. A specification of what con-
  stitutes this offence:
———— Idle and disorderly persons, how punished   442,&c.
———— Rogues and Vagabonds -   443
———— Incorrigible Rogues - -   *ib.*
Vessels, trading to the River Thames, nearly 13,500 in
   the course of a year -   215—217
Volunteers. See *Loyal Military Associations.*

3
                 War,

INDEX.

W.

	Page
War, The means of employing Criminals	99,100
—— Civil Wars seldom waged from considerations of Virtue or the security of Liberty	37
Watch-houses, Metropolis - -	414,*n.*
Watching the Metropolis, the Laws relating thereto	411,12
Watchmen and Patroles to be placed under the control of the Police - -	106,7
———— Their miserable Establishment from 8½d. to 2s. a night - -	107
———— How appointed and paid	411,12,41,7,*n.*
———— Their general unfitness -	412,13
———— The abuses which arise from this source	*ib.*
———— The number in the Metropolis -	414
———— Rewards proposed to excite vigilance	415,16
Watchmakers to be registered - -	108
Water and Waterworks - -	595
Watermen on the Thames, Act 34 Geo. III. regulating their Fares, &c. - -	596
West India Produce pilfered in a year - -	240,1, *n.*
Westminster, The Acts of Parliament relative to its Police	411, *n.* 412,*n.*
Women and Children of late years regularly frequent the Taprooms of Public Houses, a proof of the Corruption of Morals	310—314
Writs. An extraordinary Statement of the astonishing expence of Small Law-suits, exemplified by an authentic Table of the number of Writs issued in Middlesex in the course of a year	587
The subject further explained -	585,8

F I N I S.